# ANALYSING PERFORMANCE

Each chapter in this important new critical reader tackles the theory and practice of modern performance work, and enables students and teachers to see what is at stake in analysing dance, drama, music and videos using contemporary critical theories.

The commitment to cross-disciplinary approaches mirrors the breakdown of boundaries between these art forms in today's multi-media world. How do postmodernist, feminist or psychoanalytic readings construct performance worlds? What is the impact of multiculturalism on the language of theatre? What are the dynamics between AIDS, representation and live art? How does one talk about 'the body' in contemporary dance forms?

These and other issues are addressed in this star-studded and lively collection. An essential reader for every student and teacher of performance studies.

*edited by Patrick Campbell*

# ANALYSING PERFORMANCE

## A critical reader

MANCHESTER UNIVERSITY PRESS
MANCHESTER AND NEW YORK

distributed exclusively in the USA and Canada by St. Martin's Press

*Published by* Manchester University Press, Oxford Road,
Manchester M13 9NR, UK *and*
Room 400, 175 Fifth Avenue, New York, NY 10010, USA

*Distributed exclusively in the USA and Canada by* St. Martin's Press, Inc.,
175 Fifth Avenue, New York, NY 10010, USA

*British Library Cataloguing-in-Publication Data*
A catalogue record is available from the British Library

*Library of Congress Cataloging-in-Publication Data*
Analysing performance: a critical reader/edited by Patrick Campbell.
p. cm.
ISBN 0-7190-4249-6. ISBN 0-7190-4250-X (alk. paper)
1. Performing arts—Semiotics. 2. Performing arts—Philosophy.
I. Campbell, Patrick, 1935–
PN 1590.S26A52 1996
791'.014—dc20 95–12859 CIP

ISBN 0 7190 4249 6 *hardback*
ISBN 0 7190 4250 X *paperback*

First published in 1996
99 98 97 96 95 10 9 8 7 6 5 4 3 2 1

Typeset in Dante by Wyvern
Typesetting Limited, Bristol
Printed in Great Britain
by Redwood Books, Trowbridge

# CONTENTS

# CONTRIBUTORS

*Elaine Aston* is a Lecturer in Theatre Studies at the University of Loughborough where she runs a course on feminist theatre. She has published extensively on performance analysis and women's theatre. Her publications include *Sarah Bernhardt* (1989), *Theatre as Sign-System* (with George Savona) (1991) and *An Introduction to Feminism and Theatre* (1995). She has also co-edited two volumes of plays performed by The Women's Theatre Group: *Herstory*: Volumes 1 and 2 (1991).

*Valerie A. Briginshaw* is a Principal Lecturer in Dance and Head of the Dance Department at the Chichester Institute of Higher Education. She is co-author of the book *Dance Analysis* (1988). She has edited, compiled and contributed to *Post-Modernism and Dance Discussion Papers*, a conference report published by West Sussex Institute of Higher Education, and she has published reviews and articles in a number of dance magazines and journals. Her research interests include feminism and postmodernism in relation to dance.

*Patrick Campbell*, the editor of this book, is a Principal Lecturer in English at Middlesex University where he is responsible for the MA in Performing Arts and was co-editor of the journal *MTD* (Music Theatre Dance). He has been Visiting Professor at the Universities of British Columbia and Colorado. Publications include *Wordsworth and Coleridge: Lyrical Ballads* (1991) and articles in academic journals on subjects as various as Tennyson, Shakespeare, Patrick Anderson, Ian Dury, Siegfried Sassoon and Robert Lowell. He has recently updated the history of Trent Park and is currently embarked on a critical study of Sassoon's poetry.

*Alexandra Carter* is a Principal Lecturer in the School of Dance at Middlesex University. Her teaching interests are dance history, analysis, gender issues and contemporary critical perspectives on the arts. She was able to integrate all these concerns in her research on representation, hegemony and ballet in the British music hall, for which she was awarded a Ph.D. from the University of Surrey.

*Steven Connor* is a Professor of Modern Literature and Theory at Birkbeck College, London. He is the author of books on Dickens and Beckett, as well as of *Postmodernist Culture: An Introduction to Theories of the Contemporary* (1989), *Theory and Cultural Value* (1992) and *The English Novel in History: 1950 to the Present* (1995).

*Sophie Fuller* is the author of *The Pandora Guide to Women Composers: Britain and the United States, 1629–present* (1994). She studied music at King's College, London where (with Nicola LeFanu) she organised Britain's first Music and Gender Conference in July 1991. She now works as a freelance musicologist and writer, specialising in the work of late Victorian and Edwardian women composers. She also works for the national organisation Women in Music, setting up an archive, information and resource project.

*Lizbeth Goodman* is a Lecturer in Literature at the Open University, a regular academic consultant/presenter for the Open University BBC (radio, TV and video) and Producer/Director of TBA, the resident comedy company based at the Gate Theatre, Notting Hill, London. She is Chair of the Open University's Literature and Gender course, to be published (ed. Goodman) in 1996, along with original BBC videos, audio cassettes and TV programme. She is also Chair of the Open University's Gender/Politics/Performance Research Project. Publications include *Imagining Women: Cultural Representations and Gender*, eds. Bonner, Goodman *et al.* (1992), *Contemporary Feminist Theatres* (1993) and many articles in academic journals. Her two new books, *Sexuality in Performance* and her edited book of interviews with women in British theatre, *Feminist Stages*, are forthcoming in 1996. She is also active on the Editorial Committee of *New Theatre Quarterly*.

*E. Ann Kaplan*, a Professor of English and Comparative Studies at Stony Brook, State University of New York, also directs the Humanities Institute there. She has published widely on women in film and television, feminist theory, psychoanalysis and postmodernism. Her books include *Women in Film: Both Sides of the Camera*, *Rocking Around the Clock: Music Television, Postmodernism and Consumer Culture*, and *Motherhood and Representation: The Mother in Popular Culture and Melodrama*. She has written and been widely interviewed on Madonna and is currently working on a new book entitled *Travelling Cameras, Travelling Identities: Women, 'Nation' and Film*. In press is an edited volume on psychoanalysis and cultural studies.

*Sandra Kemp* is a Senior Lecturer in English Literature at the University of Glasgow. She writes on fiction and feminist literary theory. She has also edited Rudyard Kipling, E. Nesbit, Charlotte Brontë and Virginia Woolf. She is the author of *Kipling's Hidden Narratives* and *Italian Feminist Thought*. She is an editor of *Screen* magazine, and reviews literary criticism, children's books and dance for a variety of publications.

*Baz Kershaw* worked as a design engineer before reading English and Philosophy at Manchester University. He has extensive experience as a director and writer in radical theatre, including productions at the now legendary Drury Lane Arts Lab. He was the founder of the first mobile rural community arts group and of the first reminiscence theatre company, Fair Old Times. He is the co-author of *Engineers of the Imagination: the Welfare State Handbook* and the author of *The Politics of Performance*. He has taught in several universities, and he is currently Professor of Theatre and Performance at Lancaster University.

*Lucy O'Brien* is a writer, broadcaster and journalist. She has just completed *She Bop (The Definitive History of Women in Rock, Pop & Soul)* (1995) and is the author of two biographies—*Dusty* (1989) and *Annie Lennox* (1991). A former *New Musical Express* writer, she has contributed to a variety of publications including the *Guardian*, *The Face*, *Cosmopolitan*, *Vox* and *New Statesman & Society*. She was also in a very raucous all-girl punk band in 1979—but, hey, we all have to start somewhere . . .

***Sarah Rubidge*** is the Co-ordinator of the MA programme in Dance Studies at the Laban Centre, London, where she teaches Advanced Choreography and contributes to the MA Aesthetics and MA Documentation and Reconstruction programmes. She has worked with Rambert Dance Company, Second Stride, the Siobhan Davies Dance Company and the Shobana Jeyasingh Dance Company, and has taught and lectured in Eastern and Western Europe, the US, New Zealand and Tunisia. She is a regular contributor to *Dance Theatre Journal* and is currently engaged in doctoral studies at the Laban Centre.

*A.* ***Ruth Tompsett*** teaches Drama and Performing Arts on graduate and undergraduate programmes at Middlesex University. Her teaching, writing and research interests lie within Carnival Studies and Black British and African Theatres, in which connection she makes regular visits to South Africa and the Caribbean.

***Jatinder Verma*** is the Artistic Director of Tara Arts, which he founded with a group of friends in 1976 following the racist murder of a young Asian boy in Southall, west London. He has written, directed and adapted a wide range of texts, from contemporary plays informed by the Asian experience in Britain to classics of the Indian and European stages. In 1991, he became the first 'ethnic' to be invited to direct at the Royal National Theatre, producing his own adaptation of *Tartuffe* and an ancient Sanskrit classic, *The Little Clay Cart*. He migrated to Britain on St Valentine's Day, 1968 from East Africa, where he was born of Punjabi–Indian parents, took a First in History from York University and an MA in South Asian Studies from the University of Sussex. He conducts frequent workshops and lectures in colleges and universities in Britain and abroad.

***Elizabeth Wright*** is a Fellow of Girton College, Cambridge. Among her publications are *Psychoanalytic Criticism: Theory in Practice* (1984), and *Postmodern Brecht: A Re-Presentation* (1989). She has edited *Feminism and Psychoanalysis: A Critical Dictionary* (1992). She is currently co-editing *Lesbian and Gay Studies: Coming Out of Feminism?* (forthcoming, 1996).

# ACKNOWLEDGEMENTS

I would like to record my indebtedness first and foremost to the students, past and present, on the MA in Performing Arts at Middlesex University. It was a consequence both of the discussions generated in seminars over a number of years and of the sense that there existed no single critical text which could provide a context for those debates that prompted the conception of this book. The University authorities allowed me study leave to complete the editorial process. They deserve my gratitude. So too does Ann Lea who has cheerfully undertaken much of the word-processing and Helen Spackman for her encouragement in many ways. Anita Roy at Manchester University Press has been a consistently sympathetic editor. Lastly, I would like to tender my thanks to all the book's contributors who have taught me much and who will, by their efforts, render the same services to those who peruse these pages.

*Patrick Campbell*
December 1994

FOR ANTHONY AND LUCY CAMPBELL

INTRODUCTION *Patrick Campbell*

# Interpretations and issues

As though perversely to provide an illustration of the intentional fallacy, this book has ended up rather differently from how it was originally conceived. True, some intentions have taken on a palpable form. For instance, I did envisage an interdisciplinary, or at least a cross-disciplinary, compilation: at the most obvious level, a collection of separately authored yet potentially interlocking essays on dance, music, drama and multi-media performance. As the table of contents testifies, these primary and generic emphases remain. There are, crudely categorised, two essays on music, three on dance, four mainly concerned with theatre; but nearly all offer perspectives at once more plural and more relevant to the postmodern turn. While seeking connections across the performing arts, they transgress the established boundaries erected by these disciplines and, in some cases, provide arguments or examples that signal the erasure or at least the elision of traditional lines of demarcation between different areas and categories of the performative. This novel and transgressive sense of the contiguous should hardly surprise the informed reader. After all, accepted notions of what constitutes a unified and lexical culture are being rendered obsolete by the changing realities of our audio-visual, multi-mediatised, global society. As Johannes Birringer counsels, we need to re-chart our artistic topographies and 'engage in collaborative intercultural art, media and research projects'.[1]

It is easy to instance ways in which these collaborations are happening. Semiotics, despite commentators who regard it as a quasi-science or fatally limited by its gender-blindness, has provided not only a new critical vocabulary for performance but also, in tandem with the multiplex and pervasive phenomenon of the postmodern, has given an impetus—through its concern with non-canonical 'texts' such as film and popular music—to the already resonant debate about high and low art. To take another example. While the rejection of metanarratives has meant the erosion, already presaged by political realities, of Marxist foundations, poststructuralist ideas about audience reception (in a phrase by Kershaw that finds a number of echoes in this book) 'demolish the façade of the passive spectator' (see Chapter 8). The active role of an audience, linked to debates about the gendered gaze and representation of the acting body, is in turn a current preoccupation of feminist theatre.

It is scarcely surprising then, at a time of Heraclitean culture flux, when the performing arts pose more questions than answers, more strategies than univocal messages, and when representations of the real and the imaginary no longer seem separable (witness all those live art pieces in which TV images vie with acting bodies for our spectatorial gaze) that these essays should mirror a collective state of mind that is speculative and interlocutory. What is performance? How do we analyse it? And write about it? How do the live arts function in a culture where the public is assailed by images yet taught to respect words? What is real outside representation? How do we represent the body in performance? How do we bring new theoretical perspectives to performance analysis? To pose these questions is not, I suggest, to offer confident answers: a recurrent phrase one encounters in relation to the postmodern is 'the problem of definition'. Yet it is worth noting that all these general concerns, along with a host of other more specific enquiries, are addressed, either directly or implicitly, by the contributors to this book. May the debate be joined and given both a new impetus and a broader dimension by all those performers, critics and spectators who engage with its contents.

In fact, the book, by accident and design, exemplifies the very dynamics of artistic change. Thus some articles have a contextual bias: they constitute informed field surveys of a kind intended as the staple of the enterprise, accounts which adumbrate innovative artistic or critical developments that have acquired credence or notoriety in the last decade or so: for example, feminist interventions in the live arts; women's involvement in the composition and performing of music; exploratory approaches to multicultural theatre; the ongoing debates about authenticity, high/low culture or pornographic representations in the arts, in addition to the impact of the postmodern phenomenon on a wide range of performative initiatives. Other articles, narrower in scope and often prognostic as well as diagnostic, argue a position or expound a theory that reflects a new line of enquiry: spectator dynamics; the body as the site of representation; changing political strategies of the now anachronistic oppositional theatre, of the women performers or of the proponents of queer culture.

As we approach the millennium, it has become a *sine qua non* of performance that just as its praxis is being broadened and redefined, so its interpretation and analysis cannot be confined to the finished product. Lizbeth Goodman reminds us that in feminist theatre, for example, the politics also 'informs the choice of working method, topic, form and style . . . a distinct and rich field of cultural representation' (see Chapter 1). The impact of feminism on the performing arts, in terms of both theory and practice, is, inevitably and quite deliberately one of the book's main inflections—four articles refer to feminism in their titles. But the voice has many cultural accents and variations. Since the pivotal year of 1968—the year of the French cultural revolution and the liberating English Theatres Act—there have been so many reverberations within the women's movement that we now acknowledge a diversity of feminisms (Goodman lists socialist, radical, Marxist, materialist, cultural, liberal, separatist: a polyphony of voices which has espoused issues 'as various as class, race, ethnicity, ability, age, sexual orientation and privilege' (*ibid.*). If the main projects of the 1970s were, as Kaplan recalls, 'finding the female voice, rediscovering lost female texts, writing women's history; making women's images, demanding control of women's bodies', feminism in a global millennial culture is projecting its voice(s) so that a wider and more heterogeneous audience can attend, a polyvocal instrument pledged to discard such oppositional 'scores' as the politicised 'agitprop' of the previous generation. Nowhere has this propensity been more apparent than in the world of performance; it is hardly a cause for surprise that a preponderance of these essays stress women's contribution both on the stage and in feminist critical practices that now aim to analyse and interpret the live arts in the wider context of their constructions of identity, gender and race.

These propensities have meant that feminism(s), while still the most powerful force for change, now exhibit(s) more symptoms of the postmodern condition—the second major discourse, if discourse it is, to be reflected in the performing arts of the last decade and thus in these pages. After all, postmodern style, even if defined by its disruptions and evasions, by its refusal to countenance the self-contained work of art, shows no intentions of going away. True, it has taken critical issue with modernism's obsession with Western supremacy, the claims of a transcendent and often masculine reason, the hierarchical distinction between high art and mass culture. But it can be argued that both its 'style' and its 'substance', both its privileging of the eclectic and the plural, and its loss of faith in the efficacy of historical and theoretical models that legitimated modernism's control over history, have provided an impetus to feminism as it has diversified into feminisms. In short, postmodernism has offered useful strategies and approaches, 'particularly a wariness towards generalisations which transcend the boundaries of culture and reason'.[2] How feminist performance can retain a strategic political dimension within a postmodern condition that, for all its multiplexity and distrust of meta-discourses still operates largely within the dominant cultural ideology, is a question addressed by more than one voice in this book. For though the traditional disciplines associated with the performing arts remain, technological innovation—along with feminist interventions—has, in Kaplan's phrase, changed the whole 'game'; not only has the very concept of what constitutes the performative been broadened and destabilised, but the very modes and processes of production, exhibition and consumption have acquired new dimensions (see Chapter 5). Live performance must come to terms with this mediatised and reflexive culture.

Steven Connor's *Postmodern performance*, as its title implies, explores the nature of performance itself rather than its specifically political or spectatorial dimensions. Playing with two notions of 'performance'—akin to the difference between acting (doing) and enacting (impersonating)—Connor traces in the postmodern a compounding of these two dynamics of 'action and enaction, of immediacy and repetition, event and work' (see Chapter 6). Yet the range of so-called postmodern performance, indeed its very exorbitance, indicates the dangers of attempting definitions and devising taxonomies; such work, moreover, exists in a world where simulation is so pervasive that one's capacity to separate off 'instances of performance from instances of the real' is compromised. Using Stoppard's *Travesties* to illustrate some of the problems, Connor examines the play's postmodern dimension—the collision and disruption of three meta-discourses (artistic, anti-artistic, political), to the consequent ideological confusion of the audience. Yet the play itself is precisely crafted and refuses to focus attention on an open postmodern theatricality as opposed to modernist performativity. In contrast, the later work of Richard Foreman does concentrate on the intensities of present performance, not only as a strategy for resisting the 'stabilising effect of any single perspective' but to give their spectators pure unfolding action which *is* (and here we are back to Connor's original distinction) rather than performance which *means*. Foreman, in opting for exorbitance and in refusing the consolations of closure, shows how far down this particular road some postmodern artists have gone: in his plays, 'the tendency of performing to "coagulate" into performance is everywhere at work and everywhere resisted.' (*Ibid.*)

In *Postmodern dance and the politics of resistance* (Chapter 7), Valerie Briginshaw considers postmodernity in terms of dance and in particular its capacity to make political statements—an area outside Connor's remit. While many commentators see the postmodern phenomenon as essentially apolitical, Briginshaw accedes to Hal Foster's view that some of its artistic manifestations are resistant to dominant ideologies. Since postmodernism reflects and represents the socio-economic forces of late capitalist society, it is hardly surprising that some kinds of postmodern dance should reveal these processes: how, for example, power systems operate or stereotypes are created. In an analysis that evokes parallels with Kershaw's discussion of the Wooster Group's L.S.D., Briginshaw concludes that representations of reality, rather than reality itself, dominate our hyperreal postmodern consciousness. This preoccupation with signs and referents rather than real objects, with surface and simulacra, with process and reflexivity, with the way in which representations are constructed, is exemplified in a detailed analysis of Lea Anderson's *Perfect Moment*, a dance which reveals, *inter alia*, that such gender signs as masculine and feminine codes of dress or behaviour are cultural constructs and embody certain power assumptions. Moreover, by problematising such accepted norms as heterosexuality or romantic love, the dance blurs the distinction between representation and reality. In a number of ways, then, it challenges the existing 'status quo', a postmodern text that, by its resistance to dominant cultural values, thus embodies a political dimension.

Ann Kaplan's *Feminism(s)/postmodernism(s): MTV and alternate women's videos and performance art* (Chapter 5) also posits the view that 'certain texts evidence a postmodern feminist "politics" of resistance, albeit a politics not easily assimilable to old Marxist paradigms'. But since issues associated with the early feminist project are now perceived as limited and limiting—Kaplan cites the binarism of the 1970s film debates in which the proponents of documentary realism were aligned against an 'avant-garde' who saw coherence and closure as evidence of an oppressive ideology—there is a need to rethink feminist *strategies* in a multiplex, postmodern culture. For this imploding world has not only eroded the high/low culture boundary; it questions received notions of authorship and artistic coherence, and even blurs—via TV, film, advertising images, computers and surveillance screens—distinctions between the object-world and the imaginary world (see also Chapters 1 and 6). Since videated images contribute significantly to this process in the USA, women there are now exploiting the possibilities of a genre not bound by the old polarity of dominant ideology = realism; oppositional ideology = avant-garde. In examining a number of 'resisting' alternate and commercial videos and performance art pieces, as well as mixed media work, Kaplan reveals how these works share *strategies* for criticising dominant representational modes, eliding distinctions between such categories as 'society', 'artist', 'text' and 'spectator'. But if *devising* strategies for making feminist statements for the 1990s is part of the process, there is also a pressing need to create a 'space' for these performances and exhibitions. While postmodernist appropriations have permitted a blurring of artistic boundaries, they have not, in Kaplan's view, helped to develop institutional awareness. Should cutting-edge video work by women therefore be directed at the sympathetic coterie audiences of the alternate network, should it woo the commercial channels or should it find a 'space' in between? Whatever happens—and the general debate finds echoes in the UK—certain tendencies are apparent. In turning strategically to certain kinds of video and performance, women are forging connections and exploring new text–spectator relationships, rather than, as in the 1970s, concentrating on the message, on critiquing canonical texts or contesting oppressive representations within texts. Perhaps, Kaplan concludes, this 'resistant' politics needs to locate its own 'space', a space 'somewhere between the avant-garde, and commercial, theoretical and institutional modes'.

If some areas of feminist performance have developed 'resistant' strategies within the postmodern condition, music, on the evidence of Sophie Fuller's *New perspectives: feminism and music*, is a field within whose parameters many women still feel artistically marginalised. While our society's stereotype of the 'feminine' has 'given women access to certain forms of musical expression', it has perversely 'denied them access to others' (see Chapter 4). The role of the diva, for example, has been shot through with paradox—an object of worship on stage and a repository of scandal off it; a performer required to play canonical roles in which strong women are ultimately and inevitably punished for their femininity or talent. In the realm of the popular—and here the essay touches on issues taken up by Lucy O'Brien (see Chapter 14)—women are often excluded from male networks and structures or expected to operate as singers/songwriters rather than hard rockers. In the classical field, analyses of musical structures have revealed, as a consequence of the pioneering work of Susan McClary, the implicit operation of patriarchal value systems whereby, in sonata form, for example, the 'feminine' or second theme is usually grounded or resolved. Nonetheless, Fuller can point to some encouraging signs in the current cultural climate: the emergence of powerful material on the British 'indie' scene and the 'Riot Girl' movement in the US, as well as the direct expression of women's issues in some contemporary operas. While opinion remains divided over the possibility of a discrete female musical language, women are beginning to confirm their presence in a postmodern musical world which liberatory feminisms have enabled them the better to see, hear and understand.

The often tenuous links between the discipline of semiotics and the analysis of feminist performance are explored in Elaine Aston's *Gender as Sign-System: the feminist spectator as subject* (Chapter 3). While semiotics has provided commentators with an alternative vocabulary and framework for representational and communication analysis, it tends to be 'gender-blind', ignoring—despite recent emphases on decoding rather than encoding—the real spectator's active and often problematic response to the sign systems on stage. As a consequence, the feminist project has tended to politicise the formal semiotic model—as it has also been drawn to a 'resistant' postmodernism. Outlining the 'progress' of the female spectator role in feminist theatre, Aston shows how early plays by women tended to contain political messages 'likely to be didactically encoded' and have an 'every woman appeal'. More recently, feminist performances, less closed and more heteroglossic in character, have allowed spectators a greater degree of self-determination, more chance to allow their 'punctum' (Barthes' term for 'that mode of painful and compulsive pleasure that is not sought out but actively seeks out and injures the receiver')[3] to become part of the theatrical event. Thus a performance of a text by the radical lesbian writer Sarah Daniels will probably affect heterosexual and homosexual women in her audiences very differently; its enactment allows a range of active and questioning spectatorial positions among women that reflect wider matters of gender, class and race, as well as sexual orientation. Such considerations facilitate 'the possibility of bringing actual, real spectator reactions into a formal model of theatrical response' and open up new possibilities for semiotic approaches to the performing arts.

The matter of the spectator's relationship to feminist performance is also central to Lizbeth Goodman's *Feminisms and theatres: canon fodder and cultural change* (Chapter 1). For her, today's feminist theatre draws much of its strength from what she terms a 'reciprocal dynamic', a cultural exchange not only between performance and audience but beyond any given venue, a process which enriches 'the relationship between practitioners and critics'. One of the strengths of feminist theatre resides in its capacity to subvert the expectations of those male and non-feminist audience members now attending performances, as women's experience has been redirected 'from the wings to the centre of the stage'. Such a change and extension of performative focus—which Aston also finds in the work of Yvonne Rainer—has highlighted an internal conflict of aims: on the one hand, entrance into a theatrical mainstream which has marginalised women, on the other, 'maintenance of an active opposition to that mainstream'. Nonetheless, as Goodman remarks, both resistant and transgressive impulses have characterised the oppositional strategies of the movement since the 1960s and '70s. Indeed, feminist theatre's continuing development is predicated on its adaptability, its capacity to incorporate new techniques, to recognise our active capacity as spectators, to redirect the gaze, or gazes; in short, to be self-analytical in a way that established mainstream work rarely is. In these ways, feminist performance work can survive the process of 'mediatisation' and become part of a dynamic theatre practice that is constantly enriched by 'new material, stories, images and styles'.

No area of the performing arts has been more influenced by the feminist project than dance, a state of affairs less evident in the worlds of popular and classical music—as Lucy O'Brien's and Sophie Fuller's essays attest (see Chapters 14 and 4). Dance differs from music, and indeed from theatre, in other significant ways. As Alexandra Carter's *Bodies of knowledge* (Chapter 2) reminds us, dance in all its formal variety has only recently become a subject for serious academic study at all—a consequence, variously, of its ephemeral and non-replicable character, 'a Western mind–body dualism which privileges the verbal and cognitive over the sensory and physical' (a point explored in different ways by Wright and Kemp), dance's association with women and its supposed dependency on music. But a significant strength, and one reinforced by Briginshaw (see Chapter 7), is that the very physicality of dance—and there is a current proliferation of discourses on the body—means that it can expose and challenge patriarchal value systems which represent the female body as the locus of sexuality. Thus no dance analysis, no matter how formalist in intention, can ignore the cultural practices from which it emanates; no spectator can 'read' a performance and no choreographer devise one without recourse to the kind of underlying ideological assumptions present in work as different as that of Isadora Duncan or Martha Graham. Most components of a dance work, even its formal constituents of narrative and movement, dynamic and spatial elements, the aural and visual penumbra, the performers themselves—what a semiotic approach such as Aston's would define as its sign systems—are likely to be amenable to and benefit from a feminist critique, proof, if proof were needed, that dance *doubles* as both artistic product and cultural indicator, with the performative potential both to reinforce and to subvert dominant constructs of gender.

Sandra Kemp's wittily titled *Reading difficulties* (Chapter 9) also considers performance in terms of issues related to 'reading' non-literary texts. This procedure, she reminds us, has 'always been made coherent and therefore accessible'. Postmodern theory, on the other hand, holds that we no longer need to believe in a text's origin in terms of authorial intention and ideology or by comfortable reference, via a mimetic aesthetic (see also Chapter 10), to an object to be imitated. Yet this shift of attention, from text to 'reader' as a site of meaning, so often remarked upon in reception theory, is inadequate as a way of describing the *processes* that operate in the performing arts. While conceding that postmodern practice may focus on reading new sorts of performance texts in new sorts of ways, Kemp sees interpretation itself as performance, 'as the very process of bringing into meaning'. Using choreographer Yvonne Rainer's avant-garde films by way of illustration, she maintains that, in performance, 'meaning-making' is an activity based on a *collaboration* or collusion between performer and audience in which the performative text *is* the reading, and where the emphasis is on process, on meaning as *becoming*. In dissolving the traditional 'boundaries between inside and outside, subject and object, distance and intensity', these interpretative strategies also problematise other neat categorisations such as the division between high and low culture.

By remarking that 'the high art works of Rembrandt may be part of elitist culture . . . the responses they elicit are not', Kemp draws attention to one of the ways in which this high/low art debate has been fuelled anew by reception theory and semiotics. Originally stimulated by materialist noises from the cultural left which objected to the canonisation of verbal text or printed score, and latterly reflecting a postmodern condition preoccupied with the processes of mediatisation, the debate has now invaded the world of pop/rock music. As Lucy O'Brien's *Sexing the cherry* (Chapter 14) makes clear, the moronic inferno of popular music is not only being slowly if erratically admitted to the walled citadels of serious art, but has begun, in the last decade, to establish its own internal hierarchies of high and low which rely as much on market forces as on established criteria. While these shifting boundaries in part reflect the traditional divide between the artistic and the commercial, they also, as O'Brien's discussion of Madonna and the Canadian singer-songwriter Jane Siberry indicate, relate more subtly to other cultural polarisations such as the represented body versus the disembodied voice. Concluding on a polemical note which finds an echo in Fuller's article (see Chapter 4), O'Brien argues that despite the positive impact of feminism in other areas of the arts, qualitative and hierarchical distinctions persist in a phallocentric pop world which still valorises male material 'as if female artists couldn't possibly be the authors of their own work'.

If traditional demarcations between culture proper and popular culture have, despite the cries of philistinism, become more blurred, this dissolution has in turn contributed to an ongoing controversy about authenticity and the need or otherwise to respect artistic intention. Should Shakespeare be recycled as Charles Marovitz advocates?[4] Is a Bach concerto best performed only with the instruments available in his day? Should we bother to 'reconstruct' the original choreography of *Le Sacre du Printemps*? Is it defensible to transpose the key of a Kurt Weill song to suit a particular singer? Eschewing an overtly politicised stance, Sarah Rubidge's essay *Does authenticity matter?* (Chapter 13) examines the case for and against authenticity in relation to theatre, music and especially dance: she considers the fashionable view that veracity is not an objective property of a performance but something we ascribe to it, that the use of a pristine 'text' does not in itself, granted the permutations of cultural conditions, guarantee an unadulterated presentation. Live performance, she reminds us, is particularly problematic since it does not consist of permanent and replicable physical objects; in dance, even the means of 'recording' the movement 'text' is of recent provenance. In posing possible solutions to the vexed question of what kind of authenticity we want in the performing arts, Rubidge maintains that it is finally a matter of purpose. Reconstructions of canonical works clearly do have historical value. But revivals which imaginatively re-examine and re-interpret the world of the work, thereby allowing the site of the authentic to reside in the integrity of its practitioners, grant the work, in Miller's telling phrase, an 'afterlife' it might otherwise never have enjoyed.

The issue of the body in the work, present *as* the work (see Chapter 9), is also adumbrated in *Psychoanalysis and the theatrical* (Chapter 10), an essay in which Elizabeth Wright examines a post-Freudian, postmodern theatre practice that has dispensed with the notion of performance as inherently mimetic or as a Freudian safety valve for repressed desires. Suspicious of texts that lure the spectator into a collusive pact, this kind of non-narrative, non-representational performance art elides the conventional distinctions between artist, art object and spectator. In dismissing traditional emphases on the authorial voice, the text's authority and the actor's presence (a point also made by Kershaw in Chapter 8), such work, in Wright's view, questions the unity between voice and world, verbal signifier and signified. The focus is on the performer's body as a 'living embodiment of drive tensions', on all the multifarious sign systems on stage.

Pina Bausch's *The Lament of the Empress* thus typically shows traumatised figures unconsciously acting out anxieties in a world of promises in which the symbolic (even in the form of 'mother', 'father' or 'child') does not fulfil our expectations. In this performative world transitional objects have a pathological dimension in that the subjects become them, acting out regressive fantasies in cross-gender roles. This collective awakening of the audience to its own repression is, Wright attests, an altogether more radical move than Freud's sublimatory strategies when it comes to art. Just how political this discourse of the body can be is evidenced in the work of Heiner Müller whose play *Hamletmaschine* (1978) is a collage of phantasmagoric images, disconcerting noises and merging identities which 'subvert the very processes whereby language comes to mean', resisting all the old formulas for portraying character and suspending dramatic disbelief.

While Elizabeth Wright stresses the psychoanalytic dimension in postmodern performance, Baz Kershaw alerts us to the changing inflections of 'political' theatre in *The politics of performance in a postmodern age* (Chapter 8). In a mediatised world, where performance invades the everyday and where grand narratives have lost their authority, a *didactic* oppositional theatre now seems as anachronistic as the traditional polarisations between propaganda and art or high and low culture. As a consequence, we need to be alive to different kinds and degrees of political efficacy: granted the semiotic openness of postmodern performance, what might seem radical in one live context might be interpreted quite differently in another. Even Brecht's 'Epic Theatre' may require a contemporary reassessment.

Drawing on Foster's distinction between 'transgressive' and 'resistant' politics (a distinction also alluded to by Kaplan and Briginshaw), Kershaw argues that the transgressive and sometimes transcendent politics of the 'avant-garde' do not fit easily into a postmodern scenario where performance—in the widest sense—is already part of everyday experience and thus already implicated in the dominant culture formations (see Chapter 8). If feminist performance, as Goodman attests, is developing its own strategies for dealing with this, Wooster Group's L.S.D. circumvents the problem by offering a range of subverting perspectives, by juxtaposing often incompatible codes which allow spectators to 'derive contradictory meanings from the piece', by exposing *all* representations as constructed and even—though Kershaw regards this activity as eccentric—by attempting the erasure of actorial 'presence' from the performance because it can be linked, after the example of demagogues, to the idea of political charisma.

*Glasgow All Lit Up!* provides another postmodern example of political theatre of a far less sophisticated but potentially more popular kind: a street event in which the unplanned juxtapositions of processional images, floats, lanterns and so on create another kind of polyvocality which stage-manages a political sense of popular solidarity in diversity, and perhaps, in Kershaw's estimation, constitutes one way forward for democratised performance. For, he concludes, we need to accept that performances can no longer simply '"model" ideologies or reflect the politics of their context': they need to grapple (as other commentators argue feminist and ethnic performance must) with global issues, with 'inequality, injustice and servitude'.

While Kershaw reminds us that the idea of the 'political' can be applied in our postmodern condition to 'a widening range of phenomena' and their representation, Lizbeth Goodman's *AIDS and live arts* (Chapter 12) starts from the inclusive premise that most innovative and recent theatre is inherently political insofar as the interplay of ideas across the stage/world divide can and does affect social change. Focusing on AIDS and one of its principal artistic manifestations, the so-called 'Theatre of the Plague', Goodman attests that the pandemic's representation in performance art not only addresses gender and sexuality but impinges on a number of related social issues: the representation of queer culture and of women, audience response to issue-based performance, 'the theatricality of politics and the politics of theatricality'. The 'quilt' metaphor (itself the title of a piece) draws attention to this pervasiveness, to the impact of AIDS as both a shared community problem and an individual tragedy. Yet Goodman is alive to the danger that live art, whether addressing the actual crisis or symbolic of a wider social malaise, has tended, more noticeably in the UK than in the US, to represent AIDS as a predominantly male problem, thereby deflecting attention from women's issues or even from the need to explore common ground—an odd irony granted the numerical superiority of women in theatre audiences. Moreover, it is clear that the semiotics of AIDS has invested everyday objects—the quilt or the syringe, or even bodies in Mehmet Sander's intensely physicalised performance work—with new connotations. As Goodman concludes, 'wherever we look we may find the image of AIDS: a metaphor and a reality; a sign system worth analysing and a performance of daily life and death. . . .' Such a specific project can help counter the oft-iterated charge that semiotics has been too concerned with encoding or too apolitical in its applications (see Chapter 3).

In addressing the issue of multiculturalism and the performing arts, Jatinder Verma's *The Challenge of Binglish* (Chapter 11) provides insights that derive from his role as a practising and ethnically 'other' director. In offering a prognosis for an evolving form of political theatre, he takes issue with British post-imperial assumptions about so-called 'multicultural' theatre, seeing its evolution as a reaction to liberal socio-political forces that demanded 'coloured' performers and racially mixed casts. Since the very term needs re-definition Verma coins his own—'Binglish'—to characterise such initiatives in general and his work with Tara Arts in particular. Tara's productions—and Verma draws on reviews to buttress his personal observations—are provocative in that they foreground the 'hidden texts' of ethnicity and racial equality and 'provoke' other ways of seeing canonical texts at a time when postcolonial Britain is itself undergoing a crisis of identity. Such 'otherness', which, in postmodern fashion, subverts one of the meta-discourses of recent history, can offer audiences innovative forms of presentation based on a non-Western aesthetic at once more open and multidisciplinary and less text-bound, a theatrical world where 'gesture is speech, as much as a phrase of music is a sentence—or the passage of time'. For audiences, these multicultural productions, negotiating freely between the familiar (native) and unfamiliar (foreign), reflect contemporary ambivalences both *to* and *of* the 'New Britons'; moreover, by making a 'different sort of noise', they have the potential to re-invigorate conventional theatre. If postmodern and feminist performance initiatives offer ways forward—and Ann Kaplan talks of 'the increasingly non-Eurocentric women's voices moving into debates' (see Chapter 5)—such multicultural theatre provides a novel but not unrelated impetus for change.

Much wider in its remit, Ruth Tompsett's *Changing perspectives* (Chapter 15) also considers the extent to which a rich and diverse arts scene depends on diversity and difference amongst the creative artists who contribute to it. It discusses how the gender, sexuality, racial origin, class or ability/disability of creative artists can inform their creative work and demonstrates how many of the existing attitudes and structures in established contemporary arts production contribute to maintaining a narrowly based arts scene. The essay makes a case for the importance of more representative and broadly based arts production and concludes with a review of the ways in which the arts can be opened up to a wider range of voices and perspectives. The discussion is organised into three sections, each headed by a key question: 'Who speaks for who?', 'Who is in charge?' and 'What are the influences for change?' The aim is to inform, question and challenge readers, and engage them in debate, drawing on a wide range of mostly recent or contemporary reference across the arts, mainly in Britain, including theatre, cinema, dance, music and live art.

Patrick Campbell's *Bodies politic, perverse and proscribed* concludes this collection of essays. Its placement at the end is strategic: if analysis and interpretation are modes of enquiry that are generally constructive, censorship, at least in its most repressive manifestations, deals a gavel-blow to the process of debate. The essay begins by reflecting on general issues: the nature of censorship and the forms it takes, the reasons why the arts are peculiarly susceptible to censure, censorship's role as a barometer of changing cultural values, the ways in which its force can be ameliorated by arguments about artistic worth or serious purpose, by the extenuating contexts of the comedic or educational. In moving from the general to the particular, Campbell then considers the current cultural preoccupation with pornography which has divided the women's movement into, on the one hand, the pro-censorship lobby ('pornography is the theory: rape is the practice') and, on the other, the increasingly vociferous 'Feminists Against Censorship'. Such groups, here and in the US, are campaigning for an erotic art for women predicated on the belief that women should celebrate their own bodies and their own sexual experience; and that to repress this celebratory iconography is to collude in patriarchal values and to limit freedom of choice. Many of the most daring and politicised steps in this area have been taken by women performance artists of whom Annie Sprinkle is perhaps the most controversial. By such performative strategies as public orgasms and strip-(non)tease shows, she subverts the values of soft porn and the male fetishisation or aestheticisation of the naked female body in ways which have been variously called liberatory or educational.

In short, Annie Sprinkle or indeed any of the other artistic initiatives considered in this book, like 'Theatre of the Plague' or 'Live Art', offers us, as spectators, a glimpse of the exciting and often innovative directions in which performance, in this postmodern, poststructural and post-patriarchal world is moving. But as the art forms change, so too do the ways in which we talk about them. While much performing art is crossing traditional boundaries and becoming increasingly interdisciplinary and multi-mediated, procedures for analysing and interpreting performance are drawing on theoretical perspectives and approaches now seen to have a wider applicability and relevance to staged work. Conversely, as Kemp reminds us (see Chapter 9), the metaphor of performance has surreptitiously invaded criticism of all the arts. It is devoutly to be wished that this collection of essays conveys some sense of this performative and intellectual ferment, a ferment that powerfully characterises our postmodern artistic condition.

## Notes

1 Johannes Birringer, *Theatre, Theory, Postmodernism* (Bloomington, University of Indiana, 1991) p. xi.
2 Linda J. Nicholson (ed.), *Feminism/Postmodernism* (London, Routledge, 1990) p. 5.
3 Roland Barthes, quoted in K. Elam, 'Much Ado About Doing Things with Words (and Other Means): Some Problems in the Pragmatics of Theatre and Drama', in M. Issadiaroff and R. F. Jones (eds.), *Performing Texts* (Philadelphia, University of Pennsylvania Press, 1988).
4 Charles Marovitz, *Recycling Shakespeare* (London, Macmillan, 1991).

PART I

# FEMINISMS AND PERFORMANCE

I *Lizbeth Goodman*

# Feminisms and theatres: canon fodder and cultural change

'Feminism' and 'theatre' are two distinct subjects: one a form of cultural politics, the other a general category of art or performance. Yet each is political and each is performative. Indeed, most theatre can be analysed in terms of the representation of gender and power, and at that level at least, it is possible to give 'feminist' interpretations or analyses of any play or performance.[1] In most theatre, feminism is a political interpretive framework applied after the theatre is made: a way of reading politics in and of theatre, looking at performances and also the structures which produce them to show how deeply ingrained certain basic inequalities of gender and power are. But in feminist theatre, the politics is not just applied to the 'ready made' art; rather, feminism informs the making of the theatre—the choice of working method, topic, form and style. Feminist theatre is, therefore, a distinct and rich field of cultural representation. It benefits from feminist analysis, and also informs the growing body of work, academic and practical, which contributes to a changing relationship between the amorphous categories commonly called 'art' and 'life'.

In this section I shall discuss the implications of feminist theatres for academic study: what I call 'canon fodder'. I am, of course, being ironic in choosing to describe a serious subject with a pejorative and also metaphorically militaristic phrase, yet it sums up two aspects of the project of studying feminist theatres. One way of distinguishing between the field of 'feminism and theatre' and that of 'feminist theatre' is to say that the former describes a relationship between a political framework and a form of cultural representation, while the latter describes a genre or form of theatre situated in the public domain by virtue of its politics: its deliberate engagement with feminist ideas and aims, and its purposeful, change-oriented intervention in culture, as well as by virtue of the public nature of most performance.

Feminist theatre, as an academic subject, is informed by feminist theory (usually taught in women's studies courses), requires a knowledge of performance studies and drama (still often taught in 'Literature' and 'English' departments), and an awareness of social history, social policy, politics, economics and media studies. On the one hand, the genre has begun to receive attention in academic circles, particularly in the past decade, since the growth and increasing 'legitimation' of cultural studies has made way for work which is interdisciplinary and nontraditional. Yet the genre is also routinely marginalised, both as an art form and as an area of study, even within otherwise 'liberal' institutions. At the same time, feminist theatre is an art form which is performed and shaped primarily in public, outside academic institutions. It takes the personal very seriously—though it often uses comedy to make serious points—and explores the relationship between gender roles, autobiography, sexuality and identity, all the while experimenting with the public side of private performance, and the private or personal implications of the political.

### Feminist theatres

Feminist theatres are a relatively recent phenomenon, though women have been involved in theatre in many cultures, in many ways, for many generations.[2] Yet the term 'feminist', in its current usage, confines the definition of 'feminist theatre' to the past few decades.

In brief: contemporary feminist theatre as we know it in the English-speaking West began in Britain and the US in and after 1968, just after the abolition of theatre censorship in the UK (see Chapter 16), and concurrent with a wide range of important cultural revolutions including the birth of 'second wave' feminism(s) and the growth of consciousness-raising movements for women. Cultural and political movements of other kinds were also gaining momentum in this period, including demonstrations for gay and lesbian rights and the rights of single mothers, peace campaigns and student activism on a range of political issues.[3]

So, in the late 1960s and early 1970s, contemporary forms of feminism developed as women's issues began to be taken more seriously, or at least to be considered, in public and in private. At the same time, fringe theatre was developing as a challenge to mainstream theatrical and academic orthodoxies and traditions, classical and popular. Emergent feminist thought and fringe-theatre practice found each other and merged in what can be called 'early feminist theatres'. Some of the earliest organised groups included The Agitprop Street Players and The Women's Street Theatre Group. In Britain, the work of these and other agitprop groups helped to inspire a new focus on women's issues within mixed-gender socialist theatre collectives such as Red Ladder and Broadside Mobile. This change in focus led in the late 1970s and early 1980s to the formation of a number of specifically feminist companies: The Women's Theatre Group, The Feminist Theatre Group, Mrs Worthington's Daughters, Gay Sweatshop (men's and women's and mixed companies), Monstrous Regiment, Siren and many others.[4] But the very first 'feminist performances' were, in fact, political demonstrations rather than plays; they were the protests against the Miss America and Miss World beauty pageants, 'staged' in the US and Britain in 1969–71. In organising to oppose the objectification of the female body, women made a new kind of theatre: spectacular real-life theatre which aimed to re-focus society's way of seeing and depicting women.[5]

In *Contemporary Feminist Theatres* I quote Loren Kruger, an American academic who writes about gender and performance: 'There is a saying that women have always made spectacles of themselves. However, it has only been recently, and intermittently, that women have made spectacles themselves. On this difference turns the ambiguous identity of a feminist theatre'.[6]

What Kruger pinpoints in her analysis of the 'spectacle' of women's theatre is the connection between the way women are seen in society and the way they (and particularly feminist women, I would argue) choose to see and represent themselves. But before this point can be discussed in any detail, it is necessary to define my terms.

> *Spectacle*: something displayed or exhibited; impressive or unusual sight; ridiculous sight; film or theatrical show full of spectacular visual effects; pageant; (*pl*) framed optical lenses worn in front of the eyes to correct defects of vision, glasses.[7]

I chose this definition, from a popular paperback dictionary, in order to get the flavour of the word in its most common usage. The multiplicity of meanings is important, as is the combination of emphasis on exhibition and display, the theatrical framing of such displays as public events and the (plural) function of correcting defects of visions. This choice of phrases and images offers a very convenient entry into discussion of the framing of 'the gaze': a shorthand phrase for the considerable body of work on the subject of spectatorship, drawing on the metaphor of the 'eye' of the camera, and the gendered and privileged 'gaze' of the cameraman; a theory which is discussed in more detail in the next section.

With these concepts of 'spectacle' and the representation of women in place, the definition of 'feminist theatre' comes into clearer focus. Feminist theatre is written and produced by women, with some degree of political intent, in the wake of the modern women's liberation movement (i.e., since about 1968). This is a limited definition: it does not include plays by men or plays by women without political intent. However, my definition of the political extends to include most personal–political acts, from collective streets protests to the individual choices regarding sexuality and reproductive rights. This definition does not include plays written and produced before 1968, not because earlier plays were not 'feminist' (indeed, the suffrage plays were the precursors of modern feminist plays), but rather because the term itself refers to a contemporary phenomenon. Such a crude definition obviously has its limitations, some of which will be explored later. But for now it will have to do, with one major qualification: in using the word 'political', I do not mean 'about war, the economy, global issues' etc.; instead, I use the term in its particular relation to the feminist slogan 'the personal is political'. That is, I define feminist theatre as that theatre which is created by women with specifically feminist (revisionist) intent; theatre which represents some experience common to women (if it is possible to discuss the collective experiences of groups of women, without making any essentialist assumptions about women based on gender stereotyping); and which seeks to affect change in the consciousness of its audience and thereby in society as a whole. This definition is better illustrated with examples than with further qualifications, for there are many different kinds of feminist theatre.

Figure 1.1 offers an image of one particular kind of feminist theatre: scripted drama staged in the UK in the early 1980s, taking the cause of women's representation as a central aim and experimenting with form and style, while including men in the cause of rewriting classics and reassessing the canonical values which favour work by 'dead white men' over work by living women of many races and political perspectives. Of course, there are many other kinds of feminist theatre, from stage plays such as this one to much more abstract forms of movement and dance-based work; in addition, the politics of groups and individuals have shaped a number of distinct working methods for feminist theatres, from scripting to devising to collaboration.[8]

## The public perception and reception of women's theatres

Most of my writing to date has focused on British feminist theatres, but there is a corresponding—and slightly more developed—feminist

1.1] *Shakespeare's Sister*, produced by the Monstrous Regiment, 1982. *Left to right*: Anne Haydn, Patricia Donovan, John Slade, Mary McCusker, Gillian Hanna. (Mark Rusher)

theatre in the US, emerging feminist theatres in Canada and Australia, and different approaches to feminist theory in the theatre evident in various European performance traditions (those of France and Holland, for example). Even with the UK, there is not one feminism but several distinct yet often overlapping 'schools': socialist, radical, Marxist, materialist, cultural, liberal, separatist, etc. Issues of class, race, ethnicity, ability, age, sexual orientation and privilege all feed into and contribute to the shaping of many different feminisms, and many different feminist theatres. There is not one British feminist theatre, but several. There is not one set of standards, or a rule book or manual for women playwrights who write feminist work, nor for women who devise feminist performances.

Indeed, many women whose work has contributed to the feminist project of social change—in that their work has been accepted and applauded, published and made an example of—have not necessarily done so in order to be 'feminist', though their work has had (sometimes purposeful, but sometimes incidental or even unintended) feminist impact.

For example, Caryl Churchill is perhaps the most thoroughly

'mainstreamed' of British women playwrights, apart from Agatha Christie (and that is another subject altogether). Churchill is often thought of as a 'socialist feminist' playwright, but, of course, such a label captures only one element of her working life. Yet it serves a very important function, in that it describes the impact of the work on the changing social scene in which it is produced.

Churchill's work has been tremendously important as a role model for and impetus to women's theatre work, whether or not she ever intended to write as a woman or for women. Her plays are now performed all over the world and their visibility has been very influential in public perception of women writers generally, as well as in their provision of a range of strong new female parts for actresses to play. One of Churchill's most influential plays, from a feminist perspective, is *Top Girls*.[9]

The image from Churchill's play *Top Girls* [Fig. 1.2] is not taken from the most obvious source: the 1982 Royal Court Theatre première production which made the play its name. Instead, it shows a scene from a 1993 small-scale off-Broadway production. Many of the performers here are younger than those in the original cast; they are American; they have undergone a process of learning about Britain and Thatcher-era politics (the play is very much a product of the early 1980s); they have rehearsed British accents and immersed themselves in a form of feminism not familiar from everyday experience of life in New York. The canonisation of this play has taken one British woman's work into another context, setting in motion a process of valuing and reassessing women's work, women's roles in theatre and daily life (also a major theme of the play).

Modern productions of *Top Girls* tend to reflect interestingly—and almost by default—on the status of feminism, or feminisms. While none of the characters is particularly 'feminist', the conflict between work and domestic life which the play explores is still relevant, though in different contexts, and with cultural variations and generational differences in perspective. The play is not explicitly feminist in content, yet it has a considerable and enduring feminist impact attained and repeatedly reinforced through the reception and interpretation of the play in different public performance contexts.

It is just this *public* nature of theatre performance which renders it so interesting in terms of spectacle. In Greek theatre, those acts considered to be too grotesque for public presentation were performed offstage (that is to say, they were *not* performed but rather alluded to by characters on stage). In contemporary women's theatre, the definition of spectacle is much more complicated, precisely because

1.2] Caryl Churchill's *Top Girls* at the Harold Clurman Theatre, 1993, directed by April Shawhan. (Flock Theatre Company)

the growth of the women's movement, paralleled by the birth of a specifically feminist theoretical vocabulary with which such developments could be described, helped to shift the boundaries of the 'acceptable' in representational terms.

If, for example, we begin with the idea that women's traditional role has been domestic—at least in many Western societies—then the performance space for women's roles has also been circumscribed and limited to the private sphere. It has indeed been recently, and intermittently, that women have been recognised as *actors* (people who act, who do things) in the public sphere, both on stage and offstage. When we consider women's roles in the theatre, the legacy of the private can be read between the lines of the public performance. This 'publicising'—the process of making public—is itself a 'spectacle' of sorts.

I shall now move from a discussion of plays and playwrights to a discussion of two major theoretical concepts or frameworks which help to situate feminist theatre alongside other areas of cultural representation and academic study. The two areas are the concept of the 'gendered gaze' and the role of the audience in feminist theatre.

## The gendered gaze and the role of the audience in the live (feminist) theatre dynamic

The concept of the 'gaze' has been variously defined and analysed, primarily by feminist film critics such as Laura Mulvey.[10] The 'gaze' in film, TV and video refers to the directed way in which the camera frames the images presented in the frame or on the screen, effectively directing the eye of the viewer to certain objects, people or images rather than to others. Put crudely, the idea is that the camera (usually held by a man, under the direction of a man) will tend to offer the viewer a certain range of images, and to assume a gendered (implicitly male) viewer. Because live theatre is not mediated in this direct way through a camera lens, the theory of the gendered gaze cannot be so directly applied. But video removes some of the immediacy of live theatre and of the power of the individual spectator by introducing the camera which frames performances and preserves them, so that years later and miles away, they are still viewable and discussable, though they also still depict only that which the camera (-man or -woman) decided to frame.

Thus, watching a video of a live performance is more like reading an edited account of an event, rather than attending the event itself; someone (the director or cameraperson or editor) stands between the viewer and the performance. Yet videos of live performances still convey more about the dynamic of live performance than do film or television adaptations of plays, which rewrite and reframe the script in order to make it conform to a different medium altogether. Thus, while videos alter the relationship of the spectator to the performance, they serve important teaching purposes and do help to keep work archived and accessible: valuable functions in themselves, discussed in more detail later.

Of course, the 'gaze' of the viewer is altered in the transfer from live performance to video and other media, and this change in dynamic has gendered implications for feminist theatre. In live feminist theatre, in theory if not in practice, the individual audience member is, to some extent, in control of her or his own gaze. In that sense, the audience can be viewed (by the makers of the theatre) in terms of their value as active participants in the performance, by virtue of their powers of interpretation. The representation of women as subjects and objects within the theatre is thus partially inverted: the audience is viewed, just as it views; the actors and makers of the theatre depend upon the responses of their audience, just as the audience depends upon staged action to keep it engaged in the performance. In the absence of direct audience involvement, the capacity for redirecting the gendered gaze is greatly reduced.

The role of the audience in any performance, whether it be a theatre production, a political demonstration, or an academic lecture, is inevitably influenced by gender.[11] Gender is a particularly important consideration in terms of theatre audiences, due to the majority of female theatregoers. Yet the gender of the audience in feminist theatres is most significant, for in feminist theatre, it is not only the number of women which influences the stage–audience dynamic, but also the level of identification between performers and spectators, or what can be called the 'extrascenic gendered gaze'.

The theory of the gaze is useful in that it provides a framework for analysis of values associated with seeing and interpreting images. In locating the dynamics of gender and power associated with the gaze, some theorists have become caught up in analysis of visual images and points of view. This kind of approach emphasises the spectator's role in the performance, and usefully so. But an increasing emphasis on the spectator may begin to conflate the specific roles of writers, directors and performers. In effect, the importance of the spectator's active engagement within the performance may begin to displace more practical concerns: the intentions of practitioners are not best served by ignoring their 'roles' altogether. Rather, a balanced and interactive exchange between stage and audience is the most effective dynamic. The audience is important, but so is the performance. The active engagement of the audience and the active roles of practitioners are both necessary to the process of change which is the aim of feminist theatre.

The role of the audience is significant for two reasons: because it informs the making of feminist theatre and because the making of the theatre is informed by it. The process is reciprocal. The making of feminist theatre is informed by the role of the audience insofar as practitioners have conceptualised a new audience for their theatre (in the significant shift in gender, or assumed gender, of the spectator). This conceptualisation of the audience has influenced the choice of themes and the forms of representation chosen by the practitioners. Yet feminist theatre is not only received and interpreted, but also influenced by its audience. It does not merely 'preach to the converted', but also challenges traditional images and ideas, and may thereby 'convert' some members of its audience by redirecting their views on (or ways of viewing) representations of women in a particular culture. In return, the responses of audiences, in the form of applause, reviews and funding, for instance, influence the theatre itself.

An example will help to illustrate the point. One feminist theatre company which pays close attention to its choice of language and setting, and to the expectations of its audiences, is Charabanc, the best-known women's theatre company of Northern Ireland. Founded by five actresses in Belfast in 1983, Charabanc defines three strands in the company's work: 1) devising plays from and primarily for the Belfast community; 2) commissioning new Irish writing; 3) introducing and reinterpreting existing texts. Within all three strands runs the thread of putting women's experiences to the fore.[12]

In their production of Federico García Lorca's bloody and claustrophobic domestic drama *The House of Bernarda Alba*, Charabanc chose to translate the setting to Northern Ireland, deliberately calling on the associated context of political oppression and sexual repression. In choosing to alter the set, scene and language of the play, Charabanc made Lorca's work speak for and to the women (and also the men) of contemporary Belfast: a political and subversive interaction with the medium of theatre, the ideas of feminism and the politics of performance. In other words, Charabanc practised what was preached in the theoretical material above; the company recognised the gender and power dynamic of a play from another culture and generation, saw its relevance to modern-day Northern Ireland, and reframed it for a space, time and community which might identify with and respond to the domestic and cultural entrapment of the play's strong female characters.

## Theorising the feminist theatre audience

Some of the most relevant contributions to the theory of feminist theatre involve consideration of the role of the audience. Indeed, most

1.3] Emma Jordan as Adela and Carol Scanlan as Mrs Punch in *The House of Bernarda Alba* produced by Charabanc, 1993, directed by Lynne Parker. (Chris Hill)

contemporary performance theory (feminist or not) has included discussion of the audience, including the growing body of live arts work about AIDS, discussed elsewhere in this book (see Chapter 12).

Gillian Elinor has argued that feminist theatre in performance subverts the expectations of the men and nonfeminist women in its audiences, in ways which they may find pleasing despite themselves.[13] This argument is significant for two reasons: because it assumes an audience of critical spectators and because it conceives of a potential for change in relation to the perspectives of a wide range of people. Rather than argue that the feminist theatre audience is important because it is feminist (i.e., because it is composed of feminist women), Elinor argues that the audience is important because of the diversity of perspectives of its members and because of the theatre's potential to 'convert' some spectators to a feminist way of seeing. In this view, feminist theatre does more than 'preach to the converted': it affects a range of spectators in different ways.

In arguing that the feminist performer, critic and spectator all engage in the process of redirecting the gaze, Jill Dolan introduced the idea of the 'spectator as critic' into the theoretical vocabulary.[14] In some of her later work, she reformulated this idea with reference to gender, arguing that one of the most significant aspects of feminist theatre is the shift in the gendered perspective of its audience: that the traditional dramatic canon has assumed a male or male-biased spectatorship which called itself 'universal', whereas feminist performance suggests the possibility of a female spectatorship which does not call itself universal: it does not subsume the male spectator, but rather allows for differences of perspective. Dolan's work has clearly influenced academics such as Loren Kruger and her concept of the 'spectacle' of feminist performance, while social theorists including Erving Goffman have discussed the implications of 'performing self' in society. It is this complicated set of ideas, crossing performance strategies and academic disciplines, which is at the root of developing theories of self in performance such as those which inform Lesley Ferris's work on the subject of 'acting women'.[15]

The dynamic of the theatre, as opposed to the performances of everyday life, is unique in terms of the presence of an immediate and critical body of spectators. The theatre space encourages immediate reactions from the audience and permits a level of criticism which is not deemed appropriate in most forms of social interaction. Therefore, developing theories of self in performance must consider the unique qualities of the live theatre performance. When we move away from theoretical study of the gaze and the conceptual theatre audiences and look closely at the theatres themselves, a different picture begins to emerge.

### Surveying theatres and their audiences

There are only a very limited number of audience surveys available in print and these tend not to focus on women's theatre or gender balances in audiences.[16] Research conducted by Caroline Gardiner for the Policy Studies Institute is more helpful in terms of gendered analysis but not very informative about feminist theatre generally.[17] Susan Bennett's *Theatre Audiences* is written by a feminist theatre specialist, so while the subject is much wider, the implications to be drawn are most readily applicable to the study of feminist theatres.[18] The lack of published material on the subject of feminist theatre rendered it necessary to conduct my own research into these theatres and their audiences.

In 1987–90 I conducted an extensive survey of feminist and women's theatres in the UK in order to ascertain how groups defined themselves as either 'feminist' or 'women's groups'.[19] The term 'feminist theatre' was defined for the purposes of the survey as action-oriented political theatre and/or for women, concerned with one or more of the following: positive images in the representation of women; issues of women's status and rights; women's creativity; and the basic tenets of the women's liberation movement as they have filtered down into current feminist theory and practice. The range of responses received was staggering in the variety of interpretations attached to these terms, as well as in what it revealed about the status of women's theatre. Some of the results were predictable: many groups were wary of the label 'feminist', largely for fear that it would stigmatise them and possibly influence funding bodies, audiences and critics against their work (a worry which is often justified and which reveals a great deal about the negative connotations still often attached to the term 'feminist', despite its intrinsically positive meanings and aims). 'Women's theatre' was more broadly defined as theatre made by and/or about women.

At the beginning of the research, it quickly became clear that conflicting definitions of these terms would complicate any attempt to find a limited sample group for the survey. Indeed, questions pertaining to the relationship between 'feminist theatre' and 'political theatre' and to men's relationships with feminism and feminist theatre further complicated any attempt to limit the scope of the survey. Over 300 survey questionnaires were distributed and 223 groups responded in terms which could be calculated (many others self-selected themselves out of the survey). Of 223 groups, 161 were in operation and 62 disbanded by the time the survey reached them (in the past decade, of course, massive cuts to arts funding have forced the closure of many venues and the disbanding of many small companies). Of 161 companies responding, only 98 provided enough information to facilitate detailed analysis and comparison. Of those 98, 76 were in operation and 22 were disbanded. These groups identified themselves by category in the following way (some choosing two or more categories to describe themselves):

a) feminist groups (all feminist women): 34
b) women's groups (all women): 30
c) mixed groups with feminist politics: 33
d) mixed groups with left politics, fairly positive for women: 33

Of course, the definitions pose problems. Interpretation of the term 'feminism' differs, as do respondents' reasons for responding to questionnaires and their ways of responding. Even so, this information allowed me to investigate feminist theatre in concrete terms, with statistical backup.

The survey findings were particularly informative with regard to the audience. The groups with all or mostly women members had by far the highest proportion of women to men in terms of audience composition, and also the best records of producing work by women playwrights, hiring women directors and hiring women to fill backstage and technical roles. According to the survey responses on the 'woman-to-man ratio in the average audience', the majority of feminist theatre groups recorded a positive ratio. Of 98 responding groups, the number reporting having a positive ratio was 62 of which 49 were still operative.

These figures are most compelling when compared to theatre practice. Just after the completion of the survey, a new women's group (arguably a 'feminist group') was formed: the Black Mime Theatre Women's Troop. The Black Mime Theatre had existed as a mixed-gender company for some time, but many of their shows tended to showcase the men in the company. In 1990, the company's director Denise Wong decided to put together a Women's Troop, to perform all-women's shows alongside the men's and mixed-gender work. The Women's Troop's first show was *Mothers*. Co-devised and performed in 1990–1 by the women of the company, *Mothers* incorporated mime and spoken theatre, movement, dance and song, to focus on the theme of motherhood and the experience of living as black women in Britain.

Wong and the company conducted their own audience surveys, with fascinating results. The majority of audience members were, perhaps unsurprisingly, black women. But the ages and backgrounds, as well as the reasons for attending the performance, varied enormously.[20] Most informative was the survey's revelation of the means of advertising through which many audience members heard about the show: not through standard publicity sources such as posters, flyers or newspaper advertisements, but rather through word of mouth, for instance, mothers in playgroups discussing local entertainment options when they collected their children. Such a result would not have been predictable, but it makes perfect sense. It defies the logic of academic categorisation and theorisation of audience trends, and steers us back to the reality of living as women in the 'real world'. Such results also relate to a more general trend toward social interaction which affects women's theatre-going habits and ways of analysing what they see: that is, theatre is often expensive. Feminist theatre is usually cheaper but also located in out-of-the-way venues. Thus, for many women, television and video are more logistically and economically viable than

1.4] Black Mime Theatre Women's Troop in *Mothers*, co-devised by the company, directed by Denise Wong, 1990. (Desmond Ip)

theatre. Only the hard core of feminist theatre enthusiasts may be convinced to venture out at night to an inconvenient location to experience the live theatre dynamic, however exciting and challenging it may be.

### Feminist survival tips and the 'mediazation' of theatre

If the audiences are crucial in the two-way dynamic between the stage and the world, what happens when audiences stop going to the theatre in favour of watching films on video or television at home? A range of obvious answers spring to mind: closing theatres at the negative end, renewed efforts to enliven the theatre at the positive end, and a range of answers and ideas in between. But, for feminist theatre, the more interesting question is: what happens when feminist politics on stage are inaccessible because women are busy at work all day, busy at home in the evenings, often unable to afford the time to go to the theatre or the price of the ticket, and if the more convenient option is television or video, i.e., material which very rarely gives feminist politics a look in? What may result in this age of home entertainment and mass communications (which will soon offer the technology to choose videos over the phone wires via a computer modem) is a major challenge to the power of live theatre.

What will happen next is anybody's guess, but if current politics are anything to judge by, there is hope yet for feminist theatre. For theatre is not just 'drama'—scripted plays, published and reproduced from generation to generation. It is that, too, but it is also unscripted devised performance work and multi-media work. In any case, script or no script, theatre is performed. The live dynamic is what makes it unique. And that live dynamic is also a component of political activism and street protests: the root of feminist theatre as we know it, and also its greatest ally in this age of media challenges.

In the discussion of the active role of feminist theatre audiences, it was argued that the active spectator may influence the performance dynamic on stage. And, of course, theatre-goers have another means of control or direct influence at their disposal: they may choose not to go to the theatre if the performance or its politics (or price) do not suit them. This kind of 'voting with one's feet' is precisely what motivates some mainstream repertory theatres to tend towards the lowest common denominator of 'entertainment value' in choosing plays and productions. That is, much mainstream theatre assumes a middle-ground, middle-class audience; it assumes that musicals and revivals of the 'classics' are more likely to 'put bums on seats' than, for instance, radical feminist plays. This commercial reasoning has long influenced the theatre in circular fashion; audiences are used to one kind of theatre and they are not given the chance to see, and certainly not to get used to, anything so 'radical' as a feminist performance. So, when the odd feminist play does make it to the main stages (*Top Girls* for instance), the resultant success is all the greater, but also all the more likely to receive criticism for its politics, rather than praise for its innovation and originality.

In an age when all theatre is under threat due to funding cuts to the arts in general and a move towards corporate sponsorship for theatre funding—and given that few banks and commercial establishments will view companies with names such as Gay Sweatshop or Monstrous Regiment of Women as the best and most popular 'commodities' to be associated with through a sponsorship deal—feminist theatres are truly in a precarious position. Yet paradoxically, it may be the medium's long history or herstory of experimentation and adaptability which will help it to survive. For instance, most feminist performance work has always operated on a low (or no) budget. Thus, while the lack of funding for such work is still greatly inhibiting to the development of the genre, it is not a new problem. But, more importantly, because much feminist performance of recent years has incorporated multi-media performance art techniques, the genre is uniquely adaptable to a number of other media.[21] And since much of the work is self-critical and self-analytical (in a way that much mainstream work is not), it is useful in teaching situations, particularly when it is made available on video, allowing the student the means of control of the power wand, complete with fast forward, rewind and pause buttons.[22] In terms of its form and style, feminist performance work is not as seriously threatened by broadcast media as are other forms of theatre and drama.

In writing about theatre and the media, Patrice Pavis has coined the term 'the mediatization of theatre' to refer to the ways in which theatre is affected by its incorporation into media of mass communication such as radio and television.[23] John B. Thompson develops this idea in *The Media and Modernity*. He argues that the media create a distinctive kind of interaction situation which is not face-to-face in character and hence the process of 'mediazation' (*sic*) fundamentally alters the performative aspects of theatre.[24] Despite differences in phrasing, both views support a reading of the cultural context of theatre which is inextricably linked to developments in broadcast and mass communications media. The theatre, in order to preserve its unique status as an art form constructing and reacting to a live extrascenic relationship between performance and audience, must find ways to survive the process of 'mediazation'. Feminist theatre must find ways to compete with the barrage of media representations of gender and power struggles in the tabloid press and courtroom TV as they frame and transmit 'real-life dramas', from the trial of Anita Hill and Clarence Thomas to the saga of Lorena and John Wayne Bobbit.

I have discussed the theatrical implications of mediated images of women elsewhere.[25] I shall focus briefly in the next and last section on the ways in which feminist theatre and feminist performance techniques may help to keep theatre viable as a medium, part art form and part platform.

## Canon fodder: values and standards, politics and platforms

I shall focus very briefly on some of the most important issues in the academic evaluation of feminist theatre as form. Because feminist theatre is evaluated alongside mainstream work by theatre reviewers, academic critics and review panels for funding bodies, it is important to develop ways of assessing and evaluating feminist theatre which do not simply borrow from established traditions of literary criticism and art. These traditions are relevant to some extent, but so are the very different contributions of other disciplines including cultural studies, film studies and feminist theory. Thus, in evaluating feminist theatre, it is important to remember that canonical values are based in part on certain 'aesthetic criteria', but have also been influenced by the structures of the academy. By contrast, commercial values are influenced by market forces. The same play might 'suit' one set of criteria, but not the other. One play might 'suit' both or neither. Feminist theatres, like other forms of cultural representations, can be evaluated in accordance with different measures of value, depending upon the perspectives of different spectators and critics.

Because feminist theatre has developed in opposition to the hierarchical structures of patriarchal (dominant) culture, it seems particularly unjust to apply the standards of that culture to the evaluation of feminist theatre. Instead, it seems fair to outline a developing theory of feminist theatre as a distinct genre. The most useful way of approaching the subject might be to adopt a flexible definition of the term 'feminist theatre': one which allows for differences between feminists and takes the needs and interests of practitioners into account, and which accommodates the politics of production. Such a definition would incorporate the idea of the 'gendered gaze' and its relevance to the making and spectatorship of feminist theatre, as well as the many and varied roles of the active audience. In emphasising the action involved in watching and interpreting feminist performances of all kinds, live and mediated, and in recognising the political element of any such active spectatorship, we identify the life-blood of the form; that which could be drawn upon in arguing for its support in the art world and its inclusion in the academic curriculum (not only as canon fodder, but possibly also as part of a developing and ever-shifting alternative canon).

In advocating the incorporation of feminist theatre into the academic canon, I would strongly urge that it be added to the list of subjects, rather than absorbed into any existing subject such as performance studies or women's studies. I would also advocate framing the teaching of and about feminist theatre in a way which leaves open the lines of communication with women (and men) who would prefer that the theatre were treated as an 'art form' rather than a 'platform' or subject of academic study, and which makes room in theory and in practice for theatres made by women from non-English-speaking countries (where the word 'feminism' loses all meaning in linguistic/cultural translation) and in theatre groups which bring together women of different generations, and cultural, class and race backgrounds.

For example, one group which involves practitioners and academics from around the world is the Magdalena Project: Women in Theatre International. A large and loose affiliation of many women, all sharing a common interest in the expression of ideas in women's performance (dance and voice as well as theatre), the Magdalena Project has attracted many individuals and groups to its base in Cardiff, Wales. One large-scale performance piece produced by Magdalena and directed by Jill Greenhalgh was *Midnight Level Six*. This piece brought together twelve women performers who began with the factual news accounts of the rape, mutilation and murder of Cardiff prostitute Lynette White and developed a collaborative performance piece by adding images and ideas, making the story their own as individuals and as a group, weaving autobiography and personal images into the melting pot of visual and textual metaphors which became the multimedia performance.[26]

The Magdalena Project's work has emphasised the importance of finding a 'women's voice in theatre'. What the project has found through experimentation with voice, movement, dramaturgy and dance, as well as in practical and academic workshops, is a rich vein of experience shared by women of different cultures and languages.

1.5] *Midnight Level Six*, directed by Jill Greenhalgh for the Magdalena Project, 1990–1. (Brian Tarr)

Magdalena has encouraged diversity and difference within its work, teaching about the process of group devising, and dealing openly and honestly with the problems, as well as the benefits, of collaboration. The issues raised in this kind of cross-cultural work are, of course, not unique to the Magdalena Project. The same issues are often raised at international conferences on women in theatre, and at other major women's theatre forums such as Italy's Divina Project and the more academically oriented American Women in Theatre Program.[27] In all these diverse forums, feminist theatre is analysed and critiqued, as well as created and celebrated. Theatre is sometimes used as a way of teaching about gender and communication or as a form of communication when spoken and written languages are not shared.[28] But rarely are these various roles of feminist theatre considered when a reviewer criticises a play or performance for falling short of some preset 'aesthetic standard'.

Feminist theatre is a form of cultural representation affecting and affected by many and various disciplines. It is shaped and influenced by cultural, as well as literary and dramatic, factors. Thus, any useful set of criteria for assessing feminist theatre must be flexible enough to 'suit' feminist theatre over time, as both feminism and the theatre continue to change.

## Conclusions

To summarise: feminist theatres are those theatres created primarily by women with political concerns influenced by the development of the post-1968 women's movement(s) and/or by issues of real importance to the daily lives of women, in terms both of the concerns of local communities and of women around the world. These theatres may have many different functions. They may serve to entertain or to enlighten, to raise consciousness or to argue political points and/or to represent women's life experiences in ways which acknowledge them as 'real' subjects in public representation.

Feminist theatres encourage a gender-aware gaze but they do not restrict the range of possible gazes within any play or performance dynamic. As the marginalisation of many black women and women of colour, working-class women, and lesbians within feminism has been recognised and addressed—slowly but surely—so the field of feminist theatre has been informed and enriched by a wealth of new material, stories, images and styles. The reciprocal dynamic of feminist theatre is not limited to the relationship between the performance and the audience. It reaches out past the audience in any given venue or street performance or lecture hall, to inform and enrich the relationship between practitioners and critics.

With all this in mind, it becomes possible to reconsider Loren Kruger's idea of 'spectacle' in a way which builds a bridge towards a theory of feminist performance. Women have long been thought to 'make spectacles of themselves', but have only recently been recognised as the creators or 'makers' of spectacles. In the theatre, for instance, and particularly in feminist theatre, which self-consciously represents and reflects the personal and political concerns of women, the making of 'spectacles' is a doubly subversive act. It both 'usurps' the power of creation, and assumes the right to restructure the values and expectations according to which creative work tends to be judged.

In making theatre, and in watching and criticising that theatre, women and men of the past two generations of theatre-goers have witnessed a unique spectacle: the redirection of women's experience from the wings to the centre of the stage. With this 'redirection' or change of focus, the feminist theatre project has begun to recognise an internal conflict of aims between entrance into the mainstream—

i.e., breaking down the division which marginalises women from the mainstream—and maintenance of an active opposition to that mainstream. Both aims have been equally important in the development of feminist theatre as an oppositional, change-oriented project. Both stem from the oppositional techniques and strategies of the political demonstrators of the 1960s and '70s, who not only recognised and promulgated, but also *performed* their message that 'the personal is political'. The actors have watched and learned from their audiences, and vice versa, so that the urgency and political alignment of each performance may help to keep the form alive, even in the age of 'mediazation'.

Perhaps the ambiguous identity of feminist theatre is not only balanced on a recognition of difference between object and subject positions in relation to spectacle (as in Kruger's formulation), or even in relation to desire and a gendered gaze; perhaps that identity is also based on a recognition of our active roles as spectators. When it is women doing the viewing (as it usually is in live theatre) then it is in women's power to redirect the gaze in a practical as well as a theoretical sense. In viewing feminist theatres, we may see them not just as entertainment or as academic exchanges, but in all their potential as forms of cultural representation (art forms) and as political platforms and sites of intellectual engagement, created by and performed for different generations of women with different sexual orientations and political positions. The personal is political, and the active viewing of the spectacle is a creative act when it is a consciously feminist act, just as is 'making a spectacle of oneself'.

## Notes

This material has been presented in various forms over the years, in lectures and seminars for Middlesex University, Cambridge University, the Open University, the University of Calgary and the University of Turin. I am indebted to colleagues and students at all those institutions. The Open University has produced in-house monographs of two short papers on which this material is based (Arts Faculty, 1991 and 1993).

1 See, for instance, Gayle Austin, *Feminist Theories for Dramatic Criticism* (Ann Arbor, University of Michigan Press, 1990).

2 See my introduction to *Contemporary Women Dramatists*, edited by Kate Berney and Nina Templeton (London, St James Press, 1994), for a brief sweep of the history of women in theatre.

3 In my *Contemporary Feminist Theatres: To Each Her Own* (London and New York, Routledge, 1993) I analyse the impact of the post-1968 cultural revolution on the theatre in detail, drawing on the work of Michelene Wandor,

Sue-Ellen Case, Helene Keyssar, Susan Bassnett, Janet Brown, Karen Malpede *et al.*

4 *Ibid.*, pp. 24–5, 50–63.

5 *Ibid.*, pp. 24, 57.

6 Loren Kruger, 'The Dis-Play's the Thing: Gender and Public Sphere in Contemporary British Theatre', *Theater Journal*, 42:11 (1990), 27.

7 *The Penguin English Dictionary* (Harmondsworth, Penguin, 1971).

8 These and other working methods are discussed in detail in Chapter 4 of Goodman, *Contemporary Feminist Theatres*, pp. 88–113.

9 Published in association with the Royal Court Theatre production (London, Methuen, 1982). Also see Geraldine Cousin, *Churchill: The Playwright* (London, Methuen, 1989). During a 1989 research trip to Sofia, Bulgaria, I discovered that *Top Girls* was about to be performed for the first time in that country (just after the lifting of theatre censorship); my photograph of the billboard poster for the production, which hung outside the National Theatre of Bulgaria, is printed on p. 376 of Lizbeth Goodman and Gabriella Giannachi, 'Which Freedom: an Overview of Contemporary Bulgarian Theatre', *New Theatre Quarterly*, 8:32 (1992), 362–76.

10 The concept of the 'male gaze' in a media context was introduced by film theorist Laura Mulvey in 'Visual Pleasure and Narrative Cinema', *Screen*, 16:3 (1975). Also see Lorraine Gamman and Margaret Marshment (eds.), *The Female Gaze: Women as Viewers of Popular Culture* (London, The Women's Press, 1988).

11 The performative aspects of lecturing on gender are discussed in Lizbeth Goodman, 'Teaching Feminist Theatres: Stages Between Theory and Practice', *South African Theatre Journal*, 8:1 (May 1994), 3–23.

12 Company policy statement, printed in the Charabanc brochure and discussed by co-Artistic Director (with Eleanor Methven) Carol Moore in a telephone interview, 1 August 1994.

13 Gillian Elinor, 'Performance as a Subversive Activity', *Feminist Arts News* (Summer 1980), 1–2.

14 Jill Dolan, *The Feminist Spectator as Critic* (Ann Arbor, The University of Michigan Press, 1988).

15 Lesley Ferris, *Acting Women: Images of Women in Theatre* (London, Macmillan, 1990).

16 See William J. Baumol and William G. Bowen, 'Audiences: Some Fact-Sheet Data' in Elizabeth and Tom Burns (eds.), *Sociology of Literature and Drama* (London, Penguin, 1973); *Barbican Centre Research into Audience Potential* (London, Industrial Market Research, 1980); John Myerscough *et al.*, *The Economic Importance of the Arts in Britain* (London, Policy Studies Institute, 1988). None of these significantly informs a study of women in British theatre.

17 See Caroline Gardiner, *The City University Audience Survey for SWET, 1985–86* (London, Society for West End Theatres, 1986).

18 Susan Bennett, *Theatre Audiences: A Theory of Production and Reception* (London, Routledge, 1991).

19 A short version of this survey and analysis of its results is published in

Lizbeth Goodman, 'Feminist Theatre in Britain: a Survey and a Prospect', *New Theatre Quarterly*, 9:33 (1993), 66–84.

20 See discussion of *Mothers* and the audience survey in Goodman, *Contemporary Feminist Theatres*, p. 46, and more general background on the company, pp. 166–74.

21 See survey results in *New Theatre Quarterly*, 9:33 (1993), 66–84, and discussion of multi-media 'new directions' in Goodman, *Contemporary Feminist Theatres*, pp. 183, 207–8, 215.

22 New work in Performance Studies at the Open University and the BBC is exploring the use of video in teaching about gender and drama. Contact the Faculty of Arts, Literature Department, for details for the new course 'Approaching Literature' (forthcoming in 1996) which includes a block on Literature and Gender, with set texts including Susan Glaspell's *Trifles*, Ibsen's *A Doll's House* and Caryl Churchill's *Top Girls*, and a block on Shakespeare and the Canon, with texts including *As You Like It* and Aphra Behn's *The Rover*. Both course blocks will include significant broadcast (televisual, video and audio) drama workshops and performances designed for teaching purposes and available along with the co-published textbooks to other universities and to individuals.

23 Patrice Pavis, *Theatre at the Crossroads of Culture* (London, Routledge, 1992), pp. 99f.

24 John B. Thompson, *The Media and Modernity* (Cambridge, Polity Press, 1995).

25 See Lizbeth Goodman, 'Sexuality and Autobiography in Performance (Art)', *WOMEN: A Cultural Review*, 5:2, Special Issue on Women in Performance (Autumn 1994), 123–36.

26 *Midnight Level Six* was produced in Cardiff in 1991 and then went on international tour. For background information about Magdalena, see Susan Bassnett, *Magdalena: International Women's Experimental Theatre* (Oxford, Berg Publishers, 1989). Magdalena's largest festival/gathering to date (September 1994) was documented on video by Peter Hulton of Arts Archives, UK, and in print by Lizbeth Goodman *et al.* in a special issue of *Contemporary Theatre Review* (1995). The videos and journal documentation will be available for sale, individually or as a set.

27 The Divina Project is a collaborative practical and academic organisation of women in theatre and film, co-sponsored by the University of Turin, Turin City Council and Teatro Settimo: details from Professor Barbara Lanati, Department of English, the University of Turin. The American Women in Theater Program is a division of the Association of Theater Higher Education, with members from all areas of the US and Canada, as well as outside mainland North America.

28 See, for instance, Lizbeth Goodman, 'Performance Language as Communicative Gesture', in Janet Maybin and Neil Mercer (eds.), *Using English: From Conversation to Canon* (London, Routledge, 1996).

2 *Alexandra Carter*

# Bodies of knowledge: dance and feminist analysis

Dance is an art form populated by women. Although those in positions of power such as patrons, sponsors, funders, artistic directors and choreographers of mainstream companies still tend to be men, the executants of dance are primarily women. The images of women inscribed by traditional Western theatre dance forms are synonymous in our society with notions of what it is to be not just female, but feminine. Therefore, as a field which 'perpetuates some of our culture's most potent symbols of femininity, Western theatrical dance provides feminist analysis with its potentially richest material.'[1] This chapter explores the relationship of pertinent aspects of feminist theory to dance and exemplifies ways in which this approach can offer new readings of dance works. The emphasis is on analysis, that is, the activity of describing, interpreting and evaluating dance. However, as analysis is also an integral, if less clearly articulated, aspect of choreography and performance, a feminist perspective can significantly influence the making and the doing as well as the appreciating of the art form.

Although the following examples are drawn from theatre dance as practised in the West, a feminist perspective can be applied to the study of dance in all its forms, functions and contexts. Similarly, although this perspective necessarily embraces the ways in which constructs of femininity are formed, it can also offer, in aspects of methodology if not in motivation, an understanding of how gender in all its cultural manifestations and stereotypes is produced and circulated by dance.

Until recently, dance has tended to escape analytical attention. Unlike music or drama, its ephemeral nature has been compounded by the fact that there has been no score or script to study and therefore no opportunity for repeated access to the work. Further reasons for its neglect include the Western mind–body dualism which privileges the verbal and the cognitive over the sensory and the physical; the long, unquestioned heritage of ballet which has made its values and its practices almost transcendental; the perceived dependency of dance on other art forms and the low status given to any kind of women's activity. Lack of attention to dance in scholarly discourse can also be attributed to its apparent nature as a realm for experts in its practice and, by association, in its theory. Now, however, dance has become established as a discipline in its own right and open to inquiring minds, as well as questing bodies.[2] Among the many questions raised are those concerned with what kinds of images of femininity are represented in and by dance, and how these images reflect the beliefs and values of specific cultural situations. An examination of these questions may require, for example, analysis of individual works, a choreographic *œuvre*, a style or a genre.

A feminist approach can radicalise the reading of dance. Furthermore, by exposing connections between dance as an artistic product, process and event which does not simply mirror but actively produces constructs of femininity, it can identify the significant contribution which dance makes to the hegemonic practices of society.

### Feminist theory and the interpretation of dance

As the focus of this chapter is on how feminist perspectives can be applied to dance, it does not offer a detailed exposition of the general characteristics of feminist theories.[3] Pluralistic in approach and problematic in the unresolved nature of the debate, these theories do, nevertheless, have commensurate concerns which cohere around the notion that, whilst sex is a biological determinant, gender is a social construct.[4] As such, it is not simply reflected in, but produced by, cultural activity. The arts 'do not simply represent given gender identities or reproduce existing ideologies of femininity. Rather they participate in the very construction of those identities . . . consequently . . . culture is a crucial arena for the contestation of the social arrangement of gender.'[5] Furthermore, 'the representation of woman as image . . . and the concurrent representation of the female body as the locus of sexuality, site of visual pleasure, or lure of the gaze is so pervasive in our culture . . . that it necessarily constitutes a starting point for any understanding of sexual difference.'[6]

In other words, an analysis of the ways in which the female body is presented in dance can reveal dominant notions of what it is to be 'female' in particular cultural contexts. These notions are embodied in the image of the dancer which becomes a symbolic location of patriarchal ideology. As Stubbs claims in relation to the portrayal of women in literature, images are not neutral, an 'innocent pictorial guide to reality' but they 'create the world for us; they shape our consciousness.'[7] Images shape the consciousness of the doer and the viewer; the performer, the critic and the audience. While analysis can focus on ways in which women are presented in the dance itself, critical writing can also be examined for its mediation and production of concepts of gender. It is not simply the activities of women in the arts, as either producers or performers, which constitute their image, but how those images are publicly received.

In dance, images present constructs of gender which have 'become petrified in an opposition of so-called "masculine" and "feminine" movement choices' which, it can be argued, are 'social and artistic conventions rather than physical or biological fact.'[8] This perspective refutes essentialism in movement and rejects the notion of the 'natural' body. It argues that codifications of dance arise from social customs and culturally determined behaviours which are embodied and perpetuated in devices such as training systems and the methods and procedures of dance making. As Polhemus[9] so clearly explains, it is the interrelationship and mutual dependency of culture, gender and dance which makes the latter so richly rewarding for feminist analysis.

All analysis, of whatever dance form, rests on a notion that the symbols and structures of dance can only be read in relation to the cultural practices of society, for 'there is a problem with the position which assumes that the audience can read whatever they want to in a work. This position assumes an ahistorical, apolitical stance which does not take into account the dominant meanings . . . within a structure of patriarchy'.[10]

The meanings that accrue to the symbols of dance, whatever the genre, are no more transcendental or self-contained than those which are produced in any other artistic or social practice. As Shepherd argues in relation to music, not only is its status as a self-referential, socially neutral art form untenable but such a view also obliterates the hegemonic function of music.[11] In parallel, feminist analysis of music, dance or any other art form, does not rest solely in the realm of aesthetics but is a complex interplay between the aesthetic and the social. In order to make any statement about the relationship between dance and society, it has to be assumed that there are shared cultural meanings. A recognition of the specificity of audience members does not negate their shared ideologies; to refute such a premise would invalidate any notion of meaning in the arts at all. It logically follows, therefore, that if these meanings change historically and geographically then so do notions of what constitutes positive images of women. As Copeland[12] points out, the sexual politics of Isadora Duncan were very different from those of Yvonne Rainer, yet both have a validity for their time. Similarly, some of the works of Martha Graham, with their powerful, active, self-contained heroines, may seem at odds in a post-modern age which is deeply suspicious not only of the larger-than-life character and the singular psyche, but also of the meta-narratives embodied in mythology and even the manipulative artifice of the theatre experience. However, Graham's choreography did challenge notions of the passive and passionless woman. Furthermore, the theatricality of her works, and the individuality of her characters, can still speak to us today. Dance analysis, therefore, can not only be alert to negative and disempowering images of women but it can also map out changing notions of feminism itself.

Another form of social, aesthetic and artistic interplay exists in the relationship between the personal motivation of the individual who creates or performs in a work and the public reception of that work. One of the shared methodological concerns of feminist research and other contemporary critical perspectives is that of situating the place of the subject in the construction of meaning. For example, in historical or sociological research, emphasis is placed on how people themselves think and feel about their place in society. Such an approach is problematic, however, in relation to any analysis of representation. Whilst in some respects it may be important to consider what the dance maker or dance performer thinks about her/his work, personal intent or motivation is relatively powerless in the face of the cultural meanings that accrue to images of the female body.

## Feminist approaches to dance analysis

A feminist perspective on dance, as on all the arts, can illuminate many facets of its practice. A reconceptualisation of its language; a questioning of how and why its history is recorded; a consideration of how the canon was formed rather than a simple rejection of the dance heritage; a structural examination of its audiences, market, institutions and workplaces, and an analysis of the critical reception of dance, all repay enquiry.[13] As Wolff claims, in order to understand any form of representation, analysis is required of 'both texts and artists within the complex system of aesthetic and ideological discourses, institutions and structures in which they reside.'[14] However, whilst in one sense it is not logically possible to consider the artistic product outside the contextual framework of its production, performance and reception, analysis of the separate components of the dance work can be considered in order to illuminate the totality. It must be stressed that, as with any analytical project, this apparently atomistic approach serves to enhance, not destroy, the holistic experience. It is the interrelationship of these components in space and through time which constitutes the dance itself. No narrative can exist without movement; no movement without its own dynamic qualities, spatial elements and someone to perform it. Some components of the dance may warrant more attention than others, depending on the genre or style of work being observed. In some dances, for example, the *narrative* and *roles* played by the female dancer(s) may significantly define her image. In others, it is the *qualities of movement* which signify aspects of femininity.

The following identification of the key components which, to a greater or lesser extent, may be amenable to feminist analysis is a simplified form of the framework for analysis offered by Adshead.[15] This comprehensive model embraces the analytic concepts of description, interpretation and evaluation, and enables understanding of the relationship between the text and its context. The components of the dance can be identified as the *movement*; the *dynamic* and *spatial* elements; the *dancers*; the *aural* and *visual* environments and the relationship of these components through time which constitutes the *structure*, or *form*, of the dance. The treatment of these components in relation to the theme or subject matter of the dance, and their characteristic selection which constitutes the various genres and styles, offer a focus for feminist analysis.

The subject matter, theme or narrative of dance is an obvious starting point. Indeed, in some critiques of ballet, it is both the start and the finish of analysis. Questions can be raised in relation to the kinds of roles played by women in relation to the narrative: who forwards the narrative and who is its passive recipient? Another approach is to examine *how* women are portrayed; what kinds of 'characters' are they? *Petrushka* (Michel Fokine, 1911) is a key work in the twentieth-century dance canon, yet it is rarely pointed out that all identifiable female characters or groups of characters are whores, dimwits or in servicing roles of some kind. How are significant female characters presented in relation to the men in the story; how is the future, the sanity, the very existence of the heroine reliant on the agency of these men? Conversely, consider the ways in which those whose destinies are not bound up with men are identified, as they are in society, as constituting the 'other'; as representing a threat to the psychological stability of the hero (as the Sylph in *La Sylphide*, Filippo Taglioni, 1832) and/or to the very stability of society itself (Odile in *Swan Lake*, Marius Petipa/Lev Ivanov, 1895). However, although rarely read as such, the power of these disrupters of the status quo can be reinterpreted more positively. Consider, perhaps, that in *Giselle* (Jean Coralli/Jules Perrot, 1841) true moral retribution lies in the hands of the wilis; it is they and their queen who attempt to dispense justice for criminal acts of neglect and duplicity. It is not very feminine to fight for power and those who do achieve it, such as the Black Queen in *Checkmate* (Ninette de Valois, 1937), leave us a little uneasy at their singular intent. In order to vanquish the Red King and acquire his territory, she has not only to reject but remove his Knight; a kind of Margaret Thatcher of the chessboard, she is unremitting in her ambition. Such an ending, in which an independent woman achieves her desire and retains her independence, perhaps necessarily through the sacrifice of love, is unusual in our dance narratives. So often based on existing folk tales, myths and legends, they reflect the social and political ideologies embodied in those stories. If the women in *Stabat Mater* (Robert Cohan, 1975) passively wait and grieve, so do women in the Christian stories told by the fathers of the Church. However, an alternative reading of Cohan's work, with its all-female cast, reveals a mutually supportive collective. If they cannot change society, at least they can help each other through.

These examples, chosen deliberately from the ballet and modern dance canon, show how a feminist approach to specific narratives can offer different readings of works. If it is not possible to change the grand narratives embodied in our stories we can, at least, look to their origins and their reasons. By uncovering the provenance and the changes through which the most seemingly traditional tales have passed, both the stories and their 'truths' become destabilised. If we are aware that in an earlier version of the story of the Sleeping Beauty, the princess apparently bore twins by her prince,[16] her virginal image in the ballet can be seen as a parable for its time, not for all times. Similarly, even the profound connections between Indian classical dance forms and their religious roots are now being severed by those who reject the values transmitted in the male-constructed stories of female passivity and servitude. As with the Western classical dance form of ballet, there is a dilemma between acknowledging a long tradition of women's activity and questioning the forms and functions of that activity.

It is, of course, impossible to disentangle the subject matter and the roles of the dancers from the ways in which these are constituted by the components of the dance. Whether a dance has an 'exterior' subject matter, as discussed above, or whether it is concerned with the actions, qualities, designs and structures of the movement itself, it is possible to consider how the actual movement contributes to, or constitutes, the 'meanings' of the dance. Questions can be asked, for example, about what kinds of actions are performed by the women and by the men: who lifts, who supports, who leads or guides and who follows, and what is the significance of these actions in terms of notions of dependency and control? Again, there are no simple answers. In ballet, a supported promenade, whereby the male dancer holds the female who is *en pointe* and leads her around on the pivot of her foot, can be interpreted either as his manipulation of her, or as her using him to achieve and display her technical skills. Movement is always perceived in context and factors such as its qualities, the expressive interpretation of the dancers and the place of the movement within the thematic structure of the dance will all inform debate as to its meanings.

The development of release-based work and contact improvisation has meant that gender specificity and conventional partnering, found in mainstream modern dance as well as in ballet, can be subverted. In these ways of working with the body it is not simply muscular strength but how the body weight is distributed which liberates dancers from the constraints of their physiology. In the early 1990s, dance vocabularies which involved both women and men hurling their bodies through space, crashing into each other and on to the floor, became popular. It could be argued, however, that this 'Eurocrash', with its seeming democracy of movement and apparent liberation from more stylised techniques, was merely the imposition of an aesthetic which resulted in a brutalisation of both women's and men's bodies.

All movement exists with dynamic or qualitative aspects and with various elements of spatial design; these are the 'how' and 'where' of dance analysis. Again, although movement is experienced as a holistic composite of action, dynamics and space it is possible to consider these elements separately. For example, what kinds of qualities are demonstrated: who is lyrical, graceful, light and fleet and who is forceful, rhythmic and strong? Although these differences can constrain the potential of the dancers in performance and the choreographic possibilities, in themselves they need not be problematic if assigned equal value. For example, *Choreartium* (Leonide Massine, 1933) takes as its theme the interplay of feminine and masculine dance movements and qualities, and celebrates both. In *Les Noces* (Bronislava

Nijinska, 1923), blocked groups of women dancers stabbing their pointed feet with forceful intent into the earth, rather than using them to rise up from it, was a radical departure from the qualitative and spatial elements normally associated with this traditional movement of the *danse d'école*. Karole Armitage (*Watteau Duet*, 1985) used her *pointe* as symbol of dominance and aggression. These examples subvert the norm and illustrate how the interpretation of movement is contingent not on the action alone but also on factors such as how, when, where, why, who with and for what purpose it is done. Daly argues that the vocabulary of classical ballet itself is an embodiment of patriarchal ideology which renders it impossible to use for the presentation of positive images of women.[17] However, that vocabulary can, perhaps, be appropriated through a different treatment in a more sympathetic thematic or narrative context.[18]

Two dance works which perpetuate rather than challenge the cultural norms associated with qualities of masculinity and femininity are *Troy Game* (Robert North, 1974) and the previously mentioned *Stabat Mater* (Cohan, 1975), both of which were in the repertoire of the London Contemporary Dance Theatre during the same period. *Troy Game* is a bravado demonstration of masculinity which, although somewhat tongue-in-cheek, celebrates power, strength and 'machismo'. The only character who lightens and speeds up his movement in a flurry of activity, thus taking on feminine qualities, is intentionally comic. Conversely, *Stabat Mater*, which depicts Mary and a group of women waiting and sorrowing at the foot of the Cross, is an essay in grace and lyricism. The issue at stake in such a comparison is not whether the choreographers should, or even could have explored other qualities of movement, for to have done so would clearly have transformed the meaning of both works. The concern is with how these works, not just in their dynamic aspects but in their overall treatment of the subject matter, embody the cultural status quo inherent in their source material. Furthermore, the potency of our internalisation of gendered movement is realised when imagination is allowed to play with the idea of an all-female *Troy Game* or an all-male *Stabat Mater*. Difficulties encountered are not just at the simplistic level of conceiving women in shorts and thongs or men in dresses. The problems arise in transferring not only the subject matter and its psychological import from one sex to another but also in transcribing the movement. The imagination struggles, for example, with allowing women to adopt the purposeful, space-conquering strides, the wide open stances or the confrontational spatial patterning of *Troy Game*.

The spatial aspects of movement and the situation of the action in the performing space can also be considered for their significance in forming or replicating notions of gender. Experiments of the 1960s and 1970s notwithstanding, most Western theatre dance takes place on a proscenium arch stage which frames the dancer and her body. In ballet, the male dancer dominates the space not only with long travelling patterns which cross and circle the space but also with the amplitude of his movement. The ballerina tends to circle around her own axis in pirouette and crosses the stage with a series of small movements. These are, of course, generalisations, but the male *danseur* tends to be valued for his skill at occupying the public space of the stage and the *danseuse* for what she does within her personal kinesphere. Narrative meaning is achieved through another spatial device, that of focus. In *Appalachian Spring* (Martha Graham, 1944) the wife's visual and body focus is almost constantly directed at her husband, whilst he surveys the wide open spaces of his new territory. The female acolytes of the preacher relate spatially to him but the preacher himself lifts his eyes upwards to his God. Even in the seemingly democratic world of *Duets* (Merce Cunningham, 1980), the gender specificity of the actions is compounded by the orientation of the women's bodies and focus to the front and the direction of the male body and gaze to her. These duets resonate with meaning in terms of how the female body is displayed for the male gaze of the audience, with whom her partner is complicit.[19] The spatial orientation of the dancers' bodies in relation to each other is explored in relation to the film musical by Dyer.[20] Although concerned with how this partnering promotes the heterosexual ideal, the resonances of such spatial devices described by Dyer as side by side, mirroring, mutually holding or in relations of dependency are worthy of application to theatre dance.

In feminist writing on dance the area which tends to receive considerable attention is that of the physical stereotype of the female dancer. In relation to a general analysis of dance as hegemonic practice, its significance in the presentation of an ideal feminine beauty is undoubted, though historical examination will demonstrate that these notions of the ideal body change according to the cultural norms of the period. Body image can be subverted but it is a risky business; it could be argued, for example, that *Groosland* (Maguy Marin, 1989), which appears to offer possibilities for large and rotund bodies, merely succeeds in parodying them. The Cholmondeleys present real rather than manipulated varieties of body shapes and sizes but although it seemed that they might herald a new age in the body aesthetic, they remain the exception rather than the norm. Unlike the performing arts of many other cultures, the West now associates performance skills in dance with youth. At least in ballet, dancers can continue to perform by taking on mime roles but in modern and more recent forms there is still little place for the older dancer, man or woman.

One of the obvious signs of gender, in dance as in society, is dress. Costume establishes character, enhances movement qualities, enables or hinders action and defines the body image. It was Isadora Duncan who rejected the wearing of the corset in dance and in fashion generally by rebelling against 'everything it symbolised: the constraints, both physical and psychological, imposed upon women by Victorian culture.'[21] The body tights for men and women, so prevalent in British modern dance in the 1970s, reflected the unisex fashions for young people; both the title of Banes' book *Terpsichore in Sneakers* (1980) and *Redressing the Sylph*, the title of a conference on women and dance, indicate that what a dancer wears is not only related directly to the sexual politics of the day but is also a key component for the identification and subversion of gender roles.[22] An examination of footwear (or lack of it) in dance also reveals both the aesthetic concerns of a genre and the sexual politics of the time. The confining (or, a moot point, the enabling) ballet shoe; the glamorous, to-be-desired Red Shoes of the 1950s film; the liberating bare foot of early modern dance and the rowdy and aggressive Dr Martens of the 1980s all resonate with meaning about women's role in society. In dance, feet speak in more ways than one.

The dance accompaniment can also be analysed for the ways in which it endorses feminine and masculine actions and qualities. In ballet, loud, vibrant sounds from brass and wind instruments announce the male solo; tinkling arpeggios or lyrical melodies from the piano or strings accompany the female. For example, in the *grand pas classique* from Act III of *Raymonda* (Marius Petipa, 1898), it is possible to guess whether it is a male or female dancer who is about to make her/his entrance simply by the quality of the orchestral sound. Even modern dance works may offer the potential for analysis of not just who is on stage, but who is following the lyrical line of the music and who uses the rhythmic framework.

As the structure of the music can repay analysis so, too, can the overall structure of the dance itself. The common ballet *divertissement* incorporates a series of female and male solos in which each demonstrates their skills, culminating in a coda of mutual, partnered display. Whilst all the components reinforce traditional notions of femininity and masculinity, the actual structure of the *divertissement* involves both independence and partnership in a seemingly democratic co-existence. However, this democracy of structure is misleading as the actual contest (the dancers' vocabularies) is hierarchical in its gender specificity. The conscious manipulation and resultant clarity of structure, where a dance builds from discernible beginning to end through such devices as repetition, phrasing and climax, was one of the features of both modern dance and ballet which postmodernists rejected. Through aleatory processes, arbitrary decisions and conceptually-inspired rather than 'external' subject matter, the structures of postmodern works lost the traditional 'closed' forms of Western theatre dance. The fact that the great majority of choreographers creating work in this way were women is, perhaps, more significant than just historical accident. The French feminist writer, Cixous, called for language that was 'fragmentary rather than whole, ambiguous rather than clear, and interrupted rather than complete.'[23] Furthermore, as 'the feminine form seems to be without a sense of formal closure . . . without closure, the sense of beginning, middle and end or a central focus, it abandons the hierarchical organising principles of traditional form that served to elide women from discourse'.[24]

Although the making of links between so-called feminine structures of language and feminine structures of dance is a highly dubious activity in the sense that such comparisons are necessarily rooted in concepts of essentialism and biological determinism, there are interesting parallels to be made. As Shepherd suggests in relation to music, even apparently neutral structural devices are not value free but are laden with meaning and resonance (see Note 11).

## Summary

Although the different components of the dance, that is, the movement, dynamic and spatial elements, the dancers, the visual and aural environments and the devices which give the dance its structure, can be read in terms of their relationship to culturally determined notions of femininity and masculinity, none of these aspects can be analysed in isolation from each other or from the work in its entirety. Consideration of the artistic, social and historical context of the dance is also essential, for it is the values which society places on certain qualities, the cultural interpretations of movements, sights and sounds, which produce meaning. Polarities of delicate/strong; lyrical/forceful; flexible/direct; inner/outer; passive/active; emotional/rational; natural/cultural; private space/public space can be exposed as facets of the male–female binary construction in which one term, one attribute, one way of being is favoured at the expense of another. As with women's work in the wider sphere, it is not what they do but the values attributed to their actions which define their place in society. Moreover, through analysis, dance can be revealed as not just an artistic product but also as a cultural phenomenon which produces, circulates—and has the potential to subvert—dominant constructs of gender in society.

## Notes

1 A. Daly, 'Unlimited Partnership: Dance and Feminist Analysis', *Dance Research Journal*, 23:1 (1991), 2.

2 See J. Adshead, *The Study of Dance* (London, Dance Books, 1981) for an account of the development and the discrete characteristics of dance as a discipline.

3 Although somewhat reductionist in nature, there are many texts which give an overview of feminist theories. See, for example, C. Pateman and E. Gross (eds.), *Feminist Challenges: Social and Political Theory* (London, Allen and Unwin, 1986) or R. Tong, *Feminist Thought: a Comprehensive Introduction* (London, Unwin Hyman, 1989). For a direct application to dance, see C. Adair, *Women and Dance: Sylphs and Sirens* (London, Macmillan, 1992).

4 Early feminist and sociological literature tended to treat gender as an unproblematic concept but, more recently, writers such as J. Butler, *Gender Trouble: Feminism and the Subversion of Identity* (London, Routledge, 1990), have raised questions in relation to the fixed or free-will nature of this construction and the complex relationship between sex and gender.

5 J. Wolff, *Feminine Sentences: Essays on Women and Culture* (Cambridge, Polity Press, 1990), p. 1.

6 T. de Lauretis, *Alice Doesn't: Television, Semiotics, Cinema* (London, Macmillan, 1984), p. 38.

7 P. Stubbs, *Women and Fiction: Feminism and the Novel 1880–1920* (Brighton, Manchester Press, 1979), p. vix.

8 M. Goldberg, 'Ballerinas and ball passing', *Women and Performance*, 3:2 (1987/8), 8.

9 Ted Polhemus in H. Thomas (ed.), *Dance, Gender and Culture* (London, Macmillan, 1993), pp. 3–15.

10 C. Adair, V. Briginshaw and K. Lynn. 'Viewing women: the second sex', *Dance Theatre Journal*, 7:2 (1989), 29.

11 J. Shepherd, *Music as Social Text* (Cambridge, Polity Press, 1991).

12 R. M. Copeland, 'Founding mothers: Duncan, Graham, Rainer and sexual politics', *Dance Theatre Journal*, 8:3 (1990), 6–9; 27–9.

13 See A. Carter, 'Man as Creative Master, Woman as Responsive Muse', *Dance Now*, 4:1 (1994), 34–9, for an overview of possibilities for feminist perspectives on dance.

14 J. Wolff, *Feminine Sentences: Essays on Women and Culture* (Cambridge, Polity Press, 1990), p. 112.

15 J. Adshead (ed.), *Dance Analysis: Theory and Practice* (London, Dance Books, 1988).

16 M. Warner, Reith Lecture: 'Little angels, little devils: keeping childhood innocent', *The Independent* (11 Feb 1994).
17 A. Daly, 'The Balanchine Woman: of humming birds and channel swimmers', *The Drama Review*, 31:1 (1987), 9–21.
18 This device would, of course, take the dance out of the stylistic conventions of 'classical ballet' and thereby raise questions as the extent to which the boundaries of a style, or even a genre, can be redefined.
19 The concept of the gaze, now common (though contested) currency in feminist discourse, arises from Laura Mulvey's work on film. See, however, Copeland, 'Founding mothers' (Note 12) for a warning on the transference of this concept from film to dance.
20 Richard Dyer in Thomas, *Dance, Gender and Culture*, pp. 49–65.
21 Copeland, 'Founding mothers', 7.
22 'Redressing the Sylph' was the title of a symposium on women in dance held in Yorkshire in February 1994.
23 S. E. Case, *Feminism and Theatre* (London, Macmillan, 1988), p. 129.
24 Case, *Feminism and Theatre*, p. 129.

3 *Elaine Aston*

# Gender as sign-system: the feminist spectator as subject

In Jill Dolan's *The Feminist Spectator as Critic*, the concept of the feminist critic as 'resistant reader' is transposed into the theatrical context of 'resistant spectator'. The feminist spectator takes a critical look at how she is imaged on the mainstream stage, 'leaves the theatre while the audience applauds at the curtain call and goes off to develop a theory of feminist performance criticism'.[1]

To act as 'resistant spectator', the feminist critic has to challenge dominant modes of theatrical representation and communication. Among the critical tools she has at her disposal to realise her critique is the field of theatre semiotics: understanding theatre as a sign-system. Theatre semiotics has provided the vocabulary and a formal framework for representational and communicational analysis. However, as a field of study, semiotics tends to be gender blind: it neither 'sees' nor acknowledges gender in its critical and methodological paths of enquiry. Feminist intervention in this field of theory, therefore, politicises the formal semiotic model: general semiotic objectives are replaced by the specific (politicised) aims of understanding how women are represented in and how they are addressed by theatrical sign-systems.

Feminist approaches to the re-imaging of women often take the dramatic/theatrical frame of representation as their focus. In this brief study, however, I propose to take the feminist spectator as the subject, to examine how she is addressed by theatrical sign-systems in mainstream and feminist performance contexts, in order to reflect on and to propose a methodology for theatrical reception which takes account of gender, and which may be of general use to play and production analysis.

## Theatre semiotics and the spectator

The semiotic field of enquiry (understanding sign-systems) has proved a productive methodology for the study of theatre. Understanding theatre as a sign-system began with the work of the Czech semioticians of the Prague School in the 1930s and 1940s who proposed that 'all that is on the stage is a sign'.[2] Their investigations into the nature of the theatrical sign concentrated on identifying the signifying role of stage sign-vehicles and analysing their dynamic and generative capabilities.[3] This work has been developed and taken in different directions by international theatre semioticians who include Marco De Marinis, Keir Elam, Tadeusz Kowzan, Patrice Pavis and Anne Ubersfeld. Ultimately, the formal model of theatre semiotics has provided the framework and a vocabulary for identifying, classifying and analysing the 'parts' which make up the theatrical whole.

A fundamental premise of the semiotic approach is the understanding of theatre as a communication model in which a series of coded messages are sent or enacted and their meaning/s received or decoded. Most of the early work in the field of theatre semiotics was concerned with the mechanisms and processes of encodification: how meaning is encoded and transmitted through the various systems of staging—set, lighting, costume, music, props, etc. In a more recent phase of semiotic study, the emphasis has switched to the decodifying activities of the receiver: the spectator.

Despite the way in which theatre is, as the semiotician Roland Barthes has pointed out, characterised by its 'density of signs',[4] it is easier to focus on the complex encoding of theatrical sign-systems than it is to analyse the processes of decodification where what is understood and received becomes much more problematic. The spectator was, therefore, always acknowledged in the model of theatrical communication but in mechanistic or diagrammatic terms as the receiver.[5]

In the questionnaire which Patrice Pavis designed for his students to use in their analysis of theatre productions,[6] students were advised to think about the following in the audience category: where the performance takes place; their expectations of the performance; audience reactions; and the role of the spectator in the production of meaning.

Some of these issues are easier to address than others. Expectations of a theatrical event encoded in factors such as pre-publicity, knowing who is performing in a show, knowing whether a play is a comedy or tragedy, or having knowledge of the performance venue and its reputation for staging a certain kind of drama, etc., are easier elements to decode and analyse, than, for example, audience reaction. Similarly, the role of the spectator in the production of meaning, insofar as it relates to how the 'work' or 'task' of the spectator is 'fixed' or conditioned by the type of theatrical event, is an analysable element of semiotic production analysis.

Dramatic theories of spectator response have provided useful ways of identifying and analysing how an audience is expected to behave or respond in the theatre. In Brecht's theatre, for example, the spectator is required to be distanced from the event in order to leave the theatre ready for revolutionary action after the performance. The politically 'engaged' spectator of Brechtian theatre contrasts, however, with the 'passive' spectator in the West End musical who 'takes pleasure' in the event as it happens, and so on.

Spectator reaction, on the other hand, is particularly difficult to analyse within the formal mode of semiotic analysis which insists on a theoretical frame with no place for audience laughter, tears, anger, passion (as students using the Pavis questionnaire for theatre analysis have frequently observed, or, indeed, complained). Keir Elam elucidates the difficulty by using two response terms which he takes from Barthes: the *studium*, a response characterised by 'cool interest', and the *punctum*, 'that mode of painful and compulsive pleasure that is not sought out but actively seeks out and injures the receiver'.[7] He explains how theatre semiotics addresses the *studium*, but resists the *punctum*:

> The problem with much of what goes under the name of theatrical pragmatics (or theatrical semiotics in general) is that it is strictly and, one might say, strategically limited to the temperate zone of the *studium* and keeps a safe distance from the tropics or dangers of the *punctum*. . . . We as students or theorists of theatre, including theatrical reception, necessarily operate within the terms of the *studium*, a professional 'application to' or 'being interested in'. But does this mean that we must attribute an analogous cool studiousness to our model spectator or to ourselves as actual spectators? Is the semiotics of theatrical communication, in other words, destined inescapably to be a *studium* of the *studium* alone or is it not possible to conceive instead of a semiotic conception of the *punctum*, or *pathos* or, if you like, audience passion, that compulsion which . . . motivates the receiver's active participation in the artistic practice?[8]

Despite Elam's pleas for the *punctum*, traditional semiotic models have remained firmly rooted in the *studium*, in particular *studium* of the model or hypothetical spectator rather than the real one.

This distinction between the model spectator whose role can be identified and studied in the production of meaning, and the real spectator, is further clarified by De Marinis. Making use of reception theory from related fields of study, De Marinis establishes the concept of the 'model spectator' for the spectator who is intratextually constructed, inscribed or 'implied' in the performance text, as distinct from the extratextual, real spectator.[9] He also notes that a semiotics of theatrical reception ought to take account of the real (empirical) receiver, but acknowledges that the real spectator has received scant attention from the semiotician and his own analysis reinforces this.[10] Moreover, like Elam, De Marinis identifies the reactions of the real spectator as problematic for the semiotician, because they exceed the analytical frame in a way which brings its authority into question.[11]

One area where the 'implied' and 'real' spectator have both been given more consideration is in the field of feminist theory and theatre. In this field of study, the *punctum* of the real (feminist) spectator (which barely finds its way into the Pavis questionnaire) is central to the performance frame and demands our attention in production analysis.

### The female spectator and 'woman' as sign

Like many of the theatre semioticians, De Marinis does not consider gender in the semiotics of theatrical reception. Feminist analysis of spectatorship has, however, demonstrated that gender is a crucial determining factor for what De Marinis designates the intratextual (or model) and extratextual (or real) spectator in the reception of performance texts.

Feminist analysis of spectatorship was pioneered in film studies by feminist theoreticians such as Teresa De Lauretis, Mary Ann Doane, E. Ann Kaplan and Laura Mulvey. Their work makes use of post-Lacanian psychoanalysis and semiotics (referred to as psychosemiotics) to understand how the 'implied' spectator is male and how 'woman' is the object of his gaze. The issue of the 'male gaze' and its implications for the real female spectator have subsequently been explored by feminist scholarship in theatre studies. Sue-Ellen Case, leading international feminist theatre scholar, explains and summarises:

> Given the assumption that stage and audience co-produce the performance text, the meaning of the sign 'woman' is also created by the audience. The way the viewer perceives the woman on stage constitutes another theoretical enterprise . . . In the realm of theatrical production, the gaze is owned by the male: the majority of playwrights, directors and producers are men. This triumvirate determines the nature of the theatrical gaze, deriving the sign for 'woman' from their perspective. In the realm of audience reception, the gaze is encoded with culturally determined components of male sexual desire, perceiving 'woman' as a sexual object.[12]

The theatrical authorship of the 'male gaze' poses a problem for the real, 'extratextual' female spectator. De Marinis raises the issue of what happens in a performance context when real spectators react in unforeseen ways to the manner in which they are guided by the model spectator, for example, when audiences laugh in the wrong places or fail to laugh in the right ones, etc. However, the female spectator whose reactions are theatrically 'competent' generally finds herself in the position of laughing in spite of herself. Where is the pleasure in finding yourself the object of the joke? In such a theatrical frame, there is no *punctum*, no motivating passion for the female spectator.

In Anne Ubersfeld's second full-length semiotic study of theatre, *L'École du Spectateur*, she equates theatrical pleasure with the pleasure of the sign. She explains the theatrical sign in psychosemiotic terms as a 'sign-substitute'—the filling in for a 'lack', a presence which also marks an absence.[13] 'Woman' as sign in the male-authored performance context which Case describes is the sign-substitute which marks the present/absent object of male desire, fetishistically inscribed in the performance text and transforming the woman on stage into 'a kind of cultural courtesan'.[14] If the female spectator colludes in the 'co-production' of this sign, then she complies with her own victimisation and self-annihilation.[15] French feminist Hélène Cixous offers this personal response to the absence of pleasure for the female spectator in the theatrical sign:

> With even more violence than fiction, theatre, which is built according to the dictates of male fantasy, repeats and intensifies the horror of the murder scene which is at the origin of all cultural productions. It is always necessary for a woman to die in order for the play to begin. Only when she has disappeared can the curtain go up; she is relegated to repression, the grave, the asylum, oblivion and silence. When she does make an appearance, she is doomed, ostracised or in a waiting-room. She is loved only when absent or abused, a phantom or a fascinating abyss. Outside and also beside herself. That is why I stopped going to the theatre: it was like going to my own funeral.[16]

Staying away from the theatre, refusing to co-produce or co-author one's own death, is one strategy for the feminist spectator. Another is to engage in the theatrical project/s of making the sign feminist: to realise the pleasure/s and desire/s of the female/feminist spectator (as, indeed, Cixous has gone on to do by writing her own plays).

## Feminist theatre and spectatorship

In contrast to the mainstream performance context previously described, the implied and real spectators in feminist theatre are women [Goodman offers a qualification of this view in Chapter 1 (ed.)]. The real female spectator does not have to enter the theatrical frame in 'male drag': she is not coerced into producing woman as object, but is pleasured by the co-authoring of woman as subject. To understand how feminism revisions theatrical communication, it is useful to examine the roles of the model and the real spectator in the context of feminist performance.

In De Marinis's semiotic analysis of theatrical spectatorship he examines how the model spectator is constructed in two modes of performance which he identifies as the 'open' and the 'closed'.[17] These correspond to the ways in which the intratextual/model spectator is more (closed) or less (open) constructed in the performance text. Closed performances, and feminist theatre is listed as an example of this mode, are described as 'performances that predict a specific addressee, requiring definite kinds of competence for their "correct" interpretation'.[18] The prediction of a specific addressee depends upon the clear intratextual encoding of spectator response in the performance text. The intratextual receiver in feminist theatre is constructed as 'competent' in decoding the feminist message. As De Marinis observes, in closed performances 'everything works well, provided that the spectator truly corresponds to the one imagined and reacts in the predicted manner'.[19] A feminist performance attended by a team of male rugby players, for example, would initiate a very different set of responses from those constructed/desired by the theatrical text.

Feminist theatre in the wake of the Second Women's Liberation Movement provides a useful example of a 'closed' performance context and spectator response. Typically, feminist theatre at this time was group-orientated and modelled on the consciousness-raising paradigm of the feminist movement. In theatrical terms, this meant a non-hierarchical, role-sharing (rather than star-playing), collective style of performance and a collaborative working out of feminist issues or beliefs between performers and audience. The specific addressee in this performance text is the spectator who supports a feminist position, and is competent in receiving and decoding the feminist message. In this early wave of political theatre, the feminist message was likely to be didactically encoded and to have an 'everywoman' appeal—an approach subsequently challenged by the rise of identity politics.[20]

For example, Claire Luckham's *Trafford Tanzi* (1978), popular in both alternative and mainstream venues, staged the bourgeois–feminist battle for equality[21] in a wrestling ring, as Tanzi, housewife-turned-female wrestler, wins the first 'round' in her fight for equal opportunities by defeating her husband-wrestler, Dean Rebel. The role and the reaction of the feminist spectator is staged or signed in the performance text by making use of audience participation conventions associated with the sport of wrestling. The stage characters watching the fight '*chant and counter-chant, exchange insults, encourage and abuse the audience etc., particularly between the rounds*'[22] in order to get a real response from the spectators. As Michelene Wandor explains: 'at the end, the audience becomes the "real" audience, and is incited (encouraged?) to cheer either for Tanzi or Dean—in other words, the audience is drawn into participation and into taking sides'.[23] In this performance context the feminist spectator is motivated by the desire to see Tanzi win, which is intratextually inscribed as the 'correct' response, although the real spectator may always choose to respond with the 'wrong' reaction: hiss Tanzi and cheer Dean Rebel.[24]

Whilst in the *Trafford Tanzi* example the spectator response is didactically determined by the politics-as-entertainment model, other styles of feminist theatre in the late 1970s challenged the convention of using the model spectator to 'guide' the real spectator through the performance text, by allowing the real audience reactions to shape the theatrical text. For example, one of the defining characteristics of feminist theatre which gives priority to women's experiences and culture is the agency of self-determination it permits the spectator. This might, for example, mean inviting female spectators to offer their own emotional reactions or experiences relevant to a particular issue being dramatised, in order for the *punctum*, the motivating passion of the real spectator, to take on a performative role.

The American cultural-feminist theatre company At the Foot of the Mountain, for instance, created performance texts which invited the real responses of their audiences to become an integral part of their theatrical event. Their 1977 production of *The Story of a Mother*, collaboratively scripted by the group's artistic director Martha Boesing and the performers, was composed of a series of ritual-based scenes designed to examine the relationships between mothers and daughters. The performance record of this production also includes notes on audience response. For example, in the first ritual, 'The Calling Forth of the Mothers', the following instructions and responses are noted:

ACTRESS, AS MOTHER: There were certain things which I always

> said over and over again. Are there things that you always said that you would like to say again now?
>
> The audience members, speaking as their mothers, call out 'I always said' and finish it with a phrase appropriate to their own mothers. (Examples from production experience: I told you so; Now don't worry about money, money comes when you need it; If everyone else jumps off the bridge, are you going to, too?; You made your bed, now lie in it; Make your bed; But I'm not everybody else's mother; Wait till your father comes home; I hope you have three just like you; You'll never know how much I love you; This hurts me more than it hurts you; You know they're only after one thing.)[25]

Although the ritual scenes provide a framing device, these are, as Boesing describes, 'open-ended ritual segments that change shape from audience to audience'.[26] The real female spectator is therefore empowered to shape the performance text by determining her own feelings about mother/daughter relations. This kind of feminist performance belongs, as Jill Dolan has pointed out, to a particular moment in our feminist history: a moment which marks the need for self-discovery, self-exploration, which is now rather dated; 'after a decade of theorising, practising and refining our politics, this reverential stance towards ourselves as women seems simplistic and conservative'.[27]

It would be wrong to claim that all feminist theatre brings the real spectator into the performance frame in this way, which is clearly not the case, nor that this is a phenomenon restricted only to feminist theatre. However, what this type of performance does show is the concern of feminist theatre to 'actively seek out' the spectator: to initiate a response which is characterised as the *punctum* and not the *studium*. Elam comments that 'passionate or passional response to the performance is probably, and unhappily, a rare enough experience for all of us'[28] and, of course, it may well be the case that in these performance examples the spectator did not, despite the mode of address, feel a 'passionate' response. However, if, as Elam queries, it is going to be at all possible to conceive of a 'semiotic conception of the *punctum*',[29] then, in order to examine these feminist performance texts, semiotic analysis must re-draw its analytical frame to be able to note passionately motivated responses and their role in directing and shaping the performance text. The feminist spectator cannot be squeezed into the frame: rather, she exceeds, troubles and disturbs it.

These observations with respect to feminist spectatorship may, in turn, have implications for performance analysis in general. Rather than seeing spectator response as the 'end' part of the communication model or the part which will not quite fit into the frame, we might consider an approach to performance analysis which *begins* with the actual (gendered) response of the real spectator, which may then be used critically to inform the semiotic model.

In order to pursue this point, I propose to devote the remainder of this essay to a more detailed example based on spectator response to the theatre of the radical-feminist playwright Sarah Daniels.

### Case study: the theatre of Sarah Daniels and spectatorship

In his essay discussing the problems of 'a semiotic conception of the *punctum*', Elam continues his examination of this difficulty by tabulating several historical models of dramatic representation in order to pursue an analysis of spectatorial response. He deploys speech-act theory (language as action) to examine the 'perlocutionary act' of theatre on the spectator: how the drama is designed to have an effect on or act on the spectator.[30] However, rather than begin with a theorisation of how the spectator is acted upon, which brings us back again to the problem of excluding actual audience response, performance analysis might, as noted above, begin by examining real spectatorial response to frame our understanding of the desired perlocutionary effect(s).

The feminist theatre of Sarah Daniels arouses a wide range of passionate spectatorial response. Young women reading and seeing her work generally experience three main reactions.[31] Two of these are common to women irrespective of sexual orientation and are namely 1) the experience of a painful recognition (of men's behaviour towards women, of inequality, of the drudgery of women's lives, etc.); and 2) the response of laughter (characterised as 'deep', 'belly', 'gut', etc.). The third reaction, experienced by young heterosexual women, is a (pessimistic) anxiety with regard to sexual identity (questions commonly asked, for example, are 'How does this text represent me?', 'Where am I?'). I shall return to this point later.

In addition, we have on record some of the actual responses of critical reviewers which reveal a clear indication of gender-based reactions: men are mostly hostile to Daniels's work, while women react more positively.[32] What these reactions do have in common, however, is that they are all passionately experienced responses. To analyse this wide range of passionate, *actual* spectator response, we might examine how gender determines the perlocutionary effect of the drama on the addressee: how and why men and women respond differently.

Although Daniels is a playwright whose work is performed in mainstream theatre, she does not subscribe to the social and cultural values of the dominant (male) mainstream stage. She does not, for example, invite the spectator to identify with the male subject of the narrative and to collude with the objectification of the female. Rather, she invites the spectator to identify with a 'female' subject and to examine critically the representational frame which seeks to objectify her. *Masterpieces* (1983), Daniels's controversial play about pornography, for example, takes a critical look-at-women-being-looked-at, not just in pornography, but in their everyday, ordinary lives.[33]

This is an uncomfortable and disturbing experience for the male spectator. As Carole Woodis, reviewing *Masterpieces*, writes, '. . . with its heavily ironic title, it's hardly surprising that *Masterpieces* has been received with less than universal approval by male critics. It would be like asking them to applaud at their own funerals.'[34] In *Masterpieces* and other plays by Daniels, the desired perlocutionary effect is to bring the spectator to the point of recognising the harm inflicted upon women by men. The ferocity of the 'gut reactions' by the majority of male critics which Mary Remnant notes[35] indicates that the 'success' of the perlocutionary effect of *Masterpieces* is gender-determined. Whilst men are pained (and pained to the point of heated denial) by the idea that they cause suffering to women, women, on the other hand, are generally brought to the point of 'seeing' this as a painful but truthful revelation. Mary Remnant illustrates this point by contrasting one of the more sympathetic male-authored reviews of *Masterpieces* with a review by a female critic who made a note of a real, female spectator's response:

> Robin Thornber, reviewing the same play [*Masterpieces*] in Leeds for the *Guardian*, wrote: 'If it is one of the functions of drama to make you see the world in a new light, *Masterpieces* is a dazzling success', and went on to confess disarmingly: 'I came out feeling not only threatened but muddled. The play made me angry and filled me with hate for men. But then I am one.' Perhaps it might have given them a clue if, like Jill Burrows reviewing *Masterpieces* in Ipswich, also for the *Guardian*, they had overheard the woman leaving the theatre who said, 'It made me think. It made me feel ill, but it made me think.'[36]

However, Daniels's theatre is not all pain for women. As previously noted, young women studying her theatre have found her plays extremely funny; have enjoyed the experience of comedy which does not position them as the butt of the joke. Instead, much of the comedy derives from Daniels's ability to show how absurdly men seek to maintain authority over and to regulate women's lives. Whilst this comedy is less likely to appeal to men, in women it touches a chord because we are all subjected to and experience male authority on a daily basis.

The laughter/recognition response of the female spectator arises particularly in the dramatisation of domestic scenes which expose the drudgery of middle- and working-class women in the home. *Ripen Our Darkness* (1981), for example, opens in the kitchen of Mary who is constantly at the beck and call of her churchwarden husband and her sons. After reading the play for the first time, young women frequently respond with lively, often humorous, discussions of domestic scenes from their own family lives: the images of patriarchal family life, the memories of how their own mothers were/are treated in the home, etc. The painful/comic moment which these young women offer as best illustrating their laughter/recognition response, is Mary's suicide note to her husband: 'Dear David, your dinner and my head are in the oven'.[37]

Although Daniels's theatre reaches a number of women because of her ability to dramatise, painfully and pleasurably, images which reflect the reality of women's lives, her radical-lesbian politics is a dimension of her work which touches heterosexual women differently. This is not a criticism but an important observation because it highlights the need to take account of different spectatorial positions among women: to consider gender, class, race, sexual orientation, etc., as making a difference to the actual response. Life with, or rather under, men is so vigorously portrayed by Daniels as damaging to women's health and welfare, that young heterosexual women experience the 'lack' of a positive representation of what, for them, is an important part of their lives. Nevertheless, they argue that Daniels's ability to show the comic absurdity of life for women in a man-made world compensates for this 'lack'.

It is the painful/comic recognition response of having to survive in a man-made world which women spectators have as a common reference point, but which, as previously noted, is an experience which leaves men outside of and alienated by the dramatic representation. For Daniels, the woman spectator is liminally positioned between the dangers of the 'real' systems of heterosexual representation and the utopian fantasy of existing in a 'space' beyond the limits of the gender frame.[38] To be brought to an awareness of our own gender construction, to see the making of Woman and the possibilities of her unmaking, is the frightening and liberating nightmare/fantasy which Daniels's theatre offers.

Whatever the theatrical field, consideration of gender facilitates the possibility of bringing actual, real spectator reactions into a formal model of theatrical response. In turn, this may be seen as a useful way (although by no means the only way as this volume demonstrates) to approach performance analysis. How gender conditions the real and is encoded in the inscribed spectator, as these examples of feminist theatre and spectatorship have shown, may help us not only with an analysis of a specific performance text but also with our understanding of the theoretical apparatus through which we approach it.

## Notes

1 J. Dolan, *The Feminist Spectator as Critic* (Ann Arbor, the University of Michigan Press, 1988), pp. 2–3.
2 J. Veltruský, 'Man and Object in the Theatre', in P. L. Garvin (ed.), *A Prague School Reader on Esthetics, Literary Structure and Style* (Washington, Georgetown University Press [1940], 1964), p. 84.
3 For an overview of this pioneering work, see K. Elam, *The Semiotics of Theatre and Drama* (London and New York, Methuen, 1980), pp. 5–31.
4 R. Barthes, 'Literature and Signification', in R. Howard (tr.), *Critical Essays* (Evanston, Northwestern University Press, [1963], 1972), p. 261.
5 For examples of diagrammatic and tabulated models of theatrical communication see Elam, *The Semiotics of Theatre and Drama*, pp. 32–97.
6 P. Pavis, 'Theatre Analysis: Some Questions and a Questionnaire', *New Theatre Quarterly*, 1:2 (1985), 209.
7 K. Elam, 'Much Ado About Doing Things With Words (and Other Means): Some Problems in the Pragmatics of Theatre and Drama', in M. Issacharoff and R. F. Jones (eds.), *Performing Texts* (Philadelphia, University of Pennsylvania Press, 1988), p. 48.
8 *Ibid.*, p. 49.
9 M. De Marinis, *The Semiotics of Performance*, transl. A. O'Healy (Bloomington and Indianapolis, Indiana University Press [1982], 1993), p. 166.
10 De Marinis, in fact, confesses that whilst 'the real spectator requires serious, systematic, empirical investigation', such an investigation is beyond his 'actual competence in this area'. (*Ibid.*, p. 171.)
11 *Ibid.*, p. 166.
12 S. E. Case, *Feminism and Theatre* (London, Macmillan, 1988), p. 118.
13 A. Ubersfeld, *L'École du Spectateur* (Paris, Les Editions Sociales, 1991), p. 332.
14 Case, *Feminism and Theatre*, p. 120.
15 This point echoes L. Mulvey's observations on sadism, narrative and the male gaze in mainstream cinematic texts. See L. Mulvey, 'Visual Pleasure and Narrative Cinema', *Screen*, 16:3 (1975), 14.
16 H. Cixous, 'Aller à La Mer', transl. B. Kerslake, *Modern Drama*, 4 (Dec 1984), 546.
17 De Marinis, *The Semiotics of Performance*, p. 168.

18 *Ibid.*

19 *Ibid.*, p. 169.

20 The first wave of feminist activity set an all-white, middle-class, heterosexual agenda, which was later critiqued by groups of women organised around identity and difference—for example, groups of working-class women, lesbians of all classes, black women of all classes, etc.

21 Bourgeois feminism is one of the three most commonly recognised feminist positions. In brief, these are as follows: bourgeois feminism (advocates women's rights without a radical transformation of the dominant social system); radical feminism, now more frequently termed cultural feminism (seeks to overturn the patriarchal domination of women by men and emphasises women's experience and culture, etc.); and materialist feminism (critiques the material conditions of class, ethnicity, and gender, etc., and calls for a radical transformation of society). In feminist theatre, each position will initiate a different set of political or ideological concerns and performance aesthetics. For further details, see Dolan, *The Feminist Spectator as Critic*, pp. 1–18.

22 C. Luckham, *Trafford Tanzi*, in M. Wandor (ed.), *Plays by Women: Volume Two* (London, Methuen, 1983), p. 92.

23 M. Wandor, *Carry on Understudies: Theatre and Sexual Politics* (London and New York, Routledge and Kegan Paul, [1981], 1986), p. 177.

24 In the course of taking young (mixed) student groups of spectators to see *Trafford Tanzi* in the 1980s, I have noticed that the play's oversimplistic feminist position and its increasingly outdated mode of liberationist politics tend to invite the 'wrong' response!

25 M. Boesing, *et al.*, in H. K. Chinoy and L. W. Jenkins (eds.), *Women in American Theatre* (New York, Theatre Communication Group, [1981], 1987), pp. 45–6.

26 *Ibid.*, p. 44.

27 Dolan, *The Feminist Spectator as Critic*, p. 94. Moreover, the cultural-feminist position has been critiqued by materialist feminism for its reification of 'woman' as an essentialist position which fails to take account of race or class, etc.

28 Elam, 'Much Ado About Doing Things with Words', p. 49.

29 *Ibid.*

30 Speech-act theory has been developed by philosophers of language such as J. L. Austin and J. R. Searle, and has been taken up by theatre semioticians who have applied the concept of language as action to dramatic texts. The three performative levels of speech as action which have been of primary concern in this field of study are the locutionary (speaking a sentence which has meaning or makes sense), the illocutionary (the act performed in speaking the sentence), and the perlocutionary (the effect on the addressee). Elam is concerned with the concept of the perlocutionary act in different modes of dramatic representation. For further introductory detail on speech-act theory and theatre, see E. Aston and G. Savona, *Theatre as Sign-System* (London and New York, Routledge, 1991), pp. 51–70.

31 Here I am drawing on responses to Daniels's work which I have encountered among young women studying her theatre in a higher education context, i.e., women who are mostly, although not exclusively, in their early twenties, white, middle class and heterosexual.

32 On critical responses to Daniels's theatre, see M. Remnant (ed.), *Plays by Women: Volume Six* (London and New York, Methuen, 1987), pp. 7–12.

33 The pornography debate in *Masterpieces* centres on the figure of Rowena, who is used to show how women are degraded by the way in which they are represented and viewed by men in society. Rowena is so badly affected and violated by what she learns about pornography in magazines, porn videos, snuff movies, etc., that she pushes away a man who is harassing her at a London tube station. The man falls on to the track, is killed and Rowena is charged with 'murder'.

34 Quoted in M. Remnant, *Plays by Women*, p. 10.

35 *Ibid.*, p. 8.

36 *Ibid.*

37 S. Daniels, *Ripen Our Darkness & The Devil's Gateway* (London and New York, Methuen, 1986), p. 33.

38 At the close of Daniels's plays, the women are often portrayed as fleeing the 'real' man-made landscape for a feminist utopia. In *Ripen Our Darkness*, for example, Mary ends up with three blaspheming female deities in an all-female heavenly paradise, and the women in *The Devil's Gateway* (1983) all take off for Greenham Common. Daniels's most recent play, *The Madness of Esme and Shaz* (1994), takes women fleeing from the 'real' world as its central concern, which it dramatises in the fantastic adventures shared between Esme, a devout spinster, and Shaz, her lesbian niece. Both women are victims of male abuse and Shaz has been institutionalised for killing a child as a result of being systematically abused. Esme rescues Shaz and both women take flight at the end of the play for the healing powers of the Greek island of Limnos.

4 *Sophie Fuller*

# New perspectives: feminism and music

Music in its many different forms is one of the most pervasive of the arts. From hip hop to opera and from the concert hall to the supermarket, music plays a central part in our lives. Women have always been involved in making music and listening to music, as well as thinking and writing about music and what it means or tells us about our world. But why are works by women composers not part of the canon of 'great classical music' that dominates concert halls and record shops? Why are there so few women playing in heavy metal bands? Why do the female characters in so many nineteenth-century operas end up dead or mad? Can you tell if a piece of music or a song has been written by a woman or a man? How does music reflect social constructions of gender or sexuality?

These are the kinds of questions that feminist musicologists and music critics have been asking in recent years. In music, as in all disciplines, there is no one feminist orthodoxy or methodology but perhaps as many different feminisms as there are women. Moreover, academic feminist work on music covers a wide range of issues, from examining women's varied contributions to the worlds of music (and often retrieving women's work from the oblivion of the past) to the development of a feminist criticism in musicology and music analysis which, for example, can present readings of musical works in terms of gender and sexuality. In the study of most of the arts, feminist perspectives have been established for some time. It was over twenty years ago that art historian Linda Nochlin wrote:

> A feminist critique of the discipline is needed which can pierce cultural-ideological limitations, to reveal biases and inadequacies not merely in regard to the question of women artists, but in the formulation of the crucial questions of the discipline as a whole. Thus the so-called woman question, far from being a peripheral sub-issue, can become a catalyst, a potent intellectual instrument, probing the most basic and 'natural' assumptions . . .[1]

Most scholars working with disciplines such as literature, film, the visual arts or performance now take it for granted that this kind of feminist work is valid, important and exciting. It is taking much longer for these feminist challenges to be widely accepted in the fields of musicology, music history, music analysis or theory.[2]

There is, however, a much longer tradition than many people realise of a few isolated individuals working to include the contributions of women composers and musicians to a music history from which they are continually being excluded and forgotten. In 1883 Stephen Stratton read a ground-breaking paper to the Musical Association in London, entitled 'Woman in Relation to Musical Art' which challenged many Victorian beliefs about the capabilities and achievements of women.[3] Work from the earlier years of the twentieth century that looked at women's contribution to music included Arthur Elson's *Women's Work in Music* (1903) and Sophie Drinker's *Music and Women. The Story of Women in their Relation to Music* (1948).[4] Throughout the twentieth century there have been studies of individual women composers, such as Jessica Kerr's 1944 article on the seventeenth-century British composer Mary Dering.[5] Stratton's list of women composers, which includes the medieval *trobaritz* Comtessa de Dia and the sixteenth-century Italian composer Madalena Casulana, may surprise those who believe that the 'rediscovery' of women composers of the distant past started with the so-called 'second wave of feminism' in the 1960s.

But it was not really until the 1970s and early 1980s that scholars began extensive excavation of women composers and musicians of the past. Studies were made of many individual women and of groups of women such as medieval *trobaritz* (female troubadours), the professional women musicians of the sixteenth-century court at Ferrara or twentieth-century women jazz musicians. The previously forgotten music of a wide range of composers, from the twelfth-century Hildegard of Bingen through to women of the nineteenth century such as Clara Schumann, Fanny Hensel or Ethel Smyth, began to be brought to light in an ever-increasing number of articles and books, performances and recordings. At this time women began to form recording and publishing companies in order to disseminate music by women. They also founded organisations which promoted and encouraged contemporary women's music. These included groups such as the League of Women Composers (later the International League of Women Composers) and American Women Composers in the US, *Frau und Musik* in Germany and Women in Music in Britain.

But the study of women's contributions to any art practice

involves more than simply adding women's names to the accepted list of 'great' artists of the past or present. Examining the creative work of women (or of many other marginalised groups within society) inevitably leads scholars to ask searching questions about the reasons why such groups were, and still are, excluded from a cultural history that focuses on the achievements of straight, white, middle- and upper-class men. As well as exploring issues such as women's lack of access to education or performing opportunities, the study of the present neglect of women's work and their frequently overlooked achievements in the past has led many scholars to re-assess long-held assumptions about what is of value to the musical world and what is worthy of a place in the canon of 'great' composers and 'great' music. Why are symphonies and string quartets seen as more important than songs or piano pieces? Why is the study of 'classical' music often treated by scholars differently from that of 'popular' music such as rock or jazz? Why is a concert held in a public concert hall seen as more significant than one given in a drawing room? Some of the most thorough work exploring women's exclusion from the musical canon is to be found in Marcia Citron's *Gender and the Music Canon.*[6] In this book, Citron explores many fundamental issues, such as assumptions about women's ability to create works of art; the importance of recognising a female creative tradition; women's traditional placing within a private rather than a public world and their consequent exclusion from or ambivalence towards the professional world of music-making.

Women's access and contributions to the musical world have, of course, been enormously varied. Women of different classes, races, nationalities and periods of history have inevitably had very different experiences of involvement in music. Feminists working within the discipline of ethnomusicology have explored many issues surrounding the music made by women in a wide variety of cultures throughout the world.[7] Their studies place the music of women (and of men) firmly within a social and cultural context, and look at many different patterns of power and gender relationships. But in whatever culture and society they are living, throughout the world and throughout history, women have been expected to conform to what that society and culture have established as 'feminine'. This has given women access to certain forms of musical expression and denied them access to others.

In the Western musical world of the later nineteenth century, for example, it was expected that women who wrote music would produce short, tuneful songs and piano pieces. These were works that could exist within the home, the private sphere that was seen as a woman's rightful place. Such music did not challenge the widely held belief that women were physically incapable of writing complex or large-scale works.[8] Many women composers of the time, from Claribel and Carrie Jacobs-Bond to Liza Lehmann and Maude Valérie White, conformed to and internalised these and other expectations about their roles and abilities. Needless to say, there were also many women, such as Ethel Smyth, Augusta Holmès or Amy Beach, who refused to behave as society expected and who wrote and achieved performances of musical works in every style and genre. It is perhaps important to stress that both ways of working have produced equally powerful pieces of music.

In the field of popular music today there is still an expectation that women will work as singer/songwriters, often performing tuneful songs to their own guitar accompaniment, rather than in the noisy 'aggressive' genres such as hard rock. Again, although many women, from Joni Mitchell and Joan Armatrading to Tracy Chapman, Tasmin Archer and the Indigo Girls, have conformed to these expectations (see Chapter 14), there are also many women who have worked in other, less 'ladylike' genres, from heavy metal band Girlschool or '70s punks The Slits to the recent indie 'grunge' bands such as Hole, Babes in Toyland or L7. There are, of course, many different reasons why women should concentrate on smaller and less complicated genres. Women were, and still are, for example, often excluded from the male networks and structures that are so vital in achieving performances of large-scale works in both the classical and popular musical worlds. It has often been easier for women to work in genres which enable them to provide their own performances or to work within a network of friends, often other women.

The work of the composer has often been privileged above that of the many other people involved in the creation of music. This focus on a single, central artist has been challenged by some feminist scholars who have concentrated instead on the other contributions that women have made to music, from singing, conducting and playing instruments, through working as patrons and organisers, to teaching and writing about music. In some areas of the musical world, women have had to fight against gender expectations and roles. The conductor or band leader, for example, is in a position of very visible control over other musicians. Such overt power is not usually allowed to women and this is doubtless one of the reasons why so few women, even today, work in this field.[9]

Some areas in which women have traditionally played a central part have been consistently undervalued. Various studies of women as patrons, for example, have shown the importance of women's work in enabling, encouraging and influencing music.[10] In other areas, women's participation is assumed and taken for granted. Female opera singers, for example, have for many years played what is regarded as a central role in one of the most privileged of art forms. But the position of the operatic 'diva' is a complex one. Women began working as opera singers at a time when 'respectable' women did not appear on the public stage.[11] Throughout the eighteenth and the nineteenth centuries, the great divas were in the paradoxical position of being worshipped by adoring fans and at the same time being seen as somehow disreputable and scandalous.[12] Opera singers from Maria Malibran (1808–1836) through Adelina Patti (1843–1919) to Maria Callas (1923–1977) were the subject of intense media scrutiny and imagined to have personal lives that were as dramatic and passionate as the roles that they sang on stage. Divas developed reputations for being difficult and demanding, and at the same time were rarely credited for the extremely hard work involved in training their voices. Over and over again, the voice of the female opera singer has been written about as something natural or instinctive, a gift from God but never something for which the singer herself is responsible. Jean-Jacques Beineix's film *Diva* (1982) clearly demonstrates the stereotype of the female opera singer. The central character of this film is obsessed with a diva who remains throughout a mysterious figure, little more than a beautiful voice and who is, in fact, chiefly represented by the tape of her voice around which the action of the film revolves.

The roles that divas sang (and still sing) from the repertoire of nineteenth-century operas have come under intense scrutiny from feminist critics.[13] In most of these canonic works the central female character, whether it is Tosca, Violetta, Carmen, Mimi or Madame Butterfly, ends up dead, mad or, at best, betrayed and abandoned. It is as if the power of the music and the singer's voice has to be negated and the woman on the stage punished for displaying such strength and control. As Catherine Clément has put it,

> Opera is not forbidden to women. That is true. Women are its jewels, you say, the ornament indispensable for every festival. No prima donna, no opera. But the role of jewel, a decorative object, is not the deciding role; and on the opera stage women perpetually sing their eternal undoing . . . Look at these heroines. With their voices they flap their wings, their arms writhe, and then there they are, dead, on the ground.[14]

Today, the myth of the diva has perhaps moved away from the field of classical music. Contemporary female opera singers such as

Jessye Norman or Janet Baker are not surrounded by the atmosphere of scandal and obsession that haunted earlier singers. Kiri Te Kanawa has even been called the 'housewife diva'.[15] But both the word 'diva' and some of the imagery and stereotypes have been taken up by artists in the world of popular music. Annie Lennox's first solo album, for example, was entitled *Diva* and the debut album of the four-woman vocal group En Vogue was called *Funky Divas*. And perhaps it is the 'superstar' Madonna who comes closest of any artist today to taking on the mantle of the nineteenth-century diva in all its complexities and contradictions.[16]

The brief discussion of women's operatic roles above touched on the work of feminist critics. The late 1980s and early 1990s have seen the rapid growth of scholarship exploring expressions of gender and sexuality in a wide variety of music, whether written by women or men. The pioneering feminist critic Susan McClary has described her work as 'concerned with discerning how historically constituted ideas of gender, sexuality and the body have informed even the most basic of musical procedures from the sixteenth century to the present'.[17] It is this kind of work that has met with the most opposition from a notoriously conservative discipline which is opposed to certain kinds of criticism and critical theory and particularly resists any exploration of meaning in music as a reflection of society and social constructs (such as gender). Many musicologists and analysts have refused to see how music, and especially music that does not use a text or libretto, can be anything other than a transcendental art form, unsullied by contact with the 'real' world and the society that produced it.[18] But, as Ruth Solie has pointed out, if there were no meaning or value in music, why would we listen to it?[19] McClary cogently insists that 'Absolute Music articulates the same dominant social beliefs and tensions as other cultural artefacts of the nineteenth century; indeed, its patterns represent habits of thought so fundamental that they can even be transmitted without verbal cues.'[20]

These feminist studies have provided a rich and exciting variety of work, and opened up many fascinating areas of debate. McClary, in her ground-breaking book of collected essays, *Feminine Endings*, looks at expressions of gender and sexuality in music from Monteverdi through Bizet, Tchaikovsky and Laurie Anderson to Madonna. Ruth Solie has examined the musical construction of patriarchal ideas about women in Robert Schumann's song-cycle *Frauenliebe*,[21] Suzanne Cusick has looked at expressions of women's power in Francesca Caccini's *La Liberazione di Ruggiero dall'isola d'Alcina*[22] and Elizabeth Wood has discussed Ethel Smyth's representations of her lesbian sexuality in both her writings and her music.[23] Eva Rieger, McClary and Citron have all explored similar ways of reading sonata form, one of the most prevalent musical forms of the eighteenth and the nineteenth centuries, in terms of gender.[24] For many years, musicologists and analysts labelled the first, often assertive tonic theme of sonata form as 'masculine' and the second, usually more lyrical theme which introduces a different key area as 'feminine'. Whether these labels are used or not, the position of the second theme, which will reappear in the recapitulation or final section subjugated to the tonic key of the first theme, can clearly be read as relating to that of the female. As McClary has put it, 'the "masculine" tonic is predestined to triumph, the "feminine" Other to be . . . "grounded" or "resolved".'[25]

One of the questions frequently put to feminists working in any of the many fields of music is analogous to that asked in other areas of performance, namely whether music created by women is different from that created by men. Is there a musical equivalent of Hélène Cixous' *écriture féminine*? Given the diversity of women and the music that they create, this is obviously a complex question and one which many people are reluctant to answer. In the late nineteenth century, a period when men and women were widely believed to be different in many fundamental, non-biological ways, it was assumed that women's music would be different from men's. For many commentators this was an exciting prospect. An anonymous writer in *The Musical Times* of 1882 declared: 'It will be of good augury for the sex and for music when some pioneer woman arises, who, having mastered the power of musical expression, consults her own nature and not the productions of men, when determining what to say and how to speak.'[26] In *Gender and the Music Canon* Citron provides a detailed analysis of the first movement of Cécile Chaminade's Piano Sonata of 1895. While she is careful to point out that similar analyses could probably be made of works by male composers, she suggests that Chaminade's sonata 'may reconceptualise the ideologies of masculine and feminine as encoded in gendered readings of sonata form'.[27] The work of feminist critics such as Citron and McClary has begun to provide ways in which it may be possible to examine how women have articulated distinct views about issues such as gender, sexuality and power in musical works without texts or programmes. Some writers have argued that women composers have not developed a distinct language because, in the words of Renée Cox, they have 'had to adopt a masculine mode of expression in order to be taken seriously as artists'.[28]

There is a long tradition of women creating texted musical works (for example, songs or operas) which, through their relationship to the text, can be clearly seen to articulate issues relevant to their experiences as women. These range from countless anonymous folk songs to works such as Ethel Smyth's *The Boatswain's Mate* (first performed in 1916) or Ida Cox's 'One Hour Mama' (recorded in 1939). Many women composers, songwriters and musicians working today have continued to be concerned with using music in order to make a place in our culture for issues which that culture still all too rarely confronts. Melissa Etheridge's album *Yes I Am* includes the song 'All American Girl', about women 'who live and die in this man's world'. She has explained: 'I like singing about women's issues. I don't think in rock music they're ever addressed or ever brought up. I like putting it in a strong rock 'n' roll vehicle where you can move to it'.[29] The recent burst of women's activity on the British indie music scene has produced some strongly feminist songs, from the Voodoo Queen's 'Supermodel, Superficial' to Polly Harvey's explorations of female sexuality on albums such as *Dry* and *Rid of Me* (although Harvey vigorously rejects being labelled a feminist). Echobelly, a band of two women and three men, produced a powerful debut album which covered a range of issues from racism, patriarchy and abortion to the chilling anger of Sonya Aurora Madan's 'Give Her A Gun': '. . . let her anger curse the years of oppression/blame the mother, sell the sister/before she blows you away/won't someone give her a gun'. A reviewer from *Select* described this song as 'contentious' but found that it 'takes a particular (female) experience and plugs it in for even us white European males'.[30] Similar material has been a part of the defiantly feminist 'Riot Grrl' movement that started in the United States with women's bands such as Bikini Kill and Bratmobile.

'Classical' composers have also been concerned with directly expressing women's issues. Beth Anderson's opera *Queen Christina* was first performed in 1973, at the height of the women's liberation movement. This multi-media work actually involved local women's groups and a recorded speech about the women's movement, as well as focusing on the life and achievements of a strong seventeenth-century woman. Many women composers have created musical works which centre around images of powerful female characters, such as Nicola LeFanu's *The Old Woman of Beare* (1981) and *Blood Wedding* (1991–2), Thea Musgrave's *Mary Queen of Scots* (1975–7) and *Harriet, the Woman Called Moses* (1985) or Meredith Monk's *Education of the Girlchild* (1972–3) and *Atlas* (1991).

What have composers themselves said about the possibility of a woman's distinct musical language? Over sixty years ago, Ethel Smyth had typically strong views:

> . . . I fancy that even an average woman has more inward freedom than men; is less conventional, and on the other hand less haunted by the dread, if an artist or a writer, of being commonplace. None of the few women composers who have contrived to get their songs printed are afraid of melody. I think men are.[31]

Several contemporary composers refuse even to be described as 'women' composers, resisting the idea that their gender has any relevance at all to their work and rejecting any concept of a woman's musical language. Others disagree. Nicola LeFanu has written:

> Most people believe that music transcends gender, that you can't tell if a composition is by a man or a woman. I know, however, that my music is written out of the wholeness of myself, and I happen to be a woman. I'm not bothered by whether I compose better or worse than a man, because I take both possibilities for granted; but I am interested in what I can do that is different. In my thoughts and actions there is much that is similar to those of a man, and much more that is different. Can it really be otherwise in my music? Could there be a music which did not reflect its maker? If we continue to have a musical culture which draws on the creative talents of one sex, what kind of musical perspective shall we have?[32]

How much has changed since Madalena Casulana published her first book of madrigals in 1568, explaining in her dedication that she would like 'to show the world . . . the vain error of men, who so much believe themselves to be the masters of the highest gifts of the intellect, that they think those gifts cannot be shared equally by women?'[33] Women are now perhaps beginning to be able to take for granted their presence in most areas of the musical world: as composers, musicians, singers, conductors, patrons, organisers, sound engineers, teachers, DJs and critics. At the same time, the challenges, insights and demands of feminism are beginning to change how we see and hear this musical world and the ways in which we explore and understand the music that is all around us.

## Notes

1 Linda Nochlin, 'Why have there been no great women artists?' in Elizabeth Baker and Thomas B. Hess (eds.), *Art and Sexual Politics* (London, Collier, 1973), p. 2, quoted in Griselda Pollock, *Vision and Difference: Femininity, Feminism and the Histories of Art* (London and New York, Routledge, 1988), p. 2.

2 For a series of reports on the position of feminist scholarship in music see Elizabeth Wood, 'Review Essay: Women in Music', *Signs*, 6 (Winter, 1980), 283–97; Jane Bowers, 'Feminist scholarship and the field of musicology', *College Music Symposium*, 29 (1989), 81–92; Susan McClary, 'Reshaping a

Discipline: Musicology and Feminism in the 1990s', *Feminist Studies*, 19:2 (Summer, 1993), 399–423.

3 Stephen Stratton, 'Woman in Relation to Musical Art', *Proceedings of the Musical Association*, 3 (1882–3), 115–46.

4 Arthur Elson, *Women's Work in Music* (Portland, Longwood Press, [1903], 1974) and Sophie Drinker, *Music and Women. The Story of Women in their Relation to Music* (New York, Coward-McCann, 1948).

5 Jessica Kerr, 'Mary Harvey—The Lady Dering', *Music and Letters*, 25 (1944).

6 Marcia Citron, *Gender and the Music Canon* (Cambridge, Cambridge University Press, 1993).

7 See, for example, Ellen Koskoff (ed.), *Women and Music in Cross-Cultural Perspective* (Westport, CT, Greenwood Press, 1987) and Marcia Hernden and Susanne Ziegler (eds.), *Music, Gender and Culture: International Music Studies 1* (Wilhelmshaven, Florian Noetzel Verlag, 1990).

8 As can be seen by the surprise that greeted a performance of an orchestral work by Ethel Smyth in 1890, documented by George Bernard Shaw: 'When E. M. Smyth's heroically brassy overture to Antony and Cleopatra was finished, and the composer called to the platform, it was observed with stupefaction that all that tremendous noise had been made by a lady.'

9 Notable exceptions in Britain are Siân Edwards, Jane Glover, Wasfi Kani, Anne Mason and Odaline de la Martinez. Successful though these women are in their respective fields (ranging from opera to contemporary music), no woman holds an appointment as conductor of one of the major symphony orchestras, still for many people the height of achievement for a conductor.

10 See, for example, the work of Linda Whitesitt, including 'The Role of Women Impresarios in American Concert Life, 1871–1933', *American Music*, 7:12 (Summer, 1989), 159–80; 'Women's Support and Encouragement of Music and Musicians' in Karin Pendle (ed.), *Women and Music: A History* (Bloomington, Indiana University Press, 1991), pp. 301–12 and ' "The Most Potent Force" in American Music: The Role of Women's Music Clubs in American Concert Life' in Judith Lang Zaimont, Catherine Overhauser and Jane Gottlieb (eds.), *The Musical Woman: An International Perspective*, Vol. III, 1986–1990 (Westport, CT, Greenwood Press, 1991), pp. 663–81.

11 For a history of women opera singers (including the challenge of the castrati) see Rupert Christiansen, *Prima Donna. A History* (Harmondsworth, Penguin, 1986).

12 The memoirs of Clara Kathleen Rogers (1844–1931) who spent several years working as an opera singer under the name Clara Doria, provide some fascinating insights into attitudes towards singers and musicians: *Memories of a Musical Career* (Norwood, MA, Plimpton Press, 1919) and *The Story of Two Lives* (Norwood, MA, Plimpton Press, 1932).

13 See, for example, Catherine Clément, *Opera, or the Undoing of Women*, transl. Betsy Wing (London, Virago, 1989); Carolyn Abbate, 'Opera; or, the Envoicing of Women' in Ruth Solie (ed.), *Musicology and Difference: Gender and Sexuality in Music Scholarship* (Berkeley and Los Angeles, University of California Press, 1993), pp. 225–58; Susan McClary, 'Sexual Politics in Classical Music' in *Feminine Endings: Music, Gender and Sexuality* (Minneapolis, University of Minnesota Press, 1991), pp. 53–67; Nellie Furman, 'The

Languages of Love in Carmen' in Arthur Groos and Roger Parker (eds.), *Reading Opera* (Princeton, Princeton University Press, 1988); Sophie Fuller, 'The Silence of Violetta' in Nicholas John (ed.), *Violetta and her Sisters. The Lady of the Camellias: Responses to the Myth* (London, Faber, 1994), p. 263–5.

14 Clément, *Opera, or the Undoing of Women*, p. 5.

15 Alastair Macauley, 'Dame Kiri, the Housewife Diva', *Financial Times Weekend* (12–13 March, 1994), 17.

16 Madonna has been the subject of studies by a variety of scholars and theorists. See, for example, McClary, *Feminine Endings*, pp. 148–66; Cathy Switchenberg (ed.), *The Madonna Connection: Representational Politics, Subcultural Identities and Cultural Theories* (Boulder, CO, Westview Press, 1992) and Lisa Frank and Paul Smith (eds.), *Madonnarama. Essays on Sex and Popular Culture* (Pittsburgh, Cleis Press, 1993).

17 McClary, 'Reshaping a Discipline', 417.

18 See, for example, Pieter C. van den Toorn, 'Politics, Feminism, and Contemporary Music Theory', *The Journal of Musicology*, 9:3 (Summer, 1991), 275–99.

19 Ruth Solie, 'What do feminists want? A Reply to Pieter van den Toorn', *The Journal of Musicology*, 9:4 (Fall, 1991), 410.

20 Susan McClary, 'Narrative Agendas in "Absolute" Music: Identity and Difference in Brahms's Third Symphony' in Ruth Solie (ed.), *Musicology and Difference: Gender and Sexuality in Music Scholarship* (Berkeley and Los Angeles, University of California Press, 1993), p. 328.

21 Ruth Solie, 'Whose Life? The Gendered Self in Schumann's *Frauenliebe* Songs' in Steven Paul Scher (ed.), *Music and Text: Critical Inquiries* (Cambridge, Cambridge University Press, 1992), pp. 219–40.

22 Suzanne G. Cusick, 'Of Women, Music, and Power: A Model from Seicento Florence' in Solie (ed.), *Musicology and Difference*, pp. 281–304.

23 Elizabeth Wood, 'Lesbian Fugue: Ethel Smyth's Contrapuntal Arts' in Solie (ed.), *Musicology and Difference*, pp. 164–83.

24 See Eva Rieger, '*Dolce semplice?* On the Changing Role of Women in Music' in Gisela Ecker (ed.), transl. Harriet Anderson, *Feminist Aesthetics* (London, The Women's Press, 1985), 135–49; Citron, *Gender and the Music Canon*, chapter four, pp. 120–64 and McClary, *Feminine Endings*, pp. 13–16, 68–9.

25 McClary, 'Narrative Agendas in "Absolute" Music', p. 332. The words 'grounded' and 'resolved' are used by James Webster in his entry on 'Sonata Form' in *The New Grove Dictionary of Music and Musicians*, ed. Stanley Sadie (Macmillan, London and New York, 1980), vol. 17, p. 498.

26 Anon, 'The Feminine in Music', *The Musical Times* (October, 1882), p. 522.

27 Citron, *Gender and the Music Canon*, p. 144.

28 Renée Cox, 'Recovering Jouissance: An Introduction to Feminist Musical Aesthetics' in Karin Pendle (ed.), *Women and Music: A History* (Bloomington and Indianapolis, Indiana University Press, 1991), p. 333. See also McClary, *Feminine Endings*, pp. 114–16.

29 Val C. Phoenix, 'Melissa Etheridge: Yes She Is', *Deneuve*, 3:6 (Nov/Dec, 1993), 29.

30 Andrew Harrison, review of *Everyone's Got One, Select* (Sept, 1994), 89.

31 Ethel Smyth, *A Final Burning of Boats etc.* (London, Longmans, Green and Co., 1928), p. 13.

32 Nicola LeFanu, 'Master Musician: an Impregnable Taboo?' *Contact*, 31 (Autumn, 1987), 4. See also Elaine Barkin, 'Questionnaire', *Perspectives of New Music*, 19 (1980–1), 460–2, and 'Response', *Perspectives of New Music*, 20 (1981–2), 288–329.

33 Quoted in Jane Bowers, 'The Emergence of Women Composers in Italy, 1566–1700' in Jane Bowers and Judith Tick (eds.), *Women Making Music: The Western Art Tradition, 1150–1950* (London, Macmillan, 1986), p. 140.

5

E. Ann Kaplan

# Feminism(s)/postmodernism(s): MTV and alternate women's videos and performance art

The first two words of the title of this chapter, 'feminism(s)' and 'postmodernism(s)' are linked by the tell-tale slash (/) to indicate at once connection and separation or difference. Part of my purpose is to explore the relations between a particular form of 'feminism' and a particular form of 'postmodernism' (to be defined below), with a view to addressing the vexed issue of the *politics* of postmodernism. In the 1990s, feminism(s) are differentiated by politics but postmodernism is often viewed as monolithic and eschewing or resisting politics. It is therefore seen as antithetical to feminism(s), despite the efforts of scholars like Meaghan Morris to show otherwise (Morris, 1988). I will outline kinds of feminism and postmodernism pertinent to my project, going on to argue that strategies in certain texts evidence a postmodern feminist 'politics', albeit a politics not easily assimilable to old Marxist paradigms.

The two other terms—'MTV' (the 24-hour Music Television cable station)[1] and 'alternate women's videos and performance art' may also seem oddly linked. The aim is to compare and contrast strategies used by women artists in a common medium (video), working under different constraints—those of commercial television and of the independent sphere.

The two projects represent on the one hand, a 'politics of representation' and on the other, a 'politics of the (media) Institution'. They come together, first, in the links increasingly being made between the phenomena of postmodernism and video/computer technologies; second, in the attribution of the crisis in feminism(s) to the high-tech, postindustrial, postmodern age; and finally, in that both 'representation' and 'Institution' are produced through social formations and are interdependent. I will argue that postmodern aesthetic strategies can involve a kind of feminist politics, but this 'politics' will be different, depending on the context of production and exhibition of the work—

on, that is, the *institution*. What happens when postmodern strategies are deployed by women artists working independently in the relatively new modes of video and performance art? What happens when they are deployed within the constraints of MTV's commercial context? Hopefully, these questions will yield something about the links between social formations and cultural symbols.[2]

Some preliminary definitions are necessary: first, which 'feminism' is referred to? In the 1990s, we recognise many kinds of feminism, many differences among women that have earlier been repressed. What seemed a clear feminist project in the 1970s (finding the female voice, rediscovering lost female texts, writing women's history, making women's images, demanding control of women's bodies and of their lives) has been revealed as heavily Eurocentric and severely limited in its ethnic and, to a lesser extent, class biases. The links between the largely white, middle-class 1960s and 1970s movements and the then prevalent late nineteenth-century form of capitalism are now well-known. Indeed, it is precisely the postindustrial, multi-corporate mode of capitalism and the new technologies that spawned it, together with the increasingly non-Eurocentric women's voices moving into debates, that have made many 1970s feminist stances impossible. Technological and social developments, often seen as themselves part of the postmodern age, have necessitated a non-essentialising feminism—one that is fully aware that the category 'woman' is a social construct, whose meaning changes in specific contexts and historical periods; that 'feminism' itself has been layered over with representations and is open to exploitation for commercial and political ends; that the words, voices and global struggles of women of colors other than white change white women's concepts of themselves. A feminist *identity* must now be used in a deliberately *strategic* way (as, for instance, women use it in pro-choice rallies).

This paper deliberately locates itself within specific 1970s, largely white, feminist film and TV debates because I view them as essential for understanding certain women's art practices today across a spectrum of exhibition spaces. But while the texts I use are largely by and about white women, I hope that the concern with a feminist postmodern politics, and with links between cultural symbols and social formations, will have broader reference than simply the (white) subjects and (white) artists being considered. The dilemmas facing North American white female artists, as these emerge from theories developed over the past twenty years, while differing from those facing North American women artists of other colors, may have something in common, in that all female artists live and work within patriarchal contexts.

While the patriarchal frames among minority artists differ from each other, as well as from those of white women, partly because minorities (male and female) face a racism too complex to address in this context, one layer—that of gender concerns in general—may overlap these frames.

What 'postmodernism' is this paper concerned with? Like feminism(s), postmodernism is a problematic and much-debated term. I have resisted the temptation to abandon it altogether in the wake of its overuse and the resulting meaninglessness. A term is needed to distinguish our contemporary cultural context from the earlier pre-World War II period. At that time, modernism intruded upon a stultified establishment, or 'high', culture, which was constructed as in opposition to a popular culture (if one far less developed than today's). If the *players* remain essentially the same, the entire *game* is different because of the changes wrought by massive technological innovations that have drastically altered the nature of artistic apparatuses. By 'apparatuses', I mean the aesthetic modes and modes of production/exhibition/consumption that dominate both the commercial and the alternate spheres.

What I mean by a feminist postmodern politics of representation will make sense if I review briefly the feminist film debates of the 1970s: these provide the context for my positions. As is well known, the 1970s debates focused on which aesthetic strategy—the tradition of documentary realism or that of the modernist film avant-garde—was the most appropriate for feminist statements. Both strategies were seen as 'alternate' to the commercial 'classical' Hollywood film, which advocates of both groups at that time agreed was oppressive to women. The debate hinged on whether or not 'realism' as a style was inherently complicit with dominant (sexist, racist) ideology and with patriarchal/capitalist institutions like Hollywood. Those arguing for realism claimed that the style could be used by women to document their own experiences and show things 'as they really are', if such films were made outside dominant, commercial contexts of production. Those arguing for the avant-garde claimed that it was essential to interrupt the very desire for representation—that is, for narrative coherence and closure—since in capitalism, this desire could only take an Oedipal, patriarchal and ideologically oppressive representational form. Agreeing to disagree, both groups proceeded to produce formidable bodies of work in film.[3]

While I will argue below that the 1970s theoretical polarity (i.e., realism versus the avant-garde) needs to be re-thought in the postmodern context, some critics continue to debate the binarism. For instance,

Martha Gever, ultimately relying on the above 1970s arguments, pitting realism against the avant-garde, characterises certain 1980s women's videos as representing a move 'from positivism to negativity' (Gever, 1987). For Gever, 'positivism' characterises the 1970s documentary videos about women's experience of social conditions such as reproduction, healthcare, childcare, employment and domestic labor, rape, battering, and so on.[4] These are juxtaposed with select tapes by Birnbaum, Barry and others (discussed below) which, according to Gever, represent 'negativity' because they work only at the level of 'undoing' representation, not that of social conditions (*ibid.*).

Gever's notion that 'systems of representation' *can* be 'undone' is problematic. What does 'undoing' such systems mean? Her comment suggests a desire that representation be *action* or perhaps a desire for representation not to be itself. Whether intended or not, the comments recall the 1970s 'realist' position. The assumption is that realist representations, in contrast to the postmodern ones, might somehow have an activist impact on women's oppressions. That is, it is assumed that *realist* representations might do more for women than representations about representation, although this 'more' is unspecified. But deconstruction has taught us that realist texts betray how their own 'social reality' is a representation and that the ideology of the author/maker does not guarantee what a given text will show, let alone what it may 'do'. The text will manifest contradictions and ambivalences not dreamed of by the maker. What is *real* in realist texts is *who controls such a text* (to which I will return). The realist mode is an attempt to make coherent an encounter with the 'real', which, in itself, offers neither narrative nor closure. In Jameson's words, 'History is what hurts'; or, as Barbara Johnson once put it, 'the real is what you trip over; it is where ambivalences are.'[5]

Paul Ryan, meanwhile, anticipating a politics of the media *institution*, makes a useful distinction between videos which reference social change through symbol manipulation, and those that work with 'the systemics of communication'.[6] Video groups emerging from the waning 1960s counterculture used video as a tool of resistance and showed how broadcast television promoted and relied on the dynamics of an 'industrial culture'. Ryan refers to the whole institution of broadcast TV as inherently oppressive and creates a model of underground video that could have revolutionary implications. But such efforts got so little support that they never took hold: broadcast TV not only continues but has become increasingly dominant. Nevertheless, there are gaps where groups like Paper Tiger Videos (discussed below), together with Deep Dish Television in New York, represent the efforts of women in the 1980s to utilise the subversive possibilities of video and of cable television outlined by Ryan.

Understanding why the realism/avant-garde or counter-cultural/art polarities no longer pertain in the ways Gever and Ryan suggest, will be clear if I show *how* the avant-garde feminist 1970s artists conceived of their practice as 'alternate'. This, in turn, will enable me to clarify the differences between feminist-1970s and feminist-postmodern political strategies.

In the wake of May 1968, the first wave of women taking the avant-garde position turned to film as a visual form with an avant-garde tradition that could be utilised for feminist ends, as those were conceived in the period. Brecht's theories of distancing/alienation, his particular 'politics of modernism', were linked with Todorov's notion of *ostranenie* (or the device of 'making strange') and with Bakhtinian and other Russian Formalist concepts, to create a kind of text that, like many earlier modernist ones, stood in deliberate opposition to the dominant, popular Hollywood film. Certain innovative male filmmakers, particularly Godard, making use of modernist theories, paved the way for much of this feminist work. Such feminists added psychoanalysis, particularly Lacan's form of it, and French poststructuralism in their effort to explore pervasive gender constructs.

The filmic apparatus (its mode of production, processes of exhibition and consumption, its long avant-garde tradition) lent itself well to the 1970s feminist critique of the dominant patriarchal culture. But the profound alterations in American culture, noted above, as they accumulated in the 1980s, threw the 1970s concept of an 'alternative' feminist practice into question, along with the 1970s feminist positions already described. The carefully articulated polarity between 'commercial' and 'avant-garde' aesthetic practices (like that between 'realism' and the 'avant-garde' within feminist circles) no longer seemed applicable in the light of the postmodern assault on the high/low culture boundary, which both realist and avant-garde 1970s strategies ultimately retained.

'Postmodernism' connotes a cultural moment when isolated textual readings seem inadequate. Because of the complexities of their new apparatuses, texts demand to be read in terms of the network of relations that has produced them and made possible their exhibition to, and consumption by, the reader/viewer. Television, for instance, is a complex, contradictory apparatus, involving a series of layers, each in itself complex.[7] There is the layer of ownership which ranges from the multinational corporation to small, entrepreneurial ownerships; the layer of sponsors; the layer of each programme, whose production involves multi-faceted operations; the complex layer of reception/consumption which I will return to later on. One could show similar complexities in the organisation of the museum, or of performance arts spaces.

While many of the devices in postmodernism, for example, 'fragmentation', 'decentring', 'dislocation', are allied to those in modernism (the term 'postmodernism' deliberately retains the close ties to modernism), these devices take on new meanings and new implications because the network of relations in which they are enmeshed differs from the relations in modernism. For example, most modernist artists retained a clear, originally Romantic, notion of the art work as something set apart from everyday life. For them, the aesthetic was still a special, distinct sphere, created through an individual artist's genius; the viewer/spectator still inhabited a separate space. For them, 'fragmentation' was used to bemoan the loss of a coherent world. Their broken up or severely dislocated objects indicate nostalgia for the underlying whole which they perceived as at risk in the wake of World War I.

When postmodernists use the terms 'fragmentation' and 'decentring', it is not to posit any underlying whole but rather to signify that there is no longer any 'whole' to bemoan: for them, there is nothing but fragments, simulacra, no 'real' that is being imitated, and not necessarily any artistic genius behind the work (see, for example, Sherrie Levine's 'framing' of a Walker Evans photo, signed with her name).[8] One can construct a design on the computer which has no model in the world of objects and yet can be used like an object.

Partly as a result of such possibilities, the Romantic distinction between the object-world and the imaginary-world has become problematic: television images pervade our lives in the home, advertising images assault us everywhere, shop windows frame the world for us in the shopping malls that increasingly occupy our time. Inside the shops, we glimpse our own uncanny, dislocated images on surveillance video screens.

I have elsewhere called the collapsing of the fantasy-image realm and the object-world an example of a commercial (or technological) postmodernism as against a 'utopian' or transcendent postmodern form that some feminists and deconstructionists have postulated.[9] A 'utopian' postmodernism involves a movement of culture and texts beyond oppressive binary categories; it envisions texts which radically decentre the subject and which insist on a series of different spectator positions; it envisions discourses that are not hierarchically ordered.

Such devices, in bringing an end to the 'death-dealing binary opposition of masculinity and femininity',[10] are assumed to have liberating results.

But there is a third type of postmodernism, defined by Hal Foster, that, in conjunction with the above distinct types, will be useful for following arguments. Foster's concept of a *resisting* postmodernism makes space for a stage intermediate between my 'commercial' and 'utopian' postmodern categories.[11] Utopian postmodernism will only be possible once (if ever) current transitional struggles are moved through; meanwhile, the positive potentialities of the 'commercial' postmodernism, such as MTV, are still being debated, as in this paper. Foster's resisting postmodernism looks back to (and may rely on) certain strands of modernism which connoted *resistance*, *critique*, opposition to the dominant (namely Marcel Duchamp, René Magritte, Salvador Dali, Antonin Artaud, among others). But as a result of the political, industrial and social changes of the post-World War II period, perhaps only fully experienced in the 1980s, postmodern resisting artists inhabit a completely different semiotic field. 'Decentring' and other devices ultimately have different results, as I hope to show.

The postmodern violation of all hitherto sacrosanct boundaries, including that between 'realist' and 'avant-garde' modes, problematises the old arguments. The 1970s anti-realist stance essentialised realism in prohibiting it: it assumed that realism inevitably mimicked bourgeois codes and ideologies. In other words, it repeated the realist error, as was clear from its need to banish realism.

The old feminist media debate has now shifted its focus from the problem of *aesthetic mode* to that of *desire* as part of the shift away from the Romantic notion of the aesthetic object as something separate and distinct (continued by the 1970s feminists) to a focus on the subject–text relations. Some postmodern feminists now ask: why is it that we desire (realistic) representation? Why do we need narrative? Why do we desire closure? They are, furthermore, interested precisely in exploring the blurring of the subject/object-world boundaries that the term 'postmodernism' signifies.

In the commercial public terrain, television as a complex, contradictory apparatus is also implicated in the blurring of the subject/imaginary-world boundary, and represents a 'commercial' postmodernism. The proliferation of channels in the 1980s (in many places in the US, people with cable routinely have as many as eighty-six), and the increasing number of twenty-four-hour channels, are part of the acceleration of visual images in daily life. The VCR has made possible even more consumption of visual images of all kinds. The increased presence of videated visual images in the hitherto intimate sphere, conceived originally as in opposition to an external, public sphere, has made the difference. Video technology specifically, as against film technology which never entered the home in this way, has been central to the new blurring of the historical subject with the sphere of fantasy. The imaginary and the object worlds become fused.

Partly because women artists see video as the predominant mode in the 1980s, they have increasingly turned from film to video. There are simultaneous practical considerations such as cost, ready accessibility of video technology, ease of video use, etc.: but the main reason is the knowledge that video, in conjunction with the computer, is not only the mode of the future, but one that holds out some possibilities for resistance.[12]

Video is, then, the mode most implicated in the postmodern fusing of spheres noted above. Women media artists are rethinking the spaces within which they can now function, as well as what artists are (or need to be) doing in that space. Postmodern or poststructuralist arguments have shifted the terms of the debate: some artists no longer think of 'undoing' the systems of representation. Instead, they are attempting to explore, within a video representational system, the problem of specifically *video* representation. The project is analogous to that of the 1970s feminist avant-garde, some of whom also examined the filmic representational mode within their alternate films (for example, Sally Potter's *Thriller* 1979 or Mulvey/Wollen's films 1975–85). However, as noted earlier, their strategies relied on the oppositional modernist theories that no longer apply in the same way. Women video artists are not bound by the old polarity of dominant ideology = realism; oppositional ideology = avant-garde: they undertake their projects with no rigid sense of a hierarchy of forms.

Three main spaces for women artists may be distinguished for the purposes of the following textual analyses: 1) didactic video in the 'alternative' sphere; 2) artistic 'fictional' video in the commercial sphere of MTV; 3) video and performance art in the 'alternative' sphere. My main comparison will be between types 2) and 3), but a brief word about type 1) is in order. This type is well represented by Paper Tiger Videos and Deep Dish Television in New York. The creative, imaginative videos these organisations produce, routinely violate documentary realist codes, but their aim is explicitly (and deliberately) didactic. Paper Tiger videos such as *Joan Does Dynasty* or *Fina Bathrick on Working Women* remain quite close to some of the 1970s avant-garde films. However, the insistence in the text on the network of consumer relations within which (in these particular videos) soap operas and the women's magazine are produced, and the concern with the impact of TV as a technology, make a significant difference.

Videos in types 1) and 2) often have similar ends in view, even though their strategies may differ; both provide examples of a feminist (resisting) postmodern politics in the way the texts position the spectator. The viewer is made to understand her enmeshment in a consumer culture bent on her identification with images shown to be degrading, reactionary or limited.

The following comparison between types 2) and 3) has two levels: the first has to do with aesthetic strategies, the second with the level of social institutions and audience.

First, aesthetic strategies: 'fictional' videos both on MTV and in the alternative sphere may explore ways in which consumer culture constructs female subjectivity through utilising women's desire for representation, in particular woman's (socially constructed) narcissistic desire for idealised mirroring of her own body. The postmodern sensibility that is fascinated with the popular commercial images, and that appropriates these images self-consciously—sometimes with delight, sometimes with fascinated horror—can be found in both 'alternative' and 'commercial' videos. Common to both is the fascination with the hypnotic flow of the image and with the ceaseless possibility for transformation available in the video image. In both contexts of production, we find pleasure in hectic colors, in surfaces/textures/forms, in the mixing of realist and non-realist aesthetic modes. We also find blurring of the old high/low culture boundary or its clear irrelevance to what the artists are doing. All these elements make the works into very different aesthetic experiences from the alternative 1970s feminist films.

The strategy in both kinds of video (alternative and commercial) looks back to Dara Birnbaum's controversial but pioneering video *Technology/Transformation: Wonder Woman*, 1978–9. This video reworks original TV *Wonder Woman* footage, leading us to at once reenact our fascination with Wonder Woman as an *image* (something that 1970s avant-garde strategies rarely did), and then to catch ourselves in the act of being so caught up. Just as we are enjoying Wonder Woman's exploits, explosion footage is repeatedly cut in, 'sending up', as it were, our pleasure. The sounds accompanying the images also belie their intent and the full commentary of the video emerges in the written text at the end. There is no comfortable resolution to this video; rather, it leaves one a 'wondering' woman, instead of in the sure place of Wonder Woman herself.

Nevertheless, the degree to which the video distances itself from the image is ambiguous and anticipates a common problem with some postmodern texts. The political significance of ambiguous relation to the image may be illustrated by comparing two later videos (perhaps influenced by Birnbaum's pioneering art) to Birnbaum's strategies, as well as to each other: namely, Julie Brown's rock video, *The Homecoming Queen*, shown on MTV in 1986, and Judith Barry's *Casual Shopper* 1983, made independently. Like Birnbaum's, these videos play with mythic American female images, in these cases, the Homecoming Queen and 'Miss (WASP) America', the images central to shopping centres, as well as to ads and women's magazines, but each makes clear its distance from the myth. The different sites (i.e., commercial TV, the independent sphere) for each myth's expression are important (see below) but do not prevent a common concern with representation: both videos admit the fascination that the image wields—the desire to *be* the Homecoming Queen or Miss (WASP) America. Indeed, they play upon this fascination. However, the ways in which they do this vary.

*The Homecoming Queen* makes the desired image comical: it manages to insert a deliberate distance between the spectator and the image's fascination through laughter. The video generates laughter by having the 'Queen' behave in a manner directly the reverse of that expected: instead of smiles and charm, the Queen brandishes a gun and is, in turn, gunned down. The video's narrational mode (that of the tale told by the Queen's blonde-stereotype, gum-chewing girlfriend) further distances us from the awe usually associated with the mythic figure. The video spoofs the usual romance story by having the friend fall instantly in love with the police officer investigating the Homecoming Queen's wild rampage and death.

This is as far as Julie Brown can go, it seems, within the confines of the commercial station. The parody of the Homecoming Queen ritual is made, but no larger institutional or cultural critique is involved. Having made its point, the video offers a resolution, which, even if in the comic mode, permits the satisfaction of closure (and 'forgetting').

Judith Barry's *Casual Shopper* ultimately functions in a different register: the video asks us to accompany the heroine on her shopping expedition. It takes us inside the experience of the mall, imaging its seductive thrall and its sensual pleasures. The mall represents the world of the imaginary, with its overwhelming focus on desire including the Freudian 'family romance'. But, gradually, we begin to realise that our heroine is totally affectless—as passive, beautiful and vacant as a mannequin in the store window or the models in the women's

5.1, 5.2 and 5.3] Stills from Dara Birnbaum's video *Technology/Transformation: Wonder Woman* © 1978–79. (Dara Birnbaum)

magazine pages she idly glances through. In not permitting the intrusion of any world outside the mall and its fantasies, the video inserts the idea that, for the woman, there *is* nothing but herself as consuming and desiring subject—no subjectivity outside of the commodity-relation. We fully understand, then, the network of relations within which the heroine is positioned and how these relations work to produce a sense that all there is *is* representation. Or, to put it differently, the viewer gets a sense of the difficulty of knowing where representation begins and ends: a problem that did not, as such, arise in prior historical moments and which Julie Brown's video does not attempt to address.

Barry's video makes its point precisely because it first shows, and only then addresses, the fascination of the female image it ultimately aims to deconstruct. By the video's end, the dangerous, seductive aspects of the image are revealed. This differs from the relatively innocent 'joke' that *The Homecoming Queen* rests on.

A second contrast between two women's videos, Laurie Anderson's *Language Is a Virus* (1986), shown on MTV, and Julie Zando's low-budget video *Hey Bud* (also 1986), made independently, shows that the resisting postmodern video can take very different forms, while having in common a critique of dominant representational modes, and

5.4] A still from Judith Barry's video *Casual Shopper*, 1983. (Judith Barry)

of the part that consumption and communications technology play in daily life. The contradictory nature of MTV is evident in the fact that Anderson's video was played at all (although it disappeared quite quickly). But the video represents work by a number of artists such as David Byrne and Philip Glass who are part of an increasing group of 'crossovers', straddling the old commercial/avant-garde polarity—namely, artists who came out of art schools or their equivalent. The work of these artists has contributed to breaking down the polarity.

Anderson's images in *Language Is a Virus* are set to the complex but rhythmic and pleasurable beat of her music. Her own husky voice is used like a contrapuntal instrument, while her body gyrates and is constantly transformed. In this way, Anderson prevents the fetishisation of her body, or even its precise fixing as male or female (she alternates between male and female dress codes).

The video's main theme is the pollution of the world by language (which includes language on TV), and which, following William Burroughs, is seen as a virus from outer space. In Lacanian terms, since language is coterminous with culture, culture is itself diseased. The space of the video suggests an 'outer space' or a no-place, since objects and bodies float in and out of the frame in a chaotic, fragmented way.

*Hey Bud* works in an analogous manner: Julie Zando juxtaposes television newsreel footage showing an industrialist blowing his brains out in front of the news cameras (he had been caught embezzling funds) with images of two young women preparing for the prom and concerned only about their fashionable dresses, make-up and romance. The soundtrack for their scenes consists of a repeated 'I love you', until the obsessive words cease to have any meaning and become an annoyance. The juxtaposition of an obsessive male symbolic order, where machismo and violent exhibition reign, and an imaginary claustrophobic female terrain, where emptiness and cloying love are the norm, makes the point. Both these videos invite the spectator to think about the systemics of communication—about language and the media in particular—rather than drawing attention only to female icons.

Some performance artists, however, take a further step—one beyond what select MTV and alternate videos achieve—and actually implicate the spectator in a new *system of communication*. For instance, *Maelstrom*, a video installation by Judith Barry (on view at Whitney/ Equitable in 1988) comments on the depersonalisation of the electronic age through placing the spectator inside that depersonalised system. It develops and makes new use of processes of spectator involvement, deriving ultimately from the surrealists (especially Marcel Duchamp), and revitalised by the 1960s American Pop Art (the 'happenings').

*Maelstrom* gives the spectator the dizzying experience of overwhelming information and image input. The spectator has to submit voluntarily to this bombardment of the image by stepping on the floor where the images are being relayed. The verbal messages sweep up on the viewer in bits and pieces, and demand that she or he search for them and piece them together. Their gradual linguistic impact, together with the experience of invasion by the image, make the point that contemporary culture is 'invaded' by images and information.

This is a point that the passive daily consumer of media images is deliberately not made aware of, since consumerism depends precisely on desire being harnessed through the image. The Museum site (however problematic in other ways), together with the text's own desire to comment on the consumption processes it is producing, make the experience a different one from that of uni-dimensional, commercial consumption.

Other types of video, this time combined with performance, are appropriately labelled 'postmodern' because of a concern with the collapsing of boundaries analogous to that examined in the videos discussed. Now, however, the concern is specifically ontological, rather than about systems of communication *per se*. Such works are preoccupied with the problem of being versus image, inner world versus outer-world, animal versus human, with the meaning of the body and voice in contact with other bodies and voices. Often, as already mentioned, videos are linked with performance art, exploring a different postmodern sensibility that would be misnamed 'negative'.

Angelika Festa's complex work is an example. It has as much to do with a desire to demonstrate/expose woman's position in culture by affecting the spectator in a particular way as with Gever's 'negative' philosophy. It refuses the objectification and appropriation that culture usually imposes on woman by playing with codes/signifiers/assumptions about social (particularly gender) interrelationships. As such, it is again not an expression of negativity *per se*. Recalling Selma Fraiberg's work with blind infants (where mothers were forced to find new ways of interacting with babies just because the usual mutual gaze was denied),[13] Festa's denial of the spectator–performer gaze (her eyes are covered) forces the spectator into other interactive modes. One might look at the feet displayed on the video playing in the room, or at the performer's arms and hands that are uncovered. One might be drawn to a certain kind of inner meditation by the stimulus the work provides.

The work raises questions about links among the installation's parts, and many associations might come to the viewer's mind: Christ, the crucifixion, swaddling clothes, Christ's gift of bread and fish, experiences of birth, death and so on. Meanwhile, the refusal of the gaze interchange that humans rely on in interaction[14] makes the spectator uneasy. The spectator is invited to notice the woman-as-object, and that the object is precisely *unpleasurable*. The work refuses the pleasure spectators have come to expect from the display of the female body. One is forced to work at interpretation, to put together for oneself the discordant pieces that are given. One wants to ask: 'Why are you doing this? Tell me what you mean.' But the body hangs silent, motionless, blind. The refusal to communicate forces the spectator back on him- or herself, back into him- or herself.

Performances like Festa's, then, try to work outside the voyeuristic/fetishistic structure ushered in by the mirror-phase and the entry into language and the symbolic. Rather, the performance returns us to the interactive, pre-linguistic structure of mother and child studied by Daniel Stern and referred to above. If the work is postmodern in the sense of not being clear about who is speaking and to whom, or about the message, content or argument of the piece, it avoids the whole commercial/alternative blending of the first type of postmodern

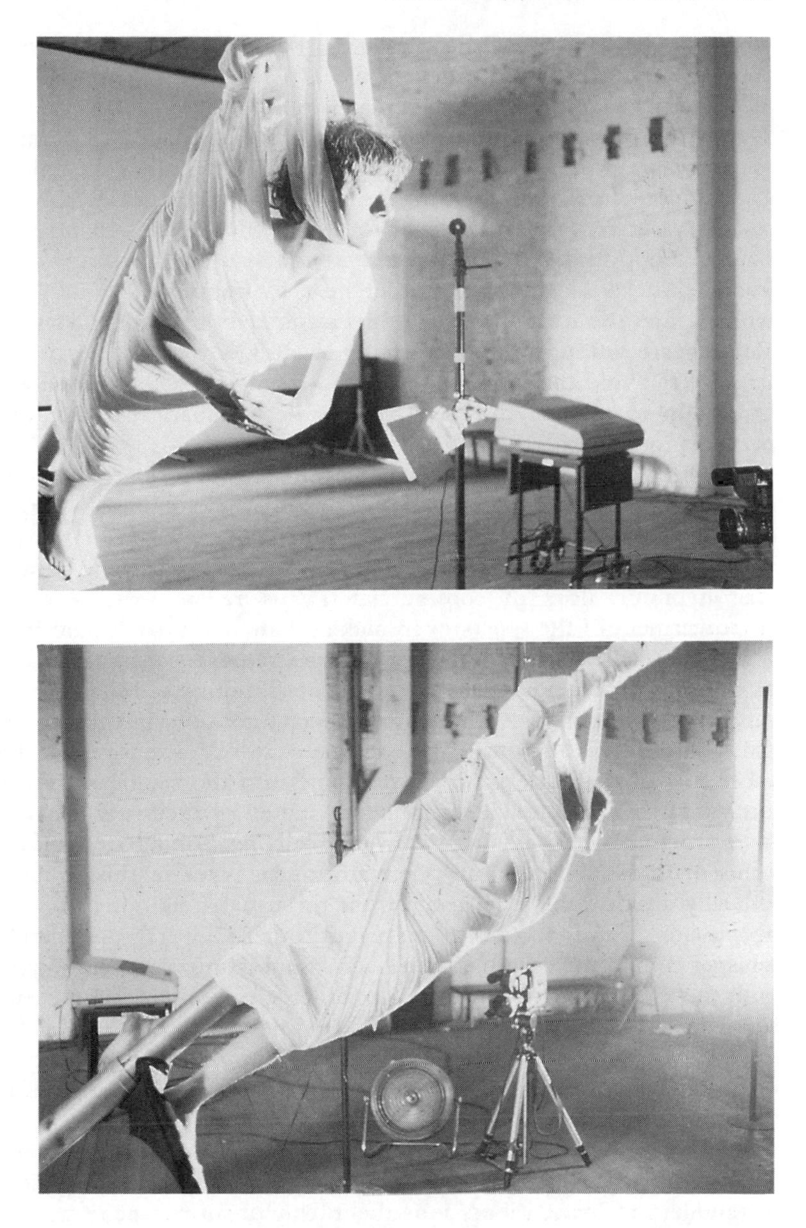

5.5 and 5.6] Untitled dance with Fish and Others: performance by Angelika Festa, May 30–1, 1987. Experimental Intermedia Foundation, New York, NY. (Hubert Hohn)

woman's text. None of the pleasures, fantasies and desires of the popular with which the previous work played are introduced. The piece simply makes enormous demands on the viewer.

The strategies are analogous to the ones employed by an artist, Mary Kelly, working in another visual field: Kelly's installation 'Corpus' (part of a larger long-term work on aging, *Interim*, which references Charcot's drawings of hysterics) chooses not to represent woman's body itself, but to exhibit a woman's clothes instead. The framed articles of clothing are set next to fragments of narratives which are in the form of retold conversations, but whose links to the clothing are left up to the spectator to decide. Kelly hopes by this strategy to avoid the problem of woman's body as object of the gaze, and again to include the spectator in the installation by requiring participation.

The video or art installation and the performance arguably offer a new system of communication in constructing a spectator position deliberately counter to that which commercial television or the conventional art gallery imposes. The enforced passivity of the continuous, hypnotic flow of commercial TV is replaced by a certain empowerment of the spectator in making him/her a participant in the work. Some installations carry this to an extreme: for instance, a work by Barry Schwartz consists of a complex positioning of mirrors, video cameras and monitors such that the spectator's own image becomes the 'content' of the work. This produces an odd situation *vis à vis* other spectators in the gallery who come into the room and see the 'art work' that the previous person has created by their presence: they then proceed to take their turn in constructing a different work. All kinds of interchanges among spectators take place in this situation, radically altering the experience from the usual museum one where people are careful to be silent, to respect other viewers' spaces and to whisper comments if with a friend. This doubly interactive mode (i.e., with the art work itself and with the other spectators in the museum) is particularly important for women, traditionally both the object of the gaze within the work and an isolated object in the text–spectator relation: woman is no longer positioned as passive consumer of her victimised place in art.[15]

If the violation of the hitherto sacrosanct separation of observer and art work (a separation initiated fully by the Romantics) is typically postmodern in installations, so is the mixing of forms—painting, photography, film and video. It is as if the history of the visual form is being collapsed or integrated as the new technologies develop. A hybrid form merges preceding ones, as Raymond Bellour has argued.[16]

Predictably enough, women artists seem more concerned with new ways of involving (and empowering) the spectator than with constructing 'hybrid' forms *per se*. They are more interested in the significance of the sites within which works are displayed.

In this limited sense, the commercial/alternative axis still has meaning, while it does not for textual strategies or even for prior modernist critical positions. One does not go to the Whitney to see soap operas, which are watched in the passive position of commercial TV at home: but one most likely will see in a museum or classroom setting Joan Braverman's commentary on soaps and prime-time serials in her *Joan Does Dynasty*, or Elain Rapping's *Soap*.

The issue of institutional mode of exhibition for women's work brings me to the second level I want to address, namely that of social institutions and audience. I have shown that the commercial and the alternative textual strategies have grown closer—that women artists have appropriated hitherto popular forms, while some explicitly commercial forms, like rock videos, have increasingly appropriated what were once considered avant-garde forms. But what about who gets to see what and through what institutional modes? I have talked about the desirability of new modes of communication: the issue now is whether or not those new modes can function within dominant commercial entertainment institutions or whether the entire construct of separate 'spheres' is no longer viable.

Difficult problems exist when we turn to the level of the *institution*. It is one thing for women artists to devise strategies they believe to be the most capable of making feminist statements in the 1990s or of constructing new female subjects; but quite another to create a space for exhibition of such works or an audience for them. Has the strategy of postmodernist appropriation, in, say, the form Dara Birnbaum or more recently (in art) Sherrie Levine or Jeff Coons have used it, exhausted its usefulness when co-opted by the art-market apparatus? Indeed, the whole postmodernist blurring of spheres offers contradictory possibilities: it seems potentially liberating *theoretically*, but potentially dangerous *practically*, because of the way the market always comes to dominate and to make what sells the only value.

While the installation and performance-art strategies seem potentially to create new possibilities, in practice, in contemporary American culture there is increasingly little space for alternate or noncommercial art, and (in the wake of debates about Robert Mapplethorpe and Karen Finley), even less possibility of the federal funding essential in enabling cutting edge work to be done. In addition, installations are extremely expensive to exhibit and to move from one location to another, while spaces and audience for performance art of the kind referred to above can only be found in large cities.

Given this situation, some women artists believe that the only viable solution is to develop their own alternative television and theatrical networks, since the commodity effect always contaminates. Others point to the fact that, in 1989, MTV hired a station manager well informed about deconstruction and recent media theories who sees a possibility for innovative slots on the commercial channel, and has developed ideas far more radical than Channel 13's 'New Television' hour, now 'Alive TV'. The debate is crucial, for on its outcome depend strategies for future video developments: if one opts for the alternative network, one resigns oneself to small, already convinced audiences; if one opts for trying to get innovative, progressive work on commercial channels, one risks losing control of one's ideas or their dilution. While the argument may be familiar from the areas of film and literature, it has taken on a new urgency in relation to video because of the real possibilities for making either strategy work.

What can we conclude from all this, on both the theoretical and institutional levels? On the theoretical level, I have shown that arguments like Gever's are misplaced. The strategies she advocates are not being used even for the political art she supports, as can be seen from Paper Tiger videos or work by artists like Martha Rosler. It is clear that the late 1980s videos by women do not necessarily provide us with the kind of feminist strategies that dominated 1970s work (whether it was radical, reformist, Marxist or poststructuralist in nature). The 1980s video artists briefly discussed here used video as a form whose nature permits the blurring of previously distinct boundaries retained by work we could still loosely call 'modernist' (in a broad sense). These boundaries could be listed as involving categories like 'society', 'artist', 'text' and 'spectator', which video artists seek to contest or transform.

Artists do not try to make statements about what woman is or could be, about how she has been misrepresented, misrecognised in patriarchy, about woman's absence from history, about the silencing of her voice, about her position as voyeuristic or fetishistic object, etc. Rather, they seek to give the spectator the experience that will allow her to discover for herself something about herself and the society she moves in—about the oppressions she daily labours under, about the processes of her objectification, a different matter from a theory of objectification.

All postmodern strategies employed by women respond to the collapse of belief in a totalising discourse such as modernists (using

Nietzsche, Freud or Marx, for example) still retained. The modernist concept of dialectical movement with a specific end to it affected strategies they used in the form and exhibition of their works.

The women artists discussed here are in deliberate reaction against modernism and therefore have increasingly turned to the performance and the installation. These strategies aim at forging connections, to use Lentricchia's phrase,[17] rather than relying on a modernist totalising discourse. The concept of 'forging connections', as against that of inevitable dialectics, suggests that human agency actually produces the effect. In the dialectical model, on the contrary, humans gain agency only as they become aware of the dialectical movement that they are involved in. They do not create the dialectic: they rather 'come upon it', so to speak.

'Forging connections' implies a lateral as opposed to a dialectical or building-steps arrangement. It implies a placing side by side, a lateral juxtaposition, leaving the connections to be made by the spectator. Some images in rock videos, like those by Laurie Anderson or Talking Heads work in this way. Videos by artists like Barry or Birnbaum also juxtapose images to 'forge connections', even if often the Other of commercial television is implied, not literally there. Artists like Festa ask the viewer to forge connections at a performance. But in none of these cases is there an assumed *a priori* position on society or the world—a specific class, race or gender stance that would function (as did such *a priori* positions in modernist texts by Eisenstein, Vertov, Buñuel, the German Expressionists) to unite artist and spectator before they even confronted one another through the text. (Perhaps among modernists, the early Soviet 'agit-prop' groups, or Artaud, Dali and Magritte come closest to the strategies of the postmodern works discussed—but even in these the clear worker identification or the *epater le bourgeois* stance was *a priori*.) Rather, gender, race and class positions are discovered in the processes of reacting to, or with, the work.

All these aspects of women's 1980s video work suggest that feminist statements can be made in ways other than the explicit message given out by a text. The feminist statement and the challenge to previous artistic modes is now taking place centrally in the text–spectator relationship, rather than in the theoretical analyses of classical texts or in the contesting of oppressive representations within texts.

The boundary between commercial and alternative spheres (conceived as an opposition) was useful to the 1970s feminist theorists and practitioners because it permitted the construction of a *position* from which to critique dominant, popular representations. The collapse of the polarity produces a new situation and a new *kind* of text—one which Gever calls 'negative', but which is better conceived as *different*: in the 1980s, video artists appropriated commercial forms in contrast to the careful and deliberate earlier modernist separation of avant-garde and popular modes. But this work may nevertheless be seen as continuing 1970s feminist politics, only it now uses strategies more suited to prevailing codes in the late 1980s postmodern moment. Griselda Pollock is right in noting that '. . . the changes for which the women's movement struggled have not come about . . . There is power, but there is resistance', and in arguing that '[w]hile the Brechtian modernism of the 1970s is being transformed tactically, as it must be, by the debates of the 1980s, its theoretical and practical contributions for a political art practice remain a valid and necessary component of the contemporary women's art movement.'[18] It is precisely such an art practice that I believe 1980s female video and performance artists were undertaking, albeit in a manner more suited to the new 1990s plural, feminist consciousness.

It is precisely this tension between theoretical postmodern possibilities for exciting new art modes, and the commercial and institutional co-opting that is also part of postmodernism, which artists urgently need to address as the new decade advances. Resistance may best be located in between the previously polarised avant-garde and commercial theoretical and institutional modes.

## Notes

1 MTV, as a non-stop cable station, was the brain-child of Bob Pittman, then of Warner Bros., in 1981. The idea of linking rock lyrics to visual images was not unprecedented, but it had not been undertaken in the ongoing, formalised manner of a cable station at first devoted only to round-the-clock music videos. See E. Ann Kaplan, *Rocking Around the Clock: Music Television, Postmodernism and Consumer Culture* (New York and London, Routledge, 1987). Gradually, in the years since 1981, the cable station has undergone some changes such as introducing comedy spots, special feature slots (such as 'Yo-Yo Raps' or 'Pirate MTV'), rerunning *The Monkees*, 'Postmodern MTV' and so on.

2 See Andrew Ross, 'Ballots, Bullets or Batmen: Can Cultural Studies do the Right Thing?', *Screen*, 13:1 (Spring, 1990), 28.

3 Compare films by *Newsreel* women filmmakers and those by the London Women Filmmakers' CO-O-, Mulvey/Wollen films and so on. For examples of this work and the feminist critique it involved, compare Annette Kuhn, *Women's Pictures* (London, Routledge, 1982) and E. Ann Kaplan, *Women and Film: Both Sides of the Camera* (London and New York, Routledge, 1983).

4 See Martha Gever, 'Seduction Hot and Cold', in *Screen*, 28:4 (Autumn, 1987), 58–9.

5 Barbara Johnson made this comment while participating in a seminar at Stony Brook in March 1989.

6 See Paul Ryan, 'A Genealogy of Video', *Leonardo*, 21:1 (1988), 40.

7 See E. Ann Kaplan, *Rocking Around the Clock: Music Television, Postmodernism and Consumer Culture* (London and New York, Routledge, 1987).

8 In this phase of her career, Levine experimented with reprinting, among other art works, a photograph by Walker Evans, framing it and hanging it in a gallery. This piece of art was signed with her name.

9 E. Ann Kaplan, 'Feminism/Oedipus/Postmodernism: The Case of MTV', in E. Ann Kaplan (ed.), *Postmodernism and Its Discontents: Theories and Practices* (London, Verso, 1988), pp. 30–44.

10 Toril Moi, *Sexual/Textual Politics* (New York, Routledge, 1987).

11 In Hal Foster (ed.), *The Anti-Aesthetic: Essays in Postmodern Culture* (Port Townsend, WA, The Bay Press, 1983).

12 This is not to deny that video can be used like film. I am not making an argument for form as *determining*, but rather exploring which forms seem linked to which kinds of social organisation and to specific phases of advanced industrial culture. Video of all kinds is a form that fits current social modes. It is circularly linked to the emergence of certain social modes such as the decentred social communities that now predominate. In these, the idea of the 'local cinema' is nearly extinct and the video rental store becomes the main vehicle for watching movies. I am interested here in links between technologies and new modes of thought, new social organisation.

13 See Selma Fraiberg, 'Parallel and Divergent Patterns in Blind and Sighted Infants' in *Psychoanalytic Study of the Child*, Vol. XXXIII (New York, International Universities Press, 1968), pp. 264–300.

14 See Fraiberg, *ibid.*, and Daniel Stern, 'A Micro-analysis of Mother–Infant Internation: Behavior Regulating Social Contact between Mother and her 3-1/2 Month-Old Twins', *Journal of the American Academy of Child Psychiatry*, 10 (1971), 501–17.

15 See Peggy Phelan, 'Feminist Theory, Poststructuralism, and Performance', *TDR*, 117 (Spring, 1988).

16 See Raymond Bellour, 'Cinema and Video: Painting the Body', paper delivered at The Humanities Institute, SUNY, Stony Brook, March 1988.

17 Dana Polan discussed this phrase in a talk at the Stony Brook Humanities Institute on 'Mediatization of the Academic', April 1988.

18 Griselda Pollock, *Vision and Difference: Feminism and History of Art* (London and New York, Routledge, 1988), p. 199.

PART II

# POSTMODERNISM, POSTSTRUCTURALISM, POLITICS AND PERFORMANCE

6 *Steven Connor*

# Postmodern performance

What does it mean to perform? It means to *do* something, to execute or carry out an action. To speak of 'performing an action' is in this sense tautologous, since 'to perform' just *means* to act in certain ways. In early usages, the verb 'to perform' carried the strong sense of accomplishment or bringing to completion, even, in one obsolete usage recorded by the Oxford English Dictionary, making something complete by supplying a deficiency in it. In other uses, 'to perform' implies the making actual of a latent condition or possibility: 'to carry out, achieve, accomplish, execute (that which is commanded, promised, undertaken, etc., or, in extended sense, any action, operation, or process undertaken or entered upon)'.

If performance implies the achievement of completeness, it may also, in some more recent usages, imply the immediacy and directness of a *present* action. Following J. L. Austin, for example, speech-act theorists are wont to distinguish the constative dimension of language (what is proposed or asserted as the content of an utterance) from its performative dimension, which is to say the nature of the action performed in and on the world by the utterance; to distinguish, in other words, what language says from what it does.[1] The constatation of the sentence 'Victor will meet you tomorrow' is the literal content of the statement. The performative force of the sentence will be defined by the kind of action performed by individuals as they utter these words with specific intentions and in specific contexts, as for example, promising, apologising, insisting or verifying: '(I promise that) Victor will . . .', or '(I'm sorry, but) Victor will . . .', '(I demand that) Victor will . . .' or '(Is it the case that) Victor will . . .?' The performance, or performative force of the sentence, indicates what the sentence actually and immediately does, in and by its very enunciation. Even where it may not be possible to specify such enunciative purposes, it may always be possible to identify a kind of intentional force in the act of utterance itself. Jacques Derrida, for example, has pointed to the effect of performative redoubling in the 'yes' that every utterance says to itself. This 'yes-function' is at work even when the word 'yes' is not employed, to bind utterance into its present actuality:

> [T]he *yes* comes from me to me, from me to the other in me, from the other to me, to confirm the primary telephonic 'Hello': yes, that's right, that's what I'm saying, I am, in fact, speaking, yes, there we are, I'm speaking, yes, yes, you can hear me, I can hear you, yes, we are in the process of speaking, there is language, you are receiving me, it's like this, it takes place, it happens, it is written, it is marked, yes, yes . . . *yes* is the transcendental condition of all performative dimensions. A promise, an oath, an order, a commitment always implies a *yes*, I sign.[2]

The closeness of the word 'perform' to the word 'act', however, may alert us to a certain tremor of equivocation in the word. For, if to perform means to act, make or do something, it also means to dissimulate or to pretend to act, to feign action. The difference between the two meanings of performance corresponds closely to the difference between 'acting', in the sense of doing something, and 'enacting', in the sense of playing out, or impersonating. The word 'performance' therefore points simultaneously towards immediate, spontaneous and ungoverned action on the one hand, and the act of doubling, and the doubling of action, in imitation, repetition or citation on the other. The very structure of Derrida's explication of the transcendental performative indicates how difficult it is to articulate the immediacy of any utterance or discursive situation without causing it to double up, or putting it in self-reflexive quotation marks.

The point of recalling this uncertainty in the meanings of the word 'perform' is not to fix and, in the eighteenth-century use of the word, to 'ascertain' its meanings, in order to be able to shear away irrelevance and distraction from each particular usage of the word. Rather, it is to suggest some of the ways in which the two opposite meanings of the word actually cross and combine, both in attitudes towards performance and in performance itself. For one of the salient features of postmodern performance, I will be wanting to suggest, is its capacity to explore the compounding of action and enaction, immediacy and repetition, event and work.

One word of caution. There is no shortage of candidates for the designation 'postmodern performance'; all of the following have been held with varying degrees of plausibility to be representatively 'postmodern': Bertolt Brecht, Jean Genet, Harold Pinter, Samuel Beckett,

Allan Kaprow, Joseph Beuys, Joe Orton, Tom Stoppard, Richard Foreman, Robert Wilson, David Mamet, Peter Handke, John Cage, Merce Cunningham, Yvonne Rainer, the Judson Dance Theatre, the Wooster Group, the Mabou Mimes company, Harry Partch, Steve Reich, Laurie Anderson, Dennis Potter, Thomas Kilroy, Caryl Churchill. I shall be referring to a number of pieces of work that seem to me both to qualify for the designation and to help in understanding the characteristic features of postmodernist performance, whether this be in traditional live theatre, dance, opera, music, performance art, or in the styles of performance characteristic of other cultural forms. But I think it is also important at the outset to attend to a much more general condition of performativity at work in contemporary culture. Put simply, it may be said that ours is a culture that is so saturated with and fascinated by techniques of representation and reproduction, that it has become difficult for us to be sure where action ends and performance begins. Ours is a world, it is commonly said, of widespread and pervasive simulation, in which the traditional means of separating off instances of performance from instances of the real seem to be compromised, if not wholly superseded. If this is the case, it may make more sense to point to a general condition of uncertainty about the boundaries between non-art and art, originals and repetitions, the real and the represented, than to attempt to preserve such distinctions in the form of a boundary between postmodern and non-postmodern performance (in other words, a boundary between an art that does cross boundaries and one that does not). Nick Kaye usefully warns us that 'in seeking to describe the "postmodern" in art and performance, the critic attempts to characterise that which is disruptive of categories and categorizations and which finds its identity through an evasion or disruption of conventions'.[3]

I would like to illustrate some of the problems involved in illustrating the nature of postmodern performance by considering Tom Stoppard's *Travesties*. This is a play whose purpose appears to be to explore the arbitrary logic of overlapping world-systems or structures. In this it adopts a procedure apparent in many other Stoppard plays, which commonly take closed and self-sufficient worlds and cause them to break in on each other. In *The Real Inspector Hound*, the conventions of the country-house murder mystery are mapped on to the world of theatrical reviewing; in *Rosencrantz and Guildenstern Are Dead*, the private perplexity of two minor characters in *Hamlet*, along with the repetitive games and routines they act out to pass the time, are set within and against the larger semantic universe constituted by the play of *Hamlet* itself; *On The Boundary* conflates lexicography and cricket;

*Every Good Boy Deserves Favour* orchestral music and politics; *Professional Foul* football and politics; and *Jumpers* moral philosophy and gymnastics. In all these plays, the rationale and comic engine is the coincidence and competition of mutually exclusive ways of being in or ordering the world, as these both interrupt and interpret each other. *Travesties* is perhaps the most complex of these intricately-designed collisions of worlds. The play is loosely governed by the unreliable reminiscences of Henry Carr of his time as a consular official in Zürich towards the end of World War I. Stoppard uses Carr's fragile memory as an excuse to manufacture a series of meetings between three characters engaged in different types of revolution: Tristan Tzara, associated with the artistic revolution of Dadaism, James Joyce, engineering his 'revolution of the word' in the writing of *Ulysses* and Lenin, planning the revolution in Russia.

The play thus has three distinct and powerful universes of discourse, artistic, anti-artistic and political, each of them claiming to be a total explanation and each therefore vulnerable to the disruptive force of the others. This basic structure is further complicated by the obtrusion of other principles of organisation. Stoppard uses the fact that Joyce was involved in an amateur production of *The Importance of Being Earnest* in which the historical figure of Henry Carr indeed took a role, as an excuse to borrow, or allow his own play to be borrowed by, the idiom and structure of Wilde's play. Similarly, he parodies many of the techniques of *Ulysses*, as, for example, when the earnest question and answer of the 'Ithaca' section of the book is used to generate a scene in which Joyce interrogates Tristan Tzara about the origins and principles of Dadaism.[4] Other principles of organisation are provided by Henry Carr's sartorial obsession, the chance procedures employed by Tristan Tzara for poetic composition, which include taking cut-up words out of a hat, and even the structure of limerick, which takes over a whole scene at the beginning of the play.[5] The fact that Tristan Tzara is about to woo Gwendolen Carr with a cut-up travesty of Shakespeare's eighteenth sonnet summons up involuntary quotations by Gwendolen from *Julius Caesar*—'You tear him for his bad verses?' and from *Hamlet*—'These are but wild and whirling words, my lord'—which in turn generates a passage of dialogue which is itself a collage of short snippets taken from a number of other Shakespeare plays.[6]

For the audience trying to make sense of the play, the emphasis may well fall on the recognition of coincidence and parallel, and the play is amply enough furnished with repetition—of lines, scenes and situations—to reward and reinforce this kind of attention. But, as its title announces, the play is just as fundamentally concerned with dislocation, displacement and mistranslation. Any coherence which the play achieves is against the principle of disarrangement and incompleteness which appears to govern it. This is comically exemplified in a scene towards the end of the play in which Tristan Tzara returns to Joyce a folder containing the typescript of a chapter from *Ulysses* which has been mistakenly exchanged for a passage of political polemic of Lenin's. The codes of dress and literature combine to image the principle of hybrid misalliance that is at work in Joyce's writing, Tzara's performances and Stoppard's play alike:

> CARR: And I have only one request to make of *you—why for God's sake cannot you contrive just once to wear the jacket that is suggested by your trousers??*
> *(It is indeed the case that* JOYCE *is now wearing the other halves of the outfit he wore in Act One.)*
> JOYCE *(with dignity):* If I could do it once, I could do it every time. My wardrobe got out of step in Trieste, and its reciprocal members pass each other endlessly in the night . . .
> TZARA (handing JOYCE *his folder):* Furthermore, your book has much in common with your dress. As an arrangement of words, it is graceless without being random; as a narrative it lacks charm or even vulgarity; as an experience it is like sharing a cell with a fanatic in search of a mania.

What makes this play so apt—and therefore, as we will see in a moment, so problematic—an example of postmodernism is the fact that it reflects upon many of the problems and conditions out of which artistic postmodernism itself is developed. It focuses on the historical conundrum that the revolutionary art of modernism, which seems to have so much in common with the political revolutions sweeping across Europe at the beginning of this century, is, in fact, in many of its manifestations, characterised and generated by a turning away from history, a refusal to allow art to be subsumed by politics. Joyce stands in Stoppard's play for the dignity of an art committed absolutely to the realisation of its own principles. Artistic modernism, as it hardened into creed and procedure, for example, in the principles set forth in the work of Clement Greenberg, and the museum and critical practices it encouraged, in the theory and practice of modern dance, in the work of Martha Graham, and in the development of the New Criticism in America and elsewhere, emphasised the autonomy and self-absorption of a work of art. For the critic Michael Fried, developing principles established by Greenberg, the task of art is progressively to purify itself of everything that is extrinsic to it. The modernist work of art strives to attain a condition of 'absorption', of autonomy, or self-sufficiency, which is threatened or diffused by any awareness of the contexts of its reception, or other form of impurity. The importance of Fried for a discussion of postmodern performance, as has been argued at length by Nick Kaye and myself, is that he so explicitly names the principle of dangerous impurity for art.[8]

> *The success, even the survival, of the arts has come increasingly to depend on their ability to defeat theater . . . Art degenerates as it approaches the condition of theater* . . . The concepts of quality and value—and to the extent that these are central to art, the concept of art itself—are meaningful, or wholly meaningful, only *within* the individual arts. What lies *between* the arts is theater.[9]

Far from attempting to defeat the condition of theatre, *Travesties* appears, like much postmodernist art, gladly to succumb to it. Against the modernist requirement of the autonomy of art, *Travesties* displays and implicates itself in the shifting play of appearance and performance that it shows characterises not just literature and art but politics too. If the title of the play intimates self-consciously that it is a forcing of reality into the structure of a game, an imaginary history put together for the purposes of spectacle, it does so in such a way as to suggest that the 'other' of theatre—the realities of politics and history that seemingly lie beyond its jurisdiction—has itself been penetrated by theatricality. *Travesties* is therefore theatrical not in the sense that it sets itself off from the real, but in precisely the sense disparaged by Michael Fried, in that it offers and exemplifies a principle of general performativity, which molests the theatrical/non-theatrical distinction itself.

And yet, in a curious way, *Travesties* also contradicts this condition. For all its seeming self-exposure to the conditions of performativity that prevail in it, and its self-designation as a travesty indistinguishable in kind from the other kinds of travesty going on in Zürich in 1917, the play also exempts itself from this condition. If the play shows modernity as an unpredictable chaos of dislocation, free association and revolutionary instability, it does so in a fashion that is itself intricately but reliably ordered. The play works to establish predictable rules and patterns which it is necessary for the audience to accept and inhabit for the play's demonstration of unpredictable dislocation to take place. One example of this is the cueing of time-shifts by certain switch-phrases, for example, the repeated entries of Carr's butler, Bennett, with the words, 'Yes sir. I have put the newspapers and telegrams on the sideboard, sir.' Stoppard's stage direction indicates the ways in which he means this to be interpreted by the audience:

> *(A note on the above: the scene (and most of the play) is under the erratic control of Old Carr's memory, which is not notably reliable, and also of his various prejudices and delusions. One result is that the story (like a toy train perhaps) occasionally jumps the rails and has to be restarted at the point where it goes wild . . . [T]he effect of these time-slips is not meant to be bewildering, and it should be made clear what is happening.)*[10]

Henry Carr's unreliable memory and testimony thus becomes a principle of functioning upon which the audience of the play may rely implicitly. Of course, it is always possible to argue that this authorial account is inconsistent, for Henry Carr's memory cannot, in fact, be held responsible for all of the shifts and dislocations of world and idiom in the play, since so many of these exceed his knowledge, understanding and experience. Like the theatrical 'Circe' episode from Joyce's *Ulysses*, which the play in certain respects resembles, the dream-work of the drama exceeds the control of any one dreamer. But the disciplining force of Carr's undisciplined memory is equivalent to the devising hold which the play exercises more generally over its internal divisiveness. The play shows us a world in which there is no all-encompassing mode of explanation—no meta-discourse or meta-narrative, whether political or artistic—which can reliably represent the totality of human affairs and connections, but each mode can do so only to the degree that its own act of showing pretends to just such a totalising perspective. The representation of the general principle of dysfunction in the mechanics of communication is engineered by a theatrical mechanism which itself whirs and spins with perfect precision.

This is to draw attention to the performativity of the play in the linguistic sense. The difference between what the play seems to say about theatricality and the performative force of the act of saying itself is the difference between the constative and the performative that I introduced at the beginning of this essay. *Travesties*, we may say, is designedly inattentive to the performative dimension of its own framing or staging of various styles of performance. Though the play shows many kinds of time-slip and interference across and between different times—the late nineteenth-century world of *The Importance of Being Earnest*, the turbulent times of modernism and modern revolution, the time of Old Carr's reminiscence—*Travesties* does not invite the audience to draw the immediate present of its own performative enunciation into this generalised theatricalisation of time. In the loophole which *Travesties* keeps open to secure its exemption from the shifting play of relativities it exemplifies, we may see a kind of reversion to something like the modernist self-definition and self-control that Fried promotes against the dissolutions and impurities of theatrical art; here modernist performativity is precipitated out of and preserved against postmodernist theatricality.

In fact, it would also be possible to put this the other way round and say that, at the level of the whole play's purpose and design, *Travesties* acts out (illustrates, represents, refers to) a mode of performativity that in the play itself declines or exceeds this kind of mimetic or referential purpose. Any performance of Stoppard's play will find itself controlling and curtailing, as well as indulging and releasing, the excess of the theatrical in it, that exorbitance ('ex-orbit-ance', breaking out of the circuit) which imperils the 'absorption', the shapeliness and presence to itself, of the well-made play. The play thus stands as an example of the compacting of the two meanings of performance, or the action of performance on performance, that I began by suggesting is unavoidable; the performance, or enaction of styles of performing that are pure action, without expressive, illustrative or referential purpose.

Typically, such postmodernist drama avoids absorption by forcing an attention to the intensities of present performance and attempting to resist the containing, stabilising effect of any single perspective by multiplying different frames of understanding and levels of performance. This can be seen as a struggle to separate out 'performing' from 'performance', pure unfolding action from enaction with a referential purpose—action which *is* from performance which *means*. Stoppard's interest in the comic incontinence of different discursive universes is shared by many different writers. One example might be Dennis Potter, whose later work for TV depends upon manipulated lurches between realistic drama and the staged artificiality of song and dance routines, which both underline and undermine the main action. An example of a different kind might be the work of Caryl Churchill, which deliberately sets realistic worlds in ironic and impossible conjuncture with historical worlds, for example in the prologue to *Top Girls* consisting of a dinner party of independent women from history, or the pinning together of a farcical pantomime history of nineteenth-century colonialism with problems in contemporary sexual politics in *Cloud Nine*. In recent works such as *The Skriker*, Churchill has also drawn on different theatrical styles and media.[11] In the work of Richard Foreman, the principle of exorbitance manifests itself as a refusal of continuity so absolute as to compel a ceaseless mobility of subject, purpose and perspective. Foreman represents a kind of limit-case of postmodernist performance, in his absolute refusal of the consolations of closure, and desire to open the theatre to the experience of unmasterable difference, or what he has called 'the web of everything interrupting everything else'.[12] Foreman's plays, of which the published texts are not so much the scores as the residues, are experiences of flux, in which lines of plot and situations can be abruptly derailed and rerouted at any moment, settings and sets can transform arbitrarily, and in which the traditional organising privilege given to characters and their speech is dissolved. The language in a Foreman play, for instance, which is recorded as well as live, circulates between actors rather than emanating from and defining characters, and must in any case make its way against many kinds of auditory distraction, including music, whistles and sirens. Foreman's account of the nature and purpose of this kind of theatre presents it as a kind of Becoming, or continuous emergence of significance rather than a fixing or manifestation of Being:

> When it seems that my plays, line by line, are changing the subject, that is true—but that changing of subject is the ground of the real subject, an openness and alertness resulting from a 'non-human' (post-humanistic) wandering over the whole field of everything-that-is-discoursing to us . . . To create that field (rather than allowing the consciousness to be hypnotized) my plays keep 'changing the subject'. But is it changed? Since the subject is the field, not spoken of directly, but articulated, layed [*sic*] out, by the writing of 'things'.[13]

Interestingly, Foreman's account of his work includes an awareness that the work can never be pure performing without performance, action without enaction. Foreman thus makes explicit what remains implicit in other postmodernist writers interested in exploring the Artaudian intensities of performance, namely that, despite his hostility to the referential function of theatre, his work is a kind of reflection of, or mimetic approximation to, what is taken to be the real, but hidden, ground or condition of our being. This ground is paradoxically groundlessness itself, and the work is said to be a specimen of that condition, rather than a referential reduction of it. But such performance, in the accounts that Foreman offers of it and that it offers of itself, cannot avoid some element of the referential: 'What I am trying to do', Foreman tells us, 'is get to the grain of thought and feeling . . . I try in my work to take dictation from the non-coagulated, still granual source: paradise'.[14]

It is for this reason that Foreman's work must proceed and represent itself not as a pure mobility of appearances, but as a series of self-contradictions or self-interruptions, in which the tendency of performing to coagulate into performance is everywhere at work and everywhere resisted:

> The pleasure I take (writing) is the pleasure of undercutting: interrupting: an impulse I want to (and do) make. The impulse is registered, but allowed to twist, turn, block itself, so that blockage, that reaction to its energy, produces a detour, and the original impulse maps new, contradictory territory.[15]

The resistance to traditional referential performance, as the acting out of some other scene, or the actualisation of some pre-existing condition, can never be total, since it so easily and necessarily precipitates into an exemplification of another truth, the truth of performance-in-itself. The pure process of performing can never be, as Herbert Blau puts it, 'the designated site of the extermination of the mimetic', since, as Blau goes on to observe, performing always involves to some degree a representation of itself *as* performance.[16] Foreman's work differs from that of other postmodernist writers for the theatre in its acknowledgement that there is always a kind of declension of performance into truth-telling, and its determination therefore to try to continue showing a truth beyond truth-telling in the sheer fact of its own failure to inhabit the truth:

> The need of the theatre to be effective, to be convincing, to testify to 'truth' . . . is the heart of the corruption and vulgarity of theatre . . . One reason I believe this is because I find myself, in my own work, imprisoned, hypnotized, fooled whenever I do something well, whenever I am (to myself) convincing in my mastery. Because at that point I sense I am, myself, hiding from truth behind the facade of the well built artistic edifice. So my work has been, over the past few years, to document my failure to really live up to the rigors of that impossible situation where one must show that all mastery is anti-truth.[17]

Richard Foreman's work for the theatre and reflections on that work (the title of the essay 'Notes on the Process of Making It: Which Is Also the Object' observes the nondifferentiation of these two) is perhaps the most powerful example that can be imagined of the exorbitance of postmodern performance.

But there is another mode of postmodern performance which is characterised not by excess and exorbitance, but rather by exaction and privation. Where the later work of Richard Foreman, along with that of Robert Wilson, makes the event of performing unavoidable by enlarging and proliferating its forms, some of the work of Samuel Beckett, Harold Pinter and Peter Handke has worked in the opposite direction, to isolate the conditions of performance by subtracting from it everything inessential and inauthentic. Ironically, such drama encounters some of the same paradoxes as the exorbitant mode of postmodern performance.

No more programmatic example of this way of proceeding could be imagined perhaps than Peter Handke's *Offending the Audience*, a play which sets out to deprive itself of everything that belongs to traditional theatrical performance, even to the point of denying the fact of performance itself. The text of the play begins with the careful specification of circumstances in the theatre prior to the performance, specification that seems intended to ensure that the performance is absolutely and entirely unexceptional in terms of the norms of behaviour in such circumstances. In an anticipation of one of the ironies of the play, this involves a certain heightening and isolation of the ordinariness of the situation, a stylised enaction of the style-less activity of non-theatrical real life: '*The usual theatre atmosphere should prevail. The ushers should be more assiduous than usual, even more formal and ceremonious . . . Yet, they are only ushers. Their actions should not appear symbolic*'.[18] Spilling over the border separating theatre and life in this way both diffuses the autonomy of the performance and also enlarges its dominion.

As the curtain rises, four speakers, of unspecified sex, dressed inconspicuously, advance to the front of the stage, mouthing, more and more audibly, passages of insult and invective. After a short pause, they begin to address the audience; the play-text gives no indication of differentiation among the speakers, or the ways in which the text is to be shared among them. What follows is a series of denials and deprivations. First of all, there is a denial of representation. The audience is told that what it sees and hears is to be exactly coincident with what is actually being shown and said. Fiction and illusion are rigorously eschewed: 'This is no play . . . We don't tell you a story. We don't perform any actions. We don't stimulate any actions. We don't represent anything. We don't put anything on for you' (p. 15). There is to be no equivocation or concealed meanings, we are told, no possibility of movement outwards to any other world than the one brought into being in the immediate actuality of what we see and hear in the theatre. The play insists that it has no intention to express anything. The objects on the stage have neither orderliness nor suggestiveness. The space of the performance is an actual, not an imaginary space: 'The emptiness of this stage is no picture of another emptiness. The emptiness of this stage signifies nothing. This stage is empty because objects would be in our way. It is empty because we don't need objects. This stage represents nothing. It represents no other emptiness. This stage *is* empty' (p. 16). Similarly, the play repudiates all artificial orderings of time, and denies even wishing to represent time. The time of the performance of this play is (the audience is told) the ordinary, irreversible, unstoppably elapsing time of real life, not the elastic, manipulable, sham time of theatrical performance:

> Time is no noose here. Time is not cut off from the outside world here. There are no two levels of time here. There are no two worlds here. While we are here, the earth continues to turn. Our time up here is your time down there. It expires from one word to the next. It expires while we, we and you, are breathing, while our hair is growing, while we are sweating, while we are smelling, while we are hearing. Time is not repeatable even if we repeat our words, even if we mention again that our time is your time, that it expires from one word to the next, while we, we and you, are breathing, while our hair is growing, while we sweat, while we smell, while we hear. We cannot repeat anything, time is expiring (p. 22).

As such, the play also denies that denial of the actual situation of address that makes most theatre possible, declines to decline to acknowledge the audience in the way that most drama does. The play thus poses addressivity against the self-absorption of dramatic performance. Instead of the concealed and indirect address to the audience, in the folded self-absorption of the dramatic spectacle that teasingly seduces as it ignores, this piece opens itself out directly to the audience, and thus closes the gap of implication and interpretation between audience and spectacle:

> We are not pretending that you don't exist. You are not thin air for us. You are of crucial importance to us because you exist. We are speaking to you because you exist ... Your presence is every moment explicitly acknowledged with every one of our words (p. 19).

Finally, the piece denies the possibility of completeness which is claimed by other kinds of dramatic performance, since to close the gap between performance and context to this degree is to relinquish the possibility of distinguishing between the performance which concludes at the end of the play and the real life which resumes. Like the stage directions which reach back into the moments before the performance begins, the text of the play looks forward to its aftermath, acknowledging itself as merely a prologue, a movement of opening on to whatever will happen subsequently to it. Since there is no limit to the things to which the play prospectively alludes without being able to include them, it will, in a sense, never end: 'It is the prologue to the plays and to the seriousness of your life. It is also the prologue to your future visits to the theatre. It is also the prologue to all other prologues. This piece is world theatre' (p. 34).

The play therefore attempts to expunge any possibility of difference, irony or lack of self-identity. To put it in terms of the two meanings of performance with which I have been working in this essay, the play aspires to the condition of pure and self-present event and action, entirely uncontaminated by any hint of reflection, imitation or enaction. But it also recognises that the pursuit of this entirety must necessarily involve it in contradiction. If, in one sense, the play aims to achieve the condition of pure performance by effacing every vestige of the theatrical, in another sense it can only be fully integrated with itself if it acknowledges the theatrical conditions which it inhabits. 'We express ourselves by speaking. Our speaking is our acting. By speaking, we become theatrical. We are theatrical because we are speaking in a theatre' (p. 26). The play acknowledges its own contradictoriness in this and other respects. In teasing the audience about its incapacity to keep up with the ironic self-doublings of its performance, *Offending the Audience* is also indicating the impossibility of keeping up with itself.

> You have recognised that we primarily negate. You have recognized that we repeat ourselves. You recognize. You see through. You have not made up your minds. You have not seen through the dialectical structure of the piece. Now you are seeing through. Your thoughts were one thought too slow. Now you have thoughts in the back of your mind (pp. 20–1).

The piece, in fact, cannot avoid the self-doubling and therefore self-estranging consequence of representing itself as non-representation. Despite its careful, drastic discarding of the resources of performance, the piece ends up asserting a kind of residual exorbitance within performance itself. Like the theatre proposed by Richard Foreman, this is a kind of performance that can only succeed to the degree that it fails to coincide with itself, doubles up against itself, so to speak. As such, it joins with other, more flamboyantly self-displaying and self-confuting forms of postmodern performance in demonstrating the essential impossibility of demonstrating or inhabiting the essence of the performing instance. In a postmodern world in which being seems to be in the process of being swallowed up by simulation, this is no mere game or conundrum. To explore the limits of performance in this way is to investigate nothing less than the possibility of truth and knowledge about ourselves.

Of course, it might be said that the paradoxes explored by Peter Handke's play derive largely from the fact that it consists almost entirely of words, rather than the physical movement and action which have traditionally been held to anchor the performing arts and maintain their close connection with shared social meanings and values. Indeed, one might point to a continuing strain of suspicion towards the word in contemporary performance, deriving perhaps from the writings of Antonin Artaud, which emphasises the essential autonomy of the corporeal facts of performance from language and defines their value in precisely these terms. But the removal of language or the reduction of its privilege is not enough to expunge the paradoxes involved in and explored by postmodern performance. The reason for this is that the very refusal of language requires the institution of a division between the linguistic and the non-linguistic, a division which continues to have effects at the heart of any performance which attempts to keep language outside. The work of performance artists such as Richard Long and Christo, both of whom enact processes in the natural and human landscape rather than fashioning durable aesthetic objects, may appear to have escaped the dominion of language; Richard Long by his ritualistic walks across various kinds of terrain, and the actions performed upon it, such as turning stones to face the wind, and Christo with his wrapping of buildings, or hanging of curtains across landscapes.[19] But the significance of the subtraction of language or representation in general from these actions is itself dependent upon representation, if only the minimal self-doubling of a photograph, description of the action, or other form of residue. The description of the action is both outside and inside it, insofar as the autonomy of the action from language can only be guaranteed by language. The wordless, objectless performance becomes framed as that-which-eludes-language, defined by the categories it appears to escape.

More profitable, because more honest, it appears, has been the attempt by various artists and in various media to use performance to reflect upon such differences and exclusions. Examples of this kind would include the configuration of discourse alongside various sorts of action or event.[20] As one example among many possible, I would like to discuss a piece of music-performance by the American composer Tom Johnson. *Failing: A Very Difficult Piece for Solo String Bass* was written in 1975. The score consists of the notation for a demanding piece of music of about ten minutes duration, full of changes in tempo and mood, accompanied by a text that the performer is required to read out loud in careful and exact synchronisation with the music. The text consists largely of an explanation of the particular requirements of the piece, which include, for example, the specification that the text should be read naturally and at an even pace no matter what changes of rhythm or timbre are undergone by the music, and that the performer should at all times pay attention to what he is saying and doing, in order to make sure that the text remains comprehensible to the audience. It then moves into an involved reflection upon the title of the piece, and on the difficulty of 'failing' in quite the way that it calls for. The text has the performer discuss the possibility of cheating by missing out the hardest parts of the music; this would be not only a failure, he says, but a failure to succeed in failing in the way required by the text. On the other hand, it will do no good to try to fail to meet the exacting requirements of the piece, since to succeed too well would be to fail in the way that the title of the piece anticipates. This leads to a reflection upon the complex interchangeability of success and failure:

> If I tried to fail, and then failed, that would be a kind of success, and not a failure at all. So I must try to succeed. That way, when I fail to succeed, I will succeed in communicating the essence of the piece, even though I will fail to accomplish the task it has set up. In other words, I will not be able to fail unless I am trying to succeed, and I won't succeed in interpreting the piece sensitively unless my performance turns out to be a failure. Or, putting it another way; I will probably succeed in failing to succeed, not only because the music is so difficult, but also because if I fail to succeed in failing to succeed, I will fail to fail, and thus miss the point, since *Failing* is obviously about failing, and since any successful performance must be a qualified failure.[21]

The performance of this piece actualises the situation spoken of in the text and will always be a different kind of fulfilment of the kind of success and failure specified there. The piece insists on the unique particularity of every performance, since every performance of the piece will always fill it out differently, precisely because of the difficulty of matching the performance to the specifications. The performance is therefore in advance and excess of the text. But the performance is also *of* the text that it exceeds; and that text succeeds in controlling or predicting the performance, precisely by making itself identical with that performance, and enumerating so exactly its contingencies. Thus, the simple distinctions between the score which comes before the performance, and the performance which enacts the score fall into comic, but slightly sinister commotion. The struggle between composer and performer becomes a struggle between the performer and himself, as he reads the text that both demands his conformity and signals his necessary failure to conform in the complex process of performance.

The language of the piece is thus both score and enactment, model and replica. It stands outside the performance, as a set of instructions for it, and a theoretical reflection on it, and yet is also at the heart of the performance. The music is no mere appendage or accompaniment, either, since the effect of having to work bicamerally in the mode of musical performance and the mode of spoken discourse is to bring about strange interferences between the voice and the fingers, as the dynamics of the music trouble the composure of the speaker, speaking through his voice, and the structure of the spoken text interrupts the rhythm of the music. The performer is split not just in having to be player and speaker at once, but also in being, as speaker, simultaneously inside and outside his performance. The piece requires him not only passively to transmit the text and music, but also to contribute to it, in the form of an improvised prologue and conclusion, for which no text is provided. 'Soon, however, I will be faced with a fresh difficulty. The text is about to run out but the music continues for another minute or so. During that time I must decide for myself what to talk about as I play.' However, the free improvisation into which the performer is launched at this point can only be successful if it meets certain stringent conditions:

> My remarks are to be genuinely improvised and should include specific references to this particular performance and to the degree to which I have been failing, or failing to fail, or failing to succeed to fail, or whatever. As before, I must continue to speak at a normal pace, in a normal tone of voice and maintain a balance between the speaking and the playing. As an additional challenge, I am supposed to link the written part of the text with the improvised part of the text so smoothly that no one will be able to tell where the improvised speaking began and the written text left off.[22]

The requirement to belong and refer to 'this particular performance' both opens the work on to the unpredictable event of the performance and also encompasses it in advance. The performance is both free and predetermined, both idiomatic and generalised. This is true, not just in the sense that it combines action and enaction in separable proportions, but in the sense that the performance brings into being (is itself brought into being by) the difference between the text and the performance that acts it out.

Like the other instances of postmodern performances that I have been considering, this text involves an exploration of the nature of performance itself. Such works neither determine the nature of performance by reference to stable distinctions between the work and its enactment, nor simply set performance 'free' from predetermining models. They thus demonstrate the limits of definitions of postmodern performance, or the postmodern in performance, which seem to assume the possibility of such free performance.[23] The various reflections on theatre and the instances of performance are no mere self-absorption, since 'performance' for all these works marks the point at which theatre opens out beyond itself, marks theatre as the very movement of opening beyond oneself. As such, they involve active and transforming reflection upon the nature of freedom, identity and action.

## Notes

1 See J. L. Austin, *How to Do Things With Words* (Oxford and New York, Oxford University Press, 1980).

2 Jacques Derrida, 'Ulysses Gramophone: Hear Say Yes in Joyce', transl. Shari Benstock and Tina Kendall, in Derek Attridge (ed.), *Acts of Literature* (London and New York, Routledge, 1992), pp. 297–8.

3 Nick Kaye, *Postmodernism and Performance* (Basingstoke and London, Macmillan, 1994), p. 3.

4 Tom Stoppard, *Travesties* (London, Faber and Faber, 1975), pp. 56–62.

5 *Ibid.*, pp. 33–6.

6 *Ibid.*, p. 54.

7 *Ibid.*, p. 96.

8 See Kaye, *Postmodernism and Performance*, pp. 26–8; Steven Connor, *Postmodernist Culture: An Introduction to Theories of the Contemporary* (Oxford, Blackwell, 1989), pp. 83–8, 132–57.

9 Michael Fried, 'Art and Objecthood', in Geoffrey Battcock (ed.), *Minimal Art: A Critical Anthology* (New York, E. P. Dutton, 1968), pp. 139–42.

10 Tom Stoppard, *Travesties* (London, Faber and Faber, 1975), p. 27.

11 Caryl Churchill, *Cloud Nine* (London, Methuen, 1984); *Top Girls* (London, Methuen, 1984); *A Mouthful of Birds* (London, Methuen, 1986); *The Skriker* (London, Methuen, 1994).

12 Richard Foreman, 'Notes on the Process of Making It: Which Is Also the

Object', *Reverberation Machines: The Later Plays and Essays* (Barrytown, NY, Station Hill, 1985), p. 191.

13 *Ibid.*, pp. 191, 193.

14 *Ibid.*, p. 191.

15 *Ibid.*, p. 193.

16 Herbert Blau, 'Universals of Performance', *The Eye of Prey: Subversions of the Postmodern* (Bloomington and Indianapolis, Indiana University Press, 1987), p. 167.

17 *Ibid.*, p. 199.

18 Peter Handke, *Offending the Audience* and *Self Accusation*, transl. Michael Roloff (London, Methuen, 1971), p. 11. References hereafter in the text.

19 See Richard Long, *Selected Works, 1979–1982* (Ottawa, National Museums of Canada, 1982), *Richard Long: Walking in Circles* (London, South Bank Centre, 1991), *Mountains and Water* (London, Anthony d'Offay, 1992) and Christo, *Valley Curtain, Rifle Colorado, 1970–72* (Stuttgart, G. Hatje, 1973), *Christo: The Running Fence* (Stuttgart, G. Hatje, 1977), *The Pont-Neuf Wrapped, Paris 1975–85* (New York, H. N. Abrams, 1990), *Works 1959–1989* (Hovikodden, Norway, Henie-Onstad Centre, 1990).

20 For discussion of the use of language in art and performance art, see Jessica Prinz, *Art Discourse/Discourse in Art* (New Brunswick, Rutgers University Press, 1991).

21 Tom Johnson, *Failing: A Very Difficult Piece for Solo String Bass*. My text comes from the performance of the piece by Robert Black at the Huddersfield Festival of Contemporary Music in 1993.

22 *Ibid.*

23 Though I have learned much from Nick Kaye's *Postmodernism and Performance*, his work falls into the error against which he warns, in assuming the availability of examples of pure, exorbitant performance.

7 *Valerie A. Briginshaw*

# Postmodern dance and the politics of resistance

While the topic of 'postmodern dance' has been addressed elsewhere,[1] little has been written about its political potential. This essay examines and illustrates this by analysing *Perfect Moment* (1992) (director: Margaret Williams, choreographer: Lea Anderson) adapted from an earlier stage piece, *Birthday* (1992) for the Cholmondeleys and the Featherstonehaughs.[2]

The political potential of some postmodern texts resides in the glimpses they can give of how power systems operate, of how major domains of power such as gender and sexuality are constructed, whilst also constructing individual subjectivities. The operation of power can be exposed and challenged in postmodern dance, through self-reflexive representation devices such as intertextuality and parody, problematising subjects no longer unified but fragmented and traversed by a complex network of power axes such as gender, sexuality, race and class. These construction processes also commodify things, by packaging them, as if for sale. Culture is commodified, art works become commodities, the cultural and the economic as major categories are merged. As this essay demonstrates, it is this collapse of major categories such as economics, politics and art that results in us being able to see politics *as* culture and vice versa.

Debates concerning definitions of postmodernism[3] often centre around the vexed relationship of postmodernism to modernism; whether postmodernism represents a break from modernism or a continuation of it, albeit in a different form. Foster distinguishes a 'postmodernism of resistance' 'which seeks to deconstruct modernism and resist the status quo', from a 'postmodernism of reaction' which repudiates modernism to celebrate the status quo.[4] The former could be seen as a continuation of modernism, retaining, where possible, its critical features, and the latter a break with it. Applying this theory to dance, it could be claimed that choreographers such as Lea Anderson, Pina Bausch and Mark Morris, who play with concepts such as gender and sexuality, thus revealing their constructed nature, seem to challenge the status quo, thereby exemplifying a postmodernism of resistance. On the other hand, choreographers such as Karole Armitage and Michael Clark tend uncritically to celebrate commodification more in sympathy with a postmodernism of reaction. This kind of categorisation is dangerous, however, as the boundaries are notoriously slippery. Debates abound.[5] Foster's 'postmodernism of resistance' which 'seeks to question rather than exploit cultural codes, to explore rather than to conceal social and political affiliations'[6] usefully characterises Anderson's work. She plays with cultural codes such as representation, thereby exposing the political affiliations apparent in constructions of key concepts like gender and sexuality.

In general terms, postmodernism can be seen as a response to the social and economic shifts evident in late capitalist society, for instance, from the production ethic to the consumption ethic.[7] It is this shift that has resulted in the 'commodification of culture', evident in the merging of key arenas such as the cultural and the economic. Some theorists, like Baudrillard, feel that as a result of this amalgamation critical distance is no longer possible, and that 'instead of producing meaning [culture] exhausts itself in the staging of meaning'.[8] However, for other theorists like H. Foster and F. Jameson, this same conflation revitalises the possibility of critical engagement because it exposes the ways in which things are socially constructed and therefore inherently political. The 'staging of meaning' reveals the construction process.

In a postmodern context, everything is seen to be constructed. The meaning, the performance, the performers and the audience are all constructed. The performers and the audience as subjects are no longer unified but fragmented and problematised. Postmodern texts persuade us to 'conceive of subjectivity as contextual, fluid, relational, constituted and annihilated through language'.[9] If dance is considered, then this statement could be read by substituting 'dance vocabularies' for 'language' in choreographic texts. For example, the vocabulary of classical ballet has played a crucial part in constructing a certain vision of femininity. Postmodern choreographic texts, by exposing this construction process, deconstruct and 'decentre' any notion of the feminine stereotype.[10] In Mark Morris's *The Hard Nut* (1991) the snowflakes, traditionally danced by ballerinas on *pointe* in *The Nutcracker* (1892), are danced by male and female dancers on *pointe* in a subtly less precise and slightly more abandoned manner. The *pointe* dancing and the precision are exposed as conventions of the construction process. The representation of the snowflakes as feminine is deconstructed and revealed for what it is.

The representation process is particularly pertinent to dance, where subjects are both represented in performance and as performers are also representing, a complex process which in certain postmodern works is being strategically exposed. As L. Hutcheon has asserted, 'Life in the post-modern world is utterly mediated through representations'.[11] It is through representations that we come to 'know' and make sense of the world. However, the fragile, artificial and *constructed* nature of representations must be stressed lest they are confused with 'reality'. 'Images dominate narratives, ephemerality and fragmentation take precedence over eternal truths'.[12] 'Reality' has ceased to be accessible, only images, representations and stagings remain. Baudrillard's 'simulacrum', meaning an image, a shadowy likeness, a deceptive substitute, mere pretence, has parallel connotations. There is only surface, no depth. This is highlighted by the role technology can play in cultural products by emphasising surface features; the look of the work, its staging, rather than its sense of depth or meaning. In *Perfect Moment*, for example, techniques such as camera angles from above, blurred images through frosted glass and accelerating or decelerating the video, all play with and emphasise the *process* of representation.

Any sense of a paramount 'reality' is here questioned through conventions of the performance medium. Performance becomes preoccupied with conventions or with performance itself. Painterly images such as 'patterns in space', 'icons' and 'tableaux' are prevalent.[13] They are played with and included for their own sake, making the performance *self-reflexive*. The work comments on itself and, by association, on other performances and representations. For example, in *Perfect Moment*, the action, when shot from overhead, makes the performers, often making identical unison movements, look like colonies of ants. The ritualistic repetition of gestures resembles patterns in space, rather than human actions. Frames are frozen forming tableaux, emphasising the importance of the image. Everyday movements such as hair-washing, judo and massage are made into a performance by conventions such as unison, rhythm, timing and framing. Individual subjects become automatons. The transformation of the everyday into dance emphasises that everything is a performance.

When the conventions of performance and representation are exposed, it is like seeing everything in inverted commas. What has previously been seen as 'natural' or 'real' is exposed as 'cultural' or socially constructed, revealing the ideologically grounded status of representation. At the end of *Perfect Moment*, the performers remove jackets, dresses and petticoats and arrange them, with bathrobes, wet suits, kilts and other costumes in a pattern which they complete by lying down amongst their clothes. The costumes on display emphasise the self-reflexive nature of the performance. Viewed from above, this tableau looks like a kit of clothes and dolls laid out to be dressed. Barbie, Sindy, Action Man and their outfits are supreme examples of the packaging, commodification and construction of gender. They illustrate the ideologically grounded status of gender representation, how femininity and masculinity are constructed from particular dominant worldviews or hegemonies that maintain certain power systems.

Parody also plays with the way things are represented. It shows that they are not 'real' but constructed; it 'foregrounds the politics of representation'.[14] For example, in 'drag' or cross-dressing, two contradictory statements are made. The male 'drag artist' is feminine outside (in dress, appearance, etc.) but masculine inside (the male body underneath); but, conversely, the inner motivation is a desire to be feminine whilst the outer body is masculine.[15] Because these statements contradict one another, any search for 'truth' or 'reality' becomes meaningless, and the imitative and constructed nature of gender is revealed. The representation process is exposed through the performance, the staging foregrounds the image as image. Cross-dressing in postmodern dance works can be read in this way.[16] At one point in *Perfect Moment*, all performers regardless of gender wear shoulder-length 'feminine' wigs; the hair is swung, flicked, played with and caressed, as in shampoo advertisements. The dancers turn and walk away from camera, swinging their hips in a consciously 'camp' parody of female backing groups like The Supremes. This also refers to an early Cholmondeleys' piece *Baby Love* and is an example of intertextuality.

Intertextuality is a representational and allusive device where one text refers to or quotes from another. The political potential of intertextuality is evident in *Perfect Moment* when a quote from Hollywood movies, a screen kiss, is used to expose the constructed nature of sexuality. This moment occurs significantly in the centre of *Perfect Moment*. Just after a single female performer in a satin slip has danced, a man in a suit enters; the woman approaches him and they go into a stereotypical clinch. The frame is frozen for a few seconds on this familiar symbol of heterosexual romantic love—the perfect moment, the climax of many a movie—then the image gradually fades away. By freezing the shot, placing it centrally and producing it quite abruptly out of nothing—there is no narrative or previous relationship between these two performers—it is seen for what it is, a construction. Later there are more kisses, echoing this moment, repeated by three couples simultaneously; a male pair, a female pair and a mixed pair. These gender mixes underline the constructed nature of sexuality; they challenge the hegemony of a heterosexual worldview. This and other examples of intertextuality, such as quotes from adverts, also remind audiences that nothing is original or 'real': meaning is constructed from other constructions.

The political potential of *Perfect Moment* is also evident when commodification is seen to contribute to construction. The radical juxtaposition of different environments in the piece—there is a street (everyday) and the TV studio (performance)—emphasises the interchangeability of the cultural and economic domains. Throughout *Perfect Moment*, advertising images appear and disappear. It is often difficult to distinguish 'reality' from media image, thus literally conflating the cultural with the economic. When the women pose in satin ballgowns, the first glimpse we get is through a slit or cut in some silk material, possibly alluding to a Silk Cut cigarette advert. The image of a slit in silk material is used as a sign for the brand name in this familiar British advert. Then various camera angles from above and below emphasise the model poses of the performers in Hartnell satin gown look-alikes, familiar from covers of magazines such as *Vogue*. The women appear on pedestals, later revealed as their male partners' shoulders. This revelation possibly alludes to the male-dominated capitalist system that both supports and relies on such advertising, but it also emphasises the self-reflexive nature of the performance, reminding the audience that this *is* a performance and of the role commodification plays in construction processes.

Other examples of the political potential of *Perfect Moment* are evident when the opening is analysed in some detail. The piece begins with Anderson in a satin ballgown and long gloves, holding up her dress and walking determinedly down an alleyway. This cuts to a shot of the profile of Frank Bock's head in an all-white TV studio where, dark suited, he is joined by Anderson. As Anderson begins to lift his arms, the image is blurred. Then, after she manipulates Bock as if he were a dummy, he raises his right arm and it becomes literally framed on screen with a textured border. A number of displacement strategies are evident: the radical juxtaposition of Anderson's costume, the alleyway and her determined walk, the blurring techniques and changes of camera angle. There is no time to focus on either Bock or Anderson; their presence and authority as individual subjects are displaced, fragmented and problematised. The blurring of the image emphasises that it is just an image, a constructed representation that is not 'real', a simulacrum. The framing is another example of self-reflexive performance—performance about performance. What is framed is an arm held up, this anti-charismatic device fragments the body or subject.

A series of male–female couples, identically clad in towelling bathrobes, adjust each other's hair and faces, and massage hands and feet in unison. This is initially seen through steamy glass, then frosted glass and then through glass with water running down it. Some couples are then reflected in fragments of broken mirror, while others are glimpsed performing behind these fragments. These multiple images are further multiplied because each piece of mirror reflects something different—they could not be reassembled into a unified whole. Finally, the performers are seen without any 'screen', except a slight mist as in a steamy bathroom. Four male–female couples are revealed working on each other (hair and face massage, manipulation of various parts of the body, etc.). In two couples, the males are behind the females 'working on them'; in the other two, the genders are reversed. The broken mirror images and steamy views recur until finally the couples are seen through cracked glass.

All the broken mirror shots, the 'glosses' or 'screens' filtering the images through condensation, frosted, cracked and watery glass, repeatedly emphasise the way images are filtered, framed, mediated and viewed in different ways from different positions, constructed by viewers from their positions. These shots also show fragmented rather than unified subjects and various 'plays' with gender occur. It is initially difficult to identify the male and female characters because all performers are dressed identically and seen only partially, either through a haze of some sort or because only parts of bodies are visible. When this does become clear, it is apparent that while in each couple one partner is active and the other relatively passive, it is not always the male who is active or vice versa; side by side, we see both genders carrying out the same roles. This, together with the identical dress, seems to imply the fluidity of gender, emphasising the constructed nature of defined masculine and feminine roles. Thus one of the key ideological axes of power that traverses subjects is undermined and revealed through the representation process. The dance gives us a glimpse of how the gender power system operates. By seeing both genders in manipulative roles, as well as manipulated ones, the 'normal' association of masculinity with manipulation and power is revealed as 'cultural' and socially constructed rather than 'natural'.

The importance of *images* is underlined not only by the use of mirrors, but also by the performance. Dancers are doing things to each other's bodies, massaging, washing, shampooing, making up—

presumably to create an image. The rapid cuts from one shot to another, never allowing the audience to dwell on any one performer or couple or to construct any sense of narrative, disrupt expectations, displace forms of identity and deconstruct and problematise any sense of unified individual subjects. The image replaces the subject.

It was claimed at the outset that the political potential of some postmodern texts resides in the glimpses they can give of how power systems operate. *Perfect Moment*, by presenting us with women manipulating men and vice versa, and by dressing them identically, reveals that gender signs—typically masculine or feminine codes of behaviour and dress—are culturally constructed and embody certain power assumptions. The ways in which major domains of power traverse individual subjects, fragmenting and problematising them as no longer unified, are exposed through self-reflexive representation (in framing and blurred and broken images) and devices such as intertextuality (the screen kiss) and parody (the wigs). The screen kiss is shown by self-reflexive devices such as framing, freezing and positioning to be a key media sign of sexuality, signifying heterosexuality as both the norm and a romantic ideal. When this is repeated by three differently composed couples, the power of the norm is challenged. We see that subjects are not all uniformly heterosexual, they are decentred and deconstructed, and revealed as constructed, complex and multifaceted. The commodification, inherent in the construction of subjects and culture, is also exposed through plays with advertising images which are mixed with 'reality' suggesting that 'real life' is also a commodity. Exposing such fundamental props of capitalism can be politically challenging and provocative in a resistant sense.

The political potential of postmodern texts such as *Perfect Moment* is emphasised by a representation process which continually foregrounds itself through various self-reflexive devices. *Perfect Moment* does not provide clear answers to questions; rather, the openness of the text poses many questions. There is no single meaning—a range of meanings can be constructed by different audiences—but, as has been shown, the dance, through its employment of various postmodern representational devices, has the political potential to challenge the status quo and hence fall into the category of a postmodern dance of resistance.

## Notes

1 See, for example, S. Banes, *Terpsichore in Sneakers* (Middleton, CN, Wesleyan University Press, 1987); D. M. Levin, 'Postmodernism in dance: dance,

discourse, democracy', in H. Silverman (ed.), *Postmodernism, Philosophy and the Arts* (New York and London, Routledge, 1990); V. A. Briginshaw, 'Do we really know what post-modern dance is?', *Dance Theatre Journal*, 6:2 (1988), 12–13 and 24; J. Mackrell, 'Postmodern dance in Britain: an historical essay', *Dance Research*, 9:1 (1991), 40–57.

2 *Perfect Moment* video of the Channel 4 1992 production, available from the Administrator, the Cholmondeleys and Featherstonehaughs, The Place Theatre, London.

3 Summarised, for example, in C. Jencks, *What is Postmodernism?* (London, Academy Editions, 1986) and P. Waugh (ed.), *Postmodernism: A Reader* (London, Edward Arnold, 1992).

4 H. Foster, *Post-Modern Culture* (London, Pluto Press, 1985), p. xii.

5 See, for example, A. Daly, 'What has become of postmodern dance?', *The Drama Review*, 133 (1992), 48–69.

6 See Note 4.

7 J. Arac (ed.), *Postmodernism & Politics* (Minneapolis, University of Minnesota Press, 1987), p. xxxi.

8 Quoted in P. Auslander, 'Toward a concept of the political in postmodern theatre', *Theatre Journal*, 39:1 (1987), 32.

9 P. Waugh, *Practising Postmodernism Reading Modernism* (London, Edward Arnold, 1992), p. 65.

10 L. Hutcheon, *The Politics of Postmodernism* (London, Routledge, 1989), p. 13.

11 *Ibid.*

12 D. Harvey, *The Condition of Postmodernity* (Oxford, Basil Blackwell, 1990), p. 328.

13 Quoted in S. Connor, *Postmodernist Culture: An Introduction to the Theories of the Contemporary* (Oxford, Basil Blackwell, 1989), p. 138.

14 Hutcheon, *The Politics of Postmodernism*, p. 94.

15 J. Butler, *Gender Trouble* (London, Routledge, 1990), p. 137.

16 For instance, in works of choreographers such as Liz Aggiss, Lea Anderson, Pina Bausch, Mark Morris and others.

8 *Baz Kershaw*

# The politics of performance in a postmodern age

## Introduction

As the millennium approaches, the place of performance and theatre in the politics of postindustrial societies seems increasingly uncertain and subject to drastic doubt. Alongside the collapse of communism in Russia and Eastern Europe, old notions of 'political theatre' are falling into intellectual disrepute. In the capitalist democracies, there is a continuing widespread crisis of confidence in the legitimacy of established political processes, and that, paradoxically, undermines any performance practice which has ambitions to be oppositional: if few people believe in the state, then it is hardly worth attacking. Simultaneously, the mediatisation of developed societies disperses the theatrical by inserting performance into everyday life—every time we switch into the media we are immediately confronted by a performative world of representational styles—and, in the process, the ideological functions of performance become ever more diverse and, perhaps, diluted. Moreover, the globalisation of communications stages the life of other cultures as unavoidably performative, as widening realms of human identity become object to the spectators' gaze, and the social and political resonances of particular crises, such as the suffering of starving Somalians or the quasi-invasion of Haiti by the US, are absorbed by the relentless opacity of the spectacle.

I am describing a few key political aspects of 'the condition of postmodernity'.[1] Dick Hebdige mordantly summarises some of its features:

> . . . morbid projections of post-war generation baby boomers confronting disillusioned middle age . . . a new phase in commodity fetishism, a fascination for images, codes and styles, a process of cultural, political or existential fragmentation, and/or crises, the 'decentring' of the subject, an 'incredulity towards metanarratives',

> the replacement of unitary power axes by a plurality of power/ discourse formations, the 'implosion of meaning', the collapse of cultural hierarchies . . .[2]

Within the postmodern all art, including theatre and performance, loses its claim to universal significance, to stand, as it were, outside the ideological, and becomes always already implicated in the particular power struggles of the social. As a consequence of radical new ways of thinking—such as in deconstructionist, feminist, post-structuralist, postcolonial and postmodernist theory—the old binary oppositions between, for example, propaganda and art, or politics and aesthetics, or the real and the imaginary, are deeply problematised. In parallel vein, the idea of the 'political' has been applied to a widening range of phenomena: now we have the politics of representation, the politics of the body, identity politics, sexual politics, cultural politics . . . and at a recent international seminar on performing sexualities a leading English gay critic gave an especially witty and ductile paper on the politics of the limp wrist![3] In this aftermath of the theoretical explosion it becomes no longer credible to box off 'political theatre' as a separate category, because in one way or another all performance and theatre can be seen to be involved in discourses of power, to be in some sense engaged with the political.

In this chapter, I shall explore the consequences of this diffusion of the 'political' for the analysis of performance. In particular, I want to discuss how we might begin to construct a critical approach to performance which both a) recognises some of the force of the post-modern paradigm as a liberation from sclerotic traditions of political theatre analysis, and b) pushes us past the unhelpful idea that 'all theatre is political' by viewing performance in the light of concepts drawn from theories of democracy. My starting point is the inevitable complexity of the political dimensions of performance when it is viewed as a dynamic interaction between text and context, performer and society. I will next consider how the best recent analyses of the political in performance have wrestled productively with the explosion of theory noted above. The rest of the chapter briefly considers two contrasting cases of 'postmodern' performance: the Wooster Group's *L.S.D. (. . . Just the High Points . . .)* and Welfare State International's *Glasgow All Lit Up!*[4]

My overall aim is not to deny that 'all performance is political' but to encourage discrimination between the different ways in which, and degrees to which, particular kinds of performance may be more or less politically efficacious. To start us in this direction I will briefly consider the case of a theatrical practitioner who resisted the new orthodoxy which insists that all theatre is political, who was exceptionally keen, in fact, to avoid the political in performance. I choose this as my starting point because such an aversion, like low angled light, might throw the object of our enquiry—the complexity of the politics of performance—into high relief.

### The politics of community plays

Consider the paradox of an important woman writer/director who consciously sought to keep politics out of performance, who went out of her way to commission socialist playwrights to write plays which were apolitical, and who stimulated a theatrical movement which aimed to empower not just individuals but whole communities. This was Ann Jellicoe, author of the seminal 1960s text *The Knack*, former literary manager of the Royal Court Theatre in London, who in 1974 decided to distance herself from metropolitan success because the theatre 'seemed totally unimportant in most people's lives.'[5] Four years later she wrote the first of a series of 'community plays', *The Reckoning*, which she staged as a large-scale production in the secondary-school hall of Lyme Regis, Dorset, involving a cast of around eighty non-professional performers. Ann Jellicoe has described in some detail how the project was taken up by almost the whole town, and also she has been admirably forthright about her ideological intentions in staging community plays:

> If we set out to challenge the basic political feelings of the communities we serve, we will alienate large sections of them and lose their support . . . Politics are divisive. We strongly feel that the humanising effect of our work is far more productive than stirring up political confrontation.[6]

Some commentators, mainly from the left, have taken her to task for the apparent naivety of the assumption that art can rise above politics.[7] This general issue of the ideological autonomy of art hovers close to the main current of my argument, but I want first to approach it obliquely by taking a tightly focused look at the 'politics' of a particular moment in *The Reckoning*.

The play's subject was the 1683 Monmouth Rebellion, and Monmouth's 1685 landing at Lyme Regis. The staging of the show was in the now familiar promenade style, with the audience standing and the actors working amongst them, especially in crowd scenes. The best of these in *The Reckoning* involved confrontations between local supporters of the rebellion and Loyalist troops. I was in the audience during one of these scenes on the third night of the play's short run, watching the Royalist soldiers hunt out the rebels, when a young woman performer playing an insurgent trying to evade arrest appeared at my shoulder. She jabbed me quite forcefully in the ribs, pointed at one of the Loyalists, and in a tone of absolute urgency and passion demanded that I should join her in an attack on his person. So good was her acting that for a moment I felt my body beginning to move aggressively in his direction and my fists starting to clench . . . before critical caution induced me to smile at her in a sickly attempt to diffuse the power of her subversion. She brushed off my weak deflection with a look of withering contempt and moved on to stir up someone else. A couple of days later I discovered that, as a pupil in the school's sixth form, recently she had been publicly humiliated by the teacher playing the Loyalist soldier.

Now I remember this scene because of its sense of *danger*, which I think was generated by the raw conflation or overlapping of several contrasting 'political' dimensions (or frames of reference) which were at play in the moment. In general thematic terms, the scene obviously took a stab at royalism, the willing subservience to the hegemony of inherited power, by urging direct revolt against militarism as a tool of imperial domination. As such, its setting as part of the Monmouth Rebellion may undermine its contemporary political relevance, because obviously today's British monarchy does not wield anything like the power that Charles II had. Yet the scene could well have gathered other political resonances from its immediate historical context. This was one of national disillusion with Jim Callaghan's Labour government (1976–9) which had failed to deliver a stable economy and was notoriously reneging on its election promises. In the tense atmosphere on the brink of the 'winter of discontent', during which a series of national strikes led to the general election which made Margaret Thatcher Prime Minister, a sense of growing outrage at incompetent authority seemed to be part of the mood of the nation.[8] Viewed as a commentary on the times, the scene and the play as a whole reflected a widespread shift towards political dissent. Viewed for its institutional politics, the scene also staged a challenge to the hierarchy of the education system. Viewed for its identity politics, the politics of the personal, this was a scene of fantasy revenge which perhaps gave the young woman access to an otherwise unattainable empowerment in her relationship with the teacher. In terms of both generation and gender the dimensions of normatively defined roles were being acutely tested.

It is clear, then, that this scene is not in any simplistic way 'political', in the sense that it tidily supports a particular ideology or party policy. From this perspective, at least, Ann Jellicoe's desire to avoid politics is satisfied. But, equally, the scene is by no means politically 'neutral' and this is because its potential meanings are produced not just by the text—an anti-royalist gesture in the Monmouth Rebellion—but in its interaction through the spectator with the multiplicity of its current socio-political context. I would say that the multiple ideological meanings held in potential by performance derives from its simultaneous occupation of various 'realms of representation', by which I mean frames of reference or, in the more strict terms of semiotics, discursive coding systems.[9] So at the same moment that the young performer was re-presenting a dissenter in the Monmouth Rebellion, she was also representing: a) one of her ancestors (as she was born into a Lyme Regis family); b) her classmates in secondary education; c) young Western women in the late seventies; and d) herself as an individual in that particular time and place—and this list does not exhaust the possibilities. It follows that the *type* of politics and therefore the *exact* ideological meaning perceived in the young woman's protest would vary according to the spectator's positioning in respect of those different realms: a classmate might mostly see institutional politics, a feminist might focus on sexual/gender politics, a party worker might gleefully (left) or regretfully (right) note its implications for the politics of state, and so on. It does not follow from this that *individual* interpretations are always primary, as some analysts maintain;[10] it would be more accurate to say that the scene provides opportunities for a collective act of recognition of 'resistance' within which there is scope to inflect 'resistance' with a variety of meanings.

I have analysed this moment from *The Reckoning* in some detail partly because, as Ann Jellicoe insists, the play could not be classed as 'political theatre' in the traditional sense. Nonetheless, we have seen that its performance was rife with potential political meanings and this throws the somewhat restrictive traditional notions of political theatre into question. We may say that in this analytical approach the idea of 'political theatre' is challenged by a more flexible notion of the politics of performance.

## Current approaches to politics in performance

Traditionally, 'political theatre' has been taken to refer mainly to 'left-wing theatre'. Erwin Piscator was one of the first writers to develop this connection in *The Political Theatre*, which describes his efforts to create a theatre that would champion the cause of the proletariat in its battle with the bourgeoisie.[11] His was a Marxist theatre which aimed to promote revolution, to overthrow the institutions of capitalism and to replace exploitation with justice, inequality with equality. Embedded in his practice was a vision of utopian democracy in which each will contribute according to ability and receive according to need. Many theatre practitioners and writers, from Brecht to Augusto Boal, have subsequently pursued similar convictions and they have established a rich and varied dialogue between theatre and politics. Sometimes this has been simplified by urgency—as in the agitprop plays of the 1930s Workers' Theatre Movement—sometimes it has been extraordinarily sophisticated—as in the best plays of Brecht or, more recently, Heiner Muller—but always it has assumed that the pictures of the world painted by Marxist and socialist political theorists are fundamentally accurate, reveal truths about 'reality'. Hence this tradition of 'political theatre' has tended to identify with the teleological 'master-narratives' of historical or dialectical materialism, in which the notion of politics is closely tied to ideas about the state.

But the diffusion of the 'political' brought about by globalisation and the explosion of theory has thrown all this into question, so that recent texts which specifically address the general issue of politics in performance tend to be uncertain and tentative. Sometimes they fall back on relatively well-worn agendas in their choice of critical perspectives, sometimes they embrace the new fluidity with a febrile excitement. For example, a recent British collection of essays entitled *The Politics of Theatre and Drama* acknowledges that the current situation offers 'a bewildering and exciting new field', but focuses its discussions on a now familiar list of topics: political (meaning mainly leftist), alternative, feminist, community and Brechtian theatres being its main categories of concern.[12] An American survey collection, *The Performance of Power*, also reports on 'redefinition and reassessment everywhere we looked' and shifts us on to newish critical ground by invoking semiotics, deconstruction and theories of the gaze as crucial to the 'political' conflicts of subjectivity and identity defined in terms of gender, race, class and sexuality.[13]

In contrast, the theorists who search for a fresh start in the general characterisation of the *radically* 'political' in performance—in the sense of a politics of performance which is deeply oppositional to the dominant formations and discourses of its particular society—tend to be interestingly subtle and tentative. For example, Dorrian Lambley identifies the 'poetic' in theatre, defined as 'a visible gap between signified and signifier', as the source of its potential as a 'credible language of opposition'.[14] Philip Auslander is only a little less cautious in an important book on the politics of postmodern performance, which, he argues, consists in the twofold ambition of 'exposing processes of cultural control' in order to discover 'traces of nonhegemonic discourses within the dominant without claiming to transcend its terms'.[15] These are especially *reflexive* views of the political in performance as they generate a critical awareness of both the protocols of performance—the rules of its particular aesthetics—and the assumptions upon which those protocols are based. Hence from this meta-analytical perspective a theatrical attack on the oppressions of the state, say, gains in political stature by demonstrating that the nature of its opposition may invoke processes of oppression almost identical to those it sets out to attack: under what circumstances could you justify killing the king for killing others?

Much of the uncertainty and vigour in recent discussions of the politics of performance stem from this type of reflexive consciousness which highlights cultural difference in the general 'scheme of things', so that all categories and relations of identity may become a matter of political contestation. This can be seen frequently in an American collection of essays entitled *Critical Theory and Performance*, where the editors assert that:

> In the face of the postmodern multiplicity of performance research, we accept responsibility for the categories we have constructed . . . These politics intensify most sharply, predictably enough, as we approach the most contested boundaries . . . We do not intend to efface important differences, but neither do we wish to create taxonomic ghettoes which contain them.[16]

Phrases such as 'taxonomic ghettoes' exactly capture a widespread critical tendency to collapse previously separate realms of discourse—and therefore the relationships between representation and power—into each other. In this case a principle derived from natural history (taxonomy) is coupled with a socio-political category (ghettoes) that has an especially horrendous history: in the process, what was formerly considered politically neutral or in some sense 'above' politics—i.e., 'nature' and our ways of talking about it—becomes ideologically charged. In the process, all performance becomes politicised.

What is gained through this new reflexivity in critical discourse is a kind of *democratisation* of the idea of the political, resulting from an increasing sensitivity to the ways in which power relations are embedded in all cultural practices, including those of theatre and performance. What is lost is a stable set of concepts which would enable us to identify once and for all the ideological or political significance of any particular performance text or practice in any context. A performance that could be considered 'radical' or 'revolutionary' or 'progressive' in one place or perspective might be seen as quite the opposite in another. This profound destabilisation of tradition threatens to cast theatre adrift in a constantly shifting sea of 'political' perspectives on performance.

The rest of this chapter briefly addresses the question of political radicalism in postmodern performance. It is useful to focus on the radical because it is the radical which is most thoroughly problematised in the breakdown of binaries and the diffusion of the political in postmodernity. My interest is *in what sense* postmodern shows such as *L.S.D. (. . . Just the High Points . . .)* and *Glasgow All Lit Up!* can be considered radical, because that may give us a measure of the kinds of political impact they hope to achieve in their specific contexts.

So the specific context for the following analysis is Glasgow, Scotland, on a wet and windy weekend in the autumn of 1990. I went to see the Wooster Group in *L.S.D. (. . . Just the High Points . . .)* at the Tramway Theatre on Friday night and was amused by the schizophrenically structured audience: avant-garde trendies in expensively tailored leather jackets rubbing shoulders with gangs of thin-frocked, streetwise teenage women, no doubt drawn by the filmic magnetism of Willem Dafoe, one of the Group's founder members! Then on Saturday I spent the evening on the streets, following *Glasgow All Lit Up!*, a huge lantern procession with a spectacular finale mounted by the veteran subversive British company Welfare State International. Over 10,000 people paraded through the puddle-strewn streets of the city centre in an event that blurred genres and juxtaposed disparate codes and obviously appealed to a huge and, I suppose, for the most part, casual audience. Both shows clearly proved, if any proof is still needed, that traditional distinctions between the experimental and the popular may sometimes no longer hold. What is less clear are the political implications, for analysis and in terms of actual effect, of that kind of breakthrough on such different 'stages'—the studio and the street—and such contrasting scales: the middle-scale and the massive.

## Postmodern performance in the studio

Philip Auslander frames his influential discussion of the Wooster Group's postmodern performance by drawing on a distinction made by Hal Foster between 'transgressive' and 'resistant' politics.[17] 'Transgressive' politics, he argues, were pursued by the modernist avant-garde of the early twentieth century, and they assumed that it was possible to transgress the limits of current social realities in order to judge them from a position which was somehow beyond them. Hence, the transgressive politics of Piscator or Brecht, for example, might be said to be founded on myths of transcendence fostered by the master-narrative of historical materialism, which produced an illusion that art could show how things *really* were. With the emergence of postmodern culture, however, which Auslander places some time in the 1970s, such meta-criticism is rendered impossible by the recognition that cultural action, including performance, is always implicated in its context and so it cannot 'place itself outside dominant cultural formations.'[18] It follows that the politics of postmodern performance, if it aims in any way to be oppositional, must be one of resistance from within the dominant. To be most effective, such politics would need to subvert, as it were, the building blocks of the dominant, to undermine the main strategies that it uses to maintain itself. The key political problem then becomes: how can performance, in being always already implicated in the dominant, avoid replicating the values of the dominant?

Auslander argues that the deconstructive techniques used by the Wooster Group in *L.S.D. (. . . Just the High Points . . .)* aim to resist the ways in which dominant ideologies have been inscribed in the performative by mainstream theatrical traditions. Hence the show is in four parts which are *not* related through narrative, storyline or plot. Part 1 juxtaposes the reminiscences of LSD guru Timothy Leary's babysitter Ann Rower, with random readings from classic 1960s texts by Allen Ginsberg, Jack Kerouac and others; Part 2 presents excerpts from Arthur Miller's *The Crucible* with the characters played or presented in totally contrasting styles; Parts 3 and 4 are similarly obliquely related to the previous parts and to each other. A brief list of the show's other deconstructive methods will suggest its mind-knotting complexity. Ann Rower's reminiscences are repeated coolly by actress Nancy Riley as she listens to Rower's recording of them on a Walkman; the reading of 1960s classics is deliberately offhand and the actual texts are held up in the air at the end of each reading; the men are in contemporary dress and most of the women in sixteenth century costume; the men speak through microphones (usually) but the women do not; Ron Vawter reads his part of Proctor from Miller's play at breakneck, unintelligible speed while Kate Valk in blackface as Tituba seems to be totally possessed by her character . . . and so on. Such complexity means that the audience is almost constantly wrong-footed by an extraordinarily adroit juxtaposition and mixing of performing styles, types of text, modes of address, performative frames, realms of representation. As all the rules of previous dramaturgies are broken in the name of such deconstructions, the precise political purpose of the show is not at all easy to determine.

Auslander addresses the politics of *L.S.D.* in two interconnected ways: in terms of its semiotics and politics of representation, and in terms of its acting styles and what we might call the politics of the performer's 'presence'. Semiotically speaking, the show's deconstructive style seems designed to promote reflexive readings—or complex seeings—by overlaying and juxtaposing contrasting and often incompatible cultural codes. Auslander illustrates this point through analysis of the Group's use of blackface to present the character of Tituba from *The Crucible*. This may be interpreted as racist (as the use of blackface in an earlier Group show, *Route 9*, had been), but Auslander argues that when

> . . . the actress who plays Tituba goes on, still in blackface, to play Mary Warren, 'the sign become separated from its object', leaving the audience to impose its own interpretive schema on the displacement. I would argue that it is precisely at this moment of the emptying of the sign that the gesture becomes political, for it is when the arbitrary character of the sign is asserted that the significance of its imposition by one group on another stands out most clearly.[19]

In other words, the use of blackface can be interpreted subsequently as opening up a critique of racism. As this aesthetic strategy appears to be a principle in the dramaturgy of *L.S.D.*, the show resolutely refuses to offer a perspective through which audiences might collectively privilege one realm of representation over another. So, theoretically, individual spectators are free to derive contradictory meanings from the piece. In this sense, the show develops a deeply radical attitude to the politics of representation, by exposing *all* representations as constructed.

The political issues raised by the performer's 'presence' are even knottier, because, as Auslander rightly argues, it is associated with the idea of 'charisma', and charisma has often been used by politicians such as Nixon and Hitler to construct systems of domination; hence, 'to invoke the power of presence is to link oneself inextricably to the workings of a repressive status quo.' It follows that in order to sever that link performance must find means to deconstruct the performer's presence. He quotes two of the key acting strategies of *L.S.D.* as significant steps in this direction. Firstly, he notes the clear refusal of the actors to make a 'greater investment of the self in one procedure [rather] than another', signalled by techniques through which 'signs of emotional commitment in acting were distanced and demystified.'

Secondly, he cites the famous Part 3 recreation from videotapes of the Group's *Crucible* rehearsal when the actors had all been high on LSD. In staging a meticulously detailed reconstruction of an experience which the actors had had, but which was not directly accessible to them as memory (due to the effects of LSD), the show problematises the nature of identity—how can we decide which is the 'real' actor: the one who was high on LSD, the one shown in the videotape or the one exactly recreating a previous experience as seen on the video? In Auslander's view, such 'blurring of identity nullifies the possibility of charismatic projection' by deconstructing the performer's presence, thus questioning oppressive uses of presence in politics.

Such intricacies of analysis of the performance text expose the potential political complexity of postmodern theatre, but the attempt to dispel 'presence' from the performative seems curiously eccentric, given that it is possibly the most powerful of all the theatre's attributes. Moreover, as Auslander's analysis reaffirms, the audience plays an unavoidable role in the making of performative meaning. So if we turn to the *context* of the Group's work, we may identify other types of construct which crucially affect the reception of the actor. For example, in an acute discussion of the links between the performer's persona and the persona's image as property, Celia Lury adopts Barry King's suggestion that in Western culture

> there has been a shift from the evaluation of acting as impersonation, in which the persona of the actor should disappear into the part, to evaluation in terms of personification, in which the performance of a part is subsumed by the actor's persona.[20]

Hence, in the very moment of deconstructing texts, Willem Dafoe and Ron Vawter may be seen by the audience as constructing a persona with all the charisma and presence of a film star. Of course, such interpretive tendencies are likely to be reinforced by the forms of evaluation of acting—the 'reading strategies' of the audience—which predominate in any particular time and place. Ironically, perhaps, the Wooster Group actors' involvement in the media, especially in film, could encourage the audience to endow them with presence/authority as an integral result of their attempts to evade it.[21]

Unfortunately, I have no empirical evidence to hand about audience constitution and reaction at the Glasgow Tramway to support this contention. But anecdotal information is not entirely useless, perhaps, and my impression that I was mixing with, on the one hand, a coterie constituency, a specialist crowd of avant-garde aficionados, and, on the other hand, an informal fan club of an international film star, suggests a counter-reading to Philip Auslander's. Given this kind of audience, it is by no means certain that the deconstructive strategies of postmodern performance will ensure the elimination of presence and its potential for oppression, or empowerment. Moreover, the Tramway as a venue has a particular niche in the institutional structure of Scottish theatre. It is the premiere experimental space in which the radical and the outrageous are *licensed* to happen, as it is a component in the system of cultural provision in Scotland maintained, in part, by state agencies. Therefore, its potential *both* for defusing the politically threatening, *and* for enhancing the cultural capital of more or less radical groupings in Scottish society, is fairly patent.

What all this means for performance analysis is that anything which appears to make absolute theoretical sense needs to be tested against the specifics of practice, especially when we are dealing with the political potential of performance. Such a sense of the specific context of performance is conspicuously missing from Auslander's discussion of the Wooster Group and, to be fair to him, this is a typical omission in a great deal of contemporary performance analysis, which tends to draw connections at a more generalised level between the performative codes of particular shows and their broader socio-cultural environment. So Auslander places *L.S.D.* in the mediatised and hyperreal culture described by Baudrillard.[22] This critical strategy often produces insights (and it is far better than others which ignore context altogether), but if we wish to discriminate the 'political' in performance more precisely, then, I think, we cannot ignore the specific conditions of the performative, particularly the kinds of people who, we hope, enjoy it, and the places in which it occurs.

This is not to suggest, of course, that the Wooster Group's postmodernism is apolitical. Their challenge to Arthur Miller's property rights in staging parts of *The Crucible* as they wished has profound political ramifications, as David Savran has pointed out.[23] In contrast, though, we may note that there *is* something curiously passive (in the sense of being primarily reactive) in Auslander's idea of resistance as the main mode of the postmodern political. His key contention in this respect is that the postmodern political artist offers 'strategies of counterhegemonic resistance by exposing processes of cultural control and emphasising the *traces* of nonhegemonic discourses within the dominant . . .'[24] But this seems to me to be a painfully reserved formulation, partly because the dominant discourse may well provide 'weapons'—such as performative presence—which can be turned back on it in the form of 'attack'. Or, if that kind of response is, from the point of view of the subordinate, strategically unwise, then we could use the language of 'negotiation' and 'exchange'. It follows that more fruitful domains for both the practice and the analysis of the politics of performance might be found in areas of culture which are crucial to the control exerted by dominant formations, but which also are chronically pervious to radical action. To explore this idea we shall turn from the studio to the street.

## Postmodern performance in the streets

*Glasgow All Lit Up!*, directed by Welfare State founder John Fox, was the 'centrepiece' of the community programme of Glasgow's year as European City of Culture. The chief creative activity of the project was lantern making. For eighteen months Welfare State artists trained local Scottish artists in techniques learned in Japan, and the local artists in turn worked with some 250 community organisations throughout Strathclyde—the greater Glasgow area. In the early evening of 6 October 1990, these groups converged in the city centre to form a single procession of 10,000 people carrying, wheeling, and driving some 8,000 lanterns. The Scottish arts correspondent of the *Guardian*, Joyce Macmillan, described it as follows:

> There were the big floats, of course; a gorgeous white reindeer, a huge unflattering image of the Prime Minister shoving a gunboat out to sea . . . a beautiful white Swan Lake float . . . But in a sense, the big set pieces were beside the point; what reduced one or two of us cynical old observers to tears, was the children, thousands and thousands of them . . . every one of them clutching a little lantern . . . There were boats and space ships and churches and mutant hero turtles, and lots of simple triangular lanterns with nothing but gorgeous, blobby abstract patterns on . . . There were rock groups and pipe bands and brass bands and steel bands . . . As the columns of light snaked . . . along towards the High Street, toothless well-oiled old codgers emerged from a sawdust-and-spit pub called the Right Half and cheered and danced on the pavement, to the kids' delight. The city beamed from ear to ear . . .[25]

The huge procession paraded to Glasgow Green, a mile and a half from the City Centre, where it was greeted by a 200-strong community choir, and the smaller lanterns were hung on to towers that were gradually hauled up by cranes to form four glowing pyramids of light over 40 feet high. The endpiece to the gathering was a spectacle staged by Welfare State artists, in which giant images from the Glasgow City crest—a tree, a bell, a fish and a bird—glowed and burned and flew through the air in a surreal animation that freed them from the rigour of their usual heraldic setting. A final big firework display ended the evening.

The procession manifested many postmodern characteristics—the wild mix of lanterns undermined aesthetic and cultural hierarchy, the subject was decentred by the massed scale, the images represented a concatenation of disparate power discourses, and so on, and—as with *L.S.D. (. . . Just the High Points . . .)*—its politics are by no means transparent. But I want to argue that while, on the one hand, its plurality of representational realms could contain many kinds of politics, some of them clearly contradictory, on the other hand its total relation to its context was marked by a kind of political coherence. I want to suggest that, in the terms of my argument so far, its politics of representation, in the semiotic sense, were resistant to dominant discourses, but its politics of representation, in the cultural, civil and governmental senses, engaged with the dominant in ways that were more challenging.

On the relatively mundane level of the semiotics of the lanterns, the politics of representation, it is clear that they constituted what we may call a multi-vocality or, to adopt a term from Bakhtin, heteroglossia.[26] They were multi-vocal in the sense of having no overall fictional narrative line or thematic structure, there was no identifiable imaginative logic in their juxtapositions: brash but beautiful political propaganda trundled cheek-by-jowl with nostalgic images of unsullied nature which in turn gave way to primitive abstractions tellingly reminiscent of the great modernist traditions in painting! They were heteroglossic in that they did not subscribe to a single set of explicit enunciations, there was no dominant language of imagery or form: a school identified itself through a string of two-foot high capitals (MILTON SCHOOL), shoals of tiny fish flew above a fleet of boats, inchoate blobs hovered between recognition as suns or lemons, smiles or canoes, trees or candyfloss. While many images were totally engaging, none of the voices represented was predominant; all were expressive of a plurality rooted in many local, distinctive communities. The power to resist homogeneous readings, to provoke contradictory interpretations, which the Wooster Group achieved through sophisticated techniques of deconstruction, was in this procession secured by the simple stratagem of random, or at least unplanned, juxtapositions.

The heteroglossia of the lanterns may also be interpreted from a more politically dynamic perspective through their representation of the kinds of cultural diversity typical of global cities.[27] It was obvious that the people were parading their own creations, statements of their own creative abilities and flair. Moreover, as they were clearly parading in groups, the lanterns signified a plethora of collective cultural identities. However, as Anne Phillips sees so clearly, the rich pluralism of such minority groups, whether defined in terms of race, class, gender, sexuality and so on, is a mixed political blessing.

> The new pluralism arises out of a radical tradition that sets its sight on future change. Because of this, it cannot rest content with a live and let live toleration that just enjoins each group to get on with its private affairs. But, inspired as it is by a far-reaching egalitarianism that wants to empower currently disadvantaged groups, it is also more likely to . . . validate an exclusive and fragmented politics of identity that blocks the development of wider solidarity.[28]

Yet there was a cohesion to the variety of the lanterns. This was partly sensory: the fact that they all had been made through greater or lesser elaborations of the same basic techniques produced a similarity of visual texture and a repetition of structural style which was unmistakable. In other, more abstract, words, the lanterns, as well as signifying a multitude of differences, all shared in a cognate aesthetic domain, a common creative language which at the very least hinted at an underlying unity of purpose.

Hence, I think that *Glasgow All Lit Up!* may have produced a kind of 'wider solidarity' in the culminating procession, signified by its visual and kinesthetic integrity, without erasing any of the many differences developed in the making of the lanterns. It achieved this by being inclusive of cultural difference, but by also furthering difference through the development of what was for each group a new creative and common language which could be called, to make a risky discursive leap, a language of quasi-citizenship. That is to say, the lanterns, through their similarity-in-difference, provided complementary realms of representation that fostered a formal equality within which all the participants gained a common identity as 'artists' or 'creative citizens'. In this way, the project may have modelled processes for the formation of a new kind of democratic collective. This analysis links the politics of semiotic representation to a politics of cultural representation, but in what ways did the procession impinge upon the politics of civil society, and upon the systems of governance which shore up the politics of the state?

We only have space to approach this question tentatively and superficially, through a few brief and somewhat formulaic comments on the relationships between the procession and the ideologies inscribed in its socio-political context. My comments relate the event to the idea of democracy through the concepts of civil society and the state, and they take as their analytical framework David Held's claim that

> civil society can never be 'separate' from the state; the latter, by providing the overall legal framework of society, to a significant degree constitutes the former. None the less, it is not unreasonable to claim that civil society retains a distinctive character to the extent that it is made up of areas of social life—the domestic world, the economic sphere, cultural activities and political interaction—which are . . . outside the direct control of the state.[29]

In an important sense, then, the law mediates the interaction of civil society and the state, and, in so doing, variously defines the extent to which any particular activity may be in, and/or out of, direct state control. It follows that any exchange between the law and *Glasgow All Lit Up!* may indicate how the event dealt with the politics of state, how its semiotic and culturally democratic processes may be related to the structures of political democracy in Scotland.

The quickest way to identify any exchange between the two processes of democracy is to look for signs of disequilibrium, and as *Glasgow All Lit Up!* wound its way through the city centre this took the form of disrupted traffic flow. Despite strenuous efforts of persuasion by Welfare State, the police had insisted that the roads of the route should remain open to vehicles, so that the procession had heavy Saturday evening traffic flowing in both directions alongside it. The roads crossing the route were to be kept open through the maintenance of agreed 'gaps' in the procession. Not surprisingly, most of the gaps disappeared once the procession was under way, and the net result was that the city centre came to a standstill—for a time, the procession became the dominant discourse in the public domain of Glasgow city centre during that damp Saturday evening. So, in David Held's terms, the law did not manage to mediate the interaction of civil society, as represented by the procession, and the state, as represented by the police and other authorities. Rather, the 'presence' of the procession was directly impacting upon the authorities and, for whatever reasons, the authorities gave way and the law was temporarily, in part, abated. So the symbolic discourse of the lantern procession was translated, as it were, into another discourse, namely, the kind we might identify as a non-violent 'political' demonstration for egalitarian rights to individual and collective identities. In temporarily transgressing—rather than just resisting—the institutions of democratic government, the procession opened up, metaphorically and literally, a new space for politically democratic action.

### The politics of democratised performance

I have been talking about the possibilities of democratised performance in a postmodern world. To do this, I have had to accept the growing predominance of a paradigm which, at first sight, may seem totally to destabilise traditional analytical perspectives on the politics of performance. We have seen, though, that such an image of acute rupture from older notions of 'political theatre' may be something of a distortion. That is to say, even if the old structures supporting the political analysis of theatre are demolished by the paradigm shift, it does not follow that the components used in their construction are now useless. An up-to-date politics of performance should, in fact, recognise the contiguities between Brecht and Baudrillard; between, say, a vision of theatre as a dynamic arena for social experiment and a view of the social as an experiment so thoroughly imbued with a sense of the performative.

I have attempted to address some of the issues for the politics of the performative embedded in this new(ish) global situation by noting some of the positive political aspects of the postmodern. I mean, for example, the democratisation of systems of representation when traditional cultural hierarchies are undermined. I mean, too, what De Marinis calls the semiotic 'openness' of postmodern performances, which in Auslander's terms allows audiences to impose their own 'interpretive schema' on the work and which is obviously a potential source for democratic empowerment through enhanced control over the politics of representation, or more accurately, the politics of semiotic representation.[30] But I have also been arguing that much more needs to be taken into account if we are to construct a convincing description of performance and theatre as effective aspects within other kinds of political process: in the processes of cultural, civil, and governmental politics particularly.

I have laid particular stress on the need to address the interaction of the art work and its specific context, especially with regards to the 'interpretative strategies' that are likely to be adopted by audiences at any specific time and place. More crucially still, attention has to be paid to the organisation and placing of the productive and distributive methods of particular theatres and performances, in order to see how they may be articulated to the wider power structures in their cultural, economic, social and political environment. Only as we do this will we begin to know how performance may actually impact on the varieties of politics in the contemporary world. And this, I think, is a prerequisite for the recognition that certain approaches to making theatre and performance do not simply 'model' ideologies or 'reflect' the politics of their context; but, rather, they are actively engaged in widening the bounds of political processes, in opening up new domains of political action.

I have focused on performance and democracy because it seems to me that with the demise of the old master-narratives any hope for a progressive prognosis for theatrical practice will lie in its attempts to grapple with the ultra-vexed global issues of inequality, injustice and servitude. If performance can illuminate some of the sources of worldwide oppression by exposing how the politics of representation, say, may be used to reinforce the marginalisation of minority groups, then it may contribute to a fairer economy of signs. If it can create fresh cultural space in which the silenced majorities might find a newly resonant and engaged voice, then it may lead to a wider liberation of humankind's most precious resource. I have concentrated on these possibilities in Western examples of performance not because they are in advance of practices elsewhere, but because when there is resistance to, and transgression of, oppression at the *heart* of the systems of global domination—and the idea of the European City of Culture that was the context of *Glasgow All Lit Up!* obviously may be seen as a part of that—then that may give added hope to parallel and complementary projects in other, less fortunate, parts of the world. In fact, there are many such projects on every continent, ranging from the famous ones of Augusto Boal to the relatively unknown ones of Zakes Mda, and from the liberalism of theatre for development to the radicalism of theatre for liberation.[31]

This international flourishing of new performative forms and approaches in part signals a widespread reaction against the established political processes. These advances in the politicisation of performance are part and parcel of a potential repoliticisation of massive but marginalised social formations everywhere. In the developed countries, the emergence of new social movements, in all their performative variety, seems to be evidence of this. In the developing countries, the struggle against neocolonialism, in all of its guises, is obviously a part of a related desire for autonomy and self-determination. And perhaps the politics of performance can have an important place in the drive for equality, justice and freedom. Because, as I hope I have shown, performance and theatre that is culturally democratic—a celebration of difference and pluralism within an always provisional unity—may become politically democratic in almost the fullest sense of the term. At this point we will not be talking about 'traces of resistance' in performance, but about performative negotiation and exchange which can, under certain circumstances, constitute a radical inflection of dominant discourses of a kind which furthers the evolution of effective democracy.

## Notes

1 David Harvey, *The Condition of Postmodernity: An Enquiry into the Origins of Cultural Change* (Oxford, Blackwell, 1990); Jean-Francois Lyotard, *The Postmodern Condition: a Report on Knowledge*, transl. Geoff Bennington and Brian Massumi (Manchester, Manchester University Press, 1984); Steven Connor, *Postmodernist Culture: An Introduction to Theories of the Contemporary* (Oxford, Blackwell, 1989).

2 Dick Hebdige, 'A Report on the Western Front: Postmodernism and the "Politics" of Style' in Chris Jenks (ed.), *Cultural Reproduction* (London, Routledge, 1993), p. 71.

3 Catherine Fowler, ' "Performing Sexualities" at Lancaster', *New Theatre Quarterly*, 10:38 (May 1994) reports briefly on Andy Medhurst's paper.

4 Tony Coult and Baz Kershaw (eds.), *Engineers of the Imagination: the Welfare State Handbook* (London, Methuen, 1990); David Savran, *Breaking the Rules: the Wooster Group* (New York, Theatre Communications Group, 1986).

5 Ann Jellicoe, *Community Plays: How to Put Them On* (London, Methuen, 1987), p. 3.

6 *Ibid.*, p. 122.

7 Graham Woodruff, 'Community, Class and Control: a View of Community Plays', *New Theatre Quarterly*, 5:20 (Nov 1989); Peter Reynolds, 'Community Theatre: Carnival or Camp?' in Graham Holderness (ed.), *The Politics of Theatre and Drama* (London, Macmillan, 1992).

8 Kenneth O. Morgan, *The People's Peace: British History 1945–1990* (Oxford, Oxford University Press, 1992), pp. 416–22.

9 Marco De Marinis, *The Semiotics of Performance*, transl. Aine O'Healy (Bloomington, Indiana University Press, 1993).

10 Martin Esslin, *The Field of Drama* (London, Methuen, 1987), p. 21; see also Howard Barker, *Arguments for a Theatre* (Manchester, Manchester University Press, 1993).

11 Erwin Piscator, *The Political Theatre*, transl. Hugh Rorrison (London, Eyre Methuen, 1980).

12 Graham Holderness (ed.), *The Politics of Theatre and Drama* (London, Macmillan, 1992).

13 Sue-Ellen Case and Janelle Reinelt (eds.), *The Performance of Power: Theatrical Discourse and Politics* (Des Moines, University of Iowa Press, 1991).

14 Dorrian Lambley, 'In Search of a Radical Discourse for Theatre', *New Theatre Quarterly*, 7:29 (Feb 1992).

15 Philip Auslander, 'Toward a Concept of the Political in Postmodern Theatre', *Theatre Journal*, 39 (March 1987); see also his *Presence and Resistance: Postmodernism and Politics in Contemporary American Performance* (Ann Arbor, University of Michigan Press, 1992).

16 Janelle G. Reinelt and Joseph R. Roach (eds.), *Critical Theory and Performance* (Ann Arbor, University of Michigan Press, 1992), p. 2.

17 Auslander, 'Toward a Concept of the Political in Postmodern Theatre', p. 22.

18 *Ibid.*, p. 27.

19 *Ibid.*

20 Celia Lury, *Cultural Rights: Technology, Legality and Personality* (London, Routledge, 1993), p. 72.

21 Willem Dafoe has starred in films such as *Platoon* and *Mississippi Burning*; Ron Vawter was in episodes of *Miami Vice*.

22 Jean Baudrillard, *Simulations* (New York, Semiotext(e), 1983).

23 Savran, *Breaking the Rules*, pp. 191–5.

24 Auslander, 'Toward a Concept of the Political in Postmodern Theatre', p. 23; my emphasis.

25 Joyce Macmillan, 'All Lit Up', *The Guardian*, 8 October 1990.

26 Mikhail Bakhtin, *The Dialogic Imagination* (Austin, University of Texas Press, 1981); Marvin Carlson, 'Theatre and Dialogism', in Reinelt and Roach, *Critical Theory and Performance*, pp. 313–23.

27 Iain Chambers, 'Cities without maps', in John Bird *et al.* (eds.), *Mapping the Futures: Local Cultures, Global Change* (London, Routledge, 1993).

28 Anne Phillips, *Democracy and Difference* (London, Polity Press, 1993), p. 17.

29 David Held, *Models of Democracy* (London, Polity Press, 1987), p. 281.

30 Marco De Marinis, 'The Dramaturgy of the Spectator', *The Drama Review*, 31:2 (Summer 1987).

31 Augusto Boal, *The Theatre of the Oppressed*, transl. Charles A. and Maria-Odilia Leal McBride (London, Pluto Press, 1979); Kees P. Epskamp, *Theatre in Search of Social Change*, transl. Corrie Donner *et al.* (The Hague, CESO, 1989); Zakes Mda, *When People Play People* (London, Zed Books, 1993); Eugene van Erven, *The Playful Revolution: Theatre and Liberation in Asia* (Bloomington, Indiana University Press, 1992); Penina Muhando Mlama, *Culture and Development: The Popular Theatre Approach in Africa* (Uppsala, Nordiska Afrikainstitutet, 1991).

9

*Sandra Kemp*

# Reading difficulties

In this paper I want to discuss performance in terms of some questions recently raised about reading. These questions—about the nature (or importance) of interpretation, about the threat (or promise) of multimedia (and multi-cultured) texts, about the freedom (or stability) of the reader—are routinely listed as aspects of postmodernism, although the 'postmodern', in the academy at least, still tends to describe analytic practices which rest on an authoritarian, literary method of reading, rather than addressing the specific issues raised by the performing arts, by theatre, dance and music. In order to get away from this literary bias, I will focus my discussion on the work of Yvonne Rainer, a dancer and choreographer turned film-maker, but I will frame my argument with reference to two recent philosophical essays on painting. In short, I do not want to suggest that in these postmodern times we must learn to read new sorts of texts in new sorts of ways; rather, I want to examine arguments in which the underlying idea of reading is challenged, in which interpretation itself is treated as a performance, as the process of *bringing into meaning*.

Take first the position developed by Andrew Benjamin.[1] Benjamin sees paintings as a philosopher: that is, he asks questions that go beyond the immediate experience of art to the issue of how that experience is possible. As his subtle readings of R. B. Kitaj's *If Not, Not* and *The Jewish School (Drawing of a Golem)* show, he is perfectly capable of making specific interpretations of specific works, but that is not his primary concern. He is in pursuit of what it means to 'interpret' a painting in the first place; he is interested in the ways in which philosophy is implicated in art. For a non-philosopher, the result is a series of scattered but stimulating questions: what does it mean to paint a mirror? To name a picture? What is the difference between seeing an object and seeing what it is? What is its 'whatness'? Behind all such questions is the central aesthetic issue: the relationship between experience and interpretation. But the questions Benjamin asks are not just designed to make sense of art. They are also driven by the need to philosophise and Benjamin defines this as not so much to clarify art through philosophy as to challenge philosophy through art. His work has therefore an embattled quality; the battleground is the history of philosophical aesthetics. Benjamin refers to 'Nietzsche's task, that is the overturning of Platonism'. It is a task he also takes on:

> Overturning Platonism does in this instance amount to a projected resistance to viewing mimesis as that which provides the means by which the work of art (or the generalised object of interpretation) are themselves to be interpreted.[2]

Benjamin's starting point, then, is that Platonic philosophy brings to art an interpretative strategy, a set of expectations about mimesis and representation, that no longer makes sense of what art (and the experience of art) may be. Indeed, art is now the source of a philosophy—an argument about interpretation—that challenges philosophical tradition, and one purpose of Benjamin's work is to 'rethink' terms like 'tradition, mimesis, affirmation, interpretation and the avant-garde' in studies of specific paintings, writing and architecture. The constant move between abstract framework and material work is a necessary aspect of his argument; his book is itself interpreting, as well as being about interpretation.

Benjamin's initial target, aesthetic 'tradition', is rooted in Plato's account of mimesis, in the development of an analytical mode in which to interpret is to relate interpretation to interpreted, either through a direct relationship of similarity and homology or through a mediated, allegorical relationship, a relation guaranteed by the artist's intention. Either way, what is involved is a belief in origin: the meaning of a painting can be traced back to its original 'object', the object that gives the work its unity, its meaning. Modernism, as Benjamin suggests, marked a crisis in this aesthetic but did not overturn it. The impossibility of unity—of stable objects—meant regret for what had been but also an impossible attempt to recapture it; art became a matter of futile repetition.

In this respect, Benjamin writes as a postmodernist (drawing on Lyotard and Derrida), but his call for an approach to art that recognises its 'original heterogeneity', his rethinking of the avant-garde not in terms of its negation of tradition but as an account of the *active* impossibility of representation, is derived from an older and more complex argument about art, about interpretation, drawn from Heidegger. The object *for* interpretation, Benjamin suggests, is an aspect *of* interpretation, and cannot exist apart from it. This does not just open up art as the plural object of plural readings, nor simply make clear that the object of interpretation cannot have 'origins' outside the interpretative act. More importantly, it redefines the art-object as a temporal matter, a *becoming-object* rather than a *being-object*. Interpretation is always a process of *bringing-into-being*. The space of art (and architecture) becomes the 'space of process'; interpretation is no longer predictable, no longer the result of an approach that guarantees in advance the discovery (or absence) of an original object. Via Heidegger, Benjamin thus brings to the fine arts issues that are central to the performing arts: music and dance have always had to be grasped as becoming-objects.

This notion of the text as a 'becoming-object' is important not least because it makes clear that postmodernism places aesthetics *against* interpretation (and is not simply a new sociology of reading). In this respect, postmodernism provides an important critique of cultural studies, which even in the 1980s was taught above all as a form *of* interpretation—the student's task was to get at the latent meanings that lay behind the surface meanings, to place texts in their wider 'discursive' context (bourgeois ideology, patriarchal ideology, colonial discourse, etc.). Texts and textual responses were judged politically (in terms of 'resistance', for example) and there was remarkably little interest in aesthetic issues as such. 'Art' was devalued, whether in its conventional transcendent sense or as a creative craft; texts were taken to write themselves (or to be written by discourse); the 'progressive' text disrupted its own rules of production; to read was to demystify rather than, as Benjamin might put it, to be mystified.

Benjamin's critique of the 'mimetic' reading of painting is important, then, for its *general* argument about the mimetic fallacy; though, given cultural studies' populist concerns, the most problematic areas for current cultural analysis are the more clearly performative arts of music and dance. Here it is obvious that the assumptions about interpretation and ideology do not hold—neither music nor dance is in any simple way a language; neither is necessarily 'about' anything; neither clearly 'represents' or 'imitates'. In the making of musical or dance meaning the immediate 'mystified' response of the viewer/listener is the reader response that matters; here the process of creation—the body in the work—is present *as* the work (the author can be seen *and* be seen through). And the further complication here is that bodily movements depend on physical capacities, on learnt competence. This is to raise the contrasting issue of the failure of interpretation, when the body will not do what we want it to do, when a performance, for that reason, does not work.

I want to focus here on the most commonly learnt form of musical movement, dance, and on the most familiar setting for performing anxiety, the dance floor. And I want to follow up two of the questions raised by Andrew Benjamin's work: first, the question of *critical* interpretation; second, the problem of translation, the translation of response into meaning. The problem of criticism is this: if the meaning of a work is brought into being in the process of interpretation itself, then it depends on a kind of *collusion* between performer and audience. How is a critical reading, with its implication of detachment, measurement, a consideration of this performance against real and imaginary others, now possible? Where does the sense of 'failure' come from? Do the terms of interpretative engagement not rule out the possibility of critical disengagement? If, however, reading is itself a performance, then the terms of the question are changed—performers, after all, do not just act spontaneously, they are both engaged with and careful about what they are doing. To perform, that is to say, is to frame what one is doing with a particular kind of self-consciousness, a certain kind of *form-consciousness* which enables both performers and their audiences to assess what is happening, to decode whether it works or not. We have no difficulty deciding whether someone is good or bad at telling jokes, for instance (and this has nothing to do with the jokes told), even as we laugh (or not); and, by analogy, people can also be said to be good or bad at hearing jokes, at understanding the conventions used. What is at issue here is a way of telling; our attention is being drawn to the *act* of meaning-making.

The point here, I think, is that as performers we do not first create something—the performance-as-text—and then assess it; rather, assessment, a *continuous* process of judgement, is what we mean by a performance in the first place. A dancer's movements are at once thoughtless (determined by the music/choreography: objectified) and thoughtful (determined by a listening to the music/choreographer: subjectified). Sport provides an interesting analogy here: the perfect race, the perfect game is that in which there is a perfect match of technique and occasion, body and mind; for a moment, the athlete or footballer *is* will-less. Performance, in short, is by necessity a matter of technique; it is *about* the body in the mind, the mind in the body. And it is a critical practice because it also involves, by necessity, the act of *giving form*, whether to a musical sound, a physical shape, a social gesture.

An apparently simple question can be asked here: what does it mean to move to music? Among pop performers we can distinguish between techniques of *interruption* and techniques of *enslavement*, between devices that signal listening to music by disrupting it, and devices that signal listening to music by being absorbed in it. In some musical genres, then, the spontaneity of a show is indicated by the performers' mistakes, their broken strings, their false starts and ruffled endings; in others the musicians' total engagement with what they are doing is indicated by the precision of their changes, the perfection of their integration of what we hear and what we see.

There is another simple question to ask here: what do musicians do when they are not playing: is their interest in their colleagues' sounds best shown by movement or stillness, by concentration or abandon? In popular music, silent singers, for example, perform their continuing stage role in various ways, but most deliberately move as musicians (rather than as listeners), grab tambourines rather than go into a choreographed routine. The relationship of 'listening' to music and 'moving' to music (both modes of interpretation) is, in short, a matter of convention, as is what sort of movement to make; even a spontaneous response has to be coded as 'spontaneous'. The next question, then, is when does a movement-to-music become a dance-to-music, and there are, I think, two issues here: first, the nature of the connection between what is heard and what is done, and second, the question of form, the relationship between one movement and another: how free are we to move, how much are we subject to rules of what is 'appropriate'? The question here is control—dancing/walking seems to be something like singing/talking. When dancing, we subject our body movements to musical rules (we are less free than when we walk) and yet in our very self-consciousness we seem to reveal more clearly our physical sense of our selves; we are thus more self-expressive. As Francis Sparshott puts it,

> dance, then, is a mode of behaviour in which people put themselves rhythmically into motion in a way that transforms their sense of their own existence in a way that is at once characteristic and strongly qualified according to the dance performed.[3]

The art and ballet critic Adrian Stokes once noted that to add music to a scene is to frame it, to make the movements in it (people walking to and fro) look different, less 'natural'. As spectators, we become more aware of people's body movements (trying without thinking to relate them to a musical shape) and these movements thus look to us more self-conscious—we assume a relationship between moving and listening. Movement to music seems more willed than music without it, more thought is going into it—when to put one's foot down, when to pause and turn—and even when held still one's posture now seems more consciously crafted. The analogy that comes to mind here is listening to a strange tongue: we distinguish between someone babbling and someone speaking an unknown language according not to what we hear but to what we assume about what we hear: language, unlike babble, is taken to be 'ruled', the words consciously chosen for their meaning. Adding music to a scene, then, gives *all* the movements in it an implied intention: babble becomes speech, a walk becomes a dance, even if we do not understand it.[4]

Dance is not simply a 'heightened' or more 'intense' form of movement, then; rather, it is movement which *draws attention to itself* (and to the act of—bodily—interpretation) in the very act of ceding control *to* the music—this is the difference between a movement that coincides with a beat and a movement that submits to it. For Adrian Stokes, a balletomane, the question therefore becomes: is a ballet dancer totally in control of her movements (all of which are decidedly 'unnatural', depend on years of training, skill and self-discipline) or totally out of control of them (*everything* she does is determined by the score and the choreographer)? The dancer's 'technique', that which allows her body to do whatever the dance requires, is precisely that which allows her to forget about her body altogether and just 'think' the music (the parallel with sport is again applicable here: the 'unnatural' fitness to which a footballer, say, brings his body, enables him to completely forget it, as a body, when he is playing—which no doubt explains why footballers, like dancers, are recurrently injured: they 'forget' what frail things their bodies really are).

Dance, in short, is willed movement (as Sparshott notes, people only 'dance' on hot bricks by analogy), but it is also unnecessary movement, an end in itself, not a means to another end (like walking to the shop for milk or passing the ball to the inside right). Dance movements are chosen for aesthetic rather than functional reasons—dancing to the store is not the quickest way to get there and dancing back may well mean dropping the bottle. There is an analogy here with the poetic use of language: describing the fire in sonnet form is not the most efficient way of clearing the building, even if the sonnet is still 'about' the fire, just as dance is still 'about' moving across a space. The anthropologist Roderyk Lange thus describes dance as 'poeticised' walking; a form of movement in which we are 'carried' by the music and experience an 'unusual degree of continuity' in our actions. Our movements relate to each other according to the logic of shape and sound rather than means and ends; again, there is an obvious analogy with the 'poetic' use of language, words chosen for the logic of a poem's rhythm, shape and sound, not just to convey meaning.[5]

What makes a dance movement attractive or, to use the key word, *graceful*? To some extent, such judgment depends on genre conventions, but whether we are describing Margot Fonteyn or Michael Jackson, Cyd Charisse or John Travolta, Will Crooks or Siobhan Davies, the common factor seems to be *ease* of movement, a sense of bodies become somehow *immaterial*, through which the music flows without any physical hindrance at all. As Cohen notes, 'To be dramatically compelling on stage, the dancer cannot allow *involuntary* movement to distract the viewer.'[6] The dancer, in other words, seeks to conceal her efforts, draws attention to the created form rather than the process of creation.

On the other hand (given the aesthetic of effort), at the populist end of dance, there clearly is pleasure to be taken in virtuosity and spectacle, in high leaps and difficult turns.[7] The work that goes into these is certainly not concealed and this is as true for Russian ballet dancers as for New York break dancers.

This is to raise general questions about the differences between various forms of stylised movement. What is the difference, for example, between dance and gymnastics?[8] Answer, the different factors *controlling* the body's movements: music rather than equipment, choreographic convention rather than competitive rules. What makes dancing different from ice dancing? Answer, in principle nothing (ice dancing is mostly performed as a competitive sport but that is not necessary to the form). But we are beginning to touch now on the aesthetic problem at the heart of dance analysis: if dance is a communicative art, what does it communicate, what is it *about*? Why, as Sparshott asks, should we *attend* to it? What, for example, do we mean by a good dancer? What are we describing? A physical skill? The dancer's ability to make us feel that she is somehow exempt from the law of gravity? Or something else—an interpretative skill, the ability to use the body to *express* something?[9]

Almost always, when we talk about dance we are talking about movement to music. As Sparshott put it, 'To say that music is one of the essentials of dance is not to say that every dance must have a musical accompaniment. It is rather that some music is expected, even if it be only a drum, and if there is no music, the dance is danced *in the absence* of music.'[10] The question therefore comes back to this: does a dancer, any sort of dancer, 'express' the music, or respond to it? If, as Lange suggested, to dance is to let oneself to be 'carried' by the music, to be 'moved' by it (rather than by where one wants to go) then in what sense is this a personal matter? Does one have a heightened sense of oneself when one dances or have no sense of oneself at all? I do not know the answer to that question but one does, without a doubt, have a heightened, more intense, above all more concentrated, sense *of the music*. Dancing (if not watching dancing), is, in this respect, a form of enhanced listening.

It follows that the translatability problem—how to translate response into meaning—is not quite what it seems, either. The problem here is again premised on a distinction between the immediate (sensual, thoughtless) reaction to a work and a secondary question about that response: why did I feel that way? How did the work get its effects? Was I, as Matthew Arnold put it, *right* to respond so? In this framework, to describe something as a performance is simply to add the response to the text as that which must be interpreted. But from a performative or rhetorical perspective the response was the interpretation. Even the most direct of emotional reactions (laughter, tears) are in themselves an interpretation; not to know what it means (a routine response to postmodern dance or theatre) describes less an inability to explain than to respond to it. The problem is not that we have nothing to say but that we have nothing to feel. In non-representational arts like dance and music we are, indeed, quite accustomed to deciding whether someone—a critic—has 'understood' a piece in terms not of their formal analysis but of their figurative description, their account of not *what* the music meant but *how* it did ('the music rose and hesitated, dropped and rose again, like a kite in flight').

The final point to note here—it is relevant to both criticism and translation—is that performance is essentially *sociable*. The literary image of the reader is individualised: interpretation is a form of detection, the lone scholar poring over texts for clues and traces, uncovering the truth that no one else has grasped. But at a performance one is grasping, so to speak, with everyone else. A joke is not a joke if no one laughs (whatever subsequent scholarly attempts to show that it was, textually, 'really' funny) but our laughter, our sense of the situation, cannot be disentangled from the fact that everyone else is laughing, too. We are embarrassed by an unshared or inappropriate response: if, for instance, we are the only person in the audience to be laughing. This is why a good club DJ can 'play' a club as if choreographing a dance (and why disco dancers on the floor are no more dancing 'apart' than ballet dancers on the stage).

A question still remains, though: how do dancers know how to listen to the music, what to listen for? And clearly the answer depends on the genre. Conventions of dance performance are genre-based, follow a combination of stylised and 'naturalised' movements, of learnt and spontaneous responses. (In my own experience, indeed, it is in learning how to dance to a music—watching what other people are doing and copying them—that we learn how best to listen to it.) And conventions here also determine what the dance is 'about'. In classical ballet, after all, the dancer is not just dancing the music, but dancing a character, a narrative role, and Edward Cone thus distinguishes the 'art dance' from the 'natural dance' and the 'ritual dance'. But certain pop performers (Madonna, Prince, Mick Jagger, most obviously) also dance a part, dancing *to* the music but *in* character, and much vernacular dance has used mime, the dancer representing the movements of an animal, a work process, a social type.[11]

Dance is an ideological way of listening; it draws our attention (not least in its use of space and spaces) to arguments about its own meaning (think of the difference between classical, modern and post-modern ballet, between ballroom and break dancing, between a hop and a rave). And dancing, like listening, does not come naturally: to dance to music is not just to move to it but to say something about it—whatever else the performer may tell us from stage, what they really think about their music is shown by how they move to it. And in terms of response, the body is, anyway, itself a social object (jokes thus commonly revolve around supposedly essential differences between men and women, ethnic groups, social classes). As Morag Shiach argues

> it is surely no longer possible to assume that simply by moving ground, from production to consumption, a space will be found in which to articulate the political and cultural identities of women . . . Abstractions of class and pleasure will be challenged by attention to questions such as 'whose labour, whose consumption and whose body?'[12]

Shiach is offering here another way of perceiving the problems of critical distance. The implication is that criticism is never able to get the right balance between inside and outside, the individual and the social, to measure the exchange between them. This is just as true of the supposedly non-performative arts. Thus, on reading Dickens, Jonathan Ree suggests that

> many readers find it almost impossible to avoid approaching novels as schema for vocal performances, comparable to play scripts or vocal scores; we imagine the words spoken in specific voices, male or female, young or old, and with particular timings, pitches,

> dynamics or pronunciations. We gesticulate, chuckle, grunt and sigh. Some of us in fact get quite hoarse after a couple of hours absorption in a good novel.[13]

This is, I think, one aspect of the continual (but philosophically incoherent) distinction between high and low culture—the former is seen, by its nature, as a kind of 'inner' spiritual experience (art and dance and music as objects of contemplation); the latter as a kind of 'outer' physical experience (art and dance and music as matters of collective entertainment). What such a distinction implies, though, is not so much a difference between texts as between ways of grasping texts, ways of which are *both* determined socially. Shakespeare and Beethoven were thus once objects of noisy public approbation, just as Madonna and Arnold Schwarzenegger can now be treated as objects for contemplation.[14] The high/low argument concerns not what we should read but *how* we should.

To illustrate these points further I want to refer to the avant-garde films of the choreographer Yvonne Rainer. Such texts are without the usual remit of 'cultural studies' (which considers the avant-garde irrelevant to its 'popular' domain) but I chose them because Rainer does, in fact, work with cultural studies (that is, with the everyday materials of cultural studies), if as an artist, not a critic. As in much postmodern work, where art *is* cultural critique (Andrew Benjamin's point), for Rainer, popular culture enacts its own criticism, its own account of critical reading. This corresponds to the kind of 'creative' criticism often demanded within modern and postmodern texts as described by Naomi Schor. If interpretation is something done *in* rather than *to* texts, Schor argues,

> it is a creative rather than a critical activity; in *In the Cage* the young woman is not content merely to encode and decode, rather she delights in filling the gaps, piecing together the fragments, in short adding something of her own to the faulty, often trivial texts in hand . . . The results of this unbridled imagination are 'stories and meanings without end'.[15]

And so, paradoxically, Rainer's avant-garde films embody or enact the mobile materials of popular culture: that is, precisely those desires or pleasures or responses that have been a problem for high cultural analysis. We have here, then, a form of critical analysis always in process, itself a 'becoming-object', a 'bringing-into-being', which foregrounds what Barbara Creed, writing of the difference between film theory and television theory, calls 'messy realities'.[16] By embodying such criticism in the text, popular cultural forms will not allow us to sanitise them or turn them into signs. This is the new 'new' of culture and of cultural response. This is the 'new' which concerns Yvonne Rainer.

In her *Film About a Woman Who . . .*, the voice-over suddenly says: 'Social interaction seems to be mostly about seduction.' What is striking about Rainer is the primacy of the body in her films, her focusing of the problems of distance and identity. Her dance background is constantly reflected in the repeated delineation of human interaction and performance. Rainer's concerns with women's place in narrative structures and with the politics of representation (self-image, intimacy, sexuality) are always bound up with a complex play of inner and outer. Thus, throughout her work, the body is never pure sign. It is always, on the one hand, implied interiority (expressiveness and therefore interpreted via identification and subjectivity); and, on the other hand, the object of the words, the music, the movement/choreography—a manipulated 'determined object' (and therefore grasped by possession and objectivity). One can generalise from this: in the performing arts, there is a continual exchange—depending on which way the gaze is operating—of identity and distance, of mind and body, of thought and non-thought. And this is the mode of attention foregrounded in popular culture: flickering concentration spans, emphasis on discrete moments (not depth or flow), a play of separation and involvement.

A feminist cultural studies student would ask: 'In what part of the space between them do we get "seduced"?' This is the place where culture is made and unmade, and where, in Rainer's words, its materials are 'both a given and a superimposition'. In conversation with Trisha Brown, she describes the analogous process of deconstruction and bricolage commonly associated with avant-garde film and with postmodern dance. Here, the subject's engagement with cultural representations of identity and sexuality is a dynamic, contradictory process of being shaped by particular historical positions. Networks of social relations (material, institutional, symbolic) form and are formed by the representations and collective definitions of the body and the subject. Readers, viewers and listeners are already socially constituted as men and women, but they are also always changing:

> The costumes bring in another dimension of not exactly a persona, but an association with personae created elsewhere and earlier, somewhere between *Les Sylphides* and *Primitive Mysteries*. And it is the dress that produces the association. There's a recurrent, fleeting transformation from a body moving to a flickering female image. I

> think that because the dress stands away from the body the image is never totally integrated or unified, so one goes back and forth in seeing movement as movement, body-inside dress, dress outside body and image of woman dancer, which is not the same thing as seeing or not seeing your work in terms of being a woman. Femaleness in *Glacial Decay* is both a given, as in your previous work, and a superimposition.[17]

I can expand on the issues Rainer's films raise by reference both to her choreography and to her collected film scripts.[18] I was always a great fan of Rainer in her dancer/choreographer incarnation. Her *Trio A* (1967) was, after all, the *Finnegan's Wake* of dance. Along with Siobhan Davies and Pina Bausch (to name just a couple), Rainer's work in the 1970s brought modernist and avant-garde modes to dance.[19] But I would agree with B. Ruby Rich and Mitchell Rosenbaum, who in their prefatory pieces to Rainer's scripts contend that it was the need to deal more intensively with *emotion* (here Rainer shares with other feminists the emphasis on emotion in art as of primary value) and with the problems of and possibilities of *narrative* that led Rainer away from dance and towards film.

S says to J in Rainer's *Film About a Woman Who . . .*, 'It is unthinkable that I live in this condition in intimacy with another person. And the possibility of living a life without intimate connections is equally intolerable . . . Is it any wonder that the most plausible solution is to remove my existence?' (p. 78). And Rainer's preoccupation with detachment and engagement in a work of art (and, in technical terms, with the handling of identification and distanciation) is part and parcel of her continuing concern with the private/public spirit (especially as this manifests itself for an artist). More recently, she has been particularly concerned with the tensions and contradictions between the individual psyche and the social/political being. In her own words, 'the personal and the political are not synonymous. They overlap and intertwine. And one must struggle constantly to assess one's power, or lack of it, in every sphere of one's life.'[20]

In Rainer's films, the public/private tension is manifest at the level of both content and form. As Lucy Lippard notes, Rainer has frequently used autobiographical fragments as props and this has caused its own problems.[21] More specifically, *Film About a Woman Who . . .* developed, in Rich's words, 'the mechanisms by which the materials of autobiography could be successfully combined with those of fictional and documentary materials to form a personal text'.[22] On the question of form/genre, Rainer herself notes that

> [f]eminist theorists like Mulvey and Kaplan have pointed out that melodrama, even soap opera, is a place where women's dilemmas are played out in every visible way. So this offers the avant-garde filmmaker a formal arena in which to make the tensions and dilemmas of women living in a patriarchy accessible and visible . . .[23]

Thus Rainer 'reinvented melodrama as a genre, accented for the contemporary psyche'; and it is worth quoting Rich at some length on what this involved:

> A provisional set of elements can be identified as intrinsic to the woman's film melodramas, indeed so implicit as to require a feminist attention. Such a set includes: the presence of a woman at the centre of the film; a domestic setting, usually the site of domestic conflict; an ellipsis of time to allow for the development of emotion, always central to the drama; extreme verbalisation, which replaces physical action as the means of communication for the now-interior movement; and finally, the woman's ultimate decision to release her emotions.[25]

At the same time, Rainer's dance background remains in the repeated delineation of human interaction and performance: 'Social interactions seems to be mostly about seduction.'[26] Again, 'Everything is about seduction or death.'[27] Again, 'Emotional relationships are relationships of desire, tainted by coercion and constraint.'[28] Rainer's concerns with woman's place in narrative structures, with the politics of representation (self-image, intimacy, sexuality), are thus always bound up with complex notions of power:

> In each case, one's personal actual power is available, to however limited a degree, and must be confronted, or acknowledged, in some fashion . . . [She] takes responsibility for her own destructiveness . . . She assumes responsibility for her own life.[29]

If, then, Rainer's films push us into considering what it means to 'read' our own lives and desires, the publication of her film scripts raises what seems at first a more mundane problem: as I was reading, an unease and an uncertainty about who might read the collection kept surfacing. Film buffs? Students/academics? That amorphous baggy monster, The General Public? In her foreword, de Lauretis claims that the book will be of interest to anyone concerned with the visual arts, women's cinema, aesthetics and cultural criticism. Perhaps. I am less sanguine about her statement that 'the scripts of the films are far more than a notation of the dialogues or the verbal support of the cinematic images; they are artistic and critical texts in their own right, as intensely and deliberately *written* as the essays of Virginia Woolf.'[30]

One obvious advantage of reading the scripts rather than seeing the films is that you can control the pace at which you read, pause at leisure for reflection. But modern technology in the shape of the remote control can produce the same freeze-frame effect. Moreover, to read the scripts is to turn them into narratives: to prioritise the verbal qualities at the expense of the visual effects, and this is where the problem becomes less mundane, returns us to the problem of translation. As Bérénice Reynaud comments on *Journeys from Berlin/1971*: 'the vividness and excitement of the soundtrack contrasts with the formal, quiet, discreet and faintly elegiac aspect of the image'.[31] And Rainer herself explains: 'at the visual level nothing is consummated. And, at the level of discourse, it is entirely about consummation'.[32] In *From The Center*, Lucy Lippard, commenting on the same effect, notes that 'Rainer uses words and images as though they were the same medium, as though you could start a sequence verbally and finish it visually.' Elsewhere, Rainer explains the 'value' of playing with the optical materiality of film—'unless you go into video, and then you get a whole other kind of imagery that's possible with electronics'.

The question here, then, is whether the script *read* can in any way be the same as the script *shot*. And this, in turn, raises other questions. Is the script a version of the film (one among many scripts)? Or is the film a version of the script (one among many films)? What difference does it make to see the film after reading the script? And in what order should we proceed? Should we read the script after seeing the film? Or, if we read the script do we not then need to see the film? Or is it best, as usually happens, to see the film and never read the script?

It is equally possible to turn the questions the other way round. One could argue (like de Lauretis) that Rainer's scripts focus our attention on what Barthes called the *scriptible* (the reader as writer, of the writerly text); and this kind of reading precisely emphasises/demonstrates Rainer's techniques of accretion, ambiguity, fragmentation and collage in process. Above all, it highlights her refusal of a 'coherent' or 'linear' plot/narrative. Despite her disclaimers ('. . . Martha Graham, Godard and Virginia Woolf, I can't say any of them were prime movers for me . . .'[34]), Rainer's style is highly modernist. As she says in voiceover in *Film About a Woman Who . . .*, what is crucial is to have an 'acute sense of the moment': 'But I don't necessarily know the end effect. That is one by-product of collage. Ambiguity is something that is my stock in trade . . .'[35]

Rainer's films are as resistant to metaphorical and symbolic modes, and to interpretation, as all classical modernist texts. 'This Foucault stuff? . . . Is it being used for bullshit purposes, or what?', she imagines people asking in *The Man Who Envied Women* (and in the same film Trisha completes Jackie's quote from Meaghan Morris: 'If a girl takes her eyes off Lacan and Derrida long enough to look, she may discover she is the invisible man'.[36] From a purely academic perspective, however, one advantage of reading the scripts in sequence (rather than watching the films one at a time on separate occasions) is that one gets a clear idea of recurrent motifs.

First, and most important, there emerges the tension between the aesthetic distance described above and the intensity of soap opera. Perhaps this is what Shirley means in *Film About a Woman Who . . .* when she says, 'only in the movies can you send your mind away'.[37]

Second—and despite all her disclaimers about feminism—Rainer's filmic work clearly comes out of a strong women's movement, and her material is clearly linked to feminist 'culture'. Rainer herself claims to be 'haranguing' her audiences for political purposes, but in my view the films are more subtle than that. Above all, what is striking about Rainer's work is her refusal to let her audiences adjust meaning to gender, and her awareness of the narrative implications of this, particularly in terms of the limitations of narrative codes. Rainer's films are often classified as 'affliction' films (films that centre on the suffering of female characters); but again I see them as more actively positive than this, and as resistant to a victimist historiography. Rainer's emphasis is always on the individual's own power and responsibility. She is constantly seeking a more rigorous documentation of the political. As Shirley says in *Film About A Woman Who . . .*, 'Not that it's a matter of victims and oppressors. She simply can't find alternatives to being inside with her fear or standing in the rain with her self-contempt.'[38]

In short, the questions that Rainer asks concern not just the translation problem—the relationship of interpretation and experience—but also the narrative problem, the relationship of interpretation and story—the stories we supposedly see unfold before us, the stories we already know. And I want to end this discussion by reference to an argument about painting which addresses precisely this issue. My text here is Mieke Bal's book of lectures on Rembrandt.[39]

*Reading Rembrandt* is a highly ambitious project. In it, Mieke Bal sets out to devise what she calls a visual rhetoric: 'a thoroughly integrated encounter between visuality, verbality and critical endeavour'.[40] She argues that to read a painting as a narrative, as art historians have traditionally done, is to misread it, or, at least, to read it only in part. In her introduction, Bal asks *what* reading means (a choice of a subject? A choice of terms of analysis?) and *what* is being analysed (the work? The artist? The critic's response?). The problem, as Bal argues, is to do with delimiting signs, delimiting interpretation, and distinguishing interpretation from description. Each of her chapters thus focuses on a particular theoretical issue. For example, what is the appropriate rhetoric for the interpretation of visual images? How can, or do, images narrate? What are the status and the effect of a represented viewer in visual and literary art?

And most importantly of all, how do the arts function in a culture where the public is constantly surrounded by images, yet trained to privilege words over images:

> The book is designed to pursue a number of intertwined goals. First, I shall practice 'reading'—that is, describing and interpreting images and stories both verbal and visual. At the same time, I shall reflect on what 'reading' means. I shall reflect on the relationship between literature and the visual arts, a relationship between different, but not opposed ways of producing signs and meaning. Thus I shall pursue insight into the rhetorical and pictorial devices used in the two arts. At the same time, I shall explore the different ways in which works by 'Rembrandt' and certain verbal texts are or can be related. These reflections will point towards unexpected but crucial relationships between technical and ideological issues.[41]

Throughout *Reading Rembrandt*, Bal's intention, then, is to find 'another narrative' which derives from an 'interaction' rather than an 'opposition' between discourse and image.[42] Text and image neither do, nor do without, each other, she argues, and the idea is to make discourse a partner, rather than a dominant opponent of visuality: 'to cut across the traditional word-image opposition in order to fill in images where words predominate, and word where images repress language'.[43] Her choice of Old Testament narrative is strategic. Reading the paintings through the well-known biblical stories, and without the help of the existing biblical texts (as one does), creates an inevitable tendency to trace motifs back to traditions and sources, and thereby to preclude active 'visual' interpretation. In other words, the viewer superimposes on the painting an underlying verbal story which the painting is then used to illustrate. Art critics, Bal argues, invoke dis course to overcome the fright of what she calls 'this primary visuality' (p. 288). The result is that paintings are inevitably given meanings other than those their immediate visual appearance suggests (a point which relates to Andrew Benjamin's discussion of titles). Bal argues that the discursivity of the painting is much more to do with its visuality than critics have previously allowed or have found a critical rhetoric for:

> I am not proposing that we ignore the evoked story in favour of some 'fresh' or 'direct' visual narrative. Rather, I would like to make a case for a double, differential reading, which juxtaposes the evoked against the narrated story, in order to let them interact and to let the tensions between the stories produce new meanings.[44]

With so little known about Rembrandt's life, and 'left only with what remains on the canvas', Bal's choice of 'Rembrandt' is also carefully made to shield her new critical poetics from 'what we might call the psychobiographical fallacy'.[45]

Bal also touches on the fact that if a new criticism could be found that undermines the gap between the word and image, it would have powerful institutional implications. In line with deconstruction and postmodernism, Bal hopes that by allowing critical traditions to be confronted with each other she will overcome the artificial boundaries between them, and break down 'the powerful and paralysing ideologies in the humanities today' which tend to have been expressed to-date in terms of philosophical dichotomies: theory and practice, literal and figurative, form and content, text and content, and above all, appearance and reality.[46]

*Reading Rembrandt* draws on feminist theory, rhetoric, narratology and psychoanalysis, but its greatest debt is to reception theory. Shifting attention from the medium to the reception, Bal sees the locus of meaning as in the interaction between text and reader, not in the text alone. Rather than locating the work in a stable conception of the sign, Bal sees the work as what she calls 'a sign event occurring between the canvas and its critics':

> Shifting attention from the question of intrinsic properties to that of response, the focus will be on the interaction between visual and verbal 'behaviour' of those who deal with, process or consume the works of art.[47]

She exhorts us to read for 'the navel' of each painting. According to Bal, the navel is a metaphor for an element, often a tiny detail, that hits the viewer, is processed by him or her and textualises the image on its own terms: 'the textualising navel is an emptiness, a little surface which the work leaves unfilled'.[48] So, the emphasis is on surface, detail, conflicting meanings. 'Reading for the navel' does not take for granted the wholeness enhanced by the detail, but makes the detail rather than the whole the dominant element. Like Derrida before her, Bal is anxious to demonstrate the defects of the concept of 'text', with its fixed relations between sign and meaning, its hierarchical structure, its suppression of details, of the marginal, of 'noise'.[49] In this context, Bal quotes illuminatingly from Elisabeth Bronfen who seeks those moments in a representational text that do not cover up the translation of the real into representation, but which rather show this as fractured and emphasise that fractured state (p. 235). Or, in another of Bal's coinages, this would be to engage in a 'hysterical reading':

> Rather than 'reading for the plot', a hysterical reading reads for the image; rather than reading for the main line or the proposition, it reads for the detail; and rather than reading for the hero or main character, it reads for the victim. Rather than reading for logic, linearity, and literality, it displaces these, replacing them with a scene orientated simultaneity in which the categories of literal and figural change places . . . Rather than placing the event in the historical past, this kind of reading places it in the 'hysterical' present of identification, which receives its figuration from the spatial.[50]

*Reading Rembrandt* re-traverses previously theorised areas such as psychoanalysis (drawing especially on feminist film theory) but Bal is particularly instructive on how the ways in which we perceive and interpret images are based on fantasy. In her thoughtful questioning of the troubled relationship between meaning and experience, between viewing, desiring and the impulse to fulfil desire, Bal thus reworks the familiar arguments about looking and being looked at—the gaze as the internalised social construction of looking; the proximity of moralism and metaphor, and the diffuse presence of stories as arguments—and lays bare the critical procedures that function as mechanisms of exclusion (in 'high'/'low' terms). The 'high' art works of Rembrandt may be part of élitist culture, that is, but the responses they elicit are not:

> issues like the relationship between storytelling and voyeurism; the thematic centrality of the nude as an object of vision, transparent representation and its limits—are all pervasively present in contemporary Western culture . . . The opposition high-low is intrinsic not to the object under scrutiny but to the assumptions we bring to these or any works.[51]

Bal's hypothesis and method, and the procedures of her cultural criticism, are best demonstrated in her analyses of those paintings where, for all the viewer's attempts to narrativise or to contextualise, the image's textuality remains out of place. Bal most frequently finds this in those paintings where the figure depicted (always a woman) is unwilling to communicate with the viewer and thereby problematises the latter's position. One striking example is the painting called *The Toilet of Bathsheba*. Here, the woman's reflectiveness is enhanced by the fact that her head turns away from the viewer while her body does not. Although the image clearly makes sense as a whole, what sense it makes cannot be easily decided. There is no obvious congruence between the biblical 'narrative' and the visual effects/mood/atmosphere of the painting:

> We are left with a sense of narrativity that is not fulfilled; with a sense of wholeness that does not satisfy; with a frustrated need to position ourselves in relation to the viewing situation the narrative should bring forth but doesn't. These dead ends leave us with a strong awareness of textuality as not quite appropriate, as alien.[52]

The notion that textuality is alien is not, of course, a new theoretical idea. The art of interpretation—hermeneutics—has always been premised on the assumption that some texts are difficult, opaque, unsettling; that reading is, as we have seen, detective work, the act of uncovering meaning, pinning it down. And what is new about postmodern theory is not so much the argument that the meaning of a text cannot be so pinned down, but the suggestion that we should not worry about it. If we can no longer believe that a text has an origin (whether in terms of authorial intention and ideology or by reference to an object to be imitated or represented), then, rather than seeking such unity in vain, we should, as Andrew Benjamin suggests, delight in original heterogeneity.

In practice, though, the interpretative move has been simpler: attention has switched from text to reader as the source of meaning, which is certainly to encourage interpretative pluralism but which is not, in the end, to challenge the distinction *between* text and reader. Hence my concern in this paper with performance, with the performing arts, in which the process of meaning-making is quite clearly based on a *collaboration* between performer and audience (and in which the 'text' *is* the 'reading'). The performative emphasis on process, on meaning as becoming, dissolves the usual boundaries between inside and outside, subject and object, distance and intensity (and thus, the point emphasised by postmodern critics, between high and low culture). These issues are at the centre of Yvonne Rainer's work, which further complicates the issue in its movement between different materials—bodies in dance, the appearance of bodies in film.

From the performance perspective, then, the issue is not the 'alienation' of the text (which never becomes an object which can be so alienated). Rather, the question is how we manage the translation of sensual and emotional response into a 'reading', an interpretation, in the first place. This is a particular problem for intellectuals: from what sort of 'critical' response does a critical reading derive? What is the source of interpretative expertise if there is no longer a 'true' or 'real' meaning to be uncovered? How does a reader know when to stop?

This is one of those questions, beloved of philosophers, which in terms of common-sense aesthetics seems unnecessary—the answer is when it *feels* right. And it may be that, for performers, for readers as performers, the translation problem that seems so intractable from a literary perspective is not a problem at all: analytic distinctions are not necessarily felt distinctions. In practice, that is to say, even the most 'immediate' sensation, the most direct aesthetic response, depends on expectations, on memories, on the sense-making power of the imagination. Reading, watching, listening—this is Bal's point—assumes narrative, assumes that a story is being told.

Rose Subotnik has observed that modern dance, even when accompanied by a 'difficult' score, has a relatively large public (compared to modern music) 'because ballet is sufficiently abstract that audiences do not panic if they fail to understand the "meaning" '.[53] I would put this differently: the reason for modern ballet's bigger audience is that the meaning of ballet is felt to be more open to each person's *own* interpretation. The body in the performed dance (like the body in Rembrandt's representational art) becomes the site of our understanding of the work—shaping from without (reading—trying to make 'sense') is experienced as shaping from within (the art of sensual production).

## Notes

1 Andrew Benjamin, *Art, Mimesis and the Avant-Garde* (London, Routledge, 1991).
2 *Ibid.*, p. 27.
3 Francis Sparshott, *Off the Ground. First Steps to a Philosophical Consideration of the Dance* (Princeton, Princeton University Press, 1988), p. 206.
4 See Adrian Stokes, *Tonight the Ballet* (London, Faber & Faber, 1942), p. 13.
5 See Roderyk Lange, 'Some Notes on the Anthropology of Dance', in John Blacking (ed.), *The Anthropology of the Body* (London, Academic Press, 1977),

p. 243. Sarah Jeanne Cohen notes another distinction between dance and sport: 'For dance, both performer and audience shift into a special time–space dimension. This is not the case with sport.' (*Next Week, Swan Lake. Reflections on Dance and Dancers* (Hanover, NH, Wesleyan University Press, 1982), p. 66.

6 Cohen, *Next Week, Swan Lake*, p. 54. My emphasis.

7 It could be argued that the emphasis on effort, rather than grace, is gendered. In classic ballet, men show the work that goes into their routines while women conceal it. Cohen (*ibid.*, p. 75) suggests that virtuosity, at least, should be seen as a personal rather than a gender quality, its 'exuberance' reflecting the dancer's 'rebellion' against 'restrictions of form', so that our attention is drawn to the 'tension' between dancer and music and not, as is more usual, to their unity.

8 See Sparshott, *Off the Ground*, pp. 317–26.

9 *Ibid.*, pp. 207–14.

10 *Ibid.*, p. 173.

11 Edward Cone, *The Composer's Voice* (Berkeley, University of California Press, 1982), pp. 140–1.

12 Morag Shiach, 'Feminism and Popular Culture', *Critical Quarterly*, 33:2 (1991), 45.

13 Jonathan Ree, 'Funny Voices: Stories, Punctuation and Personal Identity', *New Literary History*, 21 (1990), 104–6.

14 It is interesting how many post-Enlightenment philosophers from Adam Smith onwards have turned to the 'expressive' rather than 'imitative' arts to resolve problems of *knowledge*. For twentieth-century philosophers, the metaphor of *performance* has thus crept into criticism of all the arts (see, for instance, Jacques Derrida, 'Choreographies', in *Diacritics*, 12:2 (Summer 1982), 67–74, while within cultural studies, Madonna has become a clichéd example of the dissolve between inside and outside.

15 Naomi Schor, 'Fiction as Interpretation/Interpretation as Fiction', in Susan Sukeiman (ed.), *The Reader in the Text* (1989), p. 171.

16 Barbara Creed, *Camera Oscura*, 20/21 (1990), 23.

17 Trisha Brown and Yvonne Rainer, 'A Conversation About *Glacial Decay*', *October*, 10 (Fall 1979), 29–37.

18 Yvonne Rainer, *The Films of Yvonne Rainer* (Bloomington, Indiana University Press, 1989).

19 See Sally Banes, *Terpsichore in Sneakers: Postmodern Dance* (Boston, Houghton-Mifflin, 1980, revised 1987).

20 Rainer, *The Films of Yvonne Rainer*, pp. 22–3.

21 Lucy Lippard, *From the Center* (New York, E. P. Dutton, 1976), p. 267.

22 Rainer, *The Films of Yvonne Rainer*, p. 10.

23 *Ibid.*, p. 41.

24 *Ibid.*, p. 7.

25 *Ibid.*, p. 9.

26 *Ibid.*, p. 79.

27 *Ibid.*, p. 82.

28 *Ibid.*, p. 6.

29 *Ibid.*, p. 22.
30 *Ibid.*, p. vii.
31 *Ibid.*, p. 30.
32 *Ibid.*, p. 30.
33 Lippard, *From the Center*, p. 267.
34 Rainer, *The Films of Yvonne Rainer*, p. 38.
35 *Ibid.*, p. 35.
36 *Ibid.*, pp. 214–15.
37 *Ibid.*, p. 86.
38 *Ibid.*, p. 7.
39 Mieke Bal, *Reading Rembrandt* (Cambridge, Cambridge University Press, 1992).
40 *Ibid.*, p. 289.
41 *Ibid.*, p. 9.
42 *Ibid.*, p. 24.
43 *Ibid.*, p. 63.
44 *Ibid.*, p. 207.
45 *Ibid.*, p. 10.
46 *Ibid.*, p. 405.
47 *Ibid.*, p. 8.
48 *Ibid.*, p. 22.
49 *Ibid.*, p. 19.
50 *Ibid.*, p. 63.
51 *Ibid.*, p. 7.
52 *Ibid.*, p. 227.
53 Herbert Landberger, quoted in Rose Rosengard Subotnik, 'Towards a Deconstruction of Structural Listening', in E. Narmour and R. A. Solie (eds.), *Explorations in Music, the Arts and Ideas* (Stuyvesant, NY, Pendragon Press, 1988), p. 115.

10 *Elizabeth Wright*

# Psychoanalysis and the theatrical: analysing performance

What is the relation of psychoanalysis to theatricality and to representation in general? Or, to put it another way, why should the vicissitudes of identity be bound up with the dramatic? Theatricality becomes the operative factor both in the consulting room and on the stage, since both are what Jean-François Lyotard has called 'disreal spaces',[1] in the sense that in each representations are tried and the question arises of what is 'real' outside representation. Both in analysis and in drama there recur the crises that bespeak underlying conflicts of interpretation. The recognition of the implications of theatricality for life as such came relatively late, although the *theatrum mundi* analogy—'All the world's a stage,/And all the men and women merely players'—has been a platitude for centuries. This recognition emerged in the wake of Freudian theory but via a circuitous route which entailed working through a mimetic fallacy. Just as there was an assumption which entailed the imitation of a pre-given reality at the level of consciousness, so, too, by the same token, the unconscious was taken to be mirrored in the latent structure of a work, rather than being involved in a mimesis itself via the operations of a narcissistic subject. In this essay I hope to exemplify a certain correlation of artistic practice and criticism with the re-reading of psychoanalytic theories of the subject.

From the beginning, psychoanalytic theory has paid attention to the arts as employing the same processes that Freud uncovered in the workings of the unconscious. Of particular relevance to this investigation is Freud's classic account of the theatre as the scene of unconscious desire. In his essay, 'Psychopathic characters on the stage' (originally published 1905–6) Freud discusses how the audience's understanding of repressed material might affect their response. If the material is experienced as too threatening, the spectator's defences will come into play and inhibit the pleasure of purging emotions tied to unconscious wishes. This, Freud argues, is particularly the case where what he calls 'psychopathological drama' is involved. Here 'the source of the suffering in which we take part and from which we are meant to derive pleasure is no longer a conflict between two almost equally conscious impulses but between a conscious impulse and a repressed one'.[2] According to Freud, it is the dramatist's task to lower the spectators' resistance to the repressed material by 'diverting' them and thus enabling them to enter into the neurosis of the stage figure. The dramatist thereby creates a neurotic space where the spectators may live out their conflicts and even gain 'masochistic' satisfaction in identifying with the hero's defeat. Here, then, is the emergence of a psychoanalytic spectator theory. In one sense, this marks a break with Aristotle's poetics of the drama, since the socially undesirable emotions are indulged in rather than got rid of, but in another sense it is on a par with Aristotle in that the process is still adaptive and maintains the status quo.

A sophisticated version of this view can be found in the work of a psychoanalytic critic, himself an analyst, who develops the notion of theatre as 'the best embodiment of that "other scene", the unconscious'.[3] Just as the child is faced with the riddle of its parents, so the spectator is confronted by an enigma: every theatrical work is a riddle for the spectator and the invitation to solve it leads her/him to take up certain positions. The barrier of the edge of the stage sends the spectator's gaze back to her/himself as source of that enigma, thus establishing a relation between subject and object and stimulating the hope 'that the secret behind the moment of disappearance of the repressed objects will be revealed',[4] in other words, that the objects of fantasy will no longer be subject to repression. Art offers a lure, setting up a new category of object in the field of illusion, whereby the desired objects remain occult, available only in masked distorted form, to be appropriated in a way that does not disturb either the creator's or the spectator's narcissistic idealisation. According to Green, fantasy helps the creator/spectator couple to form a narcissistic pact: the objects are ejected and disappropriated by the artist in the hope that the spectator will appropriate and process them. The 'upsurge of desire that gave them birth'[5] is repeated by each spectator, thus continually validating the narcissistic idealisation of the creator via a series of mutual 'trans-narcissistic' desire-fantasies. Hence the enjoyment gained is surreptitious, effected as it is through the displacements of sublimation inherent in the work of art,[6] which enable it to negate the action of repression and afford a 'bonus of pleasure'. Green compares this with the symptom which yields a certain unpleasure when, as a return of the repressed, it irrupts into consciousness, since forbidden satisfaction carries with it a need for punishment.[7] Here, too, the moment of catharsis is pleasure tinged with pain, involving the spectator's identification with the hero (pity) and his masochistic movement (terror) in bringing punishment upon himself. For in the end there is an Oedipal dynamic at stake, in that the hero must placate the father, be *like* him, but not *be* him. Such a reading of Freud still openly stays within an Aristotelian poetics, since tragic recognition involves a passing from ignorance to knowledge. The knowledge thus acquired is an Oedipal knowledge lodged in a character dynamic, with the figures creating the dramatic world assigned to them. But although Green discusses the theatre of Artaud as a 'radical challenge' to representation,[8] seeing its chief value as pointing the way towards 'a theatre of primary process, which tends towards discharge', a non-Aristotelian theatre of desire, ignorant of time and space,[9] this reading of Artaud is still collusive, tied solely to recognition. The cathartic function is still the assuaging of unsatisfied desires, thus staying within the parameters of classical psychoanalysis.

Post-Freudian theatre, which must, of course, include the avant-garde theatre of Artaud and Brecht, dispenses with any notion of the arts as a safety valve for repressed wishes. Such wishes are rather to be seen as a revolt against oppressive systems of all kinds. In particular the post-Freudian theatre in its postmodernist form makes a radical break with the old idea of sublimation. Far from the arts being regarded as a safe channel for the redirection and the consequent taming of destructive and aggressive drives, artistic texts are suspected of being a medium of seducing the spectator/reader into a given pre-ideological structure. This theatre is radically anti-individualist, challenging the privileging of an intending individual as origin of meaning. In this, it has absorbed the performance tradition, a dramatic form based on a semiotic understanding of theatrical practice, a non-narrative, non-representational theatre in which the traditional forms, genres and practices are abandoned and the professional distinctions of actor, playwright, director, stage-manager, scene-shifter, spectator are eroded. The fictitious unity between voice and world is shown up by making speech compete with other elements on the stage, such as music, sound effects, gestures, sets, props, lighting, mime, mask. The most significant features of performance are the disturbance of the boundaries between artist and spectator, spectator and art 'object', art 'object' and artist. This form of subversively implicating the audience with what is happening on stage and vice versa has become the the basic structure of postmodern performance.

Post Freudian criticism has in its turn taken a different reading from Freud in likewise dispensing with the notion of art luring the spectator into a collusive pact. In his essay, 'Theatrum Analyticum' (1977), Philippe Lacoue-Labarthe uses late psychoanalysis to overturn the would-be reassuring nature of a simplistic catharsis theory which assumes the audience's pacification in relation to the demands of the symbolic and hence a reconciliation to their fate. Such an assumption implies a classical theoretical dependence on a pleasure principle versus a reality principle, since it is based on the notion that a better catharsis is obtained through the recognition of the repressed unconscious impulse (pleasure principle) being opposed by a conscious one (reality principle); the result is a saving of libido, what Freud calls an economic expenditure. This begs the question of the relation between the two processes. Lacoue-Labarthe argues that there is something theoretically prior to these principles. The communal belief in the symbolic, enshrined in language, hides the fact of death and the cessation of desire which it endlessly promises to fulfil. The theatrical cannot help but show this disruption at the heart of drama, so that the effect is not simply an exorcism of anger, fear and resentment, but a recognition of the risk that is at the heart of all play, with its 'economy of difference and deferral'.[10]

This economy of play, is not, however, the reassuring play of an anaesthetising form, but 'real' play, which, like the child's *Fort/Da*,[11] involves renunciation. The unbinding play of the death drive introduces the notion of deferral with its element of risk. The price of subjecthood is living out the drives within the symbolic net. However, there being no simple opposition between a pleasure principle and a reality principle, real effects, that is, outcomes hitherto unthought, break out in both, producing a dual risk, in that neither inner nor outer, libido nor law, are stable elements. Instead of two opposed principles, there is a dialectical interplay that results from the ongoing repositioning of the symbolic net upon a basically unconceptualised ground, the real. Theatricality thus turns up in the inescapable dialectic of the drives. To enter the symbolic dooms us to repetition: to desire and to the sacrifice of desire. But whereas desire is 'noisy' when directed outwards in the guise of Eros as a part of the noise of life, desire is 'silent' when working inwardly in the guise of the death drive. In the latter case, it is 'unmarked',[12], *unvorstellbar* ('unrepresentable', Freud), 'unpresentable'[13] and can only be theatricalised as the repeated attempt to re-present itself. Within the Dionysian/Apollonian struggle (Nietzsche), there is something that cancels the very notion of a utopian presence as promised by the symbolic, leaving only the possibility of 'the impossible ethical trial of the abyss'.[14] There is no ethical consolation to be had; time continually erodes all presence and necessitates beginning over again in the very face of death. Death is 'the empty form of time';[15] it is not simply something to which the living tries to return, but that of which the living tries to divest itself by means of repetition and differentiating modes of experience, by repeated attempts to enter the symbolic, only to be caught all over again.

So what are the implications of all this for theatre and criticism? The impact of post-Freudian psychoanalytic theory on the arts has been to raise consciousness in terms of artistic and critical practice. It has produced a body politics concerned with making a spectacle which reveals the relation of bodies to the symbolic and to specific cultures within the symbolic. The focus on the body in the wake of Brecht and Artaud marks a crucial point of division between theatre and performance. But whereas pre-Brechtian theatre, and to some extent Brechtian theatre as still canonically performed,[16] is controlled by the writer's text, in that the actors take part as 'characters', creating the dramatic world assigned to them, performance theatre gets rid of the author's voice, the text's 'authority', the lure of the great actor, and of both the illusion of reality and the Brechtian challenge to that illusion. Instead, the performance artist offers her/his body as a living embodiment of drive tensions and shifting sets of codes. The actor's body is no longer fitted into characterological representation as 'intended' by the author, even where this is radically utilised in terms of the Brechtian gestus. Abandoning all notions of the individual, performance shows the theatricalised subject working through a variety of fantasies, with the spectator called upon to scatter her/his own identifications from among a variety of subject positions.

Yet performance, by its very nature, cannot simply proclaim itself as raw life, although its most illustrious proponent strove to abolish mimesis from the stage. It was Artaud who most radically distanced himself from making any division between art and life, wanting to erase this distinction, so that representation would not 'show its duplicitous face'.[17] In his chapter 'The universals of performance', Herbert Blau recognises the necessity of Artaud's iconoclasm, but forcefully questions the difference between being and performing, maintaining that 'the most minimal performance is a differentiating act', producing marks of punctuation and introducing an element of consciousness, for 'there is nothing more illusory in performance than the illusion of the unmediated'[18] there is something written in the very nature of performance which 'seems embedded in the conservatism of the instincts and the linguistic operations of the unconscious'.[19]

This something is repetition. In the repetitions that are basic to performance, there is a re-presenting of the recurrences to which the unconscious is bound. This is the conservatism of the unconscious. So what is being repeated? In Green's argument, as was seen above, the Freudian subject is always guilty, because the identification with the father required from both the biological male and female is in the form of a double bind, the enjoiner of the law appearing simultaneously to uphold it and to break it. But this implies that the father's law is actually not rigid because the only way to obey it is also not to do so: 'you ought to be like this', yet 'you may not be like this', or, in other words, 'I am offering you desire, but repress it'. Hence, the ambivalent feelings arising from such an impossible identification haunt the subject for the rest of her/his life and may drive her/him into analysis in order to repeat them *ad infinitum*. The trance of the transference is the vital affective means which tempts the subject into modifying those repetitive somnambulistic acts which mark the refusal to engage in the symbolic. But rather than commit the subject to Oedipal guilt, the double bind might be actively contended with, instead of passively suffered. That is why, according to Cornelius Castoriadis,[20] psychoanalysis is a poetic practice faced with what Freud called an impossible task, the enabling of the patient to become autonomous largely through self-reflection upon the automatism of the unconscious. As a true politics, one which refuses to enforce an objective truth, it has something in the nature of a riddle, for the laws imposed on the subject are at the same time questionable by the subject, provided he/she is prepared 'to live on the edge of the abyss, within this ultimate double bind'.[21]

The performance art of the German choreographer Pina Bausch performs this double bind in that it presents figures attempting to execute social roles and failing to do so. The resulting conflict between subject and role testifies to the fact that what we are watching is the theatrical in everyday life: postmodern performance theatre explores the world as theatrically constructed, rather than the theatre as mirror of the world. Pina Bausch's company was formed in the early 1970s when she took charge of the Dance Theatre in Wuppertal, a small town in the Ruhr, since when her group has appeared all over the world. The works are long, often up to three or four hours; the scenes I am going to describe are from a two-hour-long film, made recently, her first venture into cinema. In it, she uses the same principle of montage as she does in her stage performances. One difference is that, while her stage action is always decentred, several things going on simultaneously, the camera focuses on one image at a time. An analogous decentring effect appears, however, because there are no shot-reverse shots and hence the viewer is uncertain of where to insert him/herself into the phantasmatic scenarios. Otherwise, Bausch uses the same principle of montage, alternating between swift cuts and agonisingly long ones, producing an associative but discontinuous linkage of scenic material. As in a psychoanalytic session, time is relentlessly subjectivised, stretching out in endless repetitions only to be suddenly and brutally cut. In both her theatre and film work, there is a constant lack of fit between decor, recorded music and speech or body language. Bausch has always used concrete materials on the stage, whose sound and smell can be perceived—leaves, flowers, damp earth, grass, water—in order to estrange the familiar. These invasions of the real are doubly effective when the use of film enables her to go outside. The model animals she hitherto used on the stage are replaced by actual animals, sheep, goats, dogs, and birds, acting as obstacles or milling around helplessly. She deals with that which will not be turned away, such as time, space, snow, earth, motion, weight. Her scenarios are, for example, set in actual time, which means lengthy and sometimes boring repetition, but it shows her subjects to be really exhausted by their futile efforts. She shows the traumatic element at the very core of the symbolic by staging phantasmatic scenarios, in which her subjects imaginarily act out nameless anxieties and confront specific fears. In the midst of a somnambulistic performance, when they are in thrall to the Other, to that which has determined them without their knowing it, the real takes them by surprise. They are caught up and trapped by mud, stones and leaves, automatically impeded by machines that are out of control or coming too close for comfort. The opening sequence is of a woman struggling with a huge garden-vacuum, blowing masses of leaves randomly about, now and again taking a pot shot at them from a pistol held in her hand; another scene is of a radio-controlled helicopter, emitting a menacing noise and zigzagging in front of a person in a long billowing dress, standing on a dais with her/his back against a wall. There are also figures, struggling with the challenges of weight and space: for example, a long, slow sequence of a man struggling with the dead weight of a large wardrobe, which he is endeavouring to carry across a wide green plain. The next take is of a featherlight dancer, draped in veils, endlessly and silently turning cartwheels as if the body's desire to return to a mythical weightless unity were confirmed. Then again, in another sequence, this fantasy is denied by the Other's demand that the subject take its place in the symbolic: the legs of a dancing pair are cut off by the camera as they uncannily and parodically perform a ballroom dance bawdily suggestive of the sexual act.

As traumatised figures, unaccountably driven, they stumble around, in a void filled with alienating music, either sentimentalised tunes, or primitive chants. Pina Bausch's world is a world of unfulfilled promises. The symbolic does not deliver the 'full' word the way the culture suggests, in particular the keywords of 'mother', 'father' and 'child'. Fathers seem to hold out excitement which suddenly turns into fear and anxiety, such as the paternal figure who hauls a small boy at the end of a rope up until he is swinging helplessly and out of control from the high branch of a tree, whimpering with fright. This shot raises questions, such as: what is a mother's rocking? Is it safe? What happens if a father tries to do it and introduces some excitement? What or whose fantasy uncannily transforms the familiar rocking into a helplessness, an imprisonment, even a hanging? More father-problems in a silent army of men, carrying babes into the woods—if one looks closely at the children carried by this procession of father-figures through the symbolic wood (its trees numbered and marked out from nature—for what? For preserving? For felling?), one notices that the whimpering does not actually come from the children but from the forest, like some wailing chorus. In each case, the putative father is marked with extreme ambivalence. So is the mother elsewhere: a woman is expressing milk from her own breast into her hand and continually sucking it up, followed by a shot of another woman standing in the middle of a flock of sheep, grasping a whisky bottle which she alternately drinks from and holds out to the sheep. There is no adequate holding mother, a point graphically made in a late sequence by a woman with a strained suffering expression on her face (who happens to be Pina Bausch herself) endeavouring to grasp two children in her arms, whose weight is too much for her. No beatific Madonna and Child this—the mother is inadequately dressed, the all-too-solid children are whining and squabbling, one deriving comfort from sucking its thumb, the other from clutching its genitals. This writhing, shapeless, amorphous thing cannot be motherhood. The real is resisting the forms that we would place upon it. The more-than-'good-enough' mother endlessly called for in the snow and the forest in yet another scene does not exist.

The film is entitled *The Lament of the Empress*: an empress has power within the symbolic, but this 'empress', appearing in various guises throughout the film, is a figure who has given up on her desire and continually protests and fills the air with idle chatter, unable, like everyone else in it, to perform an act of mourning, exhibiting the kind of uncanny anxiety that, according to Heidegger, is caused by 'nothing', by what the would-be authentic self has not yet done.

Pina Bausch's figures show a world where there are no consoling 'transitional objects', in which inner and outer reality can coincide in a playful illusion. The transitional objects that there are, have a pathological dimension, in that the subjects *become them*, acting out regressive fantasies in cross-gender roles, such as the male figure who wraps him/herself in a wet placenta-like veil and, in another scenario, submerges his/her body in a container full of water. In Pina Bausch's world, the symbolic injunction of language will never match the real body without a measure of fixed transgressive fantasy. What makes her work so compelling is that her dancers demonstrate, in what now might be called a post-Brechtian way, how the unconscious shows itself unconsciously: the docility of the figures comes about because the subjects do not know that the orders come from an Other. As actors, they do not 'demonstrate' their unknowingness. Their somnambulistic behaviour reveals the unconscious effects of law and language on the body. The entry into the symbolic generates transgression, which, as the examples amply illustrate, is 'enjoyed' in the symptom: the symptom yields covert enjoyment and enables the subject to avoid the reality of lack via a strictly ordered somnambulistic behaviour. Hence enjoyment is not spontaneous but marked with prohibition. 'Enjoying your symptom'[22] is covertly living out your transgression, allowing the element of the real into language by surreptitious means. The symptom is the resistance to the Other, the tell-tale sign of the law's implementation.

In its concentration on an authorless, actorless, directorless theatre, in no way subordinated to a literary text, Pina Bausch's dance theatre is an expropriation of Brecht's epic-cum-dialectical theatre: where Brecht analysed the great historical process, 'the Dance Theatre shows how the influence of these processes reaches down into the concrete individual realm', making visible 'the body conventions internalized via anxieties'.[23] The collective awakening of the audience to its own repression is, however, a more radical move than Freud's cautious sublimatory strategies when it comes to art. The question of how political the discourse of the body can be (while avoiding a metaphysics of the body in the style of Artaud) may be asked through the work of Heiner Müller, my second example of post-Freudian theatre.

The once-East-German dramatist Heiner Müller (born 1929) may be seen as representative of the way the contemporary theatre has absorbed the performance tradition in order to veer away from the dramatists of high modernism. In the late 1960s and early 1970s he produced a series of pieces in which he challenged the contradictory reality of contemporary socialism, calling into question the extent of the sacrifice that the individual has to make. In his later work, he makes a radical use of montage, producing fragmentary forms in an attempt to win back the subjective factor as an aesthetic category and to preserve the traces of subjectivity from the fossilisations of history. The project of reclaiming the subjective factor does not, however, mean a new retreat into the private and the personal. Subjectivity is rather to be seen as an eminently significant factor in politics: Müller wants to bring back the subject as part of the dialectic between the individual and history, to use it as an objective factor in political development and to get away from the private irrational. He would want to go further than Pina Bausch in not only finding forms by means of which the subjectivities of everyday experience can be traced and held, but also in showing their historical significance, though without reducing such experience to a particular plight, such as the effects of capitalism.

Müller's play *Hamletmaschine* (1978) is about the revolt of the body when exposed to the threat of violence and destruction. But this revolt has gone beyond the stage of being communicable in rational forms of language. It is a text 'in which the writing subject disintegrates into a series of identities, which merge into one another: Shakespeare, Ophelia, Hamlet, father, mother, whore, son; rebels and rulers'.[24] The play itself is brief, consisting of barely nine pages. The text produces a phantasmagoria of images and provokes the question of what a piece like this has to do with the theatre as we know it. It is indeed difficult to perform, which pleases Müller, for it is his contention that it is the task of literature to put up resistance against the theatre; 'only if a text cannot be done to suit the theatre in its present state, is it likely to be productive for the theatre, and interesting'.[25]

Müller has taken considerable interest in the performance aspect of contemporary theatre, in particular the theatre work of Robert Wilson. Wilson functions simultaneously as scriptwriter, director, stage designer and actor, and has brought about a radical change in the theatrical event, partly by the unprecedented length of his productions, which are anything up to twelve hours and are meant to be attended and attended to sporadically, often throughout the night. The verbal elements are monologic rather than dialogic: he uses both professional and non-professional actors as filters for a-signifying collective utterances. The 'text' is often initially a collective effort by those taking part and continues to call for collective endeavour on the part of the audience. His theatre produces a constant interplay of visual, verbal and auditory elements, which problematise the relation of image to language and challenge the onlookers to occupy subjectively whatever spaces are offered for their fantasies.

Müller, who admires and is intrigued by Wilson's refusal to do the work of interpretation, joined forces with him over *Hamletmaschine* in the course of 1986. Its first staging was in New York, its second in Hamburg (later televised), and its third in London (November, 1987). What is striking about the performance in general, whether staged or filmed, is the way a text barely nine sides long is converted into a session lasting well over two hours. The most noticeable feature of the production is the rigid repetition of a sequence of movements from scene to scene, whereby what starts out as random is turned into an expected pattern, re-contextualised in each scene by Müller's script. The repetition is given peculiar force by the device of re-arranging the stage perspective for each scene: everything on the stage is moved clockwise by ninety degrees. What is most striking about seeing and hearing the text, instead of reading it, is the theatricalisation of the space via light and sound, particularly sound. The hallmark of this performance is that there is hardly ever total silence because of the constant background of disconcerting noises. In the latter half of the play, these include harrowing screams and screeches (known as 'scream-songs' in the language of performance theatre), retchings, groans, sobs, whispers and finally sudden fragments of a popular tune blaring out shockingly to disrupt the silence staged at the end. There is an incessant collage of different noises—a repeated snapping sound, sporadic bangs, and a repetitive little tune with chromatic leaps played on an off-key piano—some of which are in a kind of syncopation with both the lighting effects and the speech or lack of speech. The tune evokes the failure of romantic enchantment, the noises the contingency of the real both outside and inside the subject. The monotony of all these sounds produces the effect of intermittent lapses and regainings of attention to them, which induces a general disorienting effect.

What experimental theatre has done from Artaud onwards is to play with the formation of subjective spaces in order to disrupt and invade the symbolisation that has taken place in language. The phonemic distortions of language are a powerful and original means of undermining the authority system. Müller subverts the very processes by which language comes to mean. The theatre of Wilson and Müller can thereby become the analyst of the spectator's illusory relation to language. Whereas in Pina Bausch the stage figures are in the grip of their fantasies, in *Hamletmaschine* the main characters refuse to be vehicles for the fantasies of their dramatist-creator and reject the definitions imposed on them by language: the resulting polyvocal, often a-signifying utterances are therefore far from being the symptoms of psychotics who disavow reality. The disturbance of normal speech is rather to count as an onslaught on the complacency of any self-justifying social system.

Müller's Hamlet is the intellectual gone bankrupt, bereft of his function as critic and prophet. In Scene 1 he declares at the outset 'I was Hamlet. I stood on the shore and I talked with the serf BLABLA, the ruins of Europe behind me'.[26] In Scene 3 he wants to be a woman and be dressed up in Ophelia's clothes. And in Scene 4 he no longer appears as Hamlet, but as 'Hamlet-player'. Müller's Hamlet is filled with nausea. He would like to opt out of history in analogous fashion to Shakespeare's hero. His wish to withdraw from history tropes Hamlet's desire for incest, generalising it into a larger gesture which marks a longing to escape to a timeless realm free from oppression. He stumps about, dressed like a Hell's Angel, now and again mechanically sagging at the knee, spoken by a polyphony of voices, some amplified, others not, producing a stereophonic effect. To be or not to be a machine, that is the question. On the one hand, the nausea of killing, 'I don't want to kill any more'; on the other hand, the way out, 'I want to be a machine'. Yet even to be in a position to consider these as alternatives is a betrayal, a failure of commitment, as the Hamlet-player knows: 'I am a privileged person My nausea/is a privilege' and he tears up a photograph of Heiner Müller, author of *Hamletmaschine*.[27]

Hamlet's failure to become a revolutionary subject is contrasted with Ophelia's refusal to remain a pathetic victim of male oppression. Ophelia, as Elaine Showalter's study of madness as 'the female malady' has amply documented,[28] came to typify female insanity for the Victorians, as much in medicine as in art and literature. Ophelia's passion was a source of fascination from the Elizabethan to the Freudian age, but until Müller, her stage presence had undergone no significant sea-change. For Müller, her revolutionary potential lies in the experience of oppression which defines the revolutionary subject in general and woman in particular. She therefore becomes representative of the forces of anarchism and revolt which arise out of this situation. Yet, paradoxically, she is rigidly confined to a wheelchair, herself machinic in her desire for vengeance, performing jerky robot-like movements, manically scratching her head; sometimes she is a distant inconspicuous presence, sometimes she is in full close-up—eyes staring, semi-toothless mouth gaping wide open, coarse grey hair giving off wisps of dust, spoken by a number of voices:

> I am Ophelia. The one the river didn't keep. The woman dangling from the rope. The woman with her arteries cut open. The woman with the overdose. Snow on her lips. The woman with her head in the gas oven. Yesterday I stopped killing myself. I'm alone with my breasts my thighs my womb.[29]

Though Ophelia is finally to be swathed in bandages from head to foot, she is nevertheless adopting the revolutionary position as against Hamlet's counter-revolutionary one, in that she appears as a woman, emancipated from her oppression, full of hate. The distinctions between the two are never quite clear cut, since both figures are spoken by others, as well as uttering themselves. Two languages emerge most distinctly: an official stage language which is elocuted by representative figures on the stage and which never comes from Ophelia in the chair, and another, unofficial, spasmodic, gasping, stuttering language, an intermittent echo of the first, mocking and subverting its clear enunciation. In both languages, the articulate and the inchoate, Electra/Ophelia repudiates her self-slaughter, her female functions of bearing and nursing children, and her role as sexual object, and proclaims her revolutionary commitment, taking up the stance of a terrorist:

> It is Electra who speaks. In the heart of darkness. Under the sun of torture. To the capitals of the world. In the name of the victims. I eject all the sperm I have received. I turn the milk of my breasts into lethal poison. I take back the world I gave birth to. I choke between my thighs the world I gave birth to. Down with the joy of submission. Long live hate and contempt, rebellion and death. When she walks through your bedrooms with butcher knives, you'll know the truth.[30]

These are the final words (except for stage directions, which are spoken aloud throughout) marking an ironic shift from Hamlet's initial BLABLA to Ophelia/Electra's refusal of BLABLA via a hate-filled silence.

Müller has remarked that 'if you don't come to grips with *Hamletmaschine* as a comedy, you won't make anything out of the play'.[31] Comic elements in *Hamletmaschine* might be discerned in the way sexual roles are destabilised and parodied throughout: a proliferation of voices undermines any fixed expectations of pitch matching gender.

A radical intertextuality takes the place of dialogue and opens a space for the comic. In this production, one way in which the reification of social role is parodied is via three zombie-like women, heavily made up, with an air of masquerading as something, all in unconscious agreement as to what it is. They have insane expressions on their faces, one hand rhythmically scratching or madly plucking at their hair, the other stiffly laid on the table, all in perfectly synchronised movements. They are more than mere representatives of bureaucracy and economy: the reification is internalised and going on inside their heads. Müller undermines via the unconscious, disturbing the spectator's self-image by the patent inner automatism of these crazed super-ego-figures, full of ineffectual severity, performing pointless tasks.

Müller is pessimistic about history. He updates *Hamlet*, making it relevant for our time: merely to indulge in anguish is a luxury. Like Brecht, Müller is an iconoclast, but he does more than attack the icons of the bourgeois world; he goes for the very structures of the bourgeois subject, as Freud revealed them, analysing not the economic contradictions, but the contradictions in the construction of the psyche. The subject is social, because the social comes to dwell within it, but the body is not the individual that results: Müller's polyphonic discourse demonstrates that the body is mere contingency of matter, material out of which the subject is made. He shows gruesomely the mess that results when the self-making apparatus, the machine, goes wrong, and the unsymbolised elements of the body jam the system and fill the world with noise. It is a pessimistic demonstration, since Müller makes it clear that this process is not necessarily revolutionary: the nausea of his Hamlet-player shows that modes of reaction against the system are often forms of the system, in that certain forms of revolution are bourgeois in themselves.

In what way, then, is it political rather than 'psychopathological' theatre? Far from 'diverting' the spectator and luring him into a gain of 'masochistic' satisfaction, Müller provides a theatre that (like psychoanalysis) plays out the 'true' time of the subject, its fears and fantasies, as against the 'false' time of history, including literary history with its privileging of great works as accomplices of power. Like Freud, Müller wants to retrieve the subjective from the crystallisations of history, but, unlike Freud, he does not see the artist's function as supplying a necessary consolation: it is rather to teach the unteachable, to get the spectator to confront the recalcitrant nature of the real in history and in the body.

Post-Freudian psychoanalysis challenges any simple notion of mimesis, whether applied to the conscious or the unconscious. The discontinuities in the narratives of the subject, which displace the big narratives and grand illusions of the past, betray the theatrical nature of reality: the subject is theatrical through and through. The post-Freudian theatre, in the wake of Lacan, reveals theatricality as a necessary element in the construction of the subject. Its effect is to make the subject (artist and spectator) experience the gap between the body as a discursive construct and its felt embodiment in experience, between the representational and the real, and to expose it to continual risk of re-definition.

## Notes

I should like to thank Martin Stanton for insightful comments on this paper. Some of the material concerning the playwright Hether Müller has appeared in my book on Brecht (see note 16).

1 Jean-François Lyotard, 'Beyond representation' in A. Benjamin (ed.), *The Lyotard Reader* (Oxford, Basil Blackwell, 1989), pp. 155–68; see p. 156.
2 Sigmund Freud, 'Psychopathic characters on the stage' [1905–6] in A. Dickson (ed.), *Art and Literature*, The Pelican Freud Library Vol. 14 (Harmondsworth, Penguin, 1985), pp. 129–41; see p. 125.
3 A. Green, transl. A. Sheridan, *The Tragic Effect: The Oedipus Complex in Tragedy* (Cambridge, Cambridge University Press, 1979), p. 1.
4 *Ibid.*, p. 3.
5 *Ibid.*, p. 24.
6 Sigmund Freud, 'Creative writers and day-dreaming' [1908], in A. Dickson (ed.), *Art and Literature*, The Pelican Freud Library Vol. 14 (Harmondsworth, Penguin, 1985), pp. 119–27. See also E. Wright, *Psychoanalytic Criticism: Theory in Practice* (London and New York, Routledge, 1984), pp. 27–9.
7 Green, *The Tragic Effect*, pp. 22–3.
8 *Ibid.*, p. 12.
9 *Ibid.*, p. 16.
10 P. Lacoue-Labarthe, 'Theatrum Analyticum', *Glyph*, 2 (1977), 122–43; see 133.
11 Sigmund Freud, 'Beyond the Pleasure Principle' [1920], in A. Richards (ed.), *On Metapsychology*, The Pelican Freud Library Vol. 11 (Harmondsworth, Penguin, 1985), pp. 269–338; see p. 284.
12 P. Phelan, *Unmarked: The Politics of Performance* (London and New York, Routledge, 1993).
13 Jean-François Lyotard, 'Answering the question: what is postmodernism?' in I. Hassan and S. Hassan (eds.), *Innovation/Renovation: New Perspective on the Humanities* (Madison, Wisconsin University Press, 1983), pp. 329–411.
14 Lacoue-Labarthe, 'Theatrum Analyticum', 139.
15 G. Deleuze, transl. Paul Patton, *Difference and Repetition* (London, The Athlone Press, 1994), p. 112.
16 E. Wright, *Postmodern Brecht: A Re-Presentation* (London and New York, Routledge, 1989).

17 H. Blau, *The Eye of Prey. Subversions of the Postmodern* (Bloomington and Indianapolis, Indiana University Press, 1987), p. 166.
18 *Ibid.*, p. 164.
19 *Ibid.*, p. 171.
20 Cornelius Castoriadis, 'Psychoanalysis and Politics', in Sonu Shamdasani and Michael Münchow (eds.), *Speculations after Freud: Psychoanalysis, Philosophy and Culture* (London and New York, Routledge, 1994), p. 1–11.
21 *Ibid.*, p. 11.
22 S. Žižek, *Enjoy Your Symptom: Jacques Lacan in Hollywood and Out* (London and New York, Routledge, 1992).
23 J. Féral, transl. Terese Lyons, 'Performance and theatricality: the subject demystified', *Modern Drama*, 25:1 (1982), 170–81; see p. 172.
24 G. Schulz, *Heiner Müller* (Stuttgart, Metzler, 1980), p. 149.
25 H. Müller, *Gesammelte Irrtümer: Interviews und Gespräche* (Frankfurt, Verlag der Autoren, 1986), p. 18.
26 H. Müller, *Hamletmaschine* in *Mauser* (Berlin, Rotbuch Verlag, 1986), pp. 55–69; see p. 89.
27 *Ibid.*, p. 96.
28 Elaine Showalter, *The Female Malady: Women, Madness and English Culture, 1830–1980* (New York, Pantheon, 1985).
29 Müller, *Hamletmaschine*, p. 91.
30 *Ibid.*, p. 97.
31 Müller, *Gesammelte Irrtümer*, p. 115.

# PART III

# ISSUES IN PERFORMANCE

11 *Jatinder Verma*

# The challenge of Binglish: analysing multi-cultural productions

While the analysis of performance is, at the best of times, an exercise fraught with uncertainties—who decides what is perceived?—the analysis of multi-cultural productions in contemporary Britain is fairly riddled with imprecision and muddled thinking. 'Cross-cultural', 'inter-cultural', 'intra-cultural', 'integrated', 'culturally-diverse' . . . these are all terms that, in varying ways, are descriptive of 'multi-cultural'.

In Britain, multi-cultural productions have evolved specifically as a practical response to a socio-political issue: the need to see on British stages performers from 'coloured' backgrounds: i.e., performers who are racially different from white Anglo-Saxons. In 30 years since this issue began to emerge—on the back of large-scale migration to Britain from the Indian sub-continent and the Caribbean—we have witnessed varying approaches to this new dynamic in British society. Many theatre productions today, both on main stages and small touring companies, feature some form of racially-mixed casts. This has in no small part been stimulated by the rise, also, of independent Asian and black companies since the 1970s; three of which—Black Theatre Co-operative, Talawa and Tara Arts—are now firmly part of national theatre provision in Britain.

The very diversity of current expressions of 'multi-cultural' in theatre production begs the need for clarification. Is a production by an Asian or black theatre company—directed by a black director, written by a black and featuring black performers—a 'multi-cultural' production? Is a production featuring a racially-mixed cast, directed by a white director, written by a white, more properly to be termed a 'multi-cultural' production? Or is the example offered by the work of Peter Brook and Ariane Mnouchkine in Paris the best definition of 'multi-cultural'?

I propose the following conceptual clarifications; and thereby also lay out the focus of my own enquiry in this essay:

*Multi-cultural* is a term most appropriately descriptive of those productions featuring a racially-mixed cast which, by not seeking to draw attention to the racial mix of the producing team, are not generally attempting to confront the dominant text-based convention of British theatre. The attempt here is to sustain a familiar view of the world, through use of existing conventions of British theatre and so subsume the potential for unfamiliarity created by the unconventional casting.

*Cross-cultural* productions are those which overtly draw upon the encounters between different cultural sensibilities, as these are represented in their producing teams—actors, directors, designers, writers, etc. The intention here is invariably to re-imagine the world, with the conventions of the English or European stage largely ignored, or seriously questioned.

*Binglish* is a term I propose to denote a distinct contemporary theatre praxis: featuring Asian or black casts, produced by independent Asian or black theatre companies. The attempt here, I would argue, is directly to challenge or provoke the dominant conventions of the English stage. Binglish productions can contain both the above definitions; but the former are not the same as Binglish productions.

(I appropriate the term 'Binglish' from the word used by contemporary Singaporeans to describe their spoken language, 'Singlish'. I use it to suggest a form of spoken English as much as a *process*: Asian and black life in modern Britain is self-evidently 'not-quite English'; and, equally, is characterised by a striving to 'be English'. I believe it is this ambivalent sensibility that forms a *sine qua non* of Asian and black life in Britain today; a sensibility that is at the heart of the title of my essay.)

The above definitions would suggest that the full scope of this topic is beyond the limitations of an essay-form. I will therefore confine myself to analyses of Binglish productions. Given my assertion that such productions can be both multi- and cross-cultural, I would hope that, while limiting my field of reference, there will be insights gained that could be applied to multi- and cross-cultural productions.

### How is a Binglish production to be analysed?

Irving Wardle's comments in the *Independent on Sunday* on my production of *Troilus and Cressida* provide a pithy summary of the problematic of analysing Binglish productions. I quote: '. . . in the case of Jatinder Verma's production of *Troilus and Cressida* I feel an attack of blimpish nationalism coming on; damned outsider gatecrashing the club, doesn't know the rules . . . Eventually, if not quite yet, the club will have to find room for it . . .'.[1] Wardle accurately points up the 'outsider' nature of Binglish productions, as much as, and more reluctantly perhaps, their inevitable rise.

The 'outsider' view is shared by several critics. One such, when asked how he came to shows produced by Asian and black theatre companies—did he, for example, come out of an interest in the type of theatre production that the company undertook or because of what the company represented as a type within British theatre?—replied, to his credit, that he went to shows by Asian or black companies because these were 'ethnic' companies.[2]

Viewed as 'outsiders' or, at best, marginal, Binglish productions can (among the more liberal-minded) be generically analysed as a 'good thing'; a form of political correctness that finds its correlative in the fact that many Asian and black audiences flock to Binglish productions because they can relate more readily to the producers, the themes and the manners of their expression. *Social goodwill*, then, undoubtedly forms a part of any analysis of such productions.

Another defining feature of Binglish productions is their use of 'other' texts. I use the adjective 'other' to describe a wide range of texts: existing European texts, adaptations of such texts, new texts from Asian and black writers, texts from Asia and Africa. What characterises their 'other-ness'? *Provocation*. Yvonne Brewster's Talawa Theatre Company presented in the early 1990s a production of Oscar Wilde's *Lady Windermere's Fan*. Featuring an all-black cast, the text was presented in period and 'as is': no adaptation was undertaken to justify the use of an all-black cast. As one national critic remarked, however, he could not ignore a moment of frisson, when one of the characters talked of 'gazing into your deep blue eyes'![3]

If the element of provocation is implicit in even the most conventional of Binglish productions, it achieves considerable amplification in adaptations and texts from the non-European world. It is worth here re-reading Irving Wardle's comments above on my production of *Troilus and Cressida*. The same critic also commented on my production of an ancient Indian play, *The Little Clay Cart*, for the Royal National Theatre: '. . . A few more shows like this and Western linear theatre will start looking primitive.'[4]

According to the Oxford English Dictionary, 'provocative' has the sense of 'tending to excite or enrage', as much as of 'stimulating, irritating'. I believe all these meanings are in operation in the perception of Binglish productions, in producers, audiences and critics alike. This sensibility of provocation is implicit, of course, in the very act of forming independent companies, which act, in turn, takes its impetus from contemporary British life. The impact of relatively large-scale Asian and black immigration into Britain since the late 1950s has in essence been provocative: provoking issues of race, nationality, ethnicity, identity, community, equality of opportunity, justice, law and order. These form the often 'hidden texts' of modern multi-cultural Britain. Postcolonial Britain, by an ironic act of symmetry, is undergoing the same uncertain groping towards defining itself as are the countries that were once colonised by Britain.

The provocation of Binglish productions, I would contend, is to stimulate other ways of 'seeing'. Is a French classic, with its history of translation into English theatre as a stylised comedy of manners, so bound within this defining convention as to be incapable of being seen as an 'Indian' play? Stylised according to an Indian vocabulary of gesture, mode of speech, dress, music, theatrical convention? Theoretically, one should be able to answer, why not? In practice, however, the provocation of such an act is not to be underestimated. Both my productions of Molière's comedies (*Tartuffe* for the Royal National Theatre and *Le Bourgeois Gentilhomme* for Tara Arts) were exercises in 'tradaptation', to use Robert Lepage's term.[5] Set in equivalent periods in India to when Molière originally wrote the texts, they provoked a re-perception of the Molière classic. As I overheard one irate member of the audience remark to the box-office attendant at Glasgow's Tron Theatre during the interval of the 1994 production of *Le Bourgeois Gentilhomme*, 'this is not Molière'! A sentiment echoed by Margaret Burgess in a regional paper during the tour of *Tartuffe*: 'Somewhere in France this week Molière is turning in his grave . . . For me, [the conception of *Tartuffe*] was as valid as transporting *A Passage to India* to Paris!'[6] What is 'acceptable' is here being confronted; what is being contested is the notion of the 'authentic' [see Chapter 13 (ed.)].

The 'foreign-ness' of Indian music, dress, mode of speech ('singsong English')—indeed, the very 'foreign-ness' of seeing a troupe of Indian performers flirting with the English language—these are all elements which are out-of-the-norm for the average British theatre-goer.

Aside from adaptations, 'other' texts also include themes which are new to Britain. An example is provided by Tamasha Theatre Company's production of *The Untouchable* in 1989. Based on a novel by Mulk Raj Anand, one of India's greatest living novelists (who was first introduced to British tastes by Graham Greene), the play considered the plight of the 'untouchable' community in India. As a specific social group, the 'untouchables' have no equivalent in Britain, except within the Asian community. Yet it requires no great exercise of imagination to see in this play a metaphor for the new 'untouchables' of Britain: the Britons of black or Asian origin. As in India, these are also barred from certain occupations and areas of settlement. Their touch is 'polluting'; though a pollution that, unlike in India, has no religious or cultural validation.

Underlining the other-ness of the texts, Binglish productions are also characterised by a linguistic distinction: what I alluded to above when talking of 'flirting with the English language'. *Flirtation* is the 'ambivalent sensibility' that is central to Binglish. Talawa Theatre Company's production of *King Lear* in 1993 and Tamasha's *Women of Dust* (1992) offer two contrasting though related illustrations of such flirtation. While Talawa's *King Lear* did not set out to adapt Shakespeare's text (unlike what I attempted with *Troilus*), the audience was nevertheless made to experience a variety of *langue*; Caribbean, West African, as much as an RSC-derived 'received pronunciation', vied with each other to create a rich tapestry of the *sound* of English. The resonance of the Caribbean accent, in particular, took on associative meanings for black members of the audience that made Shakespeare's text immediately their own. Here it could be claimed with some justification that ownership of the text was being contested through the sounds of the English language: when the production was employing a more conventional spoken English, white members of the audience were 'in tune'; when it was less conventional, it was time for the Black members to assert their ownership—which they often did with great vocal gusto.

In Tamasha's *Women of Dust*, conventional spoken English was distorted by the adoption of Rajasthani speech patterns (the play explored the lives of Rajasthani women migrant workers in North India). This was further distorted by exclamations in Hindi. To British ears, Indian-English speech is governed by conventions that derive ultimately from Empire days: 'singsong', a curious penchant for dropping definite articles, florid: conventions that achieved their defining caricature at the hands of Peter Sellers in the film *The Party*. Indian languages *per se*, of course, remain wholly foreign. (Though I should qualify this: waiting at a suburban London railway station recently on a cold wet night, I was astounded when an elderly Englishman came up to me and started speaking in Hindi! I took me a few beats to realise what he was doing and to reply in Hindi. He had been a trader in India during the Independence era, selling goods to both warring factions along the Indo-Pakistani border!)

One characteristic feature of spoken English-English (as opposed to American or any other form of English), it seems to me, is *understatement*, typified by the caricature of the 'stiff upper lip'. All caricatures have some basis in reality and this is no exception. The understatement of English-English is a development of Imperial times, when little England was assured of its power across the globe. This mode can therefore also be seen as a form of excluding others from power—the colonised, the working classes, those who do not belong to 'the club'. A mode which, in daily life, quintessentially expresses English racial discrimination. From this perspective, Asians and blacks, excluded therefore from English-English, have learnt the art of direct statement. Our use of English is more expressive, more emotive, more declamatory—'rhetorical'—to English-English ears. The conventional English comedy of manners for example is bound to sound provocative under such conditions.

*Langue*, as used in this essay, has therefore come to mean language, accent and mode of speech. And it is these varieties of *langue* that English-English audiences are having to negotiate in Binglish productions. Such negotiation of *langue*, I would argue, is a defining feature of Binglish—using the term here in both its senses: as a form of language and a distinctive theatre praxis. It is this negotiation that modern audiences are most obviously confronted with in Binglish productions; introducing them to a greater auditory experience and, by implication, challenging them—most especially, critics in their midst—to acquire a wider auditory range. These varying *langues*—Caribbean, Hindi, Punjabi, Gujarati, Urdu, Bengali, Tamil, Ghanaian, Nigerian, Somali—form part of the linguistic map of modern Britain: they cannot be expected to be absent from modern British theatre. Such training of the ear, I would argue, is also a challenge thrown up by 'cross-cultural' productions; as was evident in Michael Billington's response to Sotigui Kouyote's characterisation of Prospero in Peter Brook's version of *The Tempest*.[7]

If the spoken language offers a challenge to audiences of Binglish productions, then no less do the *forms of presentation*. Using imagery and other stage vocabulary derived from the non-European parts of the world, Binglish productions challenge the dominant European imagery of theatre. These challenges in form vary from company to company. I will concentrate a while on the practice of Tara Arts, a company with which I am obviously very familiar. I do so because Tara challenges forms from this perspective more consistently than any other independent Asian or black company at present. This assertion merely reflects a conscious search by Tara for a distinctive theatrical form—a search that is at least a decade old now.

Tara's search is premised on classical Indian aesthetics. The central premise of classical Indian theatre—which is shared by classical Chinese, Japanese and all South-east Asian theatres—is its eschewing of the photographic sense of 'reality'. As the earliest treatise on the theatre, the *Natya-Shastra*, puts it, drama must be 'a delight to the eyes as much as the ears'.[8]

Composed about AD 400 (the composition is attributed to Bharata, which is also a generic name for India), this treatise is the most comprehensive manual on the art of performance anywhere in the world, superseding in its practical detail and depth of theory even the works of Aristotle and Stanislavski. Bharata posits four constituent elements of theatre: *Abhinaya*—Gesture (which includes movement); *Vacikam*—Speech (which includes music); *Aharayam*—Costume (which includes make-up); and *Sattvikam*—the Mind (which includes emotion). These four achieve their classical representation in the image of the god Shiva, dancing with one foot on the earth and the other along with the arms held aloft: an image reproduced in countless sculptures and paintings, and evoked in countless poems. This fourfold conception of theatre led to a practice that Brecht, much later, in 1935, described as 'total theatre', on seeing a troupe of Beijing Opera actors in Berlin.[9] Movement and music, in this conception, are not ancillary to the spoken word but form an integral part of the 'text' of performance.

At the heart of the *Natya-Shastra* is the theory of *rasa*, translated by one modern commentary as 'aesthetic rapture'.[10] The closest modern rendering of the word would be 'flavour', as in the flavour of food—a metaphor that Bharata makes much use of in the *Natya-Shastra*. For the act of savouring food is an emotive as much as a functional act. A discussion of *rasa* is outside the scope of this article but I cannot leave the subject without offering the highly suggestive rendering by Abhinavagupta, an early medieval Indian literary critic: 'The actor . . . does not experience *rasa*, nor does the original character, nor even the author. For rasa implies distance. Without this aesthetic distance, there cannot exist literature, only the primary world.'[11]

I have gone to some lengths to sketch Tara's approach to performance, to suggest what underpins the company's rejection of the dominant convention of the modern English stage—the spoken word. Gesture is speech, as much as a phrase of music is a sentence or the passage of time. It is in this sense that the word, in Tara's productions, takes on the texture also of dance and music. Removing one element immeasurably reduces the whole production. The apparent simplicity of this assertion is dispelled the moment one pauses to consider that both the movement and music vocabularies are Indian-based. To most Western eyes and ears, these are at best, respectively, exotic and foreign.

This drawing upon other, non-European vocabularies of movement, music and imagery is in my view a defining characteristic of all Binglish productions. In Tamasha's *Women of Dust* for example, much of the play was spent by the characters sitting on the floor on their haunches. Such physical expression of manual labour is quite foreign to Britain. While Talawa and Black Theatre Co-operative do not draw upon Indian theatre practice, in their usage of African and Caribbean music, movement and ritual forms, they share a common tendency.

Such productions can therefore also be characterised as *negotiating a foreign-ness*. A foreign-ness not quite 'pure' as it is expressed in a flirtatious English (Binglish)! Thus a modern white audience in Britain experiencing a Binglish production could be said to be oscillating continuously between the sense of the native, the familiar and the foreign. It is this characteristic, more than any other, that distinguishes Binglish productions from multi-cultural ones (in the sense in which I have defined the latter). Multi-cultural productions are premised on the familiar; even their experiments in integrated casting aim to make the un-familiar (Asian or Black faces amidst White) *acceptable*. Binglish productions, on the other hand, overtly seek to establish other rules of the game.

Trevor Nunn's production of *Timon of Athens* for the Young Vic in 1991, offers an interesting example. Nunn, as he neared his retirement from the RSC, came increasingly to see the necessity for multi-cultural productions, as his celebrated *Othello* with Willard White testifies. In *Timon*, his cast included one Asian. The production, inevitably perhaps, given Nunn's history, was determined by the RSC's approach to speaking Shakespeare's text: the infamous 'received pronunciation'. Yet in its Asian member of cast, the production possessed an actor who could not speak in such a manner even if he tried: his English was clearly conditioned by the rhythms of his Gujarati mother-tongue. For me, this actor 'stood out', unfavourably, in comparison with the rest of the cast. I found myself feeling, 'why can't he speak like the others?' The failure of the production, for me, lies not in Trevor Nunn's decision to have a multi-racial cast—indeed, I would applaud him for that—but in failing to recognise the challenge such an actor posed to his own conception of how Shakespeare ought to be spoken. Had all the cast been encouraged to employ their natural accents or variants of

English speech—Lancastrian, Yorkshire, Cornish, etc.—the sense of having an integrated cast would have gone further. Instead, one was left with a faint aftertaste of having been witness to a deracinating process, which I believe to be the ultimate implication of a 'colour-blind' approach to casting. (This is a term which I must confess I have never been able to understand. How can I, as a member of the audience or as a practitioner, be oblivious to my colour or the colour of the actors I see on stage? It is part of what makes me particular in the world today. And is not theatre the art of making the particular reveal connections with other particularities?)

### Summary

In conclusion, I would argue that the particular type of multi-cultural productions I have analysed (Binglish) are characterised by their usage of 'other' texts, distinctive *langue*, and non-European stage vocabulary. What I have called their flirtation with English leads both practitioners and audiences alike to experience a constant negotiation between the familiar and the unfamiliar: between the sense of 'native' and 'foreign'. And this flirtation, I have tried to suggest, is a reflection of contemporary ambivalence to and of the new Britons: Asians and blacks. Binglish productions are, in sum, creating a 'different sort of noise' in English theatre (to use Salman Rushdie's trenchant phrase),[12] by a combination of colour, *langue* and forms of expression.

By implication, I am arguing also for the necessity of extending the current critical vocabulary of theatre, if multi-cultural productions generally, and Binglish productions in particular, are properly to be appreciated. I can only hope that this essay is a contribution to such an extension.

### Notes

1 Irving Wardle, *Independent on Sunday*, 3 October 1993.
2 A conversation with Michael Coveney of *The Observer*.
3 Alex Renton, *The Independent*, 18 May 1989.
4 Irving Wardle, *Independent on Sunday*, 8 December 1991.
5 Interview with Robert Lepage, *The Guardian*, 5 October 1994. Lepage uses the term to convey the sense of annexing old texts to new cultural contexts.
6 Review by Margaret Burgess, *Surrey Advertiser*, 28 June 1991.
7 Michael Billington, *The Guardian*, 28 May 1993.
8 *Natya-Shastra*, transl. Dr Adya Rangacharya (IBH Prakashana, Bangalore, 1986).

9 John Willett (transl. and ed.), 'Alienation Effects in Chinese Acting', *Brecht on Theatre* (London, Methuen, 1964), pp. 91–7.

10 J. L. Masson and M. V. Patwardhan, *Aesthetic Rapture*, 2 vols. (Poona, Deccan College, 1970). This excellent book analyses Abhinangupta's ideas, as found in his commentary, the *Abhinavabharati*, composed in the 9th century AD.

11 *Ibid.*, vol. 1, p. 24.

12 Interview with Jeremy Isaacs, 'Face to Face', BBC TV, 10 October 1994.

12 *Lizbeth Goodman*

# AIDS and live art

> Those who try to separate theatre from politics lead us into error—and this is a political attitude (Augusto Boal, *Theatre of the Oppressed*).[1]

All theatre is political in so far as performance influences audiences in a shared playing space and ideas communicated back and forth across the stage/world divide can affect social change.[2] The process may be slow, however, and in the age of mass communications, the proliferation of political messages and performance practice to small audiences may seem too great an effort to make; yet this way of thinking assumes that only the audience present in any given venue or playing space is affected by a live art work on AIDS. In fact, the larger impact of the collective body of work has been considerable, and can be discussed in terms of both the obvious signs and what might be called the 'accidental semiotics': the range of images, metaphors and ideas now associated with the AIDS pandemic, influenced by and influencing the development of performance practice and theory.

So, while all theatre is political, theatre and other performance work about AIDS is still a special case. More directly or actively political than most theatre, it takes an issue of social significance and demands that the audience pay attention. It reaches out to audiences across lines of gender and sexuality. Yet the impact of AIDS and performance work also reaches beyond its single-issue focus to touch on a number of related threads in the 'quilt' of social representations today: the representation of sex and queer culture, the role of the audience in the mainstream and 'alternative' performance of social issues, the representation of women by and through AIDS work, the theatricality of politics and the politics of theatricality.[3]

### Quilting and queer culture: AIDS in the public space

Current studies and statistics show that AIDS is a social problem of epic proportions with racial, as well as class and gender, implications.[4] But while it is now common knowledge that AIDS is not 'just' a gay men's problem, the representation of the pandemic in the media is still biased, still often connected to gay male sexuality: an effective strategy for marginalising what is more appropriately a mainstream subject. At the same time, live arts work in the past decade has been a visible and vocal forum for the representation of AIDS and its 'symptoms', physical and cultural. But of course, live arts are commonly marginalised as art forms, and 'special-issue groups' and individual performance artists were not, until very recently, accorded any kind of mainstream status or funding for their work. While gay and feminist theatres remained marginalised by funding bodies and West End producers, for instance, theatre work about AIDS remained, quite literally, on the fringe. In 1994, after the American import to Britain of major stage events such as *Angels in America*, live arts work about AIDS is much more acceptable; that is, the images and ideas expressed are in danger of being homogenised, sanitised to please a mainstream audience. Yet some of the most daring and provocative work about AIDS still occurs on the margins, at major and deliberately 'alternative' venues such as London's prestigious ICA (Institute of Contemporary Arts), for example, and at smaller 'fringe' venues. The work ranges enormously in style and political perspective, from large-scale plays, to small ensemble pieces, to solo work in the dance and movement arts. In all this work, however, the personal and the political are intertwined in a way which supports Boal's idea that the attempt to separate theatre from politics is itself a political action: even when the images of the work are 'political' in an inherited sense; even when they are imported from other movements to connect political lines and community perspectives.

The most obvious symbol of inherited or borrowed or associative sign-systems operative in the AIDS pandemic's cultural representation is the quilt: a craft or art form commonly associated with 'women's work', long undervalued and recently adopted by feminist literary critics and AIDS activists alike in their similar but separate struggles to find acceptable and effective fabrics or threads to bind together the many different patterns of their arguments, for the use of many different people.

'If anything good rises from AIDS, it's to remind us why we live': this statement is taken from the promotional blurb for *Quilt*,

12.1] *Quilt*, directed by Carole Charnow for Moving Target Theatre, 1994. *Left to right:* Anthony Clegg, Mindy Lee Raskin, Peter Tamm, William Folan-Conran. (Clive Granger)

billed as 'a musical celebration of the NAMES Project AIDS Memorial Quilt'; a project which has involved some 28,000 people making individual panels to commemorate victims of AIDS.

*Quilt* combines songs and stories to engage audience members with the lives of some of those lost to the disease. It is only one in a line of performance events aiming to bring AIDS into the mainstream by adding music and popular formats, though most such work (like *Quilt*, which played at London's Oval House Theatre, a small venue noted for its feminist, black and lesbian/gay performance work) plays to relatively small audiences. By contrast, some theatre and AIDS material has been enormously successful in the mainstream: *Angels in America*, for instance, and *Marvin's Room*, *Jeffrey*, and *The Baltimore Waltz*. The latter is perhaps the best-known AIDS play to date by a woman, Paula Vogel, described by one critic as 'a postmodern performance of quilting as a celebration of mourning': a description which emphasised both the positive and negative aspects of theatrical representation of AIDS.[5]

The promotional blurb for the AIDS play *Quilt* emphasises the attempt to find something to celebrate, to construct a positive framework for seeing and remembering the many individuals lost to the disease. This approach offers two different ways of seeing the impact of AIDS: as a community problem and a loss of individual lives. The former aims to foster community spirit in the face of the pandemic (an aim represented in group actions, performance and artistic projects such as creation of the AIDS Quilt), and the latter aims to commemorate individuals through symbols of their lives (the names, images and messages sewn on to the personalised patches of the AIDS Quilt). Both aims are generally recognised by AIDS workers, artists and critics alike.

The view that AIDS is 'symbolic' of other social problems has become a quiet but significant refrain in the public discussion about the symbolic significance of AIDS. Another refrain in the chorus of debate and dissent is the question, variously phrased, of whether the growing awareness of AIDS in the community is in part a reflection of its focus on men. This argument runs: why an AIDS theatre movement but not a breast cancer theatre movement (when breast cancer is a leading cause of death among women, still largely underfunded and underrepresented in the arts)? Why, indeed, not an evolving body of live arts work on subjects such as domestic violence, or eating disorders or other social issues of primary concern to women's lives?

Of course, there have been plays and dance work, photographs and paintings about these subjects, mainly produced by women artists. Louise Page's play *Tissue* tackled the subject of breast cancer in 1978,[6] and many individual artists and playwrights have handled other controversial 'women's subjects' in their work since, including Emilyn Claid's contemporary dance work which has addressed the subject of eating disorders. Yet the so-called 'women's issues' have not been treated as a major social or cultural phenomenon in the same way that AIDS has. Much of women's work in the AIDS and live arts movement has been creative but, in some sense, also behind the scenes. For example, the vast majority of those who made patches for the quilt featured in the play *Quilt* were women, as the programme note reveals, though the play depicted and featured both women and men. The remarkable book *From Media to Metaphor: Art About AIDS* includes a relatively small proportion of work by women, though women are represented in the visual images and are clearly part of the overall artistic project and political movement which inspired it.[7] As this book aptly illustrates, visual images of AIDS (and its metaphors, to borrow the phrase from Susan Sontag) convey messages of personal and political significance, sometimes depicting and sometimes inspiring public action. Perhaps the gendered disparity in treatment of AIDS as a subject for live arts work is also influenced by and responding to the semiotic power of the AIDS pandemic, and is not merely attributable to an inherent sexism and gender/power bias favouring men and 'men's issues' in the media and performance worlds.

### Gender and the representation of AIDS in theatre and the live arts

Many male artists have made AIDS the subject of their work, from Robert Mapplethorpe to Derek Jarman to Adam Mars-Jones. In the performance arts, where 'real life' and 'drama' can overlap in powerful ways, AIDS has been depicted by playwrights including Larry Kramer (*The Normal Heart*, *The Tragedy of Me*), Scott McPherson (*Marvin's Room*), and Tony Kushner (*Angels in America*), and by performance artists such as Tim Miller, Michael Kearns and Mehmet Sander. Though much international live arts work is now known in the UK and the gap between cultures is beginning to be bridged, it is still the case that most AIDS and performance work is made by men. Theatre work about AIDS, nicknamed 'Theatre of the Plague', has been made primarily—though not exclusively—by and about men.

As the statistics show, AIDS is a major concern for women as well as men. Yet women have not been quite so visible in the artistic representation of the AIDS crisis. In part, the focus of women's work may be attributed to their connection to other communities and issues (including breast cancer, domestic violence and other of the so-called 'women's issues' mentioned above, but also including the daily concerns of mothering and working for lower wages while trying to make ends meet). For women artists, AIDS is one major issue but not the only issue, either for individuals or for women as a group. This may explain why the expression of AIDS in women's art of all kinds tends to look beyond the single issue of AIDS, connecting it to the larger project of performing and analysing sexuality and gender dynamics more generally.

In the US, more than in the UK, there seems to be a much greater public awareness of AIDS as an issue for women, as well as men, and one which is commonly represented in the mass media. Indeed, the American media employ some quite theatrical and political tactics for providing a relatively high-profile representation of the AIDS crisis in which women's role is highlighted. American cable television features adverts for AIDS Awareness, including women's experiences, as well as men's. Prominent billboard displays about AIDS promoted by the

12.2] San Francisco AIDS Foundation promotional campaign photo, 1993. (Annie Leibovitz)

San Francisco AIDS Foundation make women highly visible, not as 'victims' but as survivors, as subjects and artists, and also implicitly as 'target audiences'. It is useful to consider two contrasting visual images which raise certain key ideas for later discussion of performance.

In the image in Figure 12.2, for instance, the artist (photographer Annie Leibovitz), the subjects (the women in the photos) and the subject matter (HIV-positive women) are all gender-specific and woman-focused, even though the message of the campaign is of wider social significance.[8] The image is intended to increase public awareness of AIDS as a problem for all people: not only gay men or people of colour, but also white heterosexual women and, to a lesser extent, also lesbian women and their children, and by extension, also other children affected with the HIV virus from birth. The one image says it all, and the gaze of the two women depicted is highly dramatic and readable in a performative/communicative and political framework: the HIV-positive woman looks out, directly, to the viewer/audience, while the teenage daughter looks to the side, not acknowledging the audience yet appealing to us in a different way through her implied vulnerability, with a slight and seemingly hopeful smile just visible on her lips. The image is static, yet the gaze of the subjects and the implied messages which the image has deliberately communicated all lend the image a certain power of movement or performative communication.

By contrast, the image in Figure 12.3 addresses men and the more sexual side of the AIDS awareness message. In this image, the main subject is a man, pictured moving away from a car; he is an active subject, communicating an action based on a choice: 'no condom, no date'. But this man's eyes are not a focus of the image. His head is in profile, his energy concentrated on movement away from the car, from the centre of the image out beyond its frame. Of the second man, we see only the back of his head, a bit of his arm through the car window, and his eyes, yet the eyes communicate most of the energy and emotion of the image, as they clearly convey disappointment or annoyance at his implied rejection. It is the active man choosing safe sex who we admire. He moves, he thinks, he has the power in the image. The other man merely reacts, and the camera was concerned to show his gaze only; not to frame him as an active person making choices of his own. Yet the image allows us to identify with the second man, or his eyes, reminding us that we, too, might end up alone if we don't practise safe sex. Message conveyed: another successful campaign image.

It is useful to remember these images (the messages they convey, the manner in which they seem to attach individuality to some subjects and not to others) as we move to an analysis of images in the live arts. It is also important that we consider the difference in approach to representation of AIDS (and indeed of sex) in the US and the UK. While the impact of AIDS on 'real' women's lives has not yet been taken up as a mainstream media subject in the UK, in the US, the representation of women and AIDS is more common, especially in the live arts. Perhaps the best-known play about AIDS by a woman is Paula Vogel's *The Baltimore Waltz*: a young woman's homage to the beloved brother who died of AIDS, staging an imagined shared trip to Europe (the trip the brother wanted to take, but which didn't happen before he died).[9] But plays such as this are not typical, in that the literary medium of the script lends them a certain respectability, whatever the subject matter and approach. If we look instead at live arts performances which do not rely to the same extent on the written word, analysis of AIDS imagery is more similar to that of individual visual images (and of course, in any textbook such as this one all we can hope to do is to create some sense of a live performance by offering isolated images and trying to create a context and performance dynamic with words on the page).

An extreme example of American women's live art—a deliberately provocative choice—is the work of Annie Sprinkle: an American ex-porn star and self-made performance artist who claims to try to 'deconstruct' the pornographic gaze in her performance art piece, *Post Post Porn Modernist*. The piece brings in images of AIDS almost accidentally, in slide-projected images of lovers, female and male and transsexual: a moment of harsh reality which interrupts and intervenes in the imaginative flow of the rest of the piece. This indirect reference to AIDS is powerful testimony to those now absent: some of the shadowy pageant of those lost to the art world. In contrast to the sexually explicit and deliberately provocative work of Annie Sprinkle, a wide range of live arts work by women such as Holly Hughes, Marty Pottenger, Penny Arcade, Sandra Bernstein, Holly Near, and musicians Cris Williamson and Tret Fure contributes to the growing body of work by women in North America; much of this does not mention AIDS directly but rather offers images of life and sexuality in the age of AIDS, adding more and more pieces to the larger quilt.

In the UK, women's theatre work is even less explicit about AIDS, though the Drill Hall's production of *Angels, Punks, and Raging Queens* (December 1992) did offer one notable exception. The cast included women and men in a large-scale musical benefit for and about AIDS. Women with AIDS, including a young girl, were the characters and actors, and the performance offered a powerful reminder that the theatre represents issues from 'real life'. As in Michael Kearns's *Intimacies*—in which an HIV-positive actor plays a range of characters, female and male, all of whom have AIDS—so part of the power of *Angels, Punks, and Raging Queens* is the close connection between the actors and the characters they play. Barriers of gender and sexuality are crossed within the plays, even as the actors reach out to those in

12.3] San Francisco AIDS Foundation bus shelter campaign, 1993. (David Martinez)

the audience who are or may be HIV-positive, and to their friends and lovers and families.

### Breaking boundaries, sharing breath: audiences and AIDS

Tim Miller offers a memorable image of AIDS uniting people across the stage/world divide in his powerful new performance piece *Naked Breath*: the metaphor of the shared breath between the living and the dead, crystallised in the image of the road or pathway contained in each of our memories: the road which leads to our memories of home and the past, the places where things have happened to us, where we have loved and been loved and possibly also contracted HIV.[10] In this image, both domestic and sexual, familial and familiar and fantastic, women's experience and men's may find common ground or at least a common means of expression.

The connection between performers and audiences is, as Miller's work implies, part of the live arts performance itself. The impact of theatre and AIDS work is greatest when audiences continue making connections after they leave the theatre. Indeed, the role of the audience is crucial in any investigation of the gender dynamics of AIDS and live arts, since in both the US and the UK, women make themselves very powerfully present in theatre audiences (surveys estimate that roughly 60–70% of theatre audiences are women). Women are out there watching the new 'Theatre of the Plague' and carrying the message into 'real life' as well. As women are still underrepresented in mainstream (Broadway and West End theatres), the underrepresentation of plays by women about AIDS is not really surprising. What *is* surprising is the way in which largely conservative audiences on the Broadway circuit and even in London have warmed to major plays about AIDS. What is compelling is the way in which certain visual images—what might be called 'semiotic signs'—have emerged and remerged in mainstream performance work about AIDS, from the community-created quilt (mainly but not exclusively sewed by women) of the fringe production *Quilt* to the neuter angel (played by women in both the American and British productions) of Tony Kushner's notable success, *Angels in America*.

Here, we arrive at what I call the 'accidental signs of AIDS': that is, the images and visual signs associated with AIDS in the minds of the audience.[11] The term 'semiotics', derived from the Greek word for sign, is often used in an abstract way, confusing its basic definition as the study of signs. In various different contexts, the definition of 'signs' will, of course, vary, but in performance studies semiotics can be defined as the study of performative signs—visual, musical, textual and contextual—or symbols or images connecting one set of ideas and meanings to another. What is most important about the study of semiotics in live arts is the active role of the audience in interpreting the meaning or significance or range of associations and implications of any given sign or symbol.[12] What is most interesting about the semiotics of AIDS and live arts work is the way in which everyday objects and signs most often associated with particular areas (medicine, for instance) become readable as symbolic of life and death in the face of AIDS. Thus, in analysing any AIDS and live arts work, it is important to look not only for intended sign systems set up by performers or directors, but also at the range of possible other interpretations or associations taken by audiences.

There is space here only to discuss, briefly, two more visual images (and it is hoped that readers will want to explore these ideas further by attending live performances).

### Mehmet Sander: moving images and bodily impact

Mehmet Sander's work can be discussed in terms of its deliberate sign-posting of AIDS. Sander's work is physical dance, involving violent falls, jumps, body slams against walls and solid objects: an enactment of the metaphor of entrapment by physical limitations of the body, and of the transcendence of the spirit and creative imagination. For Sander, billed as a 'Turkish-born HIV-positive choreographer', the work represents the pushing of the body to its limits in order to 'leave the audience breathless' and a 'litany of endurance and confrontation that celebrates stamina, risk and survival against the odds'. A press review quoted in the programme picks up on and develops the metaphorical aspect of AIDS performance in its observation that Sander 'pushes his body with a routine only possible with the armor of muscle', to a performance which is 'gutwrenchingly powerful'. The armour of muscle is a metaphor not only for the presence and strength of Sander's body in the playing space, but also for the 'muscle' or determined strength of representing physical risk in the face of AIDS, the strength of the struggle in the gay and lesbian communities against the deadening impact of the disease on individual lives and on the communities themselves. Sander's armour of muscle is a sign for all that is present and absent in the image of AIDS. His live performance work, like the isolated image which follows, is risky, brutal, daring; it leaves the viewer feeling breathless and concerned, as well as intrigued, afraid that the performance may take too

12.4] Mehmet Sander in *Force Solos,* part of the ICA's 'Ask the Angels' season, produced in association with Highways Performance Space, California, in 1994. (Sallie DeEtte Mackie)

much out of the performer, may contribute to and somehow implicate the audience in his eventual demise.

Sander defines his work as deliberately confrontational. He argues that being HIV-positive has excited and invigorated his work, as it has forced him to think about the limitations of the human body generally and his body in particular. In interview, Sander uses the martial arts metaphor for AIDS, arguing that fighting back at HIV is an empowering act,[13] recalling Susan Sontag's use of the metaphors of war and physical combat in her 'AIDS and its Metaphors'.[14] Practice and theory do come together in the experience of one HIV-positive performer. Yet the signs of AIDS are more polysemic, more positive and prevalent than the body of live arts and AIDS work has yet begun to recognise.

### Begging the question: Peta Lily's performance imagery

While Sander's work is deliberately charged with images and signs of AIDS, Peta Lily's production *BEG!* offers an example of 'accidental

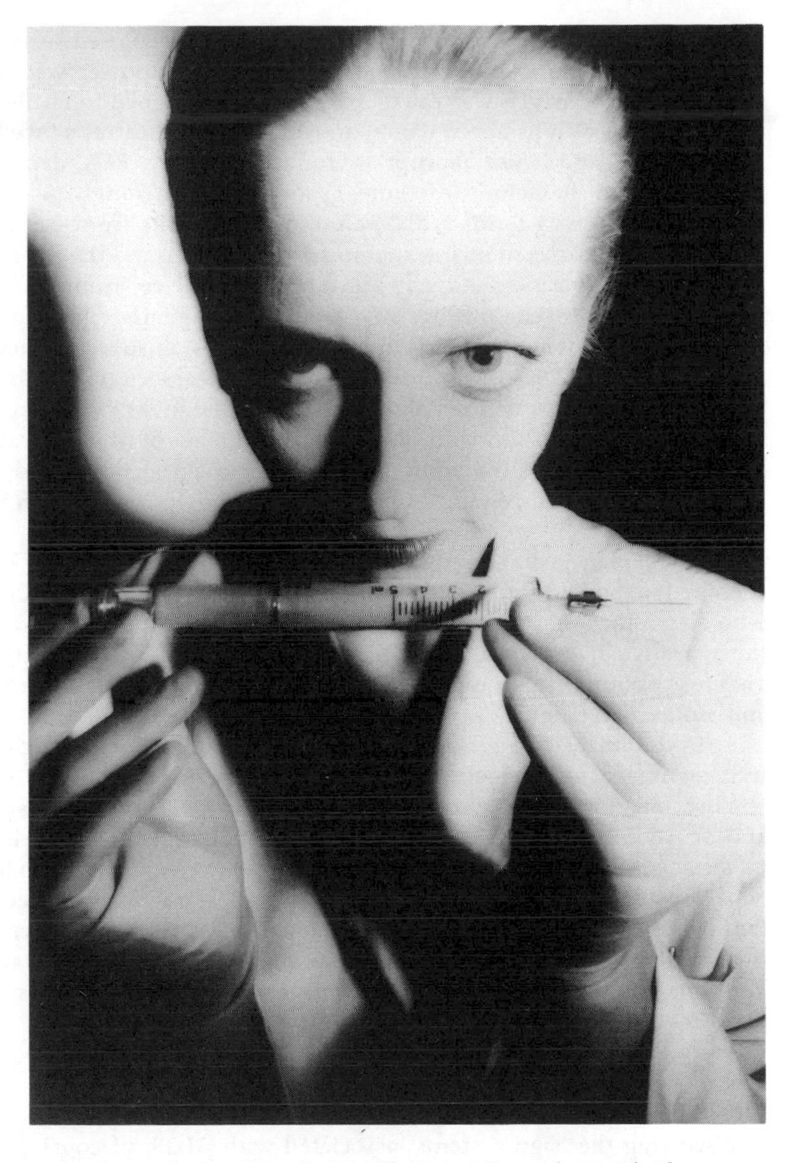

12.5] Peta Lily in *BEG!*, devised by Peta Lily with David Glass, 1993. (Colonel Kwong)

semiotic association'. This piece, produced in 1993, explored sexuality through the darker side of relationships: gender and power were critiqued in a piece which was calculated to shock, designed to challenge audience expectations about dance, movement and theatre, as well as about what is and is not appropriate for stage display. *BEG!* depicts a central woman character's (extreme, grotesque, frighteningly possible) struggle to come to terms with memories and events from her own childhood; memories of incest, memories of sexuality and the development of self identity. Peta Lily developed the piece around visual images and power relationships suggested to her by fairy tales and her own dreams: viewing the performance process as an investigation of the darker side of the psyche and its unconscious association with the representation of women in children's stories. She looks closely at the tale of Rumpelstiltskin with its narrative theme of the figurative buying and selling of the young woman (her magical talent and her beauty) by men, and reframes this gender and power dynamic in live performance.

The female protagonist, Doctor Penelope Second, played by Lily, is an active, powerful figure: 'a woman who likes sex and goes for it, who acts rather than being acted upon.'[15] She is also the murderer in the narrative framework: not the victim, but the one who acts to victimise another (in an inversion of the much more common gender and violence dynamic).

In the image in Figure 12.5, the female doctor holds the syringe. It is an image out of context—it could represent anything. It may conjure images of AID (Artificial Insemination by Donor) for some and of AIDS for others, depending on personal experience of either medical/cultural phenomenon.[16] It is a syringe: a vessel for the modern era. Not gendered, not politically aligned, yet semiotically tuned to the highest degree. It is an image of danger, of sterility, of infection. In the age of AIDS, the syringe and the quilt are equally potent symbols: one comforting, one worrying, each readable at many levels and performative contexts.

## Performing life/theorising death

In discussing the 'sign systems' associated with AIDS, of course, syringes and needles are not the only obvious negative images; we might also think of lesions, bruises, the sign system of thin-ness, also associated with (largely, but not exclusively, female) eating disorders. On the positive side, we might think of many signs or images in addition to the quilt: the angel, perhaps—a good/bad image, symbolising both death and eternal life—or the mother and daughter depicted in the AIDS Awareness campaign image, or the multi-sensual and sensational experience of sound and image as the weight of Mehmet Sander's body hits its physical opposition in the wall or the floor. We might also imagine an image not represented here, but easily described: the heart drawn in pen on Tim Miller's arm—drawn during the performance by a member of the audience, who becomes in this act a part of the performance—encompassing the words *Naked Breath*. These two words, like the performance they label and 'sign', connect the individual performer to individuals composing the group known variously as the community or audience.

These days, wherever we look we may find the image of AIDS: a metaphor and a reality; a sign system worth analysing and a performance of daily life and death, too frightening to be theorised in a purely academic or 'objective' framework, and too important not to be.

## Notes

1 Augusto Boal, *Theatre of the Oppressed* (London, Pluto Press, 1979), p. i.
2 The material of this chapter section was researched as part of the Gender/Politics/Performance Research Project, chaired by Lizbeth Goodman and funded by the Open University in 1992–4. Some of the material was recorded for the BBC Radio Series Art Works in 1993 (Lizbeth Goodman: Academic Researcher/Presenter; Jenny Bardwell: Producer, Angela Jamieson: Series Producer) and for related publications.
3 In my new book on sexuality in performance (London, Routledge, 1996).
4 See, for instance: ACT UP (eds.), *Women, AIDS and Activism* (Boston, South End Press, 1990), quoted in Andrea Blum, Julie Harrison, Barbara Ess and Gail Vachon (eds.) for the Women's Action Coalition, New York, *WAC STATS: The Facts About Women* (self published by WAC, 1993; distributed by W. W. Norton, New York).
5 Marcia Blumberg, 'Quilting: Postmodern Performance as a Celebration of Mourning', unpublished conference paper (Canada, York University, 1993).
6 In Michelene Wandor (ed.), *Plays by Women*, Volume One (London, Methuen, 1982).
7 Edited by Robert Atkins and Thomas W. Sokolowski, Guest Curators: Executive Director Susan Sollins, for Independent Curators Incorporated (New York, 1993/94); available by post from ICI, 799 Broadway, Suite 205, NY. NY 10003, USA.
8 Printed and discussed in 'Theatres of the Plague: Women, AIDS and Performance', *Everywoman* (Dec/Jan 1993), 15–16.
9 Paula Vogel, *The Baltimore Waltz*, extracts published in *The Way We Live Now* (New York, Theatre Communications Group, 1993).
10 Devised and performed by Tim Miller, 1994. Produced at Highways Performance Space in Santa Monica, California, the ICA in London and on

international tour. Miller's previous piece, 'My Queer Body' is published in Therese Jones (ed.), *Sharing the Delirium* (Heinemann, 1994). Also see 'Bodies and Stages: an Interview with Tim Miller', *Critical Quarterly* 36:1 (Spring 1994), 63–72.

11 The distinction between 'deliberate' and 'accidental' semiotic signing and sign-reading is discussed in detail in the context of a developing theory of cultural representation and interpretation in *Sexuality in Performance* (see Note 3).

12 Frits Noske discusses 'Semiotic Devices in Musical Drama', with regard to the self-contained element of semiotic signs in relation to their contextual uses, including scientific research and also the 'object-language meta-language' of musical drama, in *The Signifier and the Signified: Studies in the Operas of Mozart and Verdi* (Oxford, Clarendon Press, 1990), pp. 309–21.

13 Mehmet Sander quoted in Charles Isherwood, 'Kamikaze Choreographer', *The Advocate* (1 June, 1994), 79. Sander's piece *Force Solos* was featured in the 'Ask the Angels' series at the ICA, London (July 1994), transferred from Highways Performance Space in Santa Monica, California.

14 Susan Sontag, 'AIDS and Its Metaphors', in *Illness as Metaphor and AIDS and Its Metaphors* (New York, Anchor Books, 1988), p. 99. Sontag's argument is analysed in relation to writing on the topic by Elaine Showalter, Anthony Giddens and others in 'Death and Dancing in the Live Arts', *ibid.*

15 Interview with Peta Lily, recorded Sunday 21 February, 1993, London. The interview will be published in the forthcoming Lizbeth Goodman (ed.), *Feminist Stages: Interviews with Women in British Theatre* (London, Harwood Academic Press, 1995).

16 The theme of AID in contemporary feminist plays by Michelene Wandor, Gay Sweatshop and other companies is discussed in *Contemporary Feminist Theatres*, p. 126. On reproductive rights and and rights of lesbian mothers, see Michelene Wandor and Gay Sweatshop, 'Care and Control', in Michelene Wandor (ed.), *Strike While the Iron is Hot* (London, Journeyman Press, 1980), pp. 63–113; also Neti-Neti Theatre, 'The Memorial Gardens', unpublished, first performed London, 1988, by Mark Green and Caroline Griffin.

13

*Sarah Rubidge*

# Does authenticity matter? The case for and against authenticity in the performing arts

In this chapter I shall be addressing the question of authenticity across the performing arts. I shall look at various approaches to the notion of authenticity and in doing so I hope to elucidate the particular problems the question raises for theatre, dance and music.

In order to establish the relevance of the discussion to the performing arts, we need only to ask why we care about whether a work of music, dance or theatre is authentic or not. Is it for an intrinsic artistic value, or for its historical value or both? Our answer is likely to determine the means through which we measure authentic performances.

The notion of authenticity harbours two problematic concepts, that of authenticity itself and that of the 'work'. The description 'authentic' tends to be applied (or not) to revivals of previously performed works of music, theatre or dance. Designating a performance as 'authentic' is the outcome of a kind of judgement, one which constitutes a 'just recognition' of the work that performance purports to re-present. Authenticity is therefore not a property *of*, but something we ascribe *to* a performance.

The means through which we 'justly' recognise a work is at the centre of the debate concerning authenticity in the performing arts. Measures of authenticity, which in theatre apply as much to translations of scripts as to productions, include accurate replication of a score or script and fidelity to the spirit of the work. In recognising a performance as an authentic performance of a work, however, the implication is that, in some way or another, it communicates something of what that work has to say. The criteria upon which we make that judgement are significantly affected by the times and culture in which it is made and are inextricably linked to the work's history, which is formed and informed by its previous performances.[1]

Inasmuch as works of art are complex and frequently ambiguous, 'just recognition' is not reducible to a simple formula. At its simplest level, it can be verified by reference to some record of the work, either text, video recording or score. The criteria by which we recognise a performance as 'authentic' in its deeper sense, however, are more difficult to identify. Nevertheless, whilst it might be difficult to draw up a general formula which allows us indisputably to recognise performances as authentic (both works and their performances are too various for that), it *is* the case that we 'justly' recognise very different performances of, say, *Le Sacre du Printemps*, *King Lear* or *Giselle*, as being authentic. That they might be of variable quality does not affect this judgement. A bad performance of *Giselle* is still a performance of *Giselle*, even though this failing might affect other aesthetic judgements we make about the event.

The concept of the 'work' also requires elaboration. The notion of the 'work' in the performing arts is contentious.[2] The 'work' against which we measure authenticity in performance is an abstract concept; there is no permanent physical object to which one can refer. (The script or score are the means through which the work can be realised but not the work itself.) Several theories have been advanced in an attempt to determine what the 'work' itself is. One of the standard positions taken is that a work of music, theatre or dance is a 'type' of which there are many 'tokens' (performances or productions).[3] Certain features of the type might be indicated in a score or a script but it is not until the score is realised in performance that we have access to the work itself, and then only partially. No single performance can exhaustively realise the work, it can merely reveal one or another of its facets or 'profiles'.[4] The concept of the 'work', under this theory, is an 'open' concept.[5]

Even this relatively open position is by no means universally accepted. Jo Ellen Jacobs argues that each performance, even if it complies with a notational score, is literally a new work.[6] She posits that, just as Monet's paintings of the railway station at St Lazare (*La Gare St Lazare*) can be grouped as a family of works, but each is a work of art in its own right, so five performances of a musical work which generate from the same score are five different works of art. This analogy does not hold. Different performances of, for example, Stravinsky's *Symphony of Psalms* do not stand in the same relation to Stravinsky's symphonic work as do different paintings of La Gare St Lazare to the railway station in France which was their model.

A musical score (or a script or choreographic score) operates as a more or less detailed set of instructions from the composer to the performers. Such scores are the products of human activity, created to outline, in a shared symbol system, certain musical, choreographic or dramatic intentions which performers can then render manifest, albeit not necessarily identically from one performance to another. The subject matter of a series of paintings of a railway station or a vase of sunflowers does none of these things. Jacobs elides the difference between versions of and variations on particular subject matter, and performances of a work.

Arthur Danto takes the notion that each instantiation of a work is a new work still further. He suggests that not only each performance, but also each reception of it, constitutes a new work. Danto argues that each perceiver structures the raw perceptual data presented by the work, or performance, in a unique way and that '. . . the structure of the work . . . undergoes transformation in accordance with differences in interpretations'.[7] Although he acknowledges that there is a limit to the interpretations which can be ascribed to a work of art, he posits that certain features present in the work dominate under one interpretation but recede in another. As a result, the perceptual surface of the work is different for each viewer and each viewing. It follows from this that each individual experience of the physical manifestation of the work constitutes a new work of art. If this argument holds then the argument that each performance, or production of a work of music, dance or theatre is quite literally a new work must also hold. The question which must be asked in considering this position is whether it is possible to talk of a 'work' at all, or whether a different concept should be brought to bear.

Radical deconstructionists do just this, reducing the 'work' to a 'text', a collection of unshaped possibilities which can be arranged in any way the viewer, reader, or listener desires. Neither the author nor the text has a privileged role in guiding the interpretive response. The text is produced by the reader. This leads to what Umberto Eco calls 'interpretive drift'.[8] Deconstructionists of a less radical persuasion, however, whilst acknowledging that a text is subject to a multiplicity of readings, argue that '. . . the readings of deconstructionists are not the wilful imposition by a subjectivity of a theory on a text, but are coerced by the text itself.'[9]

Whilst accepting that the work of art, or text, is polysemic, the premise of this article is that there are such entities as works of art and that they are objects of thought and understanding, formed by individuals or group of individuals.

In the performing arts, questions of authenticity are closely concerned with the question of whether a performance is a genuine, or authentic, performance of the work of music, dance or theatre it claims to instantiate, rather than with proof of authorship, as it is in the visual arts. Each medium has subtly different problems to solve regarding the concept of authenticity. The differences are partly to do with the nature of the media themselves and partly with the history of practice in each art form. In music, for example, many, although by no means all, of the practical concerns have to do with seeking to achieve accuracy of performance in relation to the notated score and/or original performances which are presumed to be the closest to the composer's intentions. In theatre, the predominant concerns at present tend to be less to do with how a new production relates to the original performances, and more to do with whether the production is authentic in terms of 'what is going on' in the work, that is, in terms of the fictional world/s of the work. Neither position is unproblematic as we will see, nor is it unique to single art forms.

Dance, due to its history of practice, presents a more complex set of problems. Firstly, dance has many modes of presentation. Non-literal or formal dance works, such as Leonide Massine's symphonic ballets and Merce Cunningham's and Lucinda Childs' output, might be said to aspire to the condition of music. The organisation of the movement material is the focus of attention, as is the organisation of sound in music. In narrative pieces, such as Kenneth Macmillan's *Romeo and Juliet* and *Manon*, dance seems to aspire to the condition of the theatrical performance where, in general, the organisation of the movement material and its interaction with design and sound environment is in service to character, action and plot. In what could be termed semi-narrative works, such as Siobhan Davies's *Silent Partners* and Antony Tudor's *Dark Elegies*, the situation is complicated still further, for the works comment on the subtleties of human experience but do so without reference to specific characters, events or situations. It is therefore difficult to generalise when discussing requirements for authentic performances. The means through which one might judge a dance performance to be authentic are likely to differ according to the type of work under consideration.[10]

Dance also suffers from other problems which are relevant to this discussion. Means of recording the movement 'text' of a dance work, in notation (which might be seen as analogous to a script or a musical score)[11] have only recently become possible and, by virtue of the nature of the choreographic process, present certain problems. Many choreographers collaborate with the performers, particularly in the generation of movement material, when creating a dance work. The notation score is written during this period by a notator, not by the choreographer. The notator observes the movement as it is choreographed and records it using an accepted notational system such as Benesh notation or Labanotation.

Several problems attach to this method of recording dance works. A dance notation score inevitably presents an interpretation of the movement. Different ways of writing movements are possible within a single notation system. This gives the notator a range of descriptive choices. As it is notators rather than choreographers who decide how to write the movement down, it is the notators' understanding of movement which affects the notational description of the work and consequently its subsequent translation into movement by directors and/or dancers.

Further, the published score might include mistakes made by the notator when recording the movement material, or be a document of the first production and bear no record of alterations made in subsequent productions or revivals. This latter problem is common to both music and dance, where many works have been altered by the originating artist after the first performances.[12] In considering the authenticity of a revival one would need to ask whether the altered productions constitute *versions* of the same work, or *different* works, and, more pragmatically, whether the score of the original production or of the altered production should be the source for authentic performances.

In dance, however, one is fortunate if a notated score even exists. Most dance works are now preserved by their progenitors in the form of video records of performances. Video documentation presents its own problems. Video records, unlike scores and scripts, are overdetermined. They inevitably document particular realisations of works by particular performers. They also record unselectively, and are ever in danger of rendering indeterminate or contingent features of a performance, such as particular performers' interpretations of a role, mistakes in execution of the work during the performance, differences in numbers of dancers as a result of injury, set, costume, and so on, determinate features of the work.

There are various ways in which the concept of authenticity is applied in the performing arts. The notion of replication is frequently forwarded as a criterion of authenticity, particularly in music. One measure of the authenticity of a performance lies in its accurate relation to an original notation and/or production of a musical, theatrical or dance work. Another measure is the 'sound' or 'style' of the original performance. This last position has its problems inasmuch as, unless the original production took place in living memory, there is no means of authenticating a production on these grounds. Further, even an accurate reproduction of the original sound or performance text would not guarantee authenticity, for the latter was directed at an audience with very different sensibilities and interests to those held by a contemporary audience. Bruce Baugh, amongst others, argues that '[t]he original world of the work vanishes with the first public'.[13] A twentieth-century audience could not, therefore, hear the 'same' piece of music, or work of theatre, as the original audience.

A less constraining notion of authenticity is that which is proposed by writers and directors such as Raymond Leppard[14] and Jonathan Miller,[15] both of whom suggest that authenticity is achieved through fidelity to the spirit, or organising principle of a work.[16] Due to the complexity of works of music, theatre and dance, such a conception of authenticity allows for a multiplicity of interpretations to be engendered by the work, as does Gary S. Tomlinson's concept of authentic meaning.[17] This, he argues, is not fixed or permanent but is constructed by the interpreter, temporarily defined through a dialectic between the work's 'text', its culture and his or her own personal and cultural context. A work's meaning is therefore not solely reliant on authorial intention, but allows for several authentic meanings to be generated from the same script or score. These positions regard the notion of authenticity as being centrally concerned with the preservation of the internal identities of the work or with the production of the fully realised (not synonymous with exhaustive) world of the work. They are not concerned with the production of a replica of a work's original performance or production or with a performance which faithfully reproduces the creator's understanding of the work.

A further use of the term 'authentic' in the performing arts holds that the site of authentic performances is the performer. Shelley Berg,[18] discussing authenticity in dance, suggests that '. . . authentic performance reveals itself almost unconsciously as a living embodiment of past practice', although she acknowledges that it is also a revelation of present sensibilities. William Crutchfield, conversely, holds that authentic performances are to be understood in terms of the performer's immediate relation with the music both as individual and artist. He does not deny the relevance of performers' acquainting themselves with the grammar and syntax of the stylistic language in which the music is couched, nor indeed its history, but suggests that this is not an end in itself. He argues instead that it is merely the base from which performers can produce authoritative, authentic performances of the work. He concludes that authenticity is 'the *Ausstrahlung* of the performer. It joins hands with the genius of the composer and in the greatest performances seems to merge so that we feel music and musician are one.'[19]

Robert Morgan[20] notes that the way a musician thinks about music is inseparable both from assumptions about music in his or her own time and from the performers' own histories. He argues that one cannot recreate performances from previous centuries as there is '. . . no way to re-establish that fundamental, inimitable psychological and physiological relationship of the performer to a language that he has not learned but [has] absorbed unconsciously . . .'.[21]

On the basis of Morgan's argument, the possibility of 'authentic' (in the sense of historically accurate) dance performances, even from earlier in this century, is severely reduced. A significant element of the work itself is literally embodied in the dancers' movement. Personal style[22] in dance is affected by the individual dancer's preference for particular ways of moving, by dance training and, perhaps more significantly, by the cultural environment in which the dancers operate. This militates against the possibility of strictly 'authentic' performances.

The problems associated with the positions argued above are not easy to resolve. How can one know that the communion between work and performer is not misguided or that the organising principle of a work is correctly identified by performer and/or director? How can one accommodate the sensibilities of the contemporary performer to works created in the sixteenth or even early twentieth centuries and still call the performance an authentic performance of a work? How do we know that one interpretation of a work is closer to what is 'going on' in that work than another? Further, how can we test the theories themselves?

Taking a cue from Wollheim's argument that, where appropriate, aesthetic theories should be tested for adequacy against artistic theories,[23] the relevance of the various positions discussed above to practitioners, performers and audiences will now be addressed.

The argument for accuracy as a measure of authenticity is perhaps the most limiting for individual works of theatre, dance or music. Nelson Goodman argues that authentic performances of musical scores must accurately reproduce the notes written in the score which constitute a set of instructions from composer to performer. He states of authenticity in performances of musical works (and, by extension, theatre and dance works) that 'the constitutive properties demanded of a performance of the symphony are those *prescribed in* the score . . . a performance [which] has or has not all the constitutive properties of a work is or is not strictly a performance of that work'.[24]

Goodman acknowledges that scores do not specify all features of a performance but argues that, for a performance to be authentic, performers must comply with those which *are* specified. Inaccurate performances of the prescriptions recorded in the score or play text would therefore not be authentic performances of the work in question, for they would not fulfil the composer's stated musical intentions.

Notational compliance as a measure of authenticity presents problems. How can we be sure that the published score itself is a true record of the composer's musical intentions? It has been suggested that even the Urtext, the closest possible reproduction of the composer's original manuscript, does not guarantee access to the musical intentions of the composer. Raymond Leppard points out that, 'when a manuscript goes to print, editors, publishers and printers have all made decisions which can vitally affect the Urtext'.[25] These decisions are affected by the assumptions and principles under which the editors operate and may change from period to period, even, in times of rapid change, from decade to decade. Shakespeare scholar Stephen Orgel similarly argues that even the texts of Shakespeare's plays were revised for performance, even in the quartos and folios.[26] Goodman's position then has serious limitations when applied to practice in the performing arts.

Although Stephen Davies holds a similar view to Goodman's with regard to notational compliance, his conditions of authenticity differ significantly: '[a]n authentic performance of a given work must be a performance which concerns itself with producing the notes which comprise the work. The sound of an authentic performance will be the sound of those notes'.[27] He points out, however, that what is written by the composer is not necessarily an accurate notational representation of the notes the performers are expected to play or perform, by virtue of contemporary conventions regarding performance practice in relation to musical and dance notations.[28] The score therefore may only be a guide to the composer's musical intentions and strict compliance with the score, whilst it might be a necessary condition of authenticity, is not a sufficient condition. Davies argues that whilst the quest for authenticity might be characterised as aiming at the production of a particular sound, '. . . the sound to which an authentic performance aspires is that of a possible, rather than an actual, performance.'[29] Quite how we are to produce that ideal sound is not clear.

In theatre and dance, the analogy with Davies's position is the aspiration to a recreation of style of performance. Robert K. Sarlós argues that replication goes beyond adherence to play script and production text. He argues that '. . . to evoke various theatrical styles . . . one must attempt to reconstruct not only the tangible environment but also the ephemeral performance that occurred within it',[30] that is a 'dynamic, lifesize, spatial and temporal model' of the original production of the work. He suggests that the style of theatrical works which are no longer extant as performance works 'is comprehended in the bits of disconnected information that filter down to us regarding the spatial arrangement, the colour or texture of scenic elements, the breathing technique, vocal inflection, eye movement or deportment of actors and so forth.'[31]

Recapturing this style of performance in theatre and dance is difficult if not impossible to attain. This notwithstanding, Sarlós claims that evidence drawn from prompt books, reviews, reminiscences and other documentation enable us to create a spatial and temporal model of a work which, whilst not an exact replica, recaptures something of the performance milieu of the work. This, he argues, is the goal of the reconstructor.

Supporters of the replication model tend to reduce works to their observable features. Theatre works are, however, tremendously rich. Although they entail the features of which Sarlós speaks, they are more than the sum of those parts. Treatments of theatre work which diminish the play to its dynamic, spatial, and temporal features alone risk producing museum pieces which disregard that which makes a play a play, namely its fictional world/s, which are embodied both in its narrative and in the complex interplay between characters.

Leppard and Miller argue that we are unlikely ever to be in a position to determine the accuracy of performances of works for which we do not have full scores or scripts, nor to have access to the authentic sounds or performance styles created when the work was made. Even if we could, they suggest, this is not what is important about works of music, dance or theatre. What *is* important is what is 'going on' in the play, piece of music or dance.

Leppard suggests that the route to take to authenticity is less to seek to produce an accurate reproduction of what it is believed that the composers' musical intentions were, or to actualise the work's possibilities as they were actualised in the original performances, than to seek to produce 'the clearest possible revelation of that music so that its intrinsic qualities, vitality and value are presented again as vividly as they may conceivably ever have been.'[32] Such a revelation serves to allow the work to act upon the present by revealing new possibilities within, and new understandings of, the work. On this view criteria other than accurate replication of original presentations must be brought to bear if we are to judge performances as authentic. Inasmuch as it focuses its attention on the work as a work of art, an object of communication, it is the *artistic* values of the work which are proposed as the criterion of authenticity.

In music, the notion of the values of the work concerns, in Leppard's words, 'the music's vitality and meaning' in all its variety. For Leppard, the aim of any revival is to reveal that vitality to a twentieth-century audience. In order to liberate it, the conductor, or director, and performer must engage in a dialogue with the work and make choices regarding emphases to be placed on, for example, certain aspects of its dynamics, its phrasing, its texture. These choices will normally be backed up by considerable research into the historical and musical context in which the work was first produced but will proceed from the perspective of the artists' own time and artistic milieu.

In theatre, the vitality to which Leppard refers is interpreted by Orgel as lying 'in what is represented, something behind the play and beyond it that brings the play to life'.[33] This 'something' is not unidimensional. Individual plays, like works of music and dance, offer several perspectives on their subject matter. The multitude of productions of Shakespeare testify to this. Each production has the potential for bringing out new possibilities through a directorial interpretation of the world of the work as represented in the script.[34] However, the text from which the actors work is not immutable. Rather it is fluid, open to changes which arise in rehearsal and performance.

Plays are written for performance, not for publication. Orgel argues that even in Shakespeare's time 'the acting text of a play was always different from the written text, . . . not simply from the printed text but from the script, what the author wrote.'[35] Shakespeare's 'working' scripts offered the acting company a range of possibilities from which he and they could select. Their choices resulted in the 'original performance text'.[36] The original performance text, however, is only one of several possible renderings of the play. In any play, and even more so in dance works, intentions other than those of the author are involved in its creation. These include those of the designers, directors, composers as well as, of course, the performers. Further, the play (and the work of music or dance) has a multiplicity of histories, manifested in its productions. These are part of what the play, the dance, the musical work is.

Theatre offers immense possibilities for reinterpretation not only by virtue of the richness of the works themselves, the plot, dramatic discourse, cast of characters, connotative values of the text and so on, but also by virtue of its multiple channels of communication. (A change in the setting can as effectively project a new world as a change in the emphasis given to certain characters or facets of the plot.) Peter

Brook argues that Shakespeare, in particular, is an artist whose plays are open to multiple interpretations. 'The history of the plays shows them constantly being interpreted and re-interpreted, and yet remaining untouched and intact.'[37]

Many directors seek to retain a close relationship to the thesis they understand the author to be presenting in the work—as far as it can be determined. David Thacker argues that '[y]ou have to attempt to understand what the drift of the play was for Shakespeare and then search for some close contemporary equivalent that will make the play precise, clear and immediate for the audience.'[38] Nevertheless, in spite of the sometimes radical shifts in the meaning of the play, and the introduction of concepts which were unavailable to the playwright at the time of writing (for example, Freudian concepts applied to Shakespeare), implicit in this approach to interpretation is a level of fidelity to the original text. The words spoken by the actors are those written by the playwright, even though significant proportions of the text may be cut.

If 'authentic' performances of the work are to result, however, the nature of the cuts must be carefully considered. Cutting certain scenes or characters would transform a play into a different work, cutting others would not. Nonetheless, Peter Brook suggests that some plays accommodate cuts more easily than others. For example, he says, '. . . Shakespeare's plays are not all written with the same amount of finish. Some plays are looser and some are tighter . . . *Midsummer Night's Dream* . . . seemed to me to be a perfect play . . . I don't think you can change a word without losing something. However, in other plays you can move words and scenes.'[39]

Not all theatre practitioners adhere to the view that fidelity of any kind to the script or score is relevant to the preservation of the values of extant works. During the 1970s and 1980s, with the advent of postmodern theatre and dance, the very relevance of the concept of authenticity in the performing arts, whether as replication or preservation of internal identity, was challenged. Revisions, rather than revivals, of works became *de rigueur* in theatre. Theatre directors such as Richard Schechner, Julian Beck (of The Living Theatre) and Jerzy Grotowski, whilst taking plays from the classical repertoire as their starting point, abandoned the script and revised the work completely, perhaps using the broad sweep of the plot but focusing on the 'buried themes' which informed the original play in their adaptations.[40] Such revisions of work are not faithful to the original text, rather they use it as a starting point for new works which re-examine the themes presented in the original work.

Recently revisionist productions of classical dance works by choreographers such as Mats Ek, Matthew Bourne and Mark Morris have become part of the repertoire. Bourne's and Morris's versions of *The Nutcracker*, Ek's of *Swan Lake* and *Giselle* and Bourne's of *La Sylphide* retain the general lines of the narrative but re-write both the movement 'text' and the performance text in order to bring out facets of the work not evident in conventional productions. Radical revisions of dance works tend to be undertaken with works with a narrative content. In non-literal, or formal, dance work such a cavalier attitude would be more difficult to countenance if only because the materials of non-literal dance works, as with some music,[41] are themselves the subject matter of the work, rather than the medium through which the subject matter is communicated.

The question of authenticity in terms of either replication or preservation of internal identity is not pertinent in the context of such adaptations. The new productions stand in relation to the original works as do Picasso's variations of Velasquez's *Las Meninas* to the original.[42] The directors of revisions of classical theatre texts and dance works, like Picasso, acknowledge the importance of the original works, but feel free to construct radical variations on them in order to communicate more clearly the nascent insights they have derived from them.

So, what kind of authenticity is important in the performing arts? The answer to the question would seem to depend upon the purposes for which authenticity is being sought. The various senses of authenticity discussed in this article, and the production processes which facilitate them, are all important in the context of the performing arts.

Reconstructions of original productions are of real value to those interested in theatrical, musical and dance heritage, whether for scholarly or other reasons. They afford historians, practitioners and audiences access to a more complete picture of the performance traditions of the past than is available through other means of documentation, such as written and pictorial documentation. In dance and some forms of avant-garde theatre, reconstructions play an important role in preserving the history of the art form. In particular, lack of adequate recording facilities has led to serious discontinuities in the history of theatre dance.

Accurate reconstructions can also have an intrinsic value for today's audiences. Just as the survival of paintings and sculptures can offer insights into the attitudes and values current at the time of their creation, so it is with reconstructions of music, dance and theatre works. Access to such works could serve to increase our knowledge and understanding of our world, past and present. Faithful reconstruction may even aid contemporary adaptations. Ann Cooper Albright argues that, in dance, reconstructions not only refer to previous works in a way that emphasises the historical legacy of a performing art tradition but also open up new possibilities for the re-interpretation or radical revision of the original works.[43]

If the arts are a means of understanding more about our world, however, it is not mechanical replication, but access to the world of the work, in all its variety, that is important. Although the archaeology of the work might have a part to play in revealing that world, what is significant is engagement with the work as an act of communication. Revivals which re-examine the world of the work facilitate this, for they allow the work to take on what Jonathan Miller calls an afterlife.[44] Through re-interpretation a work continues to act upon and be acted upon by the world long after its original significance has ceased to be of immediate relevance. It is here, I suggest, that we can locate the *kind* of authenticity which is pertinent to the performing arts. It lies in the authentic world of the work, which is located anew in each performance.

## Notes

1 Gary S. Tomlinson, 'The Historian, the Performer and Authentic Meaning' in Nicholas Kenyon (ed.), *Authenticity and Early Music* (Oxford, Oxford University Press, 1988), pp. 115–36; Stephen Orgel, 'The Authentic Shakespeare', *Representations*, 21 (1988), 1–25.

2 For further discussion see Linda Goehr, 'Being True to the Work', *Journal of Aesthetics and Art Criticism*, 47:1 (1989).

3 The concept of type/token was first developed by C. S. Pierce. A clear way of elucidating the concept is to ask, 'How many words in the dictionary?' One's answer will depend upon whether one takes 'word' as Type, and therefore only count the words which are *defined* in the dictionary, or one takes it as Token, and therefore count every word which is printed in the dictionary. See Richard Wollheim, *Art and Its Objects* (Cambridge, Cambridge University Press, 1980) and Joseph Margolis, *Art and Philosophy* (Brighton, Harvester Press, 1981) for discussion of the type/token theory of identity.

4 Roman Ingarden, transl. Adam Czerniawski, Jean G. Harrell (ed.), *The Work of Music and the Problem of Its Identity* (London, Macmillan, 1986).

5 For further discussion see Umberto Eco, *The Open Work* (London, Hutchinson Radius, 1989) and Goehr, 'Being True to the Work'.

6 Jo Ellen Jacobs, 'Identifying Musical Works of Art', *Journal of Aesthetics and Art Criticism*, 24:4 (1990).

7 Arthur Danto, *The Transfiguration of the Commonplace* (Cambridge, MA, Harvard University Press, 1981), p. 120.

8 Umberto Eco, *The Limits of Interpretation* (Bloomington and Indianapolis, Indiana University Press, 1994).

9 For example, J. Hillis Miller, quoted in Eco, *The Limits of Interpretation*, p. 60.

10 Although the same might be said of theatre and music, the problems are not as pronounced.

11 I leave aside Physical Theatre and works such as those produced by the experimentalists of the 1960s and '70s (e.g., Trisha Brown and other members of the Judson Church Dance Theatre) which are identified not by the actual movement performed but by a set of written instructions detailing tasks to be carried out by the performers.

12 E.g., Gluck's *Orfeo*; Petipa's *Swan Lake*; Antony Tudor's *Dark Elegies*; and, more recently, Siobhan Davies's *Wyoming* and *Plainsong*.

13 Bruce Baugh, 'Authenticity Revisited', *Journal of Aesthetics and Art Criticism* (1988), 477–87.

14 Raymond Leppard, *Authenticity in Music* (London, Faber Music, 1988).

15 Jonathan Miller, *Subsequent Performances* (London, Faber and Faber, 1986).

16 The translation of theatrical works from one language to another encounters similar issues. Philippe Carden, 'Translating for Performance', *London Magazine* (Aug/Sep 1993) argues that the main criteria for evaluating a translation of a play script are that it works well as a piece of theatre (an elegant academic translation for this purpose might not suffice) and that it has respect for the original spirit or essence of the work. He cites Nick Dear's recent translation of Molière's *Le Bourgeois Gentilhomme* as an example of translation which failed to remain true to the original and Tony Harrison's translation of Molière's *Le Misanthrope* as an example of a translation which was true to the original.

17 Tomlinson, 'The Historian, the Performer and Authentic Meaning'.

18 Shelley C. Berg, 'The Real Thing: Authenticity and Dance at the Approach of the Millennium' in *Dance ReConstructed* (Conference Proceedings: Rutgers University, 1993), pp. 109–18.

19 William Crutchfield, 'Fashion, Convention and Performance Style in an Age of Revivals' in Kenyon (ed.), *Authenticity and Early Music*, pp. 19–26.

20 Robert P. Morgan, 'Tradition, Anxiety and the Musical Scene' in Kenyon (ed.), *Authenticity and Early Music*, pp. 57–82.

21 *Ibid.*, p. 70.

22 Armelagos and Sirridge argue that, in Western theatre dance, there are two styles of movement relevant to discussion of dance performance: style$_1$ (a general codified movement style such as ballet, Graham or Cunningham technique) and style$_2$ (the personal movement style of the dancer which works within those constraints). A full discussion of movement style and its effect on authentic performance can be found in Adina Armelagos and Mary Sirridge, 'The Ins and Outs of Dance: Expression as an Aspect of Style', *Journal of Aesthetics and Art Criticism*, 26 (1977) and Armelagos and Sirridge, 'Personal Style and Performance Prerogatives' in Maxine Sheets-Johnstone (ed.), *Illuminating Dance* (Lewisburg, Bucknell University Press, 1984), pp. 85–100.

23 Richard Wollheim, 'Are the Criteria of Identity that Hold for a Work of Art in the Different Arts Aesthetically Relevant?', *Ratio*, 20 (1978), 29–51.
24 Nelson Goodman, *Languages of Art* (Hackett Publishing Co., 1968), p. 117.
25 *Ibid.* For further discussion on this point see also Philip Brett, 'Text, Context and the Early Music Editor' in Kenyon (ed.), *Authenticity and Early Music*, pp. 83–114.
26 See Orgel, 'The Authentic Shakespeare'.
27 Stephen Davies, 'Authenticity in Musical Performance', *British Journal of Aesthetics*, 27:1 (1987), 40–1.
28 Early opera scores did not give full orchestration as certain performance conventions were assumed; similarly, Stepanov's dance notation gave no details of arm gestures or head movements as it was assumed that certain arm gestures and movements of the head would accompany particular steps.
29 Stephen Davies, 'Authenticity in Musical Performance', 40–1.
30 Robert K. Sarlós, 'Performance Reconstruction: The Vital Link', *Drama Review*, 28:3 (1984), 4.
31 *Ibid.*, p. 5. See also Millicent Hodgson's accounts of the reconstruction of Nijinsky's *Le Sacre du Printemps* in *Dance Research*, 3:2 (1985), 35–44 and 4:1 (1986), 63–77.
32 Leppard, *Authenticity in Music*, p. 73.
33 *Ibid.*, p. 35, p. 13.
34 See John Elsom (ed.), *Is Shakespeare Still Our Contemporary?* (London, Routledge, 1992).
35 *Ibid.*, p. 7.
36 A term used by Schechner in *Performance Theory* (London, Routledge, 1988) to differentiate between the dramatic text, that is the script, and the performance text, that is the fully determined performance, complete with setting, vocal inflection and so on.
37 Peter Brook, *The Shifting Point* (London, Methuen, 1988), p. 78.
38 David Thacker in John Elsom (ed.), *Is Shakespeare Still Our Contemporary?* (London, Routledge, 1992), p. 24.
39 Brook, *The Shifting Point*, p. 38.
40 Schechner's *Dionysus in 69* (from Euripides' *The Bacchae*), Grotowski's *Dr Faustus* (from Marlowe); Beck's *The Oresteia*.
41 Although Robert P. Morgan notes that in the late nineteenth century bars and groups of bars were omitted from, or new ones added to, Bach's music. These adjustments and compositional 'corrections' were made to bring Bach's work into conformity with the musical conventions of the day ('Tradition, Anxiety and the Musical Scene' in Kenyon (ed.), *Authenticity and Early Music*, pp. 67–8).
42 See Nelson Goodman, *Reconceptions in Philosophy* (London, Routledge, 1988) for discussion on variation.
43 Ann Cooper Albright, 'The Long Afternoon of a Faun: Reconstruction and the Discourses of Desire' in *Dance ReConstructed*, pp. 219–22.
44 Miller, *Subsequent Performances*.

14 Lucy O'Brien

# 'Sexing the Cherry': High or Low Art? Distinctions in performance

In early 1990s pop, two interesting things happened. Madonna recorded 'Justify My Love' and Jane Siberry came out with the album *When I Was A Boy*. Both releases transgressed boundaries of High and Low Art but from two seemingly opposing perspectives. The sensual territory they described, however, showed a similarity of vision and potential that undercut analytical notions about where a pop artist, particularly a female artist, fits. Women performers have traditionally been marginalised in High/Low Art debates and not seen as creative artists, therefore studying them can bring a fresh perspective to bear on the distinctions of High and Low—and why those references continue to hold cultural power. Academic analysis of pop music in media and cultural studies has elevated its status, hence making it a suitable (if not crucial) case for treatment—poised on the cusp between the academic and the popular.

In November 1993, the debate raged at the Oxford Union over the motion 'This House believes that high culture is superior to low culture.' The motion highlights criticism in crisis, where art and performance is constantly being re-evaluated. Up to the 1940s, the criterion was relatively simple. In the late nineteenth century, Matthew Arnold asserted that high culture was a civilising influence, 'the best that has been thought and said in the world.'[1] By 1946, when the Arts Council of Great Britain was established to secure 'the best for most', high/low distinctions were being eroded by movements such as the so-called New Brutalism, a postwar challenge throughout art and literature to previous consensus. Texts like John Osborne's *Look Back in Anger* (1957), with its 'kitchen-sink' drama and anti-Establishment themes, had paved the way for the supposed democratisation of culture in the 1960s, when Dylan was compared to Keats and students at the Sorbonne daubed situationist slogans on walls like: 'Art is dead, let us create everyday life'. Marxist writers such as Raymond Williams, by widening the concept of culture, helped to undermine its established association with High Art.[2] By 1968, a watershed year for High/Low Art with the emergence of poststructuralism, French theorist Roland Barthes brought into the debate consideration of non-literary 'texts'—such as advertising and wrestling.[3]

Consideration of Low Art and working-class (therefore 'mass') subcultural pluralism was enshrined in academia with the foundation in 1964 of the Birmingham Centre for Contemporary Cultural Studies. One of its most illustrious graduates, Dick Hebdige, reflected these concerns in his 1979 set text on 'yoof' culture, from teddy boy to punk, entitled *Subculture: The Meaning of Style*. High Art was viewed by the cultural Left as heritage-based, the elitist 'Grand Hotel',[4] where all cultural production was somehow orchestrated around one master system. High Art—from Beethoven to Greek urns—was increasingly seen as a fossilised Eurocentric canon of Dead White Males, while the expanding frontiers of media, music and movies meant that Low Art or popular culture was the site of change, energy, dynamism and new artistic forces. Commentators from Stuart Hall to Susan Sontag and Roland Barthes believed that any 'text', (i.e., any cultural product) could be analysed, with Dallas, MTV, shopping malls and Madonna as some of the key examples.

Interpreting pop art as a 'moronic inferno', the cultural Right, on the other hand, dismissed critics from the Left as unable to discriminate between genuine innovation and dross. While its anxiety was misdirected, it did point up the hilarious excesses of a strand of 1980s postmodern criticism, where the crypto-science of semiotics became the new orthodoxy and multi-layered meaning was found in Billy Idol's sneer or Madonna's belly button. A metatextual kinda girl, Madonna has been an easy catch-all symbol for curiously de-personalised readings of popular culture. This essay locates her as author and artist of her own destiny within the music business, as well as the depository for a thousand far-flung academic theories.

The pop industry is a good test case for arguments about modern distinctions between High and Low Art. The old 'is Dylan better than Keats?' chestnut that was wheeled out on BBC2's *The Late Show* in 1991, when playwright David Hare said, shock horror, that 'Keats was better', is still a good starting place. Hare's announcement was part of a 1980s turning point, when traditional High/Low distinctions began to creep back into cultural criticism. High/Low is perhaps a misnomer, an outdated term for a process of evaluation *within* disciplines. As writer Julian Barnes said, 'Keats is the better poet; Dylan is the better rock musician. That's it.'[5]

While Dylan may be rated 'below' Keats in the general artistic hierarchy, within rock music he is at the head of the pop Pantheon, alongside Iggy Pop, Lou Reed, Leonard Cohen and Elvis Costello. To those not directly involved in the music business, pop is a delectable mass-culture melée of ever-changing MTV videos, record company product, clothes and trends that are ripe for deconstruction. Pop may be a medium that continually re-invents itself, a Warholian industry perfectly suited to the postmodern criticism and definitions; but this multiplexity ignores the fact that within pop there exist very rigid categories of High and Low Art. These may fluctuate—one month Take That are a teen group of talentless hunks, the next they are actually OK songwriters and rather good entertainers—but at *any given time* the consensus of the music press, record industry and clubland is fixed. Pop is a more capricious medium than academic disciplines, but it has carved out its own individual signposts.

The singles charts for the week ending 4 June 1994, for instance, divided roughly in half between 'High' and 'Low' acts. Prince at number 27, with his constant interrogation of pop and the clever use of a genetic symbol instead of his name, was King of the Grand Hotel, while at number 21 acid jazz rap group Galliano followed in his High tradition with the *knowingness* of musical references on records like 'In Pursuit Of The 13th Note', the respect they displayed for Old Masters like George Clinton, Gil Scott Heron and Miles Davis.

Unashamedly Low at number 1 were teen idols Wet Wet Wet, a group who ironically began on the indie (independent label) scene with a mutant brand of Memphis blues. Moving into the slipstream of the Smash Hits market meant a dilution and polishing of their cracked surfaces, so a band that could have been High willingly became Low, along with more Campbell's Soup-type acts such as Bad Boys Inc (number 12) and World's Apart (number 29). Featured in the chart also were bands that fit Frith and Horne's High Art criteria of Rock Bohemians—those who cleave to a Romantic vision of the artist as experimenter, vanguard and someone separate from the mainstream, and Pop Situationists—performers investing in an image of cool, self-aware irony.[6] Pink Floyd, for example, the '70s supergroup of progressive art rock who through repetition and dilution of their material have veered in the 1990s dangerously close to the Low Art category; and Blur, quirky indie label lads whose mockery of Club 18–30 mass-culture ideals placed them firmly in the bracket of new Situationists.

I deliberately omitted mention of female acts, not only because there were a meagre four in that week's Top Thirty (all-girl groups Salt N Pepa and Eternal, plus solo singer/songwriters Carleen Anderson and Tori Amos), but also because women are the one constituency that until the late '80s were ignored in the intra-pop High/Low debates. One reason for this could be that the feminist movement had not fully got underway when distinctions between High and Low Art were made, and early women's liberation texts focused on socio-political rather than artistic issues.[7] As Fiske argues in *Understanding Popular Culture*, because they have traditionally been excluded by the 'dominator' high culture and ascribed roles as the Other, women have become adept at using 'low' popular culture, whether it's watching TV soaps (a springboard for discussing relationships), reading romance novels with feisty heroines (gaining a sense of desire and identity) or listening to pop music (discovering empowerment and solidarity as a fan).[8]

A young culture industry as compared to literature or fine art, pop music in Britain was perceived throughout the 1950s by High Art devotees, like TV, as a nuisance American export. Polarised from 'legitimate' classical music, rock n' roll was filed under BBC Light Entertainment until broadcasting began to open up and diversify in the early 1960s with the proliferation of radio and TV channels. Until then, jazz was the enclave of serious-minded study, High Art within Low culture, a genre for music boffins disdainful of the popular mainstream yet alienated too by the 'retro' evaluations of the élite culture. In the beat boom that followed the Beatles' 1964 'invasion' of America, a new ideology of rock was born, with arts-educated performers such as the Rolling Stones, the Yardbirds, the Who, Pink Floyd and the Kinks forming a community in which the artist wrote the songs, and was literally the purveyor of bohemian dreams and Romantic fancies.[9]

It may have been a new artistic universe—from Pink Floyd's avant-garde psychedelic beat, to Peter Blake's *Sergeant Pepper* sleeve design to Pete Townshend's claim that his guitar smashing was in the style of Gustav Metzger's 'auto-destructive' art—but it was resolutely male. Exhibiting the signs of High Art self-reflection and reference within an élite coterie, the prog rockers of the late '60s and '70s, like the self-conscious ironists of the '80s, clustered together in a way that excluded women. In 1961, commentator Francis Newton wrote of how groups of young male jazz enthusiasts 'play one another records, repeating crucial passages until they are worn out . . . endlessly discussing their comparative merits.'[10] The spirit of Hebdige's 'semiotic guerilla warfare' in his dissection of punk, mod and skin dress codes was not so different,[11] a factor picked up on by Angela McRobbie when she criticised him for inferring that style 'belongs' to men.[12]

In the grouping of High Art distinctions within pop music, women are somehow 'less', both as performers and consumers. Critics such as Frith[13] may claim that punk was a place of freedom for women, but my experience in an all-girl band on a punk scene where boys admired each other's Doc Martens and Buzzcocks' B sides was that we were novelty, that we didn't really 'know' what counted. In this air of 'dominator culture', exclusivity was even more explicit in the '60s mod territory and its revivals. In 1994, for instance, a band of roving artists, poets and musicians called PPQ ran a club at a Regent Street venue not used since its '60s heyday. It was a narcissistic scene in which modish boys admired each other's clothes and revered jazz classics, and women were not part of their 'cool' aesthetic.

If High Art in, say, sculpture, poetry or fine art is always defined by criticism, then in popular music the rock press is its bastion. For decades, the British and American figurehead publications, *New Musical Express* and *Rolling Stone*, have prioritised the activities of (nearly) Dead White Males, granting respectful space on individual terms to the clever soliloquies of artists like Lou Reed, Leonard Cohen, Bob Dylan and Elvis Costello, while black music, dance music and women were more often written about in generic or trend terms as if they were part of the mass, the Other, the 'gaping maw of the Mother.'[14]

Minor tinkerings with the apparatus have thrown up a few anomalous sensations. The May 1994 cover of post-rock bible *Q*, for instance, was spectacular in its crassness. Under the coverline 'HIPS. LIPS. TITS. POWER' (clever because it was originally a slogan dreamed up by Lesley Silverfish, a woman in an obscure 'indie' band) three fully-made up 'alternative' female stars crowded together. PJ Harvey, Bjork and Tori Amos all come from very different musical backgrounds, but they were dealt with *en masse*, as a kind of mutant Three Faces of Eve. What they spelled out was sex, separation and novelty, rather than their actual status as three figures in a respected rock tradition.

Being overlooked, however, has paradoxically created the space for women to define their own parameters of High/Low Art—if indeed that distinction for women in rock holds any meaning. In returning to Jane Siberry and Madonna, we can see how each has a place in High and Low Art respectively, but unlike their male counterparts, their movement between categories is much more slippery.

'My music is subtle. Air-placing (radio play) is a problem. The record company is missing a major tool. I'm always very respectful. When I gave them *When I Was A Boy*, they felt their hands were tied, there was nothing to work with. I said, "I'll create a front door for this record, something you can be enthusiastic about." I didn't want it to go out and disappear,' Siberry said in 1993, just after the release of her sixth album.[15] Struggling to be heard, Siberry was aware of how the High/Low Art dichotomy (or, more practically, the pull of art versus commerce) made her anxious, stifling her creativity.

Just as the nineteenth-century women consolidated their intellectual presence through literature and specifically the novel, so women in pop music have colonised the area of singer/songwriting, a broad category that has become the salubrious ghetto of the white Western educated female. Along with forerunners Joni Mitchell and Laurie Anderson, Siberry is one of the few women afforded serious study in the rock press. Most female artists (particularly black) are written about with constant reference to collaborators and producers, as if they could not possibly be the prime authors of their work: the select few, however, true to definitions of High Art, are treated like artists and sisterly seers, the caryatids on the Parthenon.

Indeed, Siberry's early work did exude a rarified aesthetic that expressed itself through shimmering, timorous, poignant soundscapes—songs full of *non sequiturs* and surreal asides that reflected a quick mind working in watercolour, the studio her haven, the control board her muse. That intimacy of observation sometimes dropped into a peculiar whimsy. An early track for instance, called 'Mimi On The Beach', with its sparse structure and graphic word pictures, is a kind of Sylvia Plath poem set to music. About a teenage girl gazing out onto the world, tense with peer pressure and despising the 'jocks' on surf boards at the beach, the song is self-conscious, wordy, arch—a failed experiment. Avant-garde and introvert, this would be the expected approach for an artist like Siberry, who took the familiar route to High Art pop via small town (Etobicoke, near Toronto, Canada), late '70s folk coffee-house circuit, a college degree and punk experimentation. These elements fuelled the conscious dissonance, the deliberately surreal in her writing. Her self-titled debut LP was financed by a waitressing job and her next two were released on a small independent before she was signed by major label Reprise (distributed by Warners), folded carefully into the 'albums artist' bracket and marketed accordingly, with well-targeted promotion and touring of selected US and European venues.

Siberry as commodity was sold as High Art, but, as she says, 'I exist in no one's ghetto.' Her humour is too sharp, her self-awareness too keen and her musicianship too strong to allow herself to be limited to the confines of pop's Grand Hotel. Realising that her escape was as much her responsibility as the record company's, Siberry admitted: 'That pattern of the introverted songwriter is hard for women to break out of. The programming goes deep when you're told that you'll be loved only if you're nice and quiet, otherwise you're considered a fishwife or homosexual. Fortunately the louder voice is getting stronger, shrugging off that worry.'[16]

Madonna, by comparison, has always had a loud voice and brashness of display that places her at the centre of 1980s popular 'low' culture. Rather than cleaving to Siberry's cerebral worldview, Madonna is rooted in 'the Body', using it to comment on instinctive sexuality and power. From the beginning of her career when she came across as an ambitious Europop *ingénue* fresh out of Patrick Hernandez's disco revue, she was a favourite of tabloid papers and glossy chart pop magazines. No mental slouch, she understood that her power as a mass-culture star relied to a great extent on manufacturing pleasure and stimulating desire—a stance that reached its apex (or nadir) with *Sex* (1992), the book of coffee-table MTV porn that featured her in various sex poses with everyone and everything from old men to Naomi Campbell, bubbling faucets and Los Angeles lesbians.

Madonna's work pulsates with principles of postmodern popular culture: smooth surfaces (playing in the surf, fashion-shoot style in the video for 'Cherish'); simple narrative (the songs 'Papa Don't Preach' or 'La Isle Bonita'); plus resistance through brash irony (the visual punning of the virgin/whore theme in 'Like A Virgin', or reflecting back male voyeurism in the peek-a-boo titillation of 'Who's That Girl'). The consummate nature of her 'knowingness' has resulted in a plethora of 'thinkpieces' in the music press, as well as a semiotic feast for pop culture critics. These comments focus on Madonna as corporate artist and a commodity of the late twentieth-century capitalism, the calculated author of a 'producerly text'.[17]

But behind the postmodern hyperbole beats a Romantic heart. Madonna as a multi-dimensional human being has aspirations towards High Art—she collects it in the form of Frida Kahlo paintings and medieval icons, and tentatively explores that impulse on records such as 'Like A Prayer' and 'Justify My Love'. If we are to describe what constitutes High or Low within her work, it lies at the level of engagement.

The 1993 album *Erotica* and its accompanying book *Sex*, for instance, show a manipulation of style, but as if Madonna herself is not there. The *Sex* pictures, blonde parodies of perversion and female fantasy coupled with a clumsy approximation of Anais Nin writings, seem curiously flat;[18] whilst the record—a thinly sung version of the taut Peggy Lee classic 'Fever', plus slow-burning disco workouts such as 'Erotic'—reflects the fact that it was recorded nine-to-five to a three-month deadline. This audio-visual package was a *job*, a product, a Warholian facsimile of the peroxide sex persona the public had come to expect.

Madonna thoroughly jolted expectations three years earlier, when, in post-divorce trauma, she had allowed her vulnerability and unconscious longings to seep through into an album that, unlike her earlier work, was widely considered to be High Art. Reminiscent of Joyce's *Portrait Of An Artist*, her 1989 album *Like A Prayer* could be re-titled *Impassioned Autobiography of a Lapsed Catholic*. From the devotional pop of the title track and its accompanying video in which Madonna kisses the face of a black Christ, to the frank re-evaluation of childhood pain on 'Promise To Try', she dealt with major life themes in a sober, poetic and aesthetic manner. Having dyed her hair a penitent black, she was rewarded with a cover on *Rolling Stone* and a serious 'artist' interview. For this project, Madonna was engaged in a full expression of self, showing an ability to cross categories more subtly than ever before.

Perhaps exclusion from pop's white male canon left her feeling less hidebound by considerations of its own High and Low Art. A year after 'Like A Prayer', Madonna released arguably the best record of her career, 'Justify My Love'. Rapping with whispered intensity to a pared-down backbeat, she voiced the deep, private nature of female fantasy and desire. Teetering between tension and sensuality, and incorporating ironic references to decadent prewar Berlin cabaret in the video, it was dance ballad as serious art form.

What is interesting is how Jane Siberry, in shifting focus from the plangent upper registers of her former material to the dance beat warmth of *When I Was A Boy*, blurred her *own* boundaries, somehow meeting Madonna in the middle. Aware that she was alienating a fan base who read dance music as anti-intellectual and vulgar, Siberry still took the risk. The track 'All The Candles In The World' is not dissimilar to 'Justify My Love', with its undertone of severe funk and low-slung fevered rap, conveying the full sensual power of '90s religious fervour. That was where Warners could have had their 'mass culture' hit with Siberry.

On one level, Madonna and Siberry could be 'read' as postmodern texts without reference to High/Low distinctions, but an array of aesthetic and literary considerations can be seen in their work, as well as the old-fashioned desire to place themselves at the centre of their story as artists. Their status as women, as Other, has meant greater flexibility in playing with and exposing the arbitrary nature of those High/Low, mass versus elite, roles. It is from these fusions that a true democratic culture of resistance can emerge.

## Notes

1 Matthew Arnold, *Culture And Anarchy* (London, 1869).
2 R. Williams, *Culture and Society* (London, Chatto and Windus, 1958).
3 R. Barthes, *Mythologies* (New York, Hill and Wang, 1972); *Image/Music/Text* (New York, Hill and Wang, 1977).
4 J. Collins, *Uncommon Cultures: Popular Culture and Post-Modernism* (New York and London, Routledge, 1989), pp. 7–27.
5 Cosmo Landesman, 'Culture Clash', *The Sunday Times* (14 Nov 1993), 11.
6 S. Frith and H. Horne, *Art Into Pop* (London, Routledge, 1989), p. 71.
7 See other essays (in this collection) by Goodman, Kaplan, Fuller.
8 J. Fiske, *Understanding Popular Culture* (London, Unwin Hyman, 1989), p. 55.
9 Frith, *Art Into Pop*, p. 71.
10 F. Newton, *The Jazz Scene* (Harmondsworth, Penguin, 1961), p. 238.
11 D. Hebdige, 'Style As Homology And Signifying Practice', in S. Frith and A. Goodwin (eds.), *On Record* (London, Routledge, 1990), pp. 56–65. Hebdige noted in detail the musical tastes, the clothes and 'boots, braces and cropped hair' that communicated the unity of a group of male working-class skinheads. He also dissected the 'semiotic guerilla warfare' of punk aggression: 'The punks wore clothes which were the sartorial equivalent of swear words, and they swore as they dressed—with calculated effect, lacing obscenities into record notes and publicity releases, interviews, and love songs. Clothed in chaos, they produced Noise in the calmly orchestrated Crisis of everyday life in the late 1970s . . .' See also the founding text: D. Hebdige, *Subculture: The Meaning Of Style* (London, Methuen, 1979).
12 A. McRobbie, 'Settling Accounts with Subcultures: A Feminist Critique (1980)', in Frith and Goodwin (eds.), *On Record*, pp. 66–81. She begins her feminist rereading of youth culture commentators such as Hebdige by stating: 'Although "youth culture" and the "sociology of youth" . . . have been central strands in the development of Cultural Studies over the past fifteen years, the emphasis . . . has remained consistently on male youth cultural forms'—then goes on to ask: 'What . . . is the nature of women's and girls' leisure? What role do hedonism, fantasy escapes, and imaginary solutions play in their lives?'
13 Frith, *Art Into Pop*, p. 155.
14 Quote from interview by author with psychoanalyst Marion Woodman for *Everywoman* magazine (February 1994) on publication of her book *Leaving My Father's House: A Journey to Conscious Femininity* (London, Rider, 1993).
15 Interview with author, London 1993.
16 *Ibid.*

17 Fiske, *Understanding Popular Culture*, p. 103.
18 Note *Sex* (New York, Martin Secker & Warburg, 1992), Madonna's letter beginning: 'Dear Johnny, Things have not been the same since you left . . .' where in the persona of dominatrix Dita she writes of a three-way affair between her, 'Ingrid' and 'Johnny'—reminiscent of Anaïs Nin's diary *Henry and June* (London, W. H. Allen, 1987), in which she described her affair with Henry Miller and his wife June.

15

*A. Ruth Tompsett*

# Changing perspectives

All art work, from popular film to contemporary dance, from rap and Shakespeare to live art and opera, is informed by the attitudes, consciousness and life experience of the person creating it. More specifically, age, class, gender, sexuality, racial origin and ability/disability will all significantly vary a person's experience of life and influence their way of representing it. This essay examines the extent to which contemporary arts reflect and derive from a genuine range of experience and perspectives and seeks to identify significant factors in the development of more diverse and representative arts activity.

Who are the creative artists in dance, drama and music today? Whose work is in production and thereby available to us? Scrutiny of listings in London's *Time Out* can offer an immediate way of finding some preliminary answers to that question. One randomly selected week's theatre listing in TO reveals, for example, that out of 155 plays in production in that week, 143 are written by men and twelve by women;[1] a similarly small proportion of plays are female-directed. Examination of several weeks' listings presents a similar picture. This simple exercise raises significant questions about the extent to which women's perspectives and experience are available in contemporary theatre production. Examination of the raw data of week by week listings of film, music, theatre or classical dance reveals a similarly disproportionate representation of male creative artists, who are, also, predominantly white and middle class. To the enquiring mind this raises a good many questions. Only contemporary dance reveals a richer and more diverse profile.

Imagine a house inhabited by a large traditional family. The head of the family occupies a room on one side of the house. The view from his window represents to him the view of the world. He gives no value or credence to the notion that other rooms have other views. He requires that the view from his window define the outside world for everyone in that house and, to a large extent, the family comply, until finally some of them believe it.

If such a metaphor for Western culture seems extreme or absurd, the more absurd fact is that it is true. Amongst their many and contested functions, the arts variously serve to represent our lives to us, to mediate experience and express feeling, to debate issues and inform, to entertain, challenge and celebrate. How effectively and valuably can plays, concerts, films begin to fulfil such functions if established art works draw predominantly on a limited range of human experience and perspectives to the exclusion of so many other voices?

This essay examines the extent to which a rich and diverse arts scene depends on diversity and difference amongst the creative artists who contribute to it. It addresses how the gender, sexuality, racial origin, class or ability/disability of creative artists informs their creative work and demonstrates how many of the existing attitudes and structures in established contemporary arts production contribute to maintaining a narrowly based arts scene. The essay makes a case for the importance of more representative and broadly based arts production and concludes with a review of the ways in which the arts can be opened up to a wider range of voices and perspectives. The discussion is organised into three sections, each headed by a key question: 'Who speaks for who?', 'Who is in charge?' and 'What are the influences for change?' The aim is to inform, question and challenge readers and engage them in debate, drawing on a wide range of predominantly recent or contemporary references across the arts, mainly in Britain, including theatre, cinema, dance, music and live art.

## Who speaks for who?

Throughout its history, American cinema has notoriously misrepresented American Indians and African–Americans. Cinema has been used in America to re-write history from the dominant white perspective and to maintain that version as the truth. In the last few years such films as *Mississippi Burning* (1988)[2] and *Dances with Wolves* (1990)[3] have been praised for 'putting the record straight' and giving a more honest account of American history. However, the heroes presented in both films are white Americans and the characters, situations and events are presented to audiences through their eyes and from the perspective of white directors and producers. It is significant that those who are prominent in African–American cinema, from Eddie Murphy to Spike Lee and Robert Townsend, tend to direct their own scripts, as well as taking acting parts. There may be several reasons for this, including difficulty with finding financial backing, but it is also likely that black film-makers feel all too keenly the risks of letting any part of their films fall into white control.

When the perspective from which a film, or song or play is created coincides with one's own, it becomes transparent, it seems merely to be 'true'. When an art work is created from a very different perspective from one's own, it can appear, at least at first, boring, confusing or irrelevant. For example, men who are accustomed to seeing films in which male characters are central to the action, or in which the male/female interaction is presented from a male director's point of view, may initially react with a lack of interest to a film from a female director, not appreciating its relevance because the content does not connect with their experience. What is invisible from one perspective may be obvious from another. A Native American watching *Dances with Wolves* may see a different film from the one most white Americans are seeing. If, amongst its many functions, art serves to enlarge our understanding of life and to represent our experience of it, a range of perspectives is crucial.

The issue is not merely one of positive images, important as that aspect is. Different perspectives derive from different sensibilities; similar events or situations can be quite differently perceived and interpreted by two people from different perspectives. For example, what is distinctly female in the directing of the film *The Piano* (1993)[4] is not the construction of positive female images (the gendered characteristics of the female characters in this film are not significantly positive or negative), but lies in the way the central character's situation and actions are explored and presented. Set down, with her daughter, in a far-flung and seemingly alien shore of the British Empire, subject to an arranged marriage to someone to whom she does not find herself attracted and who removes from her the one consolation and means of expression that she holds dear—her piano—Ada sets about acting upon circumstances, rather than remaining passive and acted upon. In trading her body, albeit by small degrees, to 'buy back' her piano, she turns around her potential role as a victim, and in a small but crucial way, takes charge of her life. The way in which the female character takes the initiative in addressing her negative situation is what suggests female authorship and direction of the film. The construction and development of the two main male characters may also be indicative of a female sensibility. The man to whom Ada is married patiently waits in vain for her to be ready to consummate the marriage. The man from whom she is 'buying back' her piano, does not, on agreeing terms, immediately seek to have full sexual intercourse and press his advantage; he touches, holds, caresses, expressing his desire with tenderness, respect and an apparent lack of haste or pressure. The actions and motivations of these two male characters derive from a female creative imagination and would be much less likely to arise from male authorship. It is just such sensibility that makes the film unusual because we are generally not accustomed to films made by women. Scenes of passion are the very stuff of movies and there are scenes of passion in *The Piano*, but the perspective is different. The act of sexual consummation is generally prioritised in films; in *The Piano*, intimacy repeatedly involves only touching or caressing. There is both sensuality and tenderness in the man's behaviour towards the woman which is paralleled by tenderness and attentiveness between mother and child. The pacing, the focus on feeling and the notion of what constitutes intimacy here, are all more characteristic of a female way of looking at sex.[5] Throughout the twentieth century, film has presented an almost exclusively white and male perspective on the world, whether real or imaginary, while a rich variety of other ways of seeing has remained unrecognised, unacknowledged, as though the white and male way of seeing was *the* way, rather than one way.

Because so little opportunity has been given to creative artists coming from a wider range of perspectives, a woman, Asian or working-class playwright, painter or songwriter may find him/herself burdened with other people's hopes or expectations; the negative responses that some British Asians brought to *My Beautiful Launderette*[6] may have had little to do with the film itself and rather more to do with a situation in which a film by a British Asian is so rare that it gets seen as an authoritative source of information or understanding on 'Asian-ness' in general, an attitude which is briefly referred to in the film itself in Nasser's irritated riposte to Johnny: 'I'm a professional businessman, not a professional Pakistani.' For this reason, creative artists using under-represented voices can feel under pressure to present specifically positive role models in their work. Good art, whether judged in terms of entertainment, aesthetics, authenticity, skill or the debate and interest it generates, does not usually result from ideological prescription. The artist must be free to work from his or her own vision and motivations. The dinner party which opens Caryl Churchill's seminal play *Top Girls* (1982)[7] is attended by five women from history celebrating the twentieth-century Marlene's promotion to managing director of an employment agency. Students of the play sometimes initially express bafflement at the choice and construction of the characters in this scene, who are not famous names nor especially attractive, who are indeed at times disagreeable or boring; they are, however, also extraordinary, each in their different ways, in what they set out to do and in what they have achieved. Dull Gret went to the jaws of hell to fight for her husband's return; the Japanese courtesan, no longer young, took to the road as a travelling Buddhist nun, as a means to independence; each of the characters, including Marlene, has had to make sacrifices and overcome difficulties that arose from her situation in a male-dominated society. They are women who made difficult decisions and who, with the exception of Griselda, took charge of their own circumstances against all the odds: these are strong women. In the 'malestream' of English-language theatre, where else can such strong women be found?

Ada and Marlene are as distinctly the creations of a female sensibility as Omar, from *My Beautiful Launderette*, derives from a British Asian perspective. They offer a glimpse of a possible diversity of experience and vision that could be widely informing and enhancing the range of arts in production. At present, much human experience is marginalised and stereotyped in the arts because the differing perspectives of men and women, black and white, gay and heterosexual, and of people of different classes and abilities are not recognised as equally valid or given equal space or opportunity. Why is it so rare to find, in production, an opera written by a woman or a play by an Asian playwright? Why, in any given week, are there only twelve plays by women out of 155 plays in production in London? Why is so little space given to other voices?

It seems likely that a white, male and middle-class perspective continues to dominate the performing arts because most of those in positions of decision-making and choice are white, male and middle class. The situation is self-perpetuating. People tend generally and more readily to find value in art work that derives from perspectives and sensibilities they share. The range of voices available to us in the performing arts is very much about who is in charge and who is doing the choosing. The next section in this essay goes on to address the question, 'Who is in charge?' and examines the connections between who is in control of choice and what range of creative work is made available to us, the potential audience.

## Who is in charge?

Few areas in the arts are as narrowly based as classical music performance. The pit, the podium and the score itself are predominantly male preserves in which women feature minimally and black musicians even more rarely. As Paul Fürst puts it,

> [t]here is no ban on women musicians playing here but the Vienna Philharmonic is by tradition an all-male orchestra. Our profession makes family life extremely difficult, so for a woman it's almost impossible. There are so many orchestras with women members so why shouldn't there be—for how long I don't know—an orchestra with no women in it. . . . A woman shouldn't play like a man but like a woman, but an all-male orchestra is bound to have a special tone.[8]

Few orchestras today actually state a case for remaining all-male, but Professor Fürst's point of view is not uncommon, nor is the collection of red herrings he offers as 'reasons' for keeping female players out of the Vienna Philharmonic Orchestra. The appeal to 'tradition' has been used to justify the rejection of women composers, conductors and players across the centuries and is not so much a reason as an excuse for not having a reason. It is prejudice dignified by the passage of time. The suggestion that the demands of playing in an orchestra may interfere with family duties makes assumptions about gender roles that people should decide for themselves and not have decided for them. Fürst's appeal for an all-male orchestra because 'there are so many orchestras with women members' is an attempt to keep a foot firmly on the brake. Finally Fürst comes to the much-voiced but little-researched notion of gendered musical tone. It may be that an all-male orchestra has a different tone from an all-female orchestra—it is an interesting research proposition—but that the male tone is 'special' is a matter of taste, or prejudice, or both.

Such attitudes as Paul Fürst demonstrates are widely evident in the still predominantly male classical music establishment. There are female members now in most national orchestras, but women conductors remain extremely rare. A major block to the progress of women conductors appears to derive from male resistance to leadership and the exercise of authority in a woman, qualities essential to conducting. Internationally respected conductor Odaline de la Martinez speaks of having constantly encountered doubt from men as to her capacity as a conductor. She refers to the jokes and tricks male orchestra members would play on her to test her out,[9] an experience echoed by other female conductors. New York (male) academic Sixten Ehrling speaks of the stamina and determination required of conductors and of the additional qualities women have to show: 'You need a strong will, and since we're talking about women conductors, more is demanded of them than men.'[10] Whether due to resistance to women being in positions of authority or for other reasons, it is hard for a woman to acquire the position of conductor; the majority of male impresarios, producers and other conductors do not choose or appoint women conductors. Martinez, to the surprise of some, has vigorously defended the BBC as one of the least prejudiced organisations she has worked for, identifying gender as a significant factor: 'There are many women bosses at the BBC, and they encourage women to enter positions of power and authority.'[11] The issue of control, the question of who is in charge of selecting or appointing, is clearly central to change.

This is most evident of all in the matter of repertoire. Few orchestral players can name a significant range of compositions by women. Many may assume few, if any, women composers exist. The evidence is that male conductors do not choose work by female composers, perpetuating a historical situation which has consistently invisibilised women's composition. Compositions by women tend only to be selected for performance when women are in charge of the choosing. It is for this reason that such organisations as Women in Music came into being and why all-women orchestras have been established.[12]

Guyanese-born black British conductor Rudolph Dunbar, who trained at the Julliard School in New York and subsequently in Paris, was initially welcomed as a conductor by the BBC, the London Philharmonic and the Berlin Philharmonic, and for several years pursued a successful career in music in Britain. With increased immigration to Britain from the West Indies in the 1950s, racial prejudice rapidly became more evident. Dunbar experienced widespread withdrawal of support and interest, and considerable shifts in attitude:

> Daring to work in the field of 'white man's music' he was never allowed to forget he was black. Sir Malcolm Sargent was one of many orchestral notabilities who questioned his credentials. 'Who is this Dunbar?' he asked impresario Harold Holt. 'Have you ever seen him conduct?' Holt replied that he hadn't, adding, 'I haven't seen Toscanini, either, but I brought him to this country for the first time.'[13]

Doubt in the capacities of black classical musicians continues today to disadvantage and discourage. In addition, works by black composers are rarely, if ever, included in concert programmes. In his time, Dunbar introduced European audiences to works by black composers. Who is introducing today's audiences to that diversity?

The pity in not recognising female and black musicianship and composition is that so much of quality and imagination remains unknown and unenjoyed that could enrich and diversify experience.

In America, Equal Opportunities Policies have led to the institution of anonymous auditioning in which musicians are positioned behind screens and as a direct result there has been a significant increase in female and black representation in orchestras. It is not so easy to use anonymous selection procedures in appointing conductors or deciding on what to include in an orchestra's repertoire.

Similar prejudice prevails in classical dance, in respect of black dancers; to be a good black ballerina is to have a limited chance of a career. In 1989, Carole Straker launched her own dance company to give opportunities to black classically trained dancers. Through such individual, black-led initiatives, black dancers can gain experience and opportunities to perform. In the 1990s, the dance establishment, however, remains little changed. Notions of what is appropriate die hard. It is as though 'white' is part of the definition of ballet. As Anthony Dowell, Artistic Director of the Royal Ballet, put it, 'Because the classical ballets are based on spectacle and geometric pattern, line, balance, I think for my eye it would be difficult if one black dancer . . . would perhaps push the balance; the eye, my eye, would be drawn.[14]

Peter Schaufuss, Danish Artistic Director of the English National Ballet, has a different perspective on the integration of black and white dancers in ballet performance: 'It's a matter of how you see things. I've sat with people out front and when some of our black dancers are dancing they see with different eyes than I do . . . I don't see that way. I see people and line and movements; it [the presence of black dancers] doesn't distract me at all.'[15]

For Peter Schaufuss, the problem lies in insufficient recruitment of black dancers to training schools. Perhaps it is a vicious circle in which young black dancers see little in professional performance that leads them to believe they would be welcome to apply to train for classical ballet. The Dance Theatre of Harlem in the US was born out of the need and enthusiasms of black dancers and choreographers to have opportunities to reach the highest standards in ballet and to explore ballet from an African–American perspective. Now an acclaimed company with an international reputation, its repertoire includes both classic and European ballets and more contemporary ballets that draw on an African heritage, as well as producing ballet which fuses European with African in a whole range of ways. Such is the diversity, richness and growth that can arise from a broader base.

In 1990, two dancers from the Dance Theatre of Harlem guested as principals with the Royal Ballet at Covent Garden. They stated a concern to be role models for younger dancers, but as Julia Pascal observed in an article in *The Guardian*, '[u]nless the Royal Ballet's directors, teachers and choreographers rethink their traditional images of ballet dancers there will be no integrated casting in the hermetically sealed world of British ballet.'[16] A notion of ballet that sees variation of skin colour as problematic is essentially racist; to take a fixed and undynamic approach to ballet is to be at odds with the very nature of creativity and art. In opera, a black Constanze pairs easily with a white Pasha Selim, but on the same stage at Covent Garden integrated casting is generally seen as 'not ballet'. It is those in charge, those who control selection and casting, who can diversify ballet's image or choose to preserve entrenched and traditional attitudes. With a wider range of perspectives and sensibilities amongst company members and wider representation at the decision-making level, new interpretations of traditional ballets might emerge and new works be added to repertoires, stimulating growth and diversity in ballet. Perhaps such development and originality is what many of those in charge most fear.

The issue of control within the arts, and of the distortions and fictions that can arise from the privileging of the white male middle-class perspective, is specifically analysed within the narrative of Hanif Kureishi's novel *The Buddha of Suburbia*, dramatised for television by Kureishi and serialised in 1993.[17] The central character, actor Karim, attracts directors' interest partly on account of what they see as his different ethnicity, an interest which turns out not to extend beyond difference of skin colour. Karim finds that he is wanted for his 'Indianness', but that it is a fictional notion of what it is to be Indian, entirely derived from the perspective of the white directors and ironically excluding Karim's own voice and experience. First he is cast as Mowgli in a 'physical theatre' production of Kipling's *Jungle Book*. At director Jeremy Shadwell's behest, Karim spends long hours attempting to acquire a phoney Indian accent, struggling to fit the caricature that has been defined for him. Not only does Shadwell refuse to address Karim's concern about using the supposed Indian accent; he also insists, in the face of Karim's protestations, that he performs with a yellowish brown concoction smeared over his naked body. 'It suits you', Shadwell says, asserting his perspective over Karim's and echoing a century-old vaudeville tradition in Western performance whereby even black performers were required to 'black up', to conform to a white caricature of being black, rather than being allowed to be themselves. The next director Karim works with seems at first to be open to the company members' own ideas and points of view: 'Collectively we invent the play', as he puts it. However, when it comes to it, Matthew Pyke acts as dictatorially as Shadwell did and Karim finds himself playing a buffoon; the situation is the more treacherous because this is a character he has created himself. Kureishi draws attention here to the manipulative nature of what on the surface appears to be a democratic process; Karim's original devised character presented a negative image which a black company member found offensive. Pyke takes the point, but the real issues are not discussed: when Karim comes up with the buffoon character, some of the same objections and analyses might apply. Pyke demonstrates that he is ultimately not interested in understanding the experience from which this character, or indeed the previous one, is drawn. The comedy in this character makes it a safer bet and Pyke can see a theatrical use for it; thus the character Karim has devised becomes hijacked to fit a creation ultimately of Pyke's devising and perspective.

*The Buddha of Suburbia* is set in the 1970s. In the 1990s, the situation is not significantly altered. *Buddha* incisively, if also humorously, demonstrates the director's power to distort reality, to privilege and perpetuate his own perspective, to the exclusion of others, while giving the appearance of being open-minded, even experimental.

The arts in the UK are part of a hierarchical and self-perpetuating distribution of power that pertains across all social organisations, including government, education and commerce. Examination of the contemporary arts scene indicates that the choosing and deciding, in terms of whose work gets into production, whose voices are heard, lies predominantly now, as it has done historically, with white, middle-class males. As a result, great potential goes unrecognised. Those who are in positions to decide and select tend to attribute value to art work which accords with their own values or perspectives, sometimes because of unacknowledged prejudice, sometimes from an unconscious lack of openness to 'the other', to art which derives from a sensibility which they do not understand or which they do not recognise as valid in its difference or with which, quite simply, they are not familiar. White directors sometimes choose to direct plays by black playwrights, heterosexual songwriters sometimes choose to write about gay love, but generally they do not or they do so tokenistically. If the greater range of voices is to be heard, there has to be more diversity at the level of management and artistic direction.[18]

Another relevant factor in any consideration of control in the arts is the critical establishment. Critics have significant, if less direct, influence on the diversity available, or not available, in the arts scene. The reading and viewing public generally look to reviews for entertainment, information, evaluation and recommendation, in varying proportions. In New York, overnight critical response to a new production can be a deciding factor in its success or failure. In London, it is less singularly determining, but it can contribute to the hype that can feed a production's success or make it less popular. Many people make choices on the basis of critics' recommendations or look to reviews and articles for guidance in interpreting art works. In particular, critics are in a position to open up new possibilities to potential audiences. Their professional knowledge and practical experience in analysing and interpreting equip them to mediate new work, analyse perspectives, identify difference and diversity, and the lack of them. The critic is crucially placed to affirm the status quo or question it, to perpetuate prejudice or to illumine and illuminate.

When men and women perceive and evaluate theatre and performance work profoundly differently, the question of gender balance in the critical cohort becomes an issue. In the mid-1990s, the ratio of female to male critics across the national press and listings magazines was 1:4. Whilst in many instances the sex of the critic is not a significant factor in differentiating response, in other instances it can result in interesting and valuable work being widely disparaged or misunderstood, or work of partial appeal receiving disproportionate praise and encouragement. Between the mid-1980s and the mid-1990s there has been an increase in female representation in reviewing, but it is noticeable that major productions, such as those at the National Theatre and from the Royal Shakespeare Company, are still generally male-reviewed, while women appear to be more often assigned to fringe and experimental theatre and to productions by black and Asian companies. It may well be that women generally bring a more open mind to bear on such a range of work, but it further aggravates the imbalance, by which a fare of predominantly male-written plays in major venues is predominantly male-reviewed, perpetuating a narrowness of perspective in the theatre establishment which remains largely unchallenged.

This limited perspective is significantly evident in the reviews of two 1993 London productions of David Mamet's *Oleanna*, directed at the Royal Court Theatre by Harold Pinter, in which a university lecturer loses his job, as a result of the female student's accusations of harassment. Male-authored and male-directed, *Oleanna* was constructed in the first instance from a distinctly gendered point of view which invited sympathy for the male character. Or did it? From the predominantly male reviewing cohort (sixteen of the seventeen reviews in the first instance were by men), it is difficult for the open-minded reader to know; the reviews mainly endorse Mamet's apparent fears of female power. When David Mamet, Harold Pinter and the leading male critics of Europe's theatre capital get together to lament and expostulate over female wiles and political correctness, any objective debate of student–tutor relations is effectively submerged and the status quo rests unchallenged. Examination of the reviewing of *Oleanna*, together with other West End productions, reveals how biased and unbalanced critical reporting on theatre in Britain distorts and obscures the meaning of plays and limits interpretation and debate.

It is possible, at least to some extent, to compare male/female perspectives on a production and to recognise the extent to which gender can be a factor in interpretation and evaluation. But a comparison between black and white British perspectives on a piece of theatre is rarely possible at all because there are no regular black critics. While this situation remains, not only do productions that come from a black or Asian perspective get inadequately reviewed, but, equally, all reviewing of arts production is thereby lacking the distinctive critical insights a black or Asian critic could bring. As C. L. R. James put it,

> [t]hose people who are in Western civilisation, who have grown up in it but yet are not completely a part, have a unique insight into their society . . . The black man or woman who is born here or grows up here has something special to contribute to Western civilisation. He or she will participate in it from birth, but will never be quite completely in it. What such persons have to say, therefore, will give a new vision, a deeper and stronger insight into both Western civilisation and the black people in it.[19]

Sometimes the absence of a black perspective is critical and the wider significance of an art work remains not merely unexplored but entirely unacknowledged and unrealised, as in the case of John Guare's *Six Degrees of Separation*, first produced in New York and subsequently in London at the Royal Court Theatre in 1992.[20] Plausible, charming Paul, pretending to be Sidney Poitier's son and a friend of Ouisa and Flan Kittredge's children, calls on the wealthy Kittredge parents claiming he has been mugged in Central Park and asking them for assistance. Through the gay, black conman Paul, playwright Guare reveals the hypocrisy in the comparable wheeling and dealing of wealthy liberal Manhattan society. Critics in the British press (again, a predominantly male, as well as entirely white, cohort), received the play with enthusiasm. Only Michael Billington was sharply critical.[21] It is not that the themes and debates that the critics identify in the play are not pertinent, but that they leave so much unexplored. No critic addressed the import and impact of Paul being African–American. Sitting in a white audience, watching this white-authored play in which the central black character cons a roomful of wealthy white Americans, is likely to be a very different experience for a white person and for a black person. The critics, perhaps the playwright himself, seem unaware of how the play unselfconsciously draws on the notion of the black man as the white man's darker self and offer no analysis of how in this play, as elsewhere, a solitary black character is a means of exposing the fear and ignorance in wealthy white society. History is written between the lines of the play's text but remains invisible and uncommented on, and its relevance to Britain is not addressed. The fact that Paul is based on a real-life character who operated very much as Paul does in the play is seen as giving a frisson, as well as authenticity, to the play; but the fact that someone like Paul exists in 'real life' doesn't make him any less of a construction, just as the play is a construction; the play and Paul's character are equally the constructions of a white perspective and sensibility. For white Britons or Americans, not to have access to black critical perspectives on the play is to miss a chance to learn about themselves. Possibly a black reviewer might have interpreted the play differently; certainly he/she would have raised other points. Lacking a black perspective, the sensibility and awareness brought to reviewing of this play was, in total, limited.

In reviewing productions that explicitly derive from a different cultural source, some critics more readily state their sense of not being appropriately equipped. Both Tara Arts' *Heer Ranjha*[22] and *Moti Roti Puttli Chunni*[23] by Keith Khan and Ali Zaida, produced at the Theatre Royal Stratford East in 1992 and 1993 respectively, won enthusiastic responses from critics, but as Malcolm Rutherford observes, 'No doubt there is more to *Moti Roti* than meets the average Anglo-Saxon eye and ear'.[24] Such awareness is more evident amongst critics in reviewing *Heer Ranjha* and *Moti Roti*, with their obvious 'otherness', than amongst the same critics in their reviews of *Six Degrees*. It is important that critics recognise the limitations of their perspectives in a range of circumstances.

From the above analyses of arts production and critical reviewing it is evident that there is a crucial connection between what is selected for performance and who is in charge of selecting; and, further, that those in control of the arts and of the critical establishment are generally white and middle class, and mostly male. It is not unusual for white, middle-class males to feel under attack in this debate; in this essay, at least, no attack is intended; a defensive situation tends to be a closed one, and here it is openness that is valuable and to be valued. The situation is not one of laying or claiming blame but of sharing an interest in broadening access to the arts and recognising the enrichment and validity of other perspectives. For the rich diversity of voices in the arts to be heard, there needs to be more diversity amongst those who are in charge. The third and final section of this essay examines existing ways of achieving that wider representation in the arts and opportunities for genuine development of hitherto undervalued arts production, by posing the question: What are the influences for change?

## What are the influences for change?

Study of alternative theatre and performance practice since the 1970s highlights a range of means and influences which have successfully effected change in the arts in terms of attitudes and opportunities, and which have led to increased diversity of perspective and sensibility. In this, as in other areas, 'the fringe' has led the establishment. This section focuses specifically on some contemporary performance practices and ways of working, the influence of education and equal opportunities policies and, in conclusion, the role of critical reviewing. Much that is positive in past and present practice provides encouragement for future development.

### *Ways of working*

Devising and rehearsal processes can be significant in broadening the sources of creative work and the inputs to it. The 1970s saw a widespread development of *ensemble* and *co-operative ways of working*; for example, a script might derive from an initial two or three weeks' period of improvisation with input from all company members; in this situation the directorial role shifts to allow, at least in the initial stages, for more sharing of ideas, and the final production is likely to be informed by the range of sensibilities of the company members and their diverse experience of life, both public and personal. In *The Buddha of Suburbia*, Hanif Kureishi illustrates how the sharing of ideas can, in practice, be more imaginary than real, especially where a director is not genuinely open to the possibilities that may emerge from such an approach, but the production achievements of such past and present companies as Joint Stock, Shared Experience, Trestle, Black Mime Theatre Company, V-tol and Forced Entertainment eloquently bear witness to the strengths of ensemble working and to the more aware, sensitive and wide-reaching theatre that can grow from it. Caryl Churchill's play *Cloud Nine* (1979)[25] originated in discussions, improvisation and exploration undertaken by members of Joint Stock who subsequently made up the cast. The honesty and complexity of the play's examination of family and colonial structures, and of their interconnections, derive not only from Churchill's notable breadth of experience and understanding, but also from the collected experience and consciousness of the cast, informed by difference of gender, age, sexuality and background. By the same token, had there been black actors in the company, and especially in the original improvisational work, the play might have offered sharper insights into relationships between people of different races in a colonial situation, an underdeveloped aspect of the play's debate.

More open and democratic ways of working in drama, dance, live art or music are to be found 'on the fringe'. The terms 'fringe' and 'alternative' suggest performance work that is peripheral, additional, somehow lesser, but nothing could be further from the truth. It is 'alternative theatre' that is constantly nudging the mores, aesthetics and processes of 'established theatre'. The fringe is more open to experiment and to giving space to different voices and different perspectives because it is generally less hierarchical. Hierarchical attitudes privilege the traditional 'pecking order' in which white comes before black, male before female and so on, preserving the status quo. The successful productions of alternative companies shift attitudes and practice in the mainstream.

Casting across race, an aspect of *non-traditional casting*, offers opportunities for introducing different perspectives into performance in several ways. Traditionally in theatre, a cast is selected by audition; men audition for male parts, children to play children, a Chinese actor for a Chinese role; actors who accept gay roles are often assumed to be gay and may find that they are subsequently seen as only suitable for gay roles. This traditional approach to casting is self-limiting and leads to casting to type or according to previous work and, even in some instances to stereotyped characterisation that the actor carries from one production to another, so that audiences expect certain kinds of characterisation from certain actors. In companies that are smaller and/or more open to experiment in how they work, the same actor may play two or more parts, may be cast against type or across race, age or gender. There are clearly practical advantages that attach to such non-traditional casting; a company is not limited in the choice of play, or in what it devises, by the gender, race or age of the company members or indeed by the number of performers in the company; an adult can play a child, a woman can play a man, black actors are not restricted to black roles. But more significantly for the discussion here, such non-traditional casting provides opportunities for valuable two-way exchanges of insight. An adult playing a child role can bring to it both 'the remembrance of things past', insider knowledge of childhood from having been there, plus adult observation of child behaviour and motivation; this was richly evident in the production of Dennis Potter's play for television *Blue Remembered Hills* (1979),[26] in which the cast of five child characters were all played by adult actors, and similarly in Trestle Theatre Company's devised mime productions *Crèche* (1981) and *Hanging Around* (1982).[27] By the same token, children and young people are able to bring a distinct perspective to playing an adult character through their often sharp observation of adult vulnerabilities. All too rarely are opportunities given to young people to play adult characters and to give us a view on ourselves informed from their experience and standpoint.[28] A black performer playing a white role can bring to the part understanding derived from shared or similar experience, together with knowledge of white life or white behaviour as observed, to some extent, 'from the outside'.

Colour-blind casting, whether in contemporary or classical work, helps to break down stereotypical views of roles and performers. Cheek by Jowl and Wild Iris are examples of multi-racial companies whose productions of Shakespeare's *As You Like It*[29] and Restoration playwright Catherine Trotter's *Love at a Loss*[30] were cast colour-blind. In these authentic productions, i.e., adhering to the original text and not operating cross-culturally, the casting defies conservative and stereotypical notions of who can or cannot perform Shakespeare or Restoration drama. In the majority of theatre companies, directors continue to have difficulty leaving their stereotypical assumptions behind and continue to see the skin colour of an actor as a significant factor in casting.

Issues of casting and of work opportunity are significant not only in respect of gender, race and age, but also pertaining to differently abled performers. Opportunities in the arts for differently abled performers are few and it is rare indeed for performers to be cast or choreographed irrespective of a disability. Were it to be more usual, audiences would soon learn not to bring special expectations to it. Michel Petrucciani, the French jazz pianist, celebratedly overcame restrictions arising from a severe bone disorder which limited his height to three foot, and speaks of his physical situation with relative unconcern: 'I think people look at my music ... They don't really care about how I am. My music overpowers my physical condition.'[31]

The dance company CanDoCo is made up of both ordinarily abled and differently abled dancers. Its choreography explores and exploits its dancers' varied capacities and attributes. A performer in a wheelchair is seen as offering a whole range of movement possibilities an ordinarily abled dancer would not have. CanDoCo recognises the equally rich choreographic potential in diverse perspectives, sensibilities and physical ability.

Thirdly, in this consideration of ways of working that can influence change, a proactive response to the continuing élitism and selectivity in the choices and decision-making of arts management and production has been the development of what is sometimes termed *separatism*. The 1970s saw the growth of companies concerned to provide opportunities for performers from self-identified groups, to present performance work from their own, hitherto largely ignored, perspectives. Such companies as Black Theatre Co-op, Tara Arts and African Dawn, Phoenix and Adzido, Gay Sweatshop and Bloolips, Graeae, Female Trouble, Fascinating Aida and Sensible Footwear, to name but a few, through the 1970s and 1980s brought an explosion of fresh experience and subject matter, styles and stories and points of view to the contemporary arts scene, challenging fixed notions of quality, identity and definition in the arts. At the sharp and often overtly political end of separate or independent development are black and Asian rap and music groups such as Ryddum Writers and Fun-Da-Mental. Though groups come and go, often transmuting as they become more successful (as did the black, all-male dance company Phoenix, which is now mixed in race and gender), separate and self-identified groups continue to emerge and establish themselves. Such 'separatism' in performance is widely viewed with unease, even sometimes with suspicion. Creative artists and performers fear the ghettoisation that may follow from their involvement in a specifically black or gay performance company; people confuse performance *by*, for example, Asians with performance *for* Asians; some are fearful of what is not familiar and the term 'separatism' can have negative political associations. For some people, perhaps especially for some white people, such fear and unease derives from not understanding why separate groups develop. It is rarely a 'first choice'; black and Asian British, women and gay performers generally form separate companies because of lack of opportunities elsewhere, not because they want to be or stay separate. Independent, self-identified groups give opportunities and training to people to whom fewer opportunities are offered elsewhere; they give space to previously unheard voices; they shift the agenda for established performance; they force the pace of change. The Dance Theatre of Harlem, discussed earlier, offers a striking example of the effectiveness of such separate or independent development.

A potentially highly effective means to challenging attitudes lies in *the use of humour.* Comedy is a two-edged sword; mother-in-law jokes and stories told at the expense of minority or immigrant groups, for example, 'Irish jokes' in Britain and 'Polish jokes' in the US, bear witness to an ancient tradition in using humour to vilify and control 'the other', and for scape-goating [see Chapter 16 (ed.)]. By the same token, humour can be used to challenge and subvert images and attitudes in the dominant culture. Through the 1980s and 1990s stand-up comedy and alternative cabaret have given increasing opportunities to a greater range of individual performers to tease, provoke, embarrass and surprise audiences into new ways of looking at themselves and other people; using irony, ridicule, story-telling, mimicry, a stand-up comedian can get an audience to see things from new standpoints. Those who were previously the butt of comedians' stories—women, gays, people from racial minorities and the differently abled—are now widely to be found working in cabaret, using humour to open up a broader view on the world. In his film *Hollywood Shuffle* (1987),[32] Robert Townsend examines white-created stereotypes of black people and through the use of humour dismantles and defuses them. The result is a film that is extremely funny, from different perspectives, to both white and black; when a white tutor sets out to teach a black acting student how to 'walk black' the resulting demonstration from the tutor is both hilarious and ludicrous; in such a tiny incident as this, Townsend offers black audiences affirmation and recognition of their repeated experience of having white people assume authority over them, while white audiences are presented with the inappropriateness and patronising nature of the assumption white people often have (and perhaps especially white teachers) that they know better, even about what it is like to be black! Townsend was once a stand-up comic and clearly draws on that experience and expertise in *Hollywood Shuffle*. In his play *The Colored Museum*,[33] American playwright George C. Wolfe makes similar use of comedy to disempower negative black stereotypes. In Britain, comedy has become a mainstream vehicle for black commentary on British life, to both black and white, as well as mixed, audiences. Lenny Henry, and more recently the comedy series *Real McCoy*[34] and *Get Up Stand Up*,[35] alongside performance companies such as The Posse and The Bibi Crew, present life and history in Britain from black perspectives, using humour that ranges from the sharply witty and analytical to the broad and bawdy. At the popular end of the performing arts, humour is possibly the most widely influential medium through which people are introduced to 'other' perspectives on everyday experience, not least because it so obviously couples entertainment with 'instruction'; in addition, the black, gay or female performer is usually performing his or her own material and is therefore in control of it and venues are often small and local which makes for much audience/performer interaction.

*Education and policies*

In considering what influences attitudes and perspectives within the performing arts, the focus so far in this section has been on action and processes within arts production itself. Also of potential influence are the *education syllabuses* in schools and universities and the introduction, wherever people work or study, of monitored *equal opportunities policies*.

Students' experience of education can significantly entrench attitudes and assumptions or open up discussion and invite enquiry, making way for different perspectives and validating other experience. Such openness needs to be broadly based and will derive from structures and processes in conjunction with the people operating them. The policies and procedures that govern admissions and recruitment of students, the nature and content of the syllabuses offered and the training, experience and selection of those who teach and lecture are all significant factors including the kinds of enquiry that are encouraged in the pursuit of learning and the nature of the educational experience offered. What is the racial mix of a given year group? What is the proportion of male to female staff, black to white? Does dance technique teaching include Asian dance? Are black playwrights and composers included in core studies? Is every student's and teacher's sexuality equally respected? The answers to questions like these indicate an institution's openness or otherwise to cultural difference and other perspectives, exclusion of which, whether through prejudice or ignorance, deprives all students of a rich and vigorous range of performing arts experience and maintains the traditional hierarchies that validate some people's experience and expression and ignores or disparages those of others.

In education, and across the arts, commerce and government, an influence for change since the early 1980s has existed wherever organisations have been interested in encouraging and assuring equality of opportunity through policies that are both supported from the top and fully monitored. In London, for example, the equal opportunities policy of the now defunct Greater London Council significantly influenced funding policy in the arts; the distribution of grants to previously unrecognised or ignored performance interests resulted in a flowering of the arts; much of the richer contemporary scene derives from support and opportunities given in the 1980s to a broader range of creative artists and their work.

### *The role of the critic*

As demonstrated earlier in this chapter, the critic is in a position to influence interpretation and evaluation of arts works, at least amongst those who read reviews and articles on the arts, and is thereby implicitly in a position of authority and control. By the same token, the critic is in a position to influence for change; by the very nature of their work, reviewers are well placed to bring past experience and expertise in analysis to bear in interpreting the new, to draw parallels, make comparisons and pose questions; they can open up new ideas and practices in the arts to wider audiences and challenge existing assumptions; an earlier reference in this chapter to a review by Julia Pascal, for example, illustrates such positive practice in critical writing. In his review of the film *Dances with Wolves* (1990), Adam Mars-Jones, writing in *The Independent*, offered a more rigorous analysis of the film's content than many of his colleagues; while recognising the advance the film makes on the old style 'western', Mars-Jones qualifies the nature of that advance: 'Costner and his team have taken a great deal of trouble to get things right—language, customs, dress—and yet the end result is less the re-creation of a vanished past than an attempt to deny history altogether.'[36]

Critical writing that questions and probes can stimulate debate and raise awareness in potential audiences and creative artists alike, especially when, as in the case of the article quoted above, the analysis is informed and detailed and the debate well reasoned. Critics are fond of disclaiming their influence on others through their writing but the widespread use people make of reviews to help them choose what to go and see is an indicator of influence at the simplest level.

### Conclusion

Perhaps dance, today, can provide a role model for the other performing arts. Exciting developments in form, style and subject matter derive from the notable diversity of creative approaches and perspectives in contemporary dance. Pina Bausch, Liz Aggiss, Yolande Snaith, Emilyn Claid, Susan Lewis, H. Patten and Michael Clark are only a few of the considerable number of choreographers who, together with such a company as CanDoCo, have broadened notions of what dance is, of what it can be about and what it can do. Drawing on a wider range of sensibilities, across gender, sexuality, race and physical ability, they have won new audiences to dance performance, who find in their work points of contact, recognition and stimulus that much previous choreography did not offer. Their work demonstrates the significant development and growth that can follow a broader representation amongst those in creative and controlling positions.

Such 'broader representation' is not easily won. Those who are satisfied with things as they are may be unsettled by the prospect of an arts scene in which new plays and symphonies, songs and dance works define life differently and stretch and challenge established notions of art, of what is good, authentic or valuable. Those who are so accustomed to being the authoritative sources of creativity and control in the arts that they believe their way of seeing to be the only way of seeing, tend to meet the challenge of other knowledges and visions with mock patronage; work that comes from a perspective they find awkwardly different from their own is labelled 'politically correct' a term often used deridingly or for comic purposes or as a cover for lack of courage to tackle the uncomfortable. The point at issue is less one of correctness, more one of mutual respect. The stereotype that is a source of broad comedy to one person is a ball and chain around the feet of another.

Wherever creative work derives from a narrow range of perspectives, we are all being 'short-changed'. Marginalisation of difference leads to a limited and limiting arts scene, from which the majority of people find their realities excluded, misrepresented or undervalued. There is a need for openness to other ways of seeing, for suspension of judgement and more willingness to listen, to respect other sensibilities, to take the risk to move off the safe ground of one's own standpoint. The prospect is exciting. Everyone stands to gain from the richer experience diversity can offer. What is it like to live in that traditional house pretending the different views from the many different windows do not exist? It is time to stop pretending and celebrate the consequences.

## Notes

1 Theatre Listings, *Time Out*, London, 27 June 1994.

2 *Mississippi Burning*, directed by Alan Parker, screenplay by Chris Gerolmo, US, 1988.

3 *Dances with Wolves*, directed by Kevin Costner, screenplay by Michael Blake, US, 1990.

4 *The Piano*, direction and screenplay by Jane Campion, NZ, 1992.

5 While director Jane Campion offers a distinctly twentieth-century feminist perspective on sexual experience and behaviour, in *The Piano*, her 'anthro-

pological perspective', in terms of her presentation of the aboriginal Maoris as childlike and generalised, is a nineteenth-century one.

6 *My Beautiful Launderette*, directed by Stephen Frears, screenplay by Hanif Kureishi, UK, 1985.

7 Caryl Churchill, *Top Girls* (London, Methuen, 1982). Theatre production: the Royal Court Theatre, London, 1982.

8 Television documentary: *A Woman is a Risky Bet*, produced by Christina Olofson for Swedish Television, shown in the UK on C4, 1992.

9 Barbara Norden, 'The Sound of Women's Music', *The Guardian* (23 May 1990).

10 *A Woman is a Risky Bet.*

11 Stephen Windos, 'Women in Charge of Men', *City Limits* (14 Aug 1986).

12 'Women in Music' was established in 1987, on the lines of a similar organisation earlier in this century. It exists to promote women's composition, conducting and musicianship. It is based at the Battersea Arts Centre, 176 Lavender Hill, London SW11.

13 Val Wilmer, 'Rudolph Dunbar', *City Limits* (7 March 1986).

14 Television documentary: *Eye to Eye: Breaking the Mould*, directed by Tim Leandro, BBC2, UK, 1989.

15 *Ibid.* The bracketed inclusion is the author's.

16 Julia Pascal, 'Blacks Swan in to Centre Stage', *The Guardian* (20 Dec 1990).

17 Television drama: Hanif Kureishi, *The Buddha of Suburbia*, BBC2, UK, 1993. Adapted from his novel of the same title (London, Faber and Faber, 1990).

18 It is observable that often those who stand outside the mainstream are more open to the range of 'other' perspectives. It may be no coincidence that such arts festivals as LIFT and Dance Umbrella, whose programming in each case is notably rich and imaginative in its diversity, have female leadership and strong female representation in their selection panels and organisational structures. Similarly, the London theatre with probably the most diverse programming in the 1990s is Theatre Royal Stratford East, headed by gay Artistic Director Philip Hedley, whose openness to diversity has brought to Theatre Royal such a rich and popular mix of black and Asian British performance and plays by working-class and young writers, together with more generally available mainstream theatre.

19 Quoted from an article by C. L. R. James in the journal *Ten* 8, 1984.

20 Theatre production: *Six Degrees of Separation* by John Guare, directed by Phyllida Lloyd at the Royal Court Theatre, 1992.

21 Review: Michael Billington, *The Guardian* (22 June 1992).

22 Theatre production: *Heer Ranjha*, adapted from an Indian original by Jatinder Verma, presented by Tara Arts at Theatre Royal, Stratford East, London, 1992 [see Chapter 11 (ed.)].

23 Theatre production: *Moti Roti Puttli Chunni*, devised and directed by Keith Khan and Ali Zaidi, at the Theatre Royal, Stratford East, London, in LIFT, 1993.

24 Malcolm Rutherford, *Financial Times* (25 June 1993).

25 Caryl Churchill, *Cloud Nine* (London, Pluto Press, 1979).

26 Television drama: *Blue Remembered Hills* by Dennis Potter, BBC, UK, 1979.

27 Theatre productions: *Crèche* (1981) and *Hanging Around* (1982), devised and presented by Trestle Theatre Company, London.

28 Notable opportunities have been offered to young writers through the Young Writers' Festivals at the Royal Court Theatre, London.
29 Theatre production: *As You Like It* by William Shakespeare, directed by Declan Donellan and presented by Cheek by Jowl, London, 1991.
30 Theatre production, *Love at a Loss*, by Catherine Trotter, directed by Polly Irvim, presented by Wild Iris, Battersea Arts Centre, London, 1993.
31 Neville Hadsley, 'Profile: Michael Petrucciani—beating all the odds', *Jazz in the South East*, 30 (30 June 1994).
32 Film: *Hollywood Shuffle*, direction and screenplay by Robert Townsend, US, 1987.
33 George C. Wolfe, *The Colored Museum* (London, Methuen, 1987). Theatre production: premiered at Crossroads Theatre Company, US, in 1986.
34 Television comedy series: *Real McCoy*, BBC2, UK, 1992–4.
35 Television comedy series: *Get Up Stand Up*, C4, UK, 1994.
36 Adam Mars-Jones, 'Getting down to the plain untruth', *The Independent* (8 February 1991).

16 *Patrick Campbell*

# Bodies politic, proscribed and perverse: censorship and the performing arts

What is censorship? Recourse to the dictionary hardly helps, though its notion of a 'censor' who 'exercises official or *officious* supervision over morals or conduct'[1] indicates the dilemma—that it is impossible to maintain a position of neutrality when considering its effects. Traditionally, censorship operates in religious, political and ethical directions but since most censoring bodies see themselves as exercising a moral imperative, these categories are rarely mutually exclusive. Moreover, censorship of the arts—our primary concern—operates in multifarious ways and in a range of diverse cultural contexts. For, as the dictionary implies, it is not always 'official', a matter of *state* control. For some, it is primarily about 'the silencing of oppositional voices in a variety of ways; for others it represents an acceptable method of controlling material that is offensive, degrading and possibly dangerous.' Certainly for anyone in the performing arts, commentator and practitioner alike, it is an area 'riven with dilemmas and potential conflict'.[2]

Censorship is generally considered to be at its most draconian when it operates a total ban on performance or text, what playwright Howard Brenton in reacting to the embargo on his *Romans in Britain* colourfully described as 'cutting out your tongue and locking you up'.[3]

But, worse still, it can lead to a situation in which Brenton's metaphor becomes a literal truth—the incarceration, exile, or even the assassination of the *artist* responsible for the work—witness the defection of the composer Schoenberg from Germany, the death threats against novelist Salman Rushdie. Such extreme cases illustrate the rough-and-ready rule that the more authoritarian a culture, regime or pressure group, the more censorious its attitude towards the arts. Nor should one forget that patriarchal cultures have been notoriously illiberal in allowing the creative efforts of women artists their proper place, often colluding in the erasure, particularly to succeeding generations, of musical compositions as well as texts and paintings.[4]

Despite the continued existence of these patriarchies, there has been a gradual liberalisation of attitudes over the years, a process which, in Western democracies at least, seems to be accelerating in the 1990s as feminist, minority and 'perverse other' lobbies make their voices heard. The climate in the UK—the main burden of this essay—is still less 'liberated' than in, say, Holland or Denmark, or in the US—where the Constitution ensures that locally repressive edicts can be overturned by the Supreme Court—but it is, despite some hiccups during Conservative rule, increasingly open to change. As long ago as 1968, the Theatres Act sounded the virtual death-knell of stage censorship; in 1974 Radclyffe Hall's lesbian work *The Well of Loneliness*, banned in the 1920s as 'obscene libel', was effectively promoted to the canon by being serialised on the radio as a 'Book at Bedtime'.[5] To peruse the current programme of events or the magazines on sale at 'art clubs' such as the Institute of Contemporary Arts (ICA) is to realise how both performance and the analysis of its sexual imagery has an outspokenness and candour unthinkable only a decade ago.[6]

But censorship is still a minefield, particularly in relation to the performing arts. Because the range of artistic expression in our post-modern culture is so diverse and multiplex, and because the very notion of what constitutes serious art is constantly being challenged and revised—never more so than now—the 'official' rules governing its public presentation are necessarily vague, even if the terms associated with these legal edicts have been the subject of frequent attempts at definition. In this country, these pivotal terms are obscenity, pornography and, to a lesser degree, blasphemy and profanity. Obscenity, broadly defined in the Official Publications Act (1959) as matter that will 'tend to deprave and corrupt persons who are likely, having regard to all relevant circumstances, to read, see or hear the matter contained within it' is a wider term than 'pornography' and has usually included bad language (profanity), gratuitous violence (particularly in combination with sex), gross racism and sexism. A Private Member's Bill of 1987 tried and failed to widen its remit still further by designating obscenity as 'whatever a reasonable person would regard as grossly offensive in relation to sex, violence or drug-taking'.

Pornography, granted its original reference to writings by and about prostitutes, is more specifically linked to sex and its public presentation. The relatively liberal Williams Report (1979) defined it as 'sexually explicit material designed for sexual arousal'. On the other hand, the Minneapolis Ordinance (1984) in the US, a product of the conviction that pornography had a deleterious effect on male social behaviour, explicitly linking it to pathological conduct, talked of 'the sexually explicit subordination of women, graphically depicted' and listed situations in which women were 'exhibited' or 'presented as sexual objects'.[7]

Despite the failure of this initiative, 'pornography' is the term now fashionably deployed in censorship debates about nudity, the sex act and more recently homoeroticism and other forms of so-called 'perverse' sex—sadomasochism, bondage and highly contentious areas such as paedophilia and bestiality. The public presentation of sex coupled with violence—rape is the most obvious example—is increasingly described as pornography in feminist discourse, where it has all but superseded 'obscenity' as a generic term. Blasphemy, 'irreverent language . . . or behaviour' directed towards something sacred or inviolable',[8] is now much less frequently invoked as a motive for censure. Though films such as *The Life of Brian* or *The Last Temptation of Christ* were deemed to be blasphemous by certain religious groups, the last successful prosecution for 'blasphemous libel' in the UK was brought in 1977 against *Gay News*.

It is not the intention of this essay to consider religious and political censorship in any detail, not because their impact on the performing arts has been less than significant, but because these forms of censure have been to some extent marginalised by the current preoccupation with pornography. Nonetheless a few observations are in order.

If the arguments about censorship, and the processes and procedures for implementing it are complicated enough in any one culture at any one time, it is clear that they assume unmanageable proportions once cultural diversity comes into play. Islam's *fatwa* against the person of Salman Rushdie, 'only procurer' of *The Satanic Verses*, is evidence of the existence of a set of values seemingly inimical to Christian ones. Western observers would find attitudes towards censorship in India just as baffling. While rape scenes are often graphically depicted in Indian films and apparently without official censure, young romantic love, particularly between lovers of different classes or creeds, is usually regarded as a taboo subject in a culture conditioned to the arranged marriage.

More surprisingly, the UK and the US—despite the common bond of language—often differ on what is and what is not acceptable in the live arts and media. There is often little discernible logic to these differences. American radio, for example, has a high tolerance for songs about drugs and sex but is generally more proscriptive than the BBC about religious allusions in pop/rock lyrics. The Beatles'

'Ballad of John and Yoko', with its line 'They're going to crucify me' was banned in 1969 by more than half the radio stations in America. The censors there, on the other hand, permit more gratuitous violence on film and tape than would be allowed by the UK Video Recording Act; conversely, a scene with two men in bed in *Thirtysomething*, considered unremarkable in Britain, caused US advertising sponsors to withdraw their support for the television series.

Of course, artists have always been adept at devising strategies for avoiding the attentions of the censor—by parable or satire, allegory or metaphor—in short, by employing a whole panoply of deflecting procedures. As Polonius knew only too well: 'By indirections find directions out'.[11] A fable provides apt illustration of the point. A king, one-eyed, hunchbacked and with a short leg, commissioned a portrait. The first artist painted him as he was, the second without imperfections. Both were executed. The third went hunting, painted the king hunched over his gun and with one foot on a tree stump. He was well rewarded.

The moral of this tale has not been lost on generations of artists who, in order to ensure the survival of their work have striven to render the inedible palatable. It is a cornerstone in the edifices of new historicist and materialist criticism that great dramatists—Shakespeare included—often supply a sub-text at odds with the received reading of their plays, thereby mediating and exploiting ideological forces. By this token *The Tempest* can be interpreted as an anti-colonialist piece, *Henry the Fifth* not as a trumpet call to Elizabethan patriots but as a pacifist chronicle, both unacceptable readings in the establishment circles in which the playwright moved. Whatever the truth of the matter, numerous modern instances abound, of which Arthur Miller's *The Crucible* is only the best known. A 'subversive' artist singled out by Senator McCarthy and his 'witch-hunters', Miller responded with *The Crucible*, an allegorical statement of the times, which took, as its central metaphor a late seventeenth-century 'witch-hunt' in Salem, Massachusetts. The play escaped censorship but no one in Miller's audiences was in any doubt as to the play's contemporary significance.

It is inevitably misleading to discuss censorship and performance without substantial reference to film, television and video. Indeed, many of the most pressing arguments—both for and against censorship—are directed at art representations in the media. For if live performance seems, on balance, to have attracted more repressive reactions than words printed on a page or paint applied to a picture, it is often maintained that filmic and, to an even greater extent, televisual or videated images require the exercise of parental or institutional control, if the young and impressionable are not to be overexposed to 'adult' material. Commercial theatre in the UK, largely a middle-class, middle-aged preserve anyway, has been left pretty much to its own devices since the demise of the Lord Chamberlain. In any case, precise 'editing' of an actual performance requires a different and inevitably more complicated approach. It is in the nature of the 'live' medium that a dance or theatrical piece will vary from performance to performance; there exists no replicable artefact beyond a text which can—quite literally—be cut or otherwise modified in the censor's office.[12] Today's signifiers are not necessarily tomorrow's signs.

The material nature of film or video also allows other and—to the viewer at least—more discernible erasing procedures. A couple of examples will illustrate the point. When Makavejec's *W.R.: Mysteries of the Organism*, an innovatory and politically prescient film was shown on English TV twenty years and much censorship on, one scene, which involved making a plaster cast of a pop star's erect penis, was starred (or at least the penis was), with the result that the potentially offensive object was obliterated. More usual is the use of a 'scan' shot whereby the image is given an unfocused or grainy appearance. A near-paedophilic moment in Oshima's *Empire of the Senses* was thus subjected to optical distortion to allay concerns that the scene, though much less shocking than others in the Japanese film, might fall foul of upholders of the Child Protection Act.

Nonetheless, once a written text becomes a performative one, the rules do seem to change. The film version of *A Clockwork Orange*, hardly inflammatory as a book (it was intended as a reformist novel and as a film attracted mainly 'highbrow' audiences) did apparently provoke—and this is grist to the mill of the moral right—a number of 'copycat' crimes, involving gang rapists chanting 'Singing in the Rain' or kicking tramps to death. Connection or not, the movie was removed from British screens. Bret Easton Ellis's *American Psycho* affords a more bizarre example. A violent and vivisectionist novel in which women are routinely mutilated, tortured and raped, the book's launch created no censorship problems for Knopf-Random House, its prestigious publishers. On the contrary, it sold in the US—predictably—in huge numbers. But when a radical feminist, Tara Baxter, protested in a Santa Cruz bookshop by 'quoting the book out loud to a hostile crowd of blurry-eyed shoppers (some boys applauded during the fuck/murder scenes)', she was arrested on a charge of trespass and briefly imprisoned. Subsequently, she expressed the wish to have 'a rat put up his [Ellis's] rectum and his genitals cut off and fried . . . in front of not only a live audience—but a video camera as well.'[13] Perhaps one kind of violence begets another. . . . More to our purpose is what Tara Baxter *actually* did. By performing the text in a public place, she laid herself open, as a performer, to legal retribution; she became a more suitable case for censure than the 'mute' author of a text or indeed than the text itself. It was her live 'act' that was censored.

Yet though a performance brings a written text 'alive', it is emphatically not a real-life event—unless 'snuff movies' really do exist. Not surprisingly, no one reacted literally to Baxter's imperative that Ellis be emasculated; indeed feminist journals everywhere refused to print the purple passage. To simulate violence or sex on stage or celluloid or videotape is not to practise it. This inherent distinction between a simulated act and a real one became the key issue in the furore over Howard Brenton's play *The Romans in Britain* in 1975. A serious political piece about the British presence in Northern Ireland in which its imperialist role was compared to that of the oppressive Roman presence in Britain, the play's provocative and anti-establishment stance became less an overt subject for censure than the scene of stage buggery involving Roman soldiers and native victims. The fact that it was intended as a *coup de theâtre* symbolising the buggery of a whole nation and was, in any case, a performative 'event', did not prevent Mary Whitehouse from attempting to get the play banned. Mr Justice Staunton, moreover, compounded her error, declaring that there was no inherent difference between the staging of such an act and the reality, thereby blurring any distinction between life and its dramatic representation. Later Nicholas de Jongh wrote in *The Guardian*:

> There is, therefore, much danger abroad when judges and lawyers try to coax dramatic and literary worlds into real life . . . A modest emendation of the Theatres Act would (and could) ensure that fidgety amateur censors cannot treat the stage and its actors as if they were respectively public thoroughfares and people who were actually murdering and raping. Until that happens who would dare to stage a new intact production of Brenton's play?[14]

It is surprising that the 'artistic merit' argument, the one most frequently cited by artists as a defence against censorship, real or anticipated, was not at the centre of the *Romans* controversy. But it was there, hovering in the wings. After all, the artistic community usually believes fervently in the seriousness of what it is doing. Kenneth Tynan, so often a prescient maverick in these matters, had, years before, remarked this 'holier than thou' attitude when noting John

Osborne's anger at the Chamberlain's cuts and revisions to his play *The World of Paul Slickey*:

> I sympathize with Osborne's rage, while regretting that he should let it trap him into implying that special privileges should be granted to serious drama and withheld from 'third-rate nude revues'. Erotic stimulation is a perfectly legitimate function of bad art as well as good, and a censor who bans a stripper is behaving just as illiberally and indefensibly as one who eviscerates a masterpiece.[15]

In 1959, that was certainly *not* a consensus view. Even today, a more usual line is that adumbrated by Harriet Gilbert who observes:

> . . . in obscenity trials it is certainly common for the defence to point out that the text in the dock has high psychological, political or literary seriousness—'artistic merit' as British law has it—and should therefore on no account be treated as though it were ordinary filth.[16]

This argument, brought forward to defend works as various as Edward Bond's *Saved* or Peter Watkins' film *The War Game*, was the nub of the very public debate in America about the Hollywood movie *The Accused*. Departing from the cinematographic convention of off-screen rape, the film's pivotal scene, a mix of what is, for censors a usually poisonous cocktail of sex and violence, provoked one American critic into calling it 'a full scale celebration of the joys of gang-banging.'[17] But its serious message, that multiple rape *is* on the increase, that all too often we—like the crowd in the film—are passive onlookers and that the rape, far from being a representation of gratuitous violence, was portrayed as an appalling degradation, won the film a reprieve.

Many of these arguments about serious purpose—a highly contentious notion anyway—are linked to contextual matters. Is Georges Bataille's porn classic *Story of the Eye* validated by its respectable appearance in a Penguin edition with '51 pages of context, both psychological and literary . . . provided not only by the author himself but by Susan Sontag and Roland Barthes'?[18] Do the collages of a group of Spanish artists, complete with 'split beavers',[19] cross the high art threshold by virtue of their public exhibition in the Atlantis Upper Gallery in East London? Is a Robert Mapplethorpe photograph of 'fist fucking' rendered immune from censorship by virtue of its aestheticisation in a 'serious' Minneapolis setting?

The issue of context is not limited to a work's physical 'frame'. It has been employed, almost to the point of obsession, on the one hand, by artists and performers anxious to preserve their work's integrity by insisting on its presentation entire; conversely, by proscribing bodies who by isolating 'bits' and thereby taking them 'out of context' present a case for suppressing the whole work. Such a *cause célèbre* was the 'trial' of *Lady Chatterley's Lover*, where the prosecution read out selected passages about sexual intercourse but failed to get the book banned on the grounds of 'obscenity'. Other cases abound. More recently, Dennis Potter's *The Singing Detective* attracted opprobrium on the grounds that an al fresco sex scene ought to ensure its non-appearance on our screens. Mary Whitehouse included it in her compilation of offensive television clips which she showed to Conservative MPs. But Lord Rees-Mogg of the Broadcasting Standards Council (BSC), when asked for his opinion, replied: 'The BBC took the view . . . that the context justified it in a serious work of art,' adding significantly: 'That does not mean that a similar scene, introduced for the sake of sensationalism in something that wasn't a work of art at all, would be acceptable.'[20] In 1989, Oshima's *Empire of the Senses* was granted an '18' certificate, complete and unabridged. Any cutting would have led its French producer to withdraw from the British cinema a film shot through with images of erections, ejaculation, vaginal penetration and finally, of genital mutilation. It was a clear case of all or nothing, the integrity of the work must be preserved.

The waters of the 'artistic merit' argument have been muddied still further by the shifting sand-barriers of high and low culture. As recent discussions have pointed out, traditional Western notions of high art have often been associated with the contemplative virtues and with so-called 'universal' values. Offering testimony to the Longford Report in 1972, Sir Kenneth Clark thus argued that 'the moment art becomes an incentive to action, it loses its true character'. Thus, by extension, Lynda Nead maintains, 'if art stands for lasting, imperishable values then pornography represents disposability, trash'.[21] It is therefore easy to see how items above the 'pulp-line' (George Steiner's term)[22] such as classical nudes, avoid any form of moral interdiction, while *Playboy*, despite its sanitised 'girl-next-door' image, is sealed in plastic wrappers; why naked bodies in performances were for so long required to remain passive and impassive—ironically bodies in motion are more likely to subvert the gendered gaze and prevent the fetishisation of the female form—or made available for the gaze of the *hoi poloi* only in club 'strip-joints' or the like. As Lynda Nead observes: 'Historically high culture has provided a space for a viable form of sexual representation: that which is aestheticized, contained and allowed'.[23]

Educational justifications—often inseparable from those about 'serious purpose' or more recently 'political correctness'—have also offered a 'space' within which performers have been allowed to operate unhindered. Whether Annie Sprinkle (discussed later) is educational or even 'political' is a moot point, but feminist critiques, both by their presence in academic books and by their high analytical tone, certainly grant her a status without which her live performances—not to mention her videos—might well be proscribed. For Linda Williams, she is therefore not only 'sex therapist' and 'sex goddess' but also 'sex educator'.[24] It is the educational aspect that has permitted, in the UK, the proliferation of sex instruction videos—readily available in high street outlets—in which the actual activities (apart from the 'money shots')[25] are not so very different from the staple of the 'soft porn' video or movie.

'Soft porn' is, however, one evidence in our materialistic culture of the taint of commercialism. The box-office factor not only means that the concept of 'artistic' or educational merit often cannot be invoked, but, more important, that it *need* not. It is true that in the UK 'soft' or 'hard' porn, like gratuitous violence, is scrutinised extremely carefully by bodies such as the Film Board (BBFC). But the situation is a complex one. While porn has come to dominate the censorship battle, control of the media is increasingly concentrated in the hands of a few multinational corporations. These are more likely to operate their own forms of repression against non-privileged groups—women, the disabled, the working classes, blacks, gays, lesbians—while at the same time validating the presentation of violent or titillating material which will attract mainstream cinema-goers or video watchers in droves.

In *Hollywood vs America*, Michael Medved expresses a commonly voiced concern about the current epidemic of 'body count' movies being made and distributed by the big Hollywood studios, on the proliferation of brutal imagery in prime-time TV, and on the violent lyrics and anarchic sentiments of many pop songs and pop videos. In *Die Hard 2* Medved totted up 264 killings, in *Rambo 3*, 106. Researchers estimate that on American television since 1955 'characters have been murdered at a rate of 1000 times higher than real world victims'.[26] But what is so worrying to Medved is the way in which graphic violence, bloodshed and brutal death are increasingly accepted; the commercial fact of life is that violence sells. It is not only what the public is inured to; it is also what it apparently wants. And even when the horror is all too graphic, it is frequently combined with a humour that appears to validate the carnage—what Medved calls 'milking laughs from lacerations'.[27] He quotes the example of *Lethal Weapon 2* (1989) in which Danny Glover punctures the skulls of two 'baddies' with a nail gun and duly reports 'I nailed 'em both.'[28]

The American film industry is aware that comedy, even of this gross kind, is an area that, if not entirely immune, has developed a resistance to the censor's red pencil. Unlike recent Eastern Bloc regimes—all too conscious of the incendiary power of political cabaret and comedy—the West is tolerant. Jerry Sadowitz, one of Britain's best-known stand-up comics, believes this acceptance is related to the way the 'genre' reflects life. While a bad-taste joke needs to be funny as well as shocking, its principal *raison d'être* stems from its capacity to raise our consciousness, to 'bring life into the open'. Offering his own extreme example: 'What's pink and hard first thing in the morning?' Answer 'a cot death', he justifies it with the comment, 'That joke would not exist if it weren't for the appalling increase in cot deaths in recent years, and *that* is what is so offensive'.[29]

The argument, which I believe applies primarily to satirical comedy, is not without its limitations. By the same token, one could justify racist jokes on the grounds that they increase audience awareness of racism. May they not simply pander to audience *prejudice*? Howard Stern, an American comic with an irreverent and salacious radio show, is testimony to the capacity of such 'comedy' to exploit some of the most deeply rooted prejudices and fantasies of American white urban males. His show is, we are told, consistently 'bigoted, plain rude, racist, offensive, homophobic, anti-feminist, anti-disease (especially . . . Aids) and anti-Semitic . . .'[30]

Apart from one fine, he has more or less dodged the punitive efforts of the censors. Needless to say, the New York-based show is massively successful in commercial terms. Yet even his act pales by comparison with that of the 'Dice Man', a comic who is not only blatantly offensive to women in his live audience, but incites his rabid supporters to a pitch of racial hatred epitomised by their chant of 'Get the fuck out of here!' There is no reformist principle at work in this reductive scenario; if ever 'comedy' merits censure, it would seem to do so here.

Earlier, mention was made of extreme forms of censorship in the form of a complete ban on an artist or on the artefact s/he creates. Such total repression usually involves stifling the work before the public has a chance to pass judgement on it—most obviously by refusing it a licence. In such cases a potential audience often remains blissfully unaware of what it has missed. On the other hand, a total embargo can be slapped on an art work as a direct consequence of official sanctions or pressure by the withdrawal of funding, or as a result of public reaction, often orchestrated by campaigners from the 'moral right'. An example of official censor and public paymaster acting in concert was afforded by Edward Bond's play *Early Morning*. After the play was banned by the Lord Chamberlain in 1967, the Arts Council then threatened to withdraw its grant if the Royal Court scheduled 'club' performances. One hardly associates the Arts Council with censorship. But this is not an isolated example. Recently asked why Susan Santoro's vaginal iconography in *Towards New Expression* had been suppressed by the Council, Director of Art Robin Campbell replied: 'On the grounds that obscenity might be alleged', adding that 'we considered . . . the avowed intention . . . was primarily a plea for sexual self-expression'.[31]

The fate of Michael Jackson's video *Black & White* illustrates that the power is not always held by officialdom. The 'crotch shots' in the eleven-minute piece caused such a public outcry in the US that the offending images had to be expunged and the video cut by four minutes. Since production costs ran to seven million dollars, the expedient proved expensive. It was public reaction from the powerful British Jewish lobby that prevented the staging of *Perdition*. A play that purported to show Jewish activities in the Holocaust in a less than favourable light, it never passed the rehearsal stages at the Royal Court. Nonetheless the Royal Court, a powerhouse of new drama in the 1960s, had long appreciated that playing to 'our house' or 'club' audiences was a way of circumventing the censor's official veto in the UK. When John Osborne's *A Patriot For Me*, a drama more homophobic than homoerotic, was put on by the Royal Court in 1965, the Lord Chamberlain took the view that the play's gay anti-hero and drag-party episode were incitements to homosexuality and insisted on the removal of five scenes. Nicholas de Jongh recalls that the Chamberlain's office argued that 'presenting homosexuals in their most attractive guise, dressed as pretty women, will to some degree cause the congregation of homosexuals and provide the means whereby the vice may be acquired.'[32] In what amounted to a test-case against the censorship of the professional theatre, John Devine, the artistic director, announced the play's performance in 'club' conditions. The drama attracted large audiences; club membership rose from 1,600 to 4,000; a blow was struck against establishment prejudice. 'Thanks to the censor', the critic Irving Wardle commented later, 'there was no need for salesmanship.'[33]

Irving Wardle's remark deserves some amplification. An argument frequently advanced against censorship and particularly in the

1990s is that it simply does not work. This may mean that ways are found of subverting the ban; more perversely, the very public threat of its implementation produces results the reverse of those intended. *A Patriot For Me* provokes both reactions. The 'trial' of *Lady Chatterley's Lover* upped sales to three million. Red Triangles, intended as a warning device to *limit* viewing of 'adult' material on British television, had the opposite effect. The prohibition syndrome is universal. In India, an apparently innocuous (by Western standards) pop-song entitled 'What's Beneath my Blouse?' (Answer: 'A Heart') which recently appeared in a film (*Khal nayak*), with lyrics mimed by star Madhuri Dixit, only survived the censor's scissors after a protracted battle and at least one private court suit. Now ten million copies of the song are in circulation.[34]

Since forbidden fruits are more tempting, they are often graded before the public can get their teeth into them. The commonest form of partial censorship thus involves removing those bad bits deemed inappropriate for public delectation. As we have seen, the theatre has, since 1968, been relatively immune to this kind of censorship, but film and video, more amenable to precise limitation, have been the main targets. The 'video nasty' scandal of 1983–4, largely generated by a tabloid press which has a well-known propensity for facing both ways, resulted in the passing of the Video Recording Act and the most vigorous of censorship initiatives. Sixty-seven films were immediately declared illegal by the Director of Public Prosecutions—totally repressed—but many more, often box-office successes—were subsequently cut by the BBFC, including such examples of the horror genre as *Terminator 2*, *Robocop* and *The Evil Dead*. The British video release *The Toxic Avenger* was much edited. Images of 'illegal' weapons—(crossbows, chainsaws and chainsticks are thus categorised) were removed from the British video of *Rambo III* and, perhaps more surprisingly, from *Teenage Mutant Ninja Turtles*, from which a total of five minutes and forty-three seconds was excised.[35]

The 'official' censor—in whatever shape or form—is often seen as some kind of demonic figure, imposing his will on a reluctant artistic community. This conveniently ignores the fact that self-censorship is practised, often as a matter of course, by editors, producers and directors, all of whom are aware of the Obscene Publications Act and the Child Protection Act; they consequently tend to exercise a degree of self-censorship before stories or programmes go out. Even the marketing of 'soft porn' is largely self-regulated by the industry. As the editors of *Pornography and Feminism* observe: 'Its range and explicitness are completely determined by what the distributors consider will be sufficiently "hot" and *risqué* to sell well, but sufficiently "acceptable" in law to be displayed in public.'[36] The most celebrated example of self-censorship was Stanley Kubrick's 1973 withdrawal of his film *A Clockwork Orange* from public screening in the UK. When London's Scala Cinema ignored the ban and screened a rogue print, Kubrick sued for breach of copyright. A spokesperson for 'Fact' (Federation Against Copyright Theft) explained: '*A Clockwork Orange* is banned from being shown in this country on the express wishes of Mr Kubrick. Why? I think he didn't like the reception it got here.'[37]

Less spectacularly, all of us exercise self-censorship via the operations of the superego, a personal regulator which exercises some control over our spectating role. I recently showed a particularly horrendous clip from *Texas Chainsaw Massacre*—a film banned in the UK only in part because of its use of 'illegal' weapons—to a group of students. Though the actual impalement of the young woman on a meat hook is not shown in the film, most of the students closed their eyes or averted their gaze in anticipation of the event. At a screening I attended of Peter Greenaway's *The Cook, The Thief, His Wife and Her Lover*, at least half the audience left the cinema at various points. Such psychical censorship is, of course, a cornerstone in the edifice of Freudian theory; in Freud's view, this is both a conscious and unconscious process and explains why the phenomena of personal censorship and dream displacement and distortion are closely related.

Censorship is not confined to visual or verbal signifiers. In fourth-century Greece, Plato declared that music was full of danger to the state, insisting in *The Republic* that it was the state's paramount duty to suppress all music of an effeminate and debasing character and to encourage only that which was pure and dignified.[38] In Georgian England, one Jeremy Collier put the matter more strongly, warning that 'musick is always as dangerous as gunpowder; it may be requires looking after no less than the press or the mint. 'Tis possible a publick regulation might not be amiss.'[39] Certainly hegemonic institutions have not been slow to recognise music's potential for generating powerful feelings and have exploited or repressed it accordingly. Jazz was for long under a cloud, not because it was a subversive form of protest—though it often was—but because it was associated with sex. As one unnamed American critic put it: 'a wave of vulgar, filthy and suggestive music has invaded the land.' The reference was to the '20s fashion for 'ragtime'!

What is perhaps a cause for surprise is the fact that music has attracted the censor's attention not only on account of its lyrics but also because of its sound textures. If the repression of unalloyed sound and of those who create its effects seems absurd, it has frequently happened—and not just to jazz. The music that was banned in Nazi Germany included anything composed by Jews or blacks, anyone influenced by jazz or 'oriental art'.

In fact, a *Dictionary of Jewish Composers* (1938), banned everyone 'suspect' from Felix Mendelssohn through Kurt Weill to Josephine Baker, and included 'orientialism' in music as an identifiable and therefore indictable characteristic. The pattern was to be repeated in other repressive regimes. In pre-*glasnost* USSR, 'socialist realism' spread its tentacles to embrace classical music and suffocate the importations of 'decadent' Western rock. Any work which did not reflect social reality—i.e., 'Soviet reality'—whatever that was in musical terms—incurred the wrath of the Head of the Union of Soviet Composers and was consigned to a kind of musical Siberia. The music of Mstislav Rostropovich, the distinguished cellist, was denied air-time, his records banned. The pianist Vladimir Ashkenazy suffered the same fate. Even in Israel the work of Richard Wagner and Richard Strauss has long been anathematised due to its apparent association with Nazism and anti-Semitism.

It is generally agreed in an area where there are almost as many opinions as people that there have historically been two main attitudes towards censorship of the arts in the West; those espoused on the one hand by the so-called 'moral right', on the other by the liberal left. The moral right, promoting family or Victorian values (which themselves posited a dichotomy between the respectable and the unregenerate—the Madonna/Magdalene polarity) was represented in the UK by the Longford Report of 1972 which embraced the values of Mary Whitehouse and 'The Festival of Light'; in the US typically by anti-porn campaigner Jerry Falwell and by 'Southern Baptist' pressure groups advocating fundamental Christian values. In general, the moral right is opposed to the public display of the naked body or of sexual activity, particularly 'illegitimate' or 'perverse' sex; such public manifestations, it believes, are symptomatic of the decay of traditional values. Sex should be related to its context—marriage, and its purpose—procreation. The proliferation of images of sex and violence are not only indicators of declining moral standards but are themselves linked to violent crimes. The furore in the US over the 'Piss Christ' imagery of Andres Serrano or Robert Mapplethorpe's photographs was a manifestation of right-wing censorship at work; in the areas of performance, a paradigmatic example of this pressure group's effect in the UK was seen in the banning—discussed elsewhere—of Howard Brenton's *The Romans in Britain*.

Two factors, one the international panic over AIDS, the other the parochial effect of Thatcherite policies, contributed to this increasingly censorious attitude towards the arts. The Local Government Act of 1982 offered more repressive guidelines to authorities on local control of 'sex establishments' and their cinematographic materials; as we have seen, the Video Act of 1984 carried this process further. Since film classification began in 1985, over 27 per cent of all '18' film videos have been cut, 47 per cent of R18 videos (soft-core sex category) have been passed only after the editing out of sections. In 1987 the introduction of Clause 28 into the Local Government Finance Bill forbade authorities to promote homosexuality or its teaching as 'a pretended family relationship'. This legislation provoked outrage in the artistic community at large. The dance group DV8 created a political piece for television, entitled *Never Again*; the 'Arts Lobby' produced a leaflet in which Simon Rattle, Julie Christie, Sir Peter Hall and Sir Michael Tippett variously condemned the clause and 'The Critics' Circle' offered the following prognosis:

> If this Clause goes through untouched, we shall have censorship of a depth, extent and malignity unknown to any democratic country and if we persist in describing ourselves as free with this clause on the statute books, we will be the laughing stock of the West and the envy of every petty totalitarian state, for we will have shown them how to silence the critics without putting them behind bars.[40]

Of course, this statement passionately espouses the liberal position on censorship, a view which most people connected with the performing arts would applaud. Though not directly concerned with the issue of homosexuality, various public policy documents have also taken a liberal line. Thus, this view has been represented, in a more sober-sided way, by the Presidential Commission of 1970 (US) and the Williams Report of 1979 (UK). Both argued that there was no proof of the assertion that pornography caused harm and thus no need to censor it. If its public display were to be circumscribed, it should be done on the basis that some adults might find it offensive.

The issue is now more complicated. While there was never a simple polarisation between the moral right on the one hand and the liberal left on the other—there were all sorts of views along and beyond this continuum—the women's movement has brought new insights to the debate and in so doing has created significant polarisations within feminism. As Carol Clore says in *Dirty Looks*:

> For better or worse, pornography has become the feminist issue of the decade. In so doing it has brought sexual matters into the spot-

> light—homosexuality, sado masochism, sex crimes and deviations as well as the central issue of the female body and its fetishization.[41]

Initially, the women's movement tended to adopt a position in which the formulation (Robin Morgan's) 'Pornography is the Theory: Rape is the Practice' became a watchword for an ideology which connected the public display of women's bodies, or selected bits, often in oppressed roles, to male narcissism, violence and exploitation. For many feminists, sexism or misogyny were causally linked to sexual representations found in soft- and hard-porn films, videos and magazines.[42]

In fact, this movement—which has given rise to such initiatives as the 'Campaign Against Pornography'—is being increasingly challenged by a counter project which, while superficially linked to liberal views, is actually striking out in much more radical and 'liberatory' ways. 'Feminists Against Censorship' in the UK and the 'Feminist Anti-Censorship Task Force' (FACT) in the US have argued that the way forward is not to censor images of women as sexual objects, not to take action against their producers or to see sexual intercourse as a key feature of women's oppression, but to challenge received assumptions and in particular the idea that sexual pleasure is a male preserve. Women should celebrate both their own bodies and their own erotic experience, and develop art forms which allow this to happen. As *Pornography and Feminism* states: 'We need sexually explicit material produced by and for women, freed from the control of right wingers and misogynists'.[43] This view takes account of the famous distinction between pornography and erotica first advanced by Gloria Steinem more than a decade ago and ever since—though it may now seem increasingly problematic—'an article of faith in the ensuing feminist debate.'[44]

> The two sorts of images are as different as love is from rape, as dignity is from humiliation, as partnership is from slavery, as pleasure is from pain.[45]

Arguing that there is no likelihood that 'the incidence of rape and violence towards women and children will decline if pornography is banned', that history proves that censorship has not worked, that 'a free and democratic society should tolerate a diversity of views and behaviour' and that pornography consists of images, not actual acts of violence, the group argues that female campaigners for censorship are unwittingly colluding in patriarchal values and limiting freedom of choice.[46]

The reclaiming of the erotic, now gathering momentum, particularly among feminists, is an appropriation that goes far beyond the precepts of liberal humanism; it has the potential to be 'liberatory', even 'libertinist' (Ross's term) in its concern to support and produce different pleasures and practices. One view is that it has been stimulated by recent theory such as Barthes' notion of *jouissance* (the ecstasy attendant on reading an open or polysemous text) but the role of feminist thinkers is probably more significant—for example, Cixous, Irigaray, Kristeva—who have foregrounded female sexuality as a source of creativity all too frequently repressed and marginalised in patriarchal cultures. According to Ross, it may also have an unlikely ancestry in de Sade who, Angela Carter argues, represented women as 'beings of power' with certain sexual rights and who thus and perhaps inadvertently 'put pornography in the service of women, or perhaps allowed it to be invaded by an ideology not inimical to women.'[47]

At all events, manifestations of this 'ideology' have begun to appear in the last decade in the performing arts. In the US, Candida Royalle, a former 'porn' star started 'Femme Distribution Inc.' with a view to creating erotic films for women; by 1991 she had produced seven movies which underlined the fact that while the production values were higher than in most pornography, women were no less averse to the sexually explicit than men. These pornographic videos aimed at women have already become big business. April de Angelis's staging of the quintessentially patriarchal *Fanny Hill*, itself sanitised as a text until the 1960s and now substantially reworked to reclaim its female perspective, showed what was becoming possible in the theatre by 1991. A perusal of alternative art magazines on sale at, say, the ICA (*Body Politic* and *Quim* are two), will reveal uncensored images of female and male bodies which are more explicit than anything in *Penthouse*, *Playboy* or *Playgirl*. *Body Politic* 4 contains the following gloss on a series of illustrations:

> The exhibition *What She Wants* is an experimental reversal of erotic traditions. It is the first exhibition to platform women artists as producers of erotic visual expression about men . . . an experimental reversal of erotic traditions . . . 64 artists have produced over a hundred images of the male body as a site of desire and fascination.[48]

In general though, the new images are of *women's* bodies rather than of men's. Feminist artist Suzanne Santoro is only one of a number of women artists whose demystifying work is based on representations of women's genitals (others include Ann Severson's film *Near the Big Chakra*, Judy Chicago's vulvic forms created in porcelain, Karen Finley's staged violations of her own body and most recently in the UK

Helen Chadwick's recreation of her own bodily functions in *Effluvia*).[49] As Rozsika Parker explains:

> For most feminists vaginal imagery signifies a rejection of images by men of women, and an exploration and affirmation of their own identity. It attacks the idea of women's genitals as mysterious, hidden and threatening and attempts to throw off a resulting shame and secrecy.[50]

In all this, many of the most daring and politicised steps have been taken by iconoclastic female performers. In France, Orlan has turned her body into a worksite, an extended performance in progress with the aid of a series of plastic surgery operations. Diamanda Galas, a New York 'live' artiste, and self-styled sex-prostitute, presented her 'Plague Mass' opera in the Cathedral of St. John the Divine in New York in 1990, coming on stage covered in blood as a tribute to the victims in the AIDS Community. Predictably, it was denounced by members of the Italian government as 'sacrilegious' and 'blasphemy' against the Catholic Church. As Galas said: 'it wasn't treated as an artwork . . . It was seen only as a mass . . . so then it became a scandal in the press.'[51]

Yet even Galas's performances—another, more avowedly sexual piece was called 'Wild Women with Steak Knives'—pales, if that be the word, in comparison with Annie Sprinkle. Pornographer and performance artist, Annie began as a masseuse and then moved, via 'porn' films, into the domain of live sex shows. What she has done and does in her one-woman performances goes far beyond anything permitted in 'commercial' UK strip shows. Penny Arcade's 1994 show at the ICA (*Bitch! Dyke! Faghag! Whore!*) with its team of erotic go-go dancers and its frank exploration of themes related to AIDS, puritanism, feminism and sex went some way along the Sprinkle road in its concluding and prolonged strip show. But Annie Sprinkle is more graphic, a very tangible manifestation of changing attitudes:

> For as gender and sexual identities have become more politicized, and as 'speaking sex' has become as important to gay, lesbian, bisexual, transexual and sadomasochistic activists as it has to Jesse Helms, drawing clear lines between what is dirty and what is clean, what is . . . on scene and what should be kept off (ob)scene, no longer seems the crux of a feminist sexual politics.[52]

Annie Sprinkle has certainly reacted to this transgressive climate. In her film *Deep Inside Annie Sprinkle*, she offers a conventional pornographic narrative of her sexual education from innocent Annie to sex-crazed exhibitionist Sprinkle. In the way of 'soft porn', the movie interlards dirty talk, sexual intercourse of various kinds and visible proof of her orgasm in a female 'money shot'. In her *Sluts and Goddesses Video Workshop*, she performs a six-minute orgasm, again complete with ejaculate (or as some interpreters argue, a 'golden shower'). In the more recent *Post-Post Porn Modernist* live piece, she invites 'members of the audience to shine a flashlight at her cervix through a speculum' and then assumes the role of a 'porn bimbo' character, who 'enjoys a solo performance in which she masturbates to climax.'[53]

This last piece was recently shown at Glasgow's Centre for Contemporary Arts, clear evidence that Annie Sprinkle *is* being treated as a serious 'political' artist. Of course, it was an 'art-house' venue; one cannot imagine her being allowed—in the UK at least—in any other kind of performance setting. But how is her work 'political'? How does it avoid the charge of being pornographic? In part, it is argued that it has an educative function: it offers women suggestions on how to enjoy sex, how to overcome their inhibitions, how to know their own bodies, how to explore new areas of erotic experience. In the process it supposedly goes far beyond male fetishisations of the female body without entirely allaying criticisms that it panders, if unintentionally, to the prurient male spectator. But indubitably Annie Sprinkle's work *does* subvert the active male/passive female paradigm of commercial porn; it humorously reveals the woman as either self-sufficient or able to take unbridled pleasure in her own powerful sexual desires, whether conventional or 'perverse'. Thus in her various roles—as active penetrator (of a man), as visible ejaculator, as purveyor of over-the-top six-minute orgasms, she parodies and transgresses both conventional gender stereotypes *and* the stylised situations of 'hard-core' porn. As Chris Straayer says: 'Annie Sprinkle's sex-life-art challenges the hegemonic categories of "heterosexual" and "male".'[54] More relevant to our debate, it challenges hypocritical notions of censorship that derive from those very patriarchal discourses that valorise a cosmeticised or aestheticised view of female genitalia and repress explicit representations below the 'pulp-line'.

What conclusions can be drawn from these examples? What is abundantly clear is that there is no longer a simple dichotomy between feminists for and against censorship. Even the binary distinction—Gloria Steinem's—between the erotic and the pornographic seems to be breaking down, indeed is being actively subverted. Ross maintains that the 'liberatory imagination' is coming to the fore, which, *inter alia*, promotes 'the idea of an expansive popular culture for women—as opposed to a restrictive mass culture'.[55] How far this can go remains to be seen. Certainly the continued erosion of the distinction between high and low art has made it increasingly difficult for the 'pulp-line' to be drawn between, the artistic and the commercial, the non-censorable and the proscribed. As Deborah Levy remarked in a recent *Guardian* piece:

> As the gap narrowed between high and low art culture and artists borrowed freely from T.V., film, sci-fi, porn mags and comic books to comment on the trashy, speedy, panicky world that both appalled and fascinated them, images of sexuality were manipulated more bravely and more boldly.[56]

Moreover, presentations of diverse sexual fantasies—formerly regarded as the unacceptable province of 'perverse others'—are now, and despite Clause 28, seen as authoritative subjectivities, 'as provoking sexual agents seeking different pleasures from those presented in mainstream representations of the norm.'[57]

In other words, a more permissive climate has opened up the whole area of performance representations, not just for female artists and their audiences but also for those 'others' whose activities in the past—even when simulated—attracted censure.

Of course, a culture and its values are in a constant state of flux; censorship of the arts is a barometer of these changing values, a touchstone for general anxieties about the changing social climate. As we have seen, the general trend, despite the efforts of the moral right in the 1980s, has been towards a more liberal attitude both in the UK and in the US: the furore over Kenneth Tynan's use of the 'f' word on British television is now seen to be as anachronistic as the American film industry's repressive 'Production Code' of 1930. Admittedly political and public attitudes to events can and on occasions *do* set the clock back. *Rambo 3* caught the backlash of public revulsion attendant upon the Hungerford massacre; the killing of James Bulger by two boys who had watched *Death Wish 3* has re-opened the '80s video violence debate; the AIDS epidemic has prompted *some* homophobic reactions to 'gay' art. Nonetheless, the prognosis indicates an inexorable movement towards 'liberatory' attitudes, attitudes that the all too often marginalised woman artist has done much to stimulate.

## Notes

1 *The Oxford English Dictionary* (Oxford, Clarendon Press, 1989), vol. 3, p. 1029.
2 J. Dickey and G. Chester (eds.), *Feminism and Censorship* (London, Prism Press, 1988), p. 1.
3 Howard Brenton, *New Statesman* (1975).
4 See Chapter 4 for an extended discussion of the topic.
5 Jolyon Jenkins, *New Statesman* (5 April 1991).

6 The June 1994 *Programme* of ICA events refers to 'Club Girls . . . performances . . . from mud wrestling to Karaoke to sex on a trapeze'.
7 See Dickey and Chester (eds.), *Feminism and Censorship*, p. 259.
8 *Longman Dictionary of the English Language* (London, Longman, 1984), p. 150.
9 James Firman, 'Poacher Turned Gamekeeper', *New Statesman* (5 April 1991), 19.
10 See *New Statesman* (5 April 1991), 17 for a complete list.
11 William Shakespeare, *Hamlet*, 2, i, 60.
12 See Chapter 13 on authenticity. *New Statesman* (5 April 1991), 11.
13 D. E. H. Russell (ed.), *Making Violence Sexy* (New York, Teachers College Press, 1993), p. 248.
14 Nicholas de Jongh, *The Guardian* (16 March 1984).
15 Kenneth Tynan, 'The Royal Smut Hound', reprinted in *A View of the English Stage* (London, Methuen, 1984), p. 375.
16 H. Gilbert, 'So Long As It's Not Sex or Violence', in L. Segal and M. McIntosh (eds.), *Sex Exposed* (London, Virago, 1992), p. 219.
17 Dorothy Wade, *The Observer* (19 February 1989).
18 Gilbert, 'So Long As It's Not Sex or Violence', p. 219.
19 A term used in the 'soft porn' industry for explicit shots of female genitalia.
20 Lord Rees-Mogg, quoted by Michael Cockerill, *The Listener* (3 November 1988).
21 Lynda Nead, 'The Female Nude' in Segal and McIntosh (eds.), *Sex Exposed*, p. 280. Also quoted by Elizabeth Wilson, 'Feminist Fundamentalism' in *Sex Exposed*, p. 23.
22 George Steiner, *Language and Silence* (New York, Atheneum, 1970), p. 70.
23 Lynda Nead, 'The Female Nude' in Segal and McIntosh (eds.), *Sex Exposed*, p. 286.
24 Linda Williams, 'A Provoking Agent' in P. and R. Gibson (eds.), *Dirty Looks: Women, Pornography, Power* (London, BFI, 1993), p. 188.
25 Visual evidence of ejaculation.
26 S. Rothman, R. and L. Lichter, *Watching America*, quoted by M. Medved, *Hollywood vs. America* (London, HarperCollins, 1994). Extract in *Sunday Times* (11 February 1993).
27 *Ibid.*
28 *Ibid.*
29 Jerry Sadowitz, *The Independent* (31 December 1988).
30 William Cash, *The Times* (23 January 1993). The argument about comedy and prejudice is corroborated by the central character Waters in Trevor Griffiths' *The Comedians* (London, Faber and Faber, 1976), p. 23:

A joke that feeds on ignorance starves its audience. We have the choice. We can say something or we can say nothing. Not everything true is funny, and not everything funny is true. Most comics feed prejudice and fear and blinkered vision, but the best ones, the best ones . . . illuminate them, make them clearer to seem easier to deal with. We've got to make people laugh till they cry. Cry. Till they find their pain and their beauty. Comedy is medicine. Not coloured sweeties to rot their teeth with.

31 Rozsika Parker, 'Censored: Feminist Art that the Arts Council is Trying to Hide' in R. Betterton (ed.), *Looking On: Images of Femininity in the Visual Arts and Media* (London, Pandora, 1987), p. 257.

32 Nicholas de Jongh, *Not in Front of the Audience* (London, Routledge, 1992), p. 106.
33 *Ibid.* Nonetheless, the production (with twenty-five scene changes and a cast of forty) cost £16,500 and never transferred to the West End.
34 Christopher Thomas, *The Times* (20 August 1993).
35 Figures quoted in 'Film Fax Special No. 1', D. Aldridge (ed.), *Film Review* (London, Orpheus Publications, 1991).
36 G. Rodgerson and E. Wilson (eds.), *Pornography and Feminism* (London, Lawrence and Wishart, 1991), p. 25.
37 Tony Parsons, *The Times*, 30 January 1993.
38 Plato, *The Republic*.
39 Jeremy Collier (1650–1726), *A Short View of the Immorality and Profaneness of the English Stage*, quoted in F. Muir, *The Frank Muir Book* (London, Heinemann, 1976), p. 2.
40 The Critics' Circle, quotation in *Section 28: Its Impact on the Arts* (The Arts Lobby, The Drill Hall Arts Centre, 1987).
41 Carol Clover, 'Introduction' in P. and R. Gibson (eds.), *Dirty Looks*, p. 1.
42 In 1984, Minneapolis City Council passed an ordinance, drafted by Andrea Dworkin and Catherine MacKinnon, allowing women to take civil action against producers or distributors of pornography. The Supreme Court eventually rejected the ordinance but the debate has continued unabated.
43 G. Rodgerson and E. Wilson (eds.), *Pornography and Feminism*, p. 15.
44 Andrew Ross, 'The Popularity of Pornography' in Simon During (ed.), *The Cultural Studies Reader* (London, Routledge, 1993), p. 232.
45 Gloria Steinem, 'Erotica and Pornography: A Clear and Present Difference' in C. Kramerae and P. A. Treichler (eds.), *A Feminist Dictionary* (London, Pandora, 1985), quoted by Janine de Giovanni, *The Sunday Times* (30 Aug 1992). For a full discussion of Steinem's distinction see Lizbeth Goodman, 'The Pornography Problem' in F. Bonner *et al.* (eds.), *Imagining Women* (London, Polity Press, 1992), pp. 274–83.
46 G. Rodgerson and E. Wilson (eds.), *Pornography and Feminism*, pp. 67–9.
47 Ross, 'The Popularity of Pornography', p. 232.
48 *Body Politic*, 4 (Oct 1993), 9.
49 This recent exhibition at the Serpentine Gallery Hyde Park, London (July/August 1994) contains, inter alia, an erotic exhibit 'Cacao', described as a 'molten bubbling fountain of 750 kilos of liquid chocolate', and 'Piss Flowers' which 'sprout obscenely from a vivid green carpet . . . crystalline blooms . . . derived by urinating in the snow, and casting the resulting holes . . . The central female hole produces a hugely protuberant phallic stamen surrounded by the more delicate, diffuse "labial" fringe created by the man . . . a strangely sexual artificial botany.' (*Exhibition Guide* by Adrian Searle).
50 Betterton (ed.), *Looking On*, p. 255.
51 Elsie Owusu talking to 'Diamanda Galas' in *Body Politic*, 4 (Oct 1993), 28.
52 Linda Williams, 'A Provoking Agent' in *Dirty Looks*, p. 177.
53 See Williams, 'A Provoking Agent' in *Dirty Looks*, pp. 176–89 for a detailed discussion of Annie Sprinkle's work.
54 Chris Straayer, 'The Seduction of Boundaries' in *Dirty Looks*, p. 156.
55 Ross, 'The Popularity of Pornography', p. 235.

56 Deborah Levy, the *Guardian* (27 Sept 1993).
57 Linda Williams, 'Pornographers on/scene' in Segal and McIntosh (eds.), *Sex Exposed*, p. 232.

# SELECT BIBLIOGRAPHY

The works listed below constitute the *main* sources. Details of all cited titles are given in the notes at the end of each chapter.

## PART I Feminisms and performance


Adair, C., V. Briginshaw and K. Lynn, 'Viewing Women: The Second Sex', *Dance Theatre Journal* 7:2 (1982)

Adshead, J., *The Study of Dance* (London, Dance Books, 1981)

Adshead, J. (ed.), *Dance Analysis: Theory and Practice* (London, Dance Books, 1988)

Alderson, E., 'Ballet as Ideology: Giselle Act II', *Dance Chronicle* 10:3 (1987)

Aston, E., and G. Savona, *Theatre as Sign-System* (London and New York, Routledge, 1991)

Banes, S., *Terpsichore in Sneakers* (Boston, Houghton Mifflin, 1980)

Barkin, Elaine, 'Questionnaire', *Perspectives of New Music* 19 (1980–1) and 'Response', *Perspectives of New Music* 20 (1981–2)

Barkin, Elaine, 'Either/Other' (critical essay on work by Susan McClary), *Perspectives of New Music* 30 (Summer 1992)

Barthes, R., 'Literature and Signification' in R. Howard (transl.), *Critical Essays* (Evanston, Northwestern University Press, [1963] 1972)

Baudrillard, J., *America* (transl. C. Turner) (New York, Verso, 1988)

Best, S., 'Jameson, Totality and Poststructuralist Critique' in D. Kellner (ed.), *Postmodernism/Jameson/Critique* (Washington, D.C., Maisonneuve Press, 1989)

Blau, H., *The Eye of Prey: Subversions of the Postmodern* (Bloomington and Indianapolis, Indiana University Press, 1987)

Bowers, Jane, and Judith Tick (eds.), *Women Making Music: The Western Art Tradition, 1150–1950* (London, Macmillan, 1986)

Bradby, Barbara, 'Sampling Sexuality: Gender, Technology and the Body in Dance Music', *Popular Music* 12:2 (May 1993)

Brett, Philip, Elizabeth Wood, and Gary Thomas (eds.), *Queering the Pitch: The New Gay and Lesbian Musicology* (New York and London, Routledge, 1994)

Briginshaw, V. A. (ed.), *Postmodernism and Dance: Discussion Papers* (Chichester, West Sussex Institute of Higher Education, 1991)

Butler, J., *Gender Trouble: Feminism and the Subversion of Identity* (London, Routledge, 1990)

Carter, A., 'Man as Creative Master, Woman as Responsive Muse', *Dance Now* 4:1 (1994)

Case, S.-E., *Feminism and Theatre* (London, Macmillan, 1988)

Castoriadis, C., 'Psychoanalysis and Politics' in Sonu Shamdasani and Michael Munchow (eds.), *Speculations after Freud: Psychoanalysis, Philosophy and Culture* (London and New York, Routledge, 1994)

Chinov, H. K., and L. W. Jenkins (eds.), *Women in American Theatre* (New York, Theatre Communications Group, [1981] 1987)

Citron, Marcia, *Gender and the Music Canon* (Cambridge, Cambridge University Press, 1993)
Cixous, H., 'Aller à la mer' (transl. B. Kerslake), *Modern Drama*, 4 (December 1984)
Clément, Catherine, *Opera, or the Undoing of Women* (transl. Betsy Wing) (London, Virago, 1989)
Connor, S., *Postmodernist Culture: An Introduction to the Theories of the Contemporary* (Oxford, Basil Blackwell, 1989)
Cook, Susan C., and Judy S. Tsou (eds.), *Cecilia Reclaimed: Feminist Perspectives on Gender and Music* (Urbana and Chicago, University of Illinois Press, 1994)
Copeland, R., 'The Objective Temperament', *Dance Theatre Journal* 4:3 (1986)
Copeland, R. M., 'Founding Mothers: Duncan, Graham, Rainer and Sexual Politics', *Dance Theatre Journal* 8:3 (1990)
Curry, R., 'Madonna from Marilyn to Marlene—Pastiche and/or Parody', *Journal of Film and Video* 42:2 (Summer)
Dahl, Linda, *Stormy Weather: The Music and Lives of a Century of Jazzwomen* (New York, Pantheon Books, 1984)
Daly, A., 'The Balanchine Woman: of Hummingbirds and Channel Swimmers', *The Drama Review* 31:1 (1987)
Daly, A., 'Unlimited Partnership: Dance and Feminist Analysis', *Dance Research Journal* 23:1 (1991)
Daniels, S., *Ripen Our Darkness and the Devil's Gateway* (London and New York, Methuen, 1986)
De Lauretis, T., *Alice Doesn't: Feminism, Semiotics, Cinema* (Bloomington, Indiana University Press, 1984)
De Lauretis, T., *Technologies of Gender: Essays on Theory, Film and Fiction* (Bloomington, Indiana University Press, 1987)
Deleuze, G., *Difference and Repetition* (transl. Paul Patton) (London, The Athlone Press, 1994)
Dolan, J., *The Feminist Spectator as Critic* (Ann Arbor, The University of Michigan Press, 1988)
Dunn, Leslie, and Nancy A. Jones (eds.), *Embodied Voices: Female Vocality in Western Culture* (Cambridge, Cambridge University Press, 1994)
Evans, Liz, *Women, Sex and Rock 'n' Roll* (London, Pandora, 1994)
Féral, J., 'Performances and Theatricality: The Subject Demystified' (transl. Teresa Lyons), *Modern Drama* 25:1 (1982).
Foster, H., *Post-Modern Culture* (London, Pluto Press, 1985)
Freud, S. (1905/6), 'Psychopathic Characters on the Stage' in A. Dickson (ed.), *Art and Literature*, The Pelican Freud Library, Vol. 14 (Harmondsworth, Penguin Books, 1985)
Freud, S. (1908), 'Creative Writers and Day-Dreaming' in A. Dickson (ed.), *Art and Literature*, The Pelican Freud Library, Vol. 14 (Harmondsworth, Penguin Books, 1985)
Freud, S. (1920), 'Beyond the Pleasure Principle' in A. Richards (ed.), *On Metapsychology*, The Pelican Freud Library, Vol. 11 (Harmondsworth, Penguin Books, 1984)
Frith, S., 'Art Ideology and Pop Practice' in C. Nelson and L. Grossberg (eds.), *Marxism and the Interpretation of Culture* (Urbana, University of Illinois Press, 1988)

Frith, S. (ed.), 'Video Pop: Picking up the Pieces', *Facing the Music* (New York, Pantheon, 1988)

Frith, S., and A. Goodwin (eds.), 'Sample and Hold: Pop Music in the Digital Age of Reproduction', in *On Record: Rock, Pop and the Written Word* (New York, Pantheon)

Fuller, Sophie, *The Pandora Guide to Women Composers: Britain and the United States, 1629–present* (London, Pandora, 1994)

Gaar, Gillian G., *She's a Rebel: The History of Women in Rock and Roll* (London, Blandford, 1993)

Goldberg, M., 'Ballerinas and Ball Passing', *Women and Performance* 3:2 (1987/8)

Green, A., *The Tragic Effect: The Oedipus Complex in Tragedy* (transl. A. Sheridan) (Cambridge, Cambridge University Press)

Grieg, Charlotte, *Will You Still Love Me Tomorrow?: Girl Groups From the '50s On* (London, Virago, 1989)

Handy, D. Antoinette, *Black Women in American Bands and Orchestras* (Metuchen, NJ, Scarecrow Press, 1981)

Harrison, Daphne Duval, *Black Pearls: Blues Queens of the 1920s* (New Brunswick, Rutgers University Press, 1988)

Hernden, Marica, and Susanne Ziegler (eds.) (International Council for Traditional Music/Study Group on Music and Gender), *Music, Gender and Culture*, International Music Studies 1 (Wilhelmshaven, Florian Noetzel Verlag, 1990)

Jezic, Diane, *Women Composers: The Lost Tradition Found* (New York, The Feminist Press, 1988)

Kallberg, Jeffrey, 'The Harmony of the Tea Table: Gender and Ideology in the Piano Nocturne', *Representations* 39 (1992)

King, B., 'The Star and the Commodity: Notes Towards a Performance Theory of Stardom', *Cultural Studies* 1:2 (May 1987)

Koskoff, Ellen (ed.), *Women and Music in Cross-Cultural Perspective* (Westport, CT, Greenwood Press, 1987)

Lacoue-Labarthe, P., 'Theatrum Analyticum', *Glyph* 2 (1977)

LeFanu, Nicola, 'Master Musician: An Impregnable Taboo?', *Contact* 31 (Autumn 1987). See also responses by Diana Burrell, 'Accepting Androgyny', and Rhian Samuel, 'Women Composers Today: A Personal View', *Contact* 32 (Spring 1988)

LeFanu, Nicola, and Sophie Fuller (eds.), 'Reclaiming the Muse', *Contemporary Music Review* 11 (1994)

Lepert, Richard, *Music and Image: Domesticity, Ideology and Sociocultural Formation in Eighteenth Century England* (Cambridge, Cambridge University Press, 1988)

Lewis, L. A., 'Female Address in Music Video', *Journal of Communication Inquiry 11* 1 (Winter 1987)

Luckham, C., 'Trafford Tanzi' in M. Wandor (ed.), *Plays By Women: Volume Two* (London, Methuen, 1983)

Lyotard, J. F., 'Beyond Representation' in A. Benjamin (ed.), *The Lyotard Reader* (Oxford, Basil Blackwell, 1989)

Lyotard, J. F., 'Answering the Question: What Is Postmodernism?' in I. Hassan and S. Hassan (eds.), *Innovation/Renovation: New Perspectives on the Humanities* (Madison, Wisconsin University Press)

McClary, Susan, *Feminine Endings: Music, Gender, and Sexuality* (Minneapolis, University of Minnesota Press, 1991)
McClary, Susan, 'Reshaping a Discipline: Musicology and Feminism in the 1990s', *Feminist Studies* 19:2 (Summer 1993)
McClary, Susan, 'Of Patriarchs . . . and Matriarchs, Too', *The Musical Times* (June 1994)
Marshall, Kimberly (ed.), *Rediscovering the Muses: Women's Musical Traditions* (Boston, Northeastern University Press, 1993)
Morris, Meaghan, *Pirate's Fiancée: Feminism and Postmodernism* (New York and London, Routledge, 1988)
Müller, H., 'Hamletmaschine', in *Mauser* (Berlin, Rotbuch Verlag, 1978)
Müller, H., *Gesammelt Irrtümer: Interviews und Gespräche* (Frankfurt, Verlag der Autoren)
Mulvey, L., 'Visual Pleasure and Narrative Cinema', *Screen* 16:3 (Autumn 1975)
Neuls-Bates, Carol (ed.), *Women in Music: An Anthology of Source Readings from the Middle Ages to the Present* (New York, Harper and Row, 1982)
Pateman, C. and E. Gross (eds.), *Feminist Challenges: Social and Political Theory* (London, Allen and Unwin, 1986)
Pavis, P., 'Theatre Analysis: Some Questions and a Questionnaire', *New Theatre Quarterly* 1:2 (1985)
Pendle, Krin (ed.), *Women and Music: A History* (Bloomington and Indianapolis, Indiana University Press, 1991)
Phelan, P., *Unmarked: The Politics of Performance* (London and New York, Routledge, 1993)
Placksin, Sally, *Jazzwomen, 1990 to the Present: Their Words, Lives and Music* (London, Pluto Press, 1985)
Remnant, M., 'Introduction' in M. Remnant (ed.), *Plays by Women: Volume Six* (London and New York, 1987)
Rieger, Eva, 'Dolce Semplice? On the Changing Role of Women in Music', in Gisela Ecker (ed.), *Feminist Aesthetics*, transl. Harriet Anderson (London, The Women's Press, 1985)
Rubey, D., 'Voguing at the Carnival: Desire and Pleasure on MTV', *South Atlantic Quarterly* 90:4 (Fall 1991)
Sadie, Julie Anne, and Samuel Rhian (eds.), *The New Grove Dictionary of Women Composers* (London, Macmillan, 1994)
Savage King, C., 'Classical Muscle', *Women's Review* 2 (1985)
Schultz, G., *Heiner Müller* (Stuttgart, Metzler, 1980)
Schwichthenberg, C. R., 'Madonna's Postmodern Feminism: Bringing the Margins to the Center', *Southern Communication Journal* 1:57 (2) (Winter 1991)
Schwichthenberg, C. R., *The Madonna Connection: Representational Politics, Subcultural Identities and Cultural Theory* (Boulder, CO, Westview Press, 1993)
Shepherd, J., *Music as Social Text* (Cambridge, Polity Press, 1991)
Showalter, E., *The Female Malady: Women, Madness and English Culture, 1839–1980* (New York, Pantheon)
Solie, Ruth (ed.), *Musicology and Difference: Gender and Sexuality in Music Scholarship* (Berkeley and Los Angeles, University of California Press, 1993)
'Sounds Australian', *The Woman's Issue* 40 (Summer 1993–4)

Steward, Sue and Sheryl Garratt, *Signed Sealed and Delivered: True Life Stories of Women in Pop* (London, Pluto Press, 1984)
Stubbs, P., *Women and Fiction: Feminism and the Novel, 1880–1920* (Brighton, Harvester Press, 1979)
Thomas, H. (ed.), *Dance, Gender and Culture* (London, Macmillan, 1993)
Tong, R., *Feminist Thought: A Comprehensive Introduction* (London, Unwin Hyman, 1989)
Toorn, Pieter C. van den, 'Politics, Feminism and Contemporary Music Theory', *The Journal of Musicology* 9:3 (Summer 1991). See also Ruth Solie, 'What Do Feminists Want? A Reply to Pieter van den Toorn', *The Journal of Musicology* 9:4 (Fall 1991)
Ubersfield, A., *L'École du Spectateur* (Paris, Les Editions Sociales, 1991)
Veltrusky, J., 'Man and Object in the Theatre' in L. L. Garvin (ed.), *A Prague School Reader on Aesthetics, Literary Structure and Style* (Washington, Georgetown University Press, 1940)
Wandor, M., *Carry on Understudies: Theatre and Sexual Politics* (London and New York, Routledge and Kegan Paul, 1981)
Warner, M., 'Little Angels: Little Devils: Keeping Childhood Innocent', Reith Lecture, the *Independent*, 11 February 1994
Wolff, J., *Feminine Sentences: Essays on Women and Culture* (Cambridge, Polity Press, 1990)
'Women: A Cultural Review', *Women and Music* 3:1 (Summer 1992)
*Women and Performance* (various articles) 3:2 (1987/8)
Wright, E., *Psychoanalytic Criticism: Theory in Practice* (London and New York, Routledge, 1984)
Wright, E., *Postmodern Brecht: A Re-Presentation* (London and New York, Routledge, 1989)
Zaimont, Judith Lang, Catherine Overhauser, and Jane Gottlieb (eds.), *The Musical Woman: An International Perspective 1983* (Westport, CT, Greenwood Press, 1984); Vol. 2, *1984–85* (1987); Vol. 3, *1986–1990* (1991)
Žižek, S., *Enjoy Your Symptom: Jacques Lacan in Hollywood and Out* (New York and London, Routledge, 1992)
Zuidervaart, L., 'Realism, Modernism, and the Empty Chair' in D. Kellner (ed.), *Postmodernism/Jameson/Critique* (Washington, D.C., Maisonneuve Press)

## PART II Postmodernism, poststructuralism, politics and performance

Auslander, P., *Presence and Resistance: Postmodernism and Politics in Contemporary American Performance* (Ann Arbor, University of Michigan Press, 1992)
Banes, S., *Terpsichore in Sneakers: Post-Modern Dance* (Middletown, Wesleyan University Press, 1989)
Benamou, M., and C. Carmello, *Performance in Postmodern Culture* (Milwaukee, Centre for Twentieth-Century Studies, 1977)
Birrenger, J., *Theatre, Theory, Postmodernism* (Bloomington, University of Indiana Press, 1991)
Blau, H., *The Eye of Prey: Subversions of the Postmodern* (Bloomington, University of Indiana Press, 1982)

Brater, E., and R. Cohn (eds.), *Around the Absurd: Essays on Modern and Postmodern Drama* (Ann Arbor, University of Michigan Press, 1990)
Cage, J., *Silence: Lectures and Writings* (Middletown, Wesleyan University Press, 1961)
Connor, S., *Postmodernist Culture* (Oxford, Blackwell, 1989)
Davy, K., *Richard Foreman and the Ontological-Hysteric Theatre* (Ann Arbor, UMI Research Press, 1981)
Derrida, J., *Writing and Difference* (London, Routledge, 1978)
Foreman, R., *Reverberation Machines: The Later Plays and Essays* (Barrytown, Station Hill, 1985)
Foreman, R., *Unbalancing Acts: Foundations for Theatre* (New York, Theater Communications Group, 1993)
Grossberg, L., 'History, Politics, and Postmodernism: Stuart Hall and Cultural Studies', *Journal of Communication Inquiry* 10:2 (Summer 1986)
Grossberg, L., 'MTV: Swinging on the [Postmodern] Star' in I. Angus and S. Jhally (eds.), *Cultural Politics in Contemporary America* (New York, Routledge, 1989)
Harvey, D., *The Condition of Postmodernity* (Oxford, Blackwell, 1990)
Heuvel, M., *Performing Drama/Dramatizing Performance: Alternate Theatre and the Dramatic Text* (Ann Arbor, University of Michigan Press, 1991)
Hutcheon, L., *The Politics of Postmodernism* (London, Routledge, 1988)
Jameson, F., *Postmodernism* (Durham, NC, Duke University Press, 1991)
Jencks, F., *What is Postmodernism?* (London, Academy Editions, 1986)
Kaplan, E. A., *Rocking Around the Clock* (London, Routledge, 1987)
Kaplan, E. A., 'Madonna Politics: Perversion, Repression, or Subversion?', in C. Schwichthenberg (ed.), *The Madonna Connection* (Boulder, CO, Westview Press, 1993)
Kaplan, E. A. (ed.), *Postmodernism and its Discontents: Theories and Practices* (London, Verso, 1988)
Kaprow, A., *Assemblages, Environments and Happenings* (New York, Abrams, 1966)
Kaprow, A., *Essays on the Blurring of Art and Life* (Berkeley, University of California Press, 1993)
Kaye, N., *Postmodernism and Performance* (London, Macmillan, 1994)
Kershaw, B., *The Politics of Performance* (London, Routledge, 1992)
MacDonald, E., *Theatre at the Margins: Text and the Post-structured Stage* (Ann Arbor, University of Michigan Press, 1993)
Mackrell, J., 'Postmodern Dance in Britain: An Historical Essay', *Dance Research* 9:1 (1991)
Mackrell, J., *Out of Line: the Story of New British Dance* (London, Dance Books, 1992)
Madan, S., *An Introductory Guide to Post-structuralism and Post-modernism* (Athens, Georgia University Press, 1988)
Manning, 'Modernist Dogma and Post-modern Rhetoric', *The Drama Review* T12 (1988)
Marranca, B., *Theatrewritings* (New York, Performing Arts Journal Publications, 1984)
Nicholson, L. (ed.), *Feminism/Postmodernism* (London, Routledge, 1990)
Prinz, J., *Art Discourse/Discourse in Art* (New Brunswick, Rutgers University Press, 1991)

Savran, D., *The Wooster Group, 1975–1985: Breaking the Rules* (New York, Theater Communications Group, 1988)
Sayre, H., *The Object of Performance* (Chicago, Chicago University Press, 1989)
Silverman, H., *Postmodernism—Philosophy and the Arts* (London, Routledge, 1990)
Simard, R., *Postmodern Drama: Contemporary Playwrights in America and Britain* (Lanham, University Presses of America, 1984)
Waugh, P., (ed.), *Postmodernism: A Reader* (London, Arnold, 1992)
Waugh, P., *Practising Postmodernism, Reading Modernism* (London, 1992)
Wright, E., *Postmodern Brecht: A Re-Presentation* (London, Routledge, 1988)

## PART III Issues in performance

Barker, H., *Arguments for a Theatre* (London, Calder, 1989; 2nd ed. Manchester, Manchester University Press, 1993)
Barthes, R., *Image, Music, Text* (London, Fontana, 1970)
Barthes, R., *Mythologies* (London, Jonathan Cape, 1957)
Betterton, R. (ed.), *Looking On: Images of Femininity in the Visual Arts and Media* (London, Pandora, 1987)
Boal, A., *Theatre of the Oppressed* (London, Pluto Press, 1970)
Brook, P., *The Shifting Point* (London, Methuen, 1988)
Brook, P., *There Are No Secrets* (London, Methuen, 1993)
Chester, G., and J. Dickey (eds.), *Feminism and Censorship* (Dorset, Prism Press, 1988)
Collins, J., *Uncommon Cultures: Popular Culture and Post-Modernism* (London, Routledge, 1989)
De Jongh, N., *Not in Front of the Audience* (London, Routledge, 1992)
Dent, G., and M. Wallace (eds.), *Black Popular Culture* (Seattle, Bay Press, 1992)
Elsom, J. (ed.), *Is Shakespeare Still Our Contemporary?* (London, Routledge, 1992)
Esslin, M., *The Field of Drama* (London, Methuen, 1987)
Fiske, J., *Understanding Popular Culture* (London, Unwin Hyman, 1989)
Frith, S., and H. Horne, *Art into Pop* (London, Routledge, 1989)
Gibson, P., and R. Gibson (eds.), *Dirty Looks: Women, Pornography, Power* (London, BFI, 1993)
Goodman, L., *Feminist Stages: Interviews With Women in British Theatre* (London, Harwood Press, 1995)
Goodman, L., *Sexuality in Performance* (London, Routledge, 1996)
Griffin, S., *Pornography and Silence* (London, Women's Press, 1987)
Hebdige, D., *Subculture: The Meaning of Style* (London, Methuen, 1979)
Kappeler, S., *The Pornography of Representation* (Cambridge, Polity Press, 1986)
Leppard, R., *Authenticity in Music* (London, Faber, 1988)
Marovitz, C., *Recycling Shakespeare* (London, Macmillan, 1992)
Mathews, T., *Censored* (London, Chatto, 1994)
Meyer, M., *The Politics and Poetics of Camp* (London, Routledge, 1994)
Miller, J., *Subsequent Performances* (London, Faber, 1986)
Owesi, K., *The Struggle for Black Arts in Britain* (London, Commedia, 1986)
Pateman, *Key Concepts: A Guide to Aesthetics, Criticism, and the Arts in Education* (London, Falmer Press, 1991)

Rodgerson, G., and E. Wilson, *The Case Against Censorship* (London, Lawrence and Wishart, 1991)
Segal, L., and M. McIntosh (eds.), *Sex Exposed* (London, Virago, 1992)
Sontag, S., *Illness as Metaphor* (New York, Anchor, 1988)
Willett, J. (ed.), *Brecht on Theatre* (London, Methuen, 1964)
Wollheim, R., *Art and Its Objects* (Cambridge, Cambridge University Press, 1980)

# INDEX